A Law Enforcement Sourcebook of **ASIAN CRIME and CULTURES** *Tactics and Mindsets*

W. C. Drug Task Force

A Law Enforcement Sourcebook of ASIAN CRIME and CULTURES *Tactics and Mindsets*

Douglas D. Daye, Ph.D.

With a Foreword by
Inspector John E. McKenna (Retired)
Officer-In-Charge, First Asian Crime Task Force
San Francisco Police Department

CRC Press
Boca Raton New York London Tokyo

Cover photos courtesy of Al Lotz, Houston P.D. Back cover photo from the collection of Tom Perdue, San Francisco P.D.

Publisher:	Robert B. Stern
Editorial Assistant	Jean Jarboe
Project Editor:	Helen Linna
Marketing Manager:	Greg Daurelle
Direct Marketing Manager:	Becky McEldowney
Cover design:	Denise Craig
PrePress:	Kevin Luong
Manufacturing:	Sheri Schwartz

Library of Congress Cataloging-in-Publication Data

Daye, Douglas D.
A law enforcement sourcebook of Asian crime and cultures: tactics and mindsets / Douglas D. Daye
p. cm.
Includes bibliographical references and index.
ISBN 0-8493-8116-9
1. Criminal justice—investigation. 2. Criminal science—intelligence.
3. Sociology. 4. Asian studies. 5. Forensic science. I. Daye, Douglas D. II. Title.
QP112.4.M43 1996
616′.0149—dc20
for Library of Congress 96-57137
CIP

International Standard Book Number 0-8493-8116-9
Library of Congress Card Number 96-57137
Printed in the United States of America 1 2 3 4 5 6 7 8 9 0
Printed on acid-free paper

Contents

Part III: Mindsets, Profiles, and Religions

Part IV: Recording, Preserving, Training, and Planning

Foreword

Within the unfolding events affecting modern society, our law enforcement fraternity cannot be watching from the sideline when Asian criminal matters disrupt the well-being of their communities. These criminals are also students of these events, and today are able to communicate their travel worldwide, and flout the international border controls of any country.

A number of years ago only a handful of law enforcement officers worldwide envisioned the happenings by Asian crime figures that confront us today. Time has thinned out the lack of awareness, but law enforcement is still troubled by a lack of cultural and historical perspectives in these matters. With time, it has become more and more apparent that police procedures should be coupled with a cultural and historical understanding of the Asian criminal's ethnic background, his nation's culture, and history.

The book before you has moved Dr. Doug Daye to the forefront in this approach to contemporary law enforcement problems. It is a learned document for law enforcement to use and study in combating this lack of knowledge. Dr. Daye is one of the very few academics attempting to redress the practical problems of coupling cultural skills and knowledge with a wide range of relevant investigative techniques.

The book is full of practical ideas, tactics and suggestions, including checklists, over 130 "Do's and Don'ts", strategies for identification, interview, interrogation and trials, brief introductions to Asian Buddhism and Confucianism and Standard Telegraphic Code, comparative profiles of Chinese and Vietnamese mindsets, and cultural sketches of "Face", Guanxi, law, economic power, medicine, languages and holidays. In short, it is exactly what every prosecutor, prison trainer, or what every police department dealing with Asian crime will want to have in its squad room. The last part of the book addresses the broad administrative concerns of those in law enforcement who must move from an understanding of tactical needs, through an expanded appreciation of Asian mindsets and cultural habits, and formulate new strategic plans in intelligence and multi-purpose training programs which more closely meet both the changing professional responsibilities of police, prisons and courts and also meet the needs of our growing multicultural population.

Dr. Daye's writings are reasoned and timely, and the book reaches out to assist a broad spectrum of law enforcement who valiantly combat this increasingly frequent type of Asian and Asian-American crime. In my opinion, Dr. Daye epitomizes the words of Cicero in *De Divinatione, II*:

> "What nobler employment, or more valuable to the state, than that of the man who instructs the rising generation?"

Inspector John E. McKenna (Retired)
Officer-In-Charge, First Asian Gang Task Force
San Franscisco Police Department

Preface

As most law enforcement people are well aware, in the 1920s and 1930s, federal, state, and municipal law enforcement generally ignored the growth of the Italian Mafia and the Italian-American La Cosa Nostra. Few attempts were made to identify, understand, and infiltrate these criminal subcultures. Today, when most Caucasian, African-American, and Hispanic police view Asian crime, they find Asian and Asian-American criminals the most "foreign of the foreign", and the temptation is strong to ignore Asian crime just as La Cosa Nostra was once ignored.

Furthermore, the unfamiliar complexities of various Asian multinational ethnic networks, their languages and numerous dialects, customs, and their insular reluctance to cooperate with police render Asians difficult to help and difficult to understand and predict. One aim of this book is to prevent Asian crime from being ignored in the way in which La Cosa Nostra was ignored and to assist police in understanding Asian cultures and thus Asian and Asian-American crime. Some of the means for such prevention and assistance are the development of such cross-cultural (XC) resources as this book, Asian crime conferences, and XC training programs.

As a result of the continued growth of professional law enforcement interest in the cross-cultural aspects of Asian crime (AC), paralleled by the pervasive growth in Asian crime, many police officers are poised to expand their participation in professional training services. To meet that interest, our initial focus to gather information about police needs should be to survey a wider range of AC investigators regarding: (1) their perceptions of their AC problems particular to their regions; (2) the range, adequacy, and types of their reference sources (Asian name transliteration guides, gang tattoos); and (3) their linguistic and XC training needs as they see them. This information would allow us to develop training and educational programs that have direct relevance to the particular needs of these specialists. I have tried to address some of these issues in this book, but an enormous amount remains to be done.

As these varied programs are being developed, small groups of AC specialists would continue to supply police with XC aspects of Asian crime intelligence and advisory information about XC differences among the various Asian communities as well as outlines of the multicultural background of Asian and Asian-American criminals. Simultaneously, we ought to continue to assist and encourage greater intelligence networking among Asian crime investigators.

Thus, the goal of this book is to contribute to the development and strengthening of North America's law enforcement capabilities to respond to expanding Asian crime problems. This, in turn, requires that the analytic services of many different professional organizations and individuals be developed and coordinated to create more effective training and education programs and to establish a more extensive law enforcement network of Asian crime investigators. In turn, they would be able to share more highly specialized information and discuss relevant issues in a more cross-culturally sophisticated and, thus, effective manner. While some of this has begun, once again there still remains an enormous amount of work to be done.

After several years of asking federal, domestic, state, and municipal police for examples of both their XC training guidelines and specific XC "Do's and Don'ts", I have come to the conclusion that, at best, there are only scattered, isolated XC points usually buried in other training materials. Much of what XC information and training there is, is usually conveyed in the one-to-one interchanges of "on-the-job" training by experienced Asian investigators. To pursue those sources, I have interviewed and ridden with as many law enforcement personnel as possible to learn from them and blend their insights with my own background as an Asian specialist. Thus, after asking and searching for such written police XC materials, I find, in effect, that there are almost none, certainly none nearly as inclusive nor arranged in the multi-leveled manner which ranges from the less complex to the more complex as is found in this book.

Also in writing this book, I have operated under the assumption that an inclusive summary of good XC data is better than (almost) none and that in some small way this book and the others that will follow will help to compensate for the absence of wide-ranging XC materials published for law enforcement personnel. Thus, I offer this sourcebook as an expanding project with the hope that it will be improved by further research and, most importantly, by incorporating suggestions and criticisms of federal, state, and municipal law enforcement people — intelligence analysts, agents, street-smart "street cops", detectives, prison guards, administrators, prosecutors, and other "Asian hands" of various backgrounds and persuasions. Therefore, if you send me your suggestions and examples about interconnected details of Asian crime and cultures, I will try to use them and (if you wish) I will explicitly acknowledge you and your agency or department.

As noted in the Senate hearings on Asian organized crime, I selected the Chinese and Vietnamese groups to focus this work because:

> "... the Chinese and Vietnamese crime groups pose the most immediate and serious threat.... the difficulty [in penetration and prosecution] can be partially attributed to the closed nature of the Asian community and to law enforcement's inability to communicate in Asian languages, as well as its *general lack of understanding of Asian culture.*"

The reader will find that while the legitimate focus of the book is upon Asian criminal activities, my admiration and respect for Asians and Asian cultures is also clear and evident. Since *all* cultures produce criminals, this book should neither be construed as a wholesale disparagement of Asian traditions or Asian peoples nor a wholesale endorsement of Asian traditions or Asian peoples.

Many law enforcement personnel — just sharp, kick-ass cops and Federal agents — have directly and indirectly contributed to the writing of this book, and I appreciate their contributions. Because I cannot compensate them (nor would they accept it), as a gesture of my appreciation, I shall contribute 5% of the small royalties of this book to the National Law Enforcement Officers Memorial Fund, 605 E. St., N.W., Washington, D.C., 20004.

Finally, a sizable number of law enforcement personnel have told me that this sourcebook is a new, unique approach for law enforcement training materials. Future comments will determine whether the book is useful enough to merit that praise, for, as the Buddhists said: "Everything is impermanent [sarvo'nityam]," including judgments and praise. Therefore, suggestions and additions are most welcome and will be explicitly acknowledged in any future editions. Criticisms are also welcome: no pain, no gain!

The Author

Having enjoyed extensive travel while using the research languages of Sanskrit, Buddhist Chinese, and Pali, Douglas D. Daye (M.A., University of Michigan; Ph.D., University of Wisconsin) has amassed a substantial record in international education, cross-cultural research, teaching, administration, applied intercultural training, foreign residency, government service and law enforcement training.

In addition to this book, he has also published over 30 research articles in comparative formal logics and epistemology, and has been invited to lecture at many Universities and Colleges, including: Berkeley (U. California), Columbia University, Oxford and East Anglia, Haverford, Wisconsin-Madison, Southern Methodist (Dallas), University College, Dublin, Gujarat (India), and Hawaii. Two of his articles on Asian organized crime have appeared in the publications of the International Association of Asian Crime Investigators (IAACI). He has also presented papers at meetings of the American Philosophical Association, Association for Asian Studies, the Canadian Society for the Study of Religion, Society for Comparative Philosophy, American Academy of Religion, and the International Association of Asian Crime Investigators.

He has been a University Visiting Professor/Scholar at California at Berkeley, Colorado at Boulder, Southern Methodist, Gujarat (India), and East Anglia. In 1975–1976, he was awarded a Senior Research Fellowship (Sanskrit) at the American Institute of Indian Studies (New Delhi) and, in 1989–1990, a 15-month research grant (Chinese) from the National Endowment for the Humanities. Having traveled extensively in the Middle East, Africa, South America, Europe, Australia, and throughout Asia, his university teaching has included courses in Indian and Chinese Philosophy and Religion, Global Philosophy of Religion (Buddhism-Christianity-Humanism), Philosophical Anthropology, Medical Ethics, Formal Logic(s), and Death and Dying, with a special focus on the cross-cultural aspects of medical ethics, epistemology, and communication. In England, and during an around-the-world teaching cruise, he taught a special course, "Across Cultures", which examined cross-cultural modes of communication and the behavioral effects of culture-specific world views.

A full Professor since 1979 at Bowling Green State University, Ohio (18,000 students), Dr. Daye was, for five years, Director, Center for International Programs. He was responsible for all foreign students, various aspects of governmental and international relations for the university, study-abroad programs, and the international recruiting needs of academic programs. He was responsible for all university relations with the National Association for Foreign Student Affairs, the U.S. State Department, and Immigration and Naturalization Service.

In 1989, he was Special Assistant to the Executive Director of the Federal Interagency Committee on Education (FICE), the U.S. Department of Education, and coordinated FICE projects with such government agencies as the Foreign Service Institute (Department of State), U.S. Information Agency, Department of Commerce, and the Federal Interagency Foreign Language Roundtable. He maintained contacts with such professional agencies as the National Governor's Association Task Force in International Educational, Federal Interagency Cross Cultural Roundtable, Center for Applied Linguistics, NALGCU, and SEITAR. In 1992, he retired with the rank of Professor Emeritus, as a member of the graduate faculty in the department's M.A. and Ph.D. programs.

Since early 1990, Dr. Daye has been engaged in writing training materials related to cross-cultural aspects of Asian and Asian-American crime and cultures. He has been invited to present Asian crime workshops co-sponsored by the FBI, BATF, INS, MAGLOCLEN, RISS, U.S. Attorney (Southern District, Ohio), FinCEN (Department of the Treasury), the State of Virginia, Department of Youth and Family Services, Boston Police Department, the University of Houston, the University of Illinois at Chicago, Metropolitan Toronto Police Advanced Homicide Seminar, Toledo Police Department, Florida Gang Investigators Association, Mongomery County P.D., and at various training conferences co-sponsored by the International Association of Asian Crime Investigators. He was a speaker at the annual 1995 and 1996 Asian Organized Crime Conferences in Anaheim and Boston and was invited to be a speaker at the 1994 Asian Organized Crime Conference in San Francisco (co-sponsored by the BATF). He was a speaker for the International Asian Organized Crime Conference in 1993, (co-sponsored by the FBI). In 1992, he helped to arrange Ohio's first Asian crime intelligence conference in Columbus and has taught various in-service training classes for individual police departments. In 1994, in Dublin, Ireland, with Dr. Paul Moore (FBI) and Cordell Hart (FinCEN, Treasury), he presented a paper on aspects of Chinese and American cultures that may influence attempts at deception during the John E. Reid method of interrogation. He completed the Reid interrogation course, a Police Intelligence Training course sponsored by the Pennsylvania State Police and the 60-hour Private Investigator course required for Virginia.

Dr. Daye has conducted extensive field interviews of law enforcement personnel and ridden with Asian crime investigators during their operations. He has attended many Asian organized crime conferences and has been a non-sworn member of a special team of Asian crime investigators for the last four years. This team investigates Asian gang members and Asian-American criminals at the Marion Days Festival, an annual meeting of over 40,000 Vietnamese and Southeast Asians in Carthage, Missouri, this team consisted of officers from the FBI-Chicago Police Department Joint Asian Gang Task Force and specialists form INS, S.S., BATF, and the Houston, Kansas City, New Orleans, and Dallas police departments. In the greater Washington, D.C., area, he is a volunteer consultant and trainer for the Montgomery County Police Department, Maryland, where he lives and from which he travels as a national consultant, cross-cultural trainer, and lecturer for law enforcement agencies.

E-mail address: dddaye@ix.NETCOM.com

Dedications

First, I wish to dedicate whatever merit this book may have to my lovely wife, Jane Loren MacDonald-Daye, a sweet Celt of the first order, and to my beautiful, mahācitta daughter, Loren Elizabeth Daye, both of whom have traveled with me in both beautiful and disagreeable parts of the world and who have lovingly accommodated themselves to my absences, my scholarly preoccupations, and field work during the last 25 years. In addition, my wife has focused her considerable analytical skills as a senior federal policy analyst by reading and criticizing the entire manuscript. Together, they have enriched and fulfilled my life and have falsified my vague recollection of the Chinese proverb that "other people's wives and children always seem the best."

Second, I also wish to dedicate any merit this book may have to sworn "gun-and-badge" cops, those law enforcement personnel who protect us. Furthermore, let no one think that I use the word "cops" with anything but respect and affection, for it is those men and women — those overworked and underpaid patrolmen, gang specialists, under-appreciated intelligence specialists, detectives, and those operational administrators in the trenches, the sergeants — who keep us reasonably safe while some of them risk their lives every night. Furthermore, among these action-oriented "street cops" — and this may be embarrassing to some tough-talking cops and is certainly not applicable to a few others — I have found an amazing and unexpected degree of old-fashioned idealism: simply "to do the right thing" under terrible situations. Thus, in my eyes, most cops and their long-suffering families deserve our gratitude and our thanks. They certainly have mine.

Acknowledgments

It is difficult to acknowledge and thank all those who have contributed to the formulation of a wide-ranging series of opinons, factual reports, and recommendations contained in this book. However, with a generic (if implicit) "thank you" to any not mentioned here, I shall try. I apologize for any omissions.

Among all those municipal, state, and federal law enforcement people with whom I have become friends and who have extended so much assistance, none have exceeded the help of M. Cordell Hart, Senior Analyst, Financial Crimes Enforcement Network (FinCEN), U.S. Department of the Treasury, the author of the excellent monograph *Chinese.* Not only has he been a helpful critic and a good friend and made a fine contribution to the Appendices, he also has been an initial reader of the whole manuscript. Furthermore, he reread parts and offered additional suggestions and detailed comments which the reader will find throughout the book. Also, Lt. Jack Willoughby (aka "Wo Fat"), Violent Gang Task Force, New Orleans P.D., took time to read the entire manuscript and offer valuable comments, corrections, and photographs; he, too, has been a good friend, an outspoken friendly critic, and is an author of excellent training materials on Vietnamese-American crime: *Wo Fat's Incomplete Cultural Guide* and *Vietnamese Gangs and Criminals.* Equally helpful with suggestions and friendly criticisms was a widely respected pioneer in Asian crime enforcement, Inspector John McKenna (Retired) San Francisco P.D., who kindly wrote the Foreword.

Furthermore, whatever merit the book may have could not have been acquired without the friendly instruction, advice, and detailed information about the "do's and don'ts" of police tactics and attitudes offered to me by my good friends Detective Al Lotz, Houston P.D.; Pat McCarthy, Asian Gang Specialist, Chicago P.D. and the Joint Asian Task Force with the FBI; the clever crime tactician, Phillip Hannum, former Investigator, Falls Church P.D., Virginia, former editor of the *IAACI Newsletter,* and, with Al Lotz, co-author of *Nightmare: Vietnamese Home Invasion Robberies.* Other Asian crime specialists who have been equally friendly and extremely helpful were two cross-culturally sophisticated, excellent Asian linguists and Asian sojourners,

George Harkin and Robert Hearn. Both are experienced federal administrators and analysts who (with permission from their agencies) willingly offered their knowledge and experience and opinions and whose outstanding materials regarding Chinese Triads and Asian names (respectively) are reproduced in the Appendices. Another friend and contributor to the Appendicies is Dr. Paul Moore, Senior Analyst, FBI, whose article regarding Chinese counterintelligence is both lucid, insightful and rare. Sergeant Tom Perdue, San Francisco Police Department, kindly offered photos and other materials from his extensive knowledge and library of Asian crime materials. All these men — Cord, Jack, Al, Pat, Phil, John, Tom, George, Bob, and Paul — are amiable critics and crime tacticians of the first order, but, more importantly, they are good friends who explained things and took me places I could never have found nor entered without their help. Most of all, without their assistance I could not have talked with members of the understandably closed circles of both the Blue Brotherhood of Police and razor-sharp members of the intelligence community.

Equally friendly and helpful were Jose Lema and Dan Bellich of the FBI and Chris Heart of the BATF. With Wyatt Evans and Gil Bartosh of the BATF, Jerry Rodin and Jesse Stoker of the INS, Mike Carew and Dan Nguyen of the Dallas P.D., An Truong and Juan DeLeon of the Tarrant County D.A.'s office, guided by the careful coordination of Chief Ed Ellefsen and Detective Rob Harmon of the Carthage P.D., and accompanied by the cop jokes and cool tactics of Al Lotz, Pat McCarthy, and Jack Willoughby, I watched and talked with many, great cops, lots of fine Vietnamese people, and with Viet-Ching gang bangers during the last five summers of great Missouri hospitality and heat at the Southeast Asian Roman Catholic celebration, Marian Days.

Chick Sheehan of Diplomatic Language Services gave me lots of practical insights and excellent constructive criticism. With great admiration and profit, I read William Cassidy's excellent monographs on things Vietnamese and Willard H. Meyers' insightful analyses of Chinese Fukienese alien smuggling and emic guanxi relations. With admiration, I read materials from and attended the training workshops of Marcus Frank, Westminster, California P. D.; Charlie Villagracia, Seattle, Washington P.D.; and Michael Smith, Philadelphia P.D., regarding Vietnamese culture and gangs. The clear, well-written works of all of the above should be in every law enforcement library. Special thanks should go to Joseph Buckeley, Professor Fred Imbau, and Bryan James of John E. Ried and Associates, Inc., who allowed me to attend their interview and interrogation training classes and begin a new book on culture and interrogation. Always helpful and friendly were Dale Zlock, Washington State Gambling Commission (an author of an excellent monograph on Asian gambling); Mark Randel of the Denver Prosecutor's office; Wayne Baber, Treasury; Jonathan Chen, Pennsylvania State Police; Lt. Bruce

Martin, Marina Police Service; Al Rock, MAGLOCLEN; and Brad Cary, Wichita P.D. Federal officials Tom Rynne, Mort Moriarty and especially Rich(ard) La Magna were very generous in their cordial, knowledgeable responses. Among our Canadian friends, always equally helpful were cross-cultural trainer Glynn Davis; Detective David Stamp, who taught me more than he knew; and Henry Hollinger, all of the Calgary Police Service, and "Gus" Riddell, Asian Unit, Ontario; Sgt. Ron Nicholson, RCMP, Asian Investigative Unit; and members of the Metropolitan Toronto Homicide Unit.

Others who deserve my sincere thanks for their friendly help and for what they have taught me in one way or another are Jeannette Chu, Immigration and Naturalization Service; the late David Collier and Dr. "Mike" Heyman, both retired CIA personnel; David O'Malie, U.S. Customs Service; Detective Paul Jarosiewicz, Cambridge P.D.; Mike Mormello, Attorney General's Office of Pennsylvania; Ken Ellis, INS; Dan Green, Missouri State Highway Patrol; Dennis Matko and Craig Reese, Columbus, Ohio P.D.; Sgt. Bob Muhlenhart and Officer Steve Colferai, Montgomery County P.D.; my former neighbor, Police Chief Galen Ash, Bowling Green, Ohio P.D.; Dr. Bob Enoch, Sharonville, Ohio P.D., and several other regulars of the Annual Virginia Beach Organized Crime conferences. Other law enforcement personnel have been helpful and generous on many important details which are reflected in the "Do's and Don'ts." Other former CIA personnel and federal and municipal investigators were equally generous with their insights into cross-cultural (XC) matters, but have preferred to remain anonymous.

By providing this list of genial sources, I do not wish to suggest that contents of this work represent the views of any or all of these people or organizations. All my kind teachers, former students, and friends — law enforcement and academic — know quite well that my second-generation Welsh-American impulses and akuśalacitta prejudices are quite capable of generating a plethora of self-inflicted mistakes and inelegancies in both style and content. Thus, I, and no one else, bear full responsibility for the content of this book.

However, to all these professional law enforcement and intelligence personnel, for their penetrating cross-cultural insights, their friendliness, and their willingness to share what could be shared I gratefully offer my sincere thanks.

關係

Guanxi: "Connections and Networking"

The idea of guanxi lies at the heart of Asian culture and Asian and Asian-American crime. It also lies at the heart of law enforcement tactics, strategies, intelligence, and training; it is at the heart of relations between cops and communities, detectives and informants, and underlies the relations between police, analysts, prison guards, and prosecutors. Thus, guanxi is the foundation of your professional work in law enforcement, your trust of other professionals, the training that you receive to connect and integrate your knowledge, skills, hunches, and maximize your safety. So, just as guanxi lies at the heart of law enforcement training, it lies at the heart of this book.

The book is designed to help you to expand your knowledge and your skills in dealing with Asian crime and with Asians and Asian-Americans. To illustrate, you should note the ways guanxi, as well as many other ideas, are introduced and developed. Guanxi is initially introduced on pages 41, 61, and 70, in discussions related to dealing with witnesses and informants, it is discussed more fully on page 157 in discussions of Face and high- and low-context cultures, and again on page 120 in discussion of the La Cosa Nostra and the Mafia. As the book unfolds, these ideas are connected ("guanxied") with a variety of relevant facts, tactics, strategies, and mindsets—from the simple to the more complex, from the isolated to the connected. Thus, the book generates an understanding of the importance of internal connections between cops and Asians and encourages more good cops, guards, analysts, and prosecutors to become good Asian crime specialists.

Therefore, the characters for guanxi at the beginning of each chapter will serve to remind us of two things: first, the need for increased North American and international law enforcement guanxi, and second, that the contents of this book are all interconnected — just as your law enforcement work and your experience is interconnected legally, socially, experientially, and professionally.

I

Introduction

1 "If You Don't Have Much Time … "

關係

…read the next five pages, then go to Part II, "Do's and Don'ts", page 35.

Things to Keep in Mind

This is a *sourcebook* of suggested tactics, strategies, profiles, and explanations to assist police in combating Asian and Asian-American criminal activities and improving a variety of police relationships with the different Asian-American communities. At different levels of complexity, the book contains crime-relevant descriptions of Asian ideas including Chinese criminal "networking" and Vietnamese "village mentality" and cross-cultural aspects of interviewing, interrogation, intelligence, records, trials, name-identification codes (STC), Triads and Tongs, gangs, personal relations, funerals, family, food, colors, numbers, holidays, calendars, and general social behavior with police. Street-relevant cultural knowledge for gang specialists, detectives, and intelligence analysts is provided in brief overviews about Asian religions, legal systems, medicine, and languages and scripts and an explanation of why differences between cultures are important for them. To help in cross-cultural understanding, there are substantial ethnic profiles and comparisons among American, Chinese, and Vietnamese world-views or *mindsets*. Also, the need for the preservation of hard-won, street-wise strategies police *already* possess, but which are usually ignored and seldom preserved, is considered. Finally, suggestions are offered regarding the expansion and coordination of additional sources and topics in planning cross-cultural, in-service training programs to meet the challenge of increasing cultural diversity in North America and the expanding internationalization of organized crime.

To turn to a more familiar example, it may be helpful to think of this sourcebook as an expanded version of a federal law enforcement Profile, such as the Japanese Boryokudan (Yakuza) Profile, which is divided into: "Manner and Attitude, Group Travel, Facial Features, Clothing, Fingers, Travel Patterns, Occupations, Business Cards, Tattoos, Language". Notice that only some of these categories will be relevant to spotting an individual Yakuza member at one time. However, these descriptions constitute a list of possibly relevant items about which you should be *aware* if you are working Japanese organized crime. Combined with hands-on-experience, these descriptions will supplement your experience, expand your expectations, and sharpen your observations.

> "Individually, these characteristics may not be conclusive; however, when considered collectively together with officer experience, reasonable suspicion may be established to support further investigation."

The Feds think so, too; they wrote the previous sentence.

You do not need to read straight through the whole book. It is a source of possible solutions to problems; that is why it has tactics, strategies, profiles, and explanations. This is not a textbook about an academic specialty. So skip around and read what is relevant to you at the time. Use the Index for specific topics and the Glossary for specific ideas or words, and leave the rest for another day.

Different readers have different amounts of time available and different feelings about written materials. Do not try to memorize everything. Dip back into different parts of the book from time to time and test your experience against these generalizations. What is described or recommended here may not apply to your special situation.

Starting with the "Do's and Don'ts" in Part II, the book contains a wide range of problems, topics, and levels of complexity — like an ocean, it starts with shallow surf, then odd tide pools, and finally goes on to deeper, more difficult depths. The book starts from familiar problems and concrete suggestions and moves toward more general patterns of information. It is written to offer something to readers of very different backgrounds and levels of education. And, of course, there will always be examples and counter-examples not covered here. Also, throughout the whole book, the words "cross cultural" will be abbreviated as "XC".

First, take a look at the Table of Contents; it will give you an idea of the topics in the book and how they are organized. Reviewing the contents or the index will help you choose which sections are relevant to your interests and the amount of time you have available. Suggestions for further reading are listed at the end of several chapters.

Some Reasons to Be Cautious

Remember that there are enormous differences between Asian cultures (Chinese, Japanese, Korean, Vietnamese, Thai, Laotian, Cambodian, Hmong, Burmese, Philippine, Malaysian, Indonesian) and what holds for one does not necessarily hold for all. Moreover, there are great differences *within the "same" Asian groups, clans, villagers, or even between speakers of the same dialect.* Regional differences hold true between Asian cultures just as they hold true between different American cultures, for example, the deep South; Garden Grove, Orange Co.; Aspen-Vail; New York; Fort Worth-Dallas; Vermont; Miami, Dade Co.; San Francisco-Berkeley; North Dakota; and Boston-Cape Cod.

There are no "magic wands" that will enable you to reduce the complexity of Asian Crime and XC communication to a simple formula. Like scotch, XC complexity is an acquired taste.

All true generalizations have true counter-examples. In other words, no sensory-based empirical descriptions of cultures fit everybody, everything, everywhere all the time. Be cautious and take these generalizations with a grain of salt. Try them out and see whether they actually apply to your situation.

Understanding something about religion is certainly important in understanding a culture, but religious thought and practices are shaped by culture as much as they help to shape a culture. For example, assume that you picked up a book on Buddhism to better understand Vietnam or Japan; then ask yourself how much would a similar book on Christianity (or Judaism) help you understand or predict criminal behavior in Oakland, the Bronx, or in Chicago? Obviously, it might help, but one would be ill-advised to make too many causal connections between specific behaviors and the form and content of religious beliefs. Bastards remain bastards with or without Kuan Yin or Yahweh, Karma or Aseity.

To Others, We Have a Peculiar Culture Too!

We all wear culturally tinted sunglasses. We do not see foreigners the way they see themselves and foreigners do not always see us the way we see ourselves. Many Asians and Asian-Americans do not always share our mainstream U.S. emphases upon hyper-individuality, personal uniqueness, "doing our own thing", legalistic demands for social entitlements, or cries for various freedoms and "rights" with little emphasis upon personal responsibility and duties. Various reactions to these viewpoints are not necessarily *wrong*, but they *are* very different.

For example, some Asians consider quite odd our "incomplete" families consisting of only the parents and children (and perhaps grandparents), our amazing social and geographical mobility, our YUPPIEism and DINKism, our giving of blood, our public militancy about parading our style of individualism as if it were universally desired, and our inclination to appeal to courts, bloated legions of lawyers, our bail system, and our "letter-of-the-law" approaches to solving social problems. They sometimes wonder at the apparent loss of our sense of clan/family and ethnic loyalty, strong mutual support between long-term friends, intra-family dependence, public manners, and neighborhood self-reliance.

In short, we, and they, wear culturally tinted sunglasses which may filter our views and expectations of each other. As a consequence, we may actually see each other quite differently. However, since we all wear cultural sunglasses, the explicit realization that there *are* XC differences will help us to become alert and sensitive to cultural differences which produce "static" in our communications, excess stress on the job, and lower "stats" and make it harder to get the bad guys.

How Much Cross-Cultural Understanding Is Enough?

To keep your feet on the ground as you read these generalizations about Asians and Asian-American crime, ask yourself the three questions that follow. If you were to read the same sort of generalizations about members of a familiar criminal group such as the Mafia/La Cosa Nostra or the Colombians, the Haitians, or the Bloods and Crips, etc.:

1. How closely would you apply this information?
2. What problems would you see between what you read and what you know happens on the street?
3. How and to what extent would you act upon what you read?

A Checklist of Our Own Tolerances for Differences

On a scale of 1 (little tolerance) through 10 (a lot), how much tolerance do you have for:

1. New things — or do you think that if it is not broken, do not change it?
2. Complexity — or do you insist that all explanations must be simple and "obvious"?
3. Refutation — or do you seldom suspend judgment and always have the "final word" on foreign things?

4. Abstract Reasoning — or must all evidence for decisions be something you can touch, taste, see, or hear?
5. Non- "common sense" — or do you think that all Asian peoples are "basically" the same as ourselves?
6. Seeing our own cultural styles — or are our American ways of doing things actually just the way things *really* are, everywhere?
7. Different levels of exposition — or do you always want "just enough" information (and no more) for your job as you *now* see it?
8. Different analytical viewpoints? — or do the boundaries of your present job dictate the boundaries of what you will need to know and how you should get it?

To all the above, add: "NOT"! Thus, if you responded affirmatively to more than 50% of the above, we have a lot of work to do to understand what is different about Asian vs. non-Asian crime.

Be Skeptical!

Take *everything* in this book with a grain of salt. All generalizations have *at least* a few true counter-examples. Furthermore, we all fly by the seat of our pants even though we all try to learn as much as we can. But the relationships between Asian crime and Asian cultures are too complicated to be captured in a single book. No one has all the answers about these varied, complex relationships. Nor is anyone more than a fledgling expert, including the author. This includes Asians too, who, except for knowing their own home culture, are usually as ignorant about other Asians as are we North Americans.

At this point, if you do not have much time, turn to the "Do's and Don'ts" in Part II, starting on page 35.

Basics — What? Why? How? — Benefits, and Sources

2

關係

The purpose of this chapter is to tell you what is in the book, how it is organized, and its benefits and limitations.

Seven Basic Questions: What? Why? How?

Question 1: What Are the Cross-Cultural (XC) Aspects of Asian Crime?

We have an expanding, law-abiding, hardworking Asian-American population which is unevenly distributed and whose varied cultures are felt to be the most "foreign of the foreign (ethnically distinct)" from most North American Eurocentric law enforcement personnel, whether the latter are of Hispanic, African-American, or Caucasian decent.

The XC aspects of Asian crime (AC) are a limited but unrecognized problem for police because Asian-Americans and Asian-Canadians are often the fearful, but silent and uncooperative, victims of under-reported Asian-based crime for which the perceptions of cultural differences are important for community-police relations and police intelligence; for example, in New York about 70% of Chinese restaurants are extorted and 60% of the Chinese businesses are pressured by such criminal activities, but little is reported to the police.

Question 2: What Kind of Information is Cross-Cultural Information?

Any crime-relevant perceptions and actions resulting from different cultural assumptions, mindsets, and procedures.

Question 3: Why Is Cross-Cultural Information Important?

North America is becoming increasingly culturally diverse; this means that law enforcement people will observe more foreign customs and languages, and come into contact with increasing numbers of distinct ethnic groups. Furthermore, many of these ethnic groups will play greater economic, social, political, and cultural roles than ever before. As this diversity increases, cultural differences also become more important, not less important. Cultural differences do not "even out" as cultural diversity increases. Thus, cross-cultural knowledge and skills will become increasingly important for *all* Americans — native born *and* foreign born.

To understand, but not necessarily *agree* with, behaviors which are culturally different, it is helpful to know that cultural traits, behaviors, and mindsets which may be productive in one culture (for example, individual competitiveness) may not be productive in another culture, one which emphasizes quiet group consensus about collective goals.

It is simply a fact that all peoples do not have the same basic traits, as is assumed inaccurately in some theories and their applications in psychology, sociology, criminology, and personnel management. This fact is usually ignored, and we tend to project our own cultural assumptions upon others. Sometimes it does not matter; sometimes it is a disaster.

Question 4: Why Are the Cross-Cultural Aspects of Asian Crime Important?

As stated in the Preface, there are increasing problems with many forms of domestic and international Asian-based crime committed by a small number of Asian and Asian-American criminals. For example, Chinese Triads are presently the largest and oldest criminal organizations in the world, although not necessarily in North America. Thus, Triads actually represent "traditional" crime, whereas the Johnny-come-lately La Cosa Nostra (LCN) and Mafia are relative newcomers. We North Americans simply "discovered" Asian organized crime sometime after we finally admitted that the Mafia and the LCN actually exist.

Organized attempts to investigate and integrate those crime relevant but limited aspects of XC skills and knowledge to reduce Asian victimization and to increase police efficiency are usually unfamiliar to, generally ignored by, and seldom integrated within most law enforcement training programs. However, *they should be* integrated, for the characteristics of Asian crime requires a change in the characteristics of training.

Question 5: How Would Police Be Trained in Cross-Cultural Aspects of Asian Crime?

Various types of integrated instruction through discussion, case studies, lectures, reading, role playing, and the uses of interactive videos and CD-ROMs could be developed to assimilate and enhance XC skills and knowledge about the good and bad effects of cultural differences between Asians, Asian-Americans, Asian-Canadians, and North American law enforcement organizations.

Question 6: What Assumptions Should Guide Cross-Cultural Training Programs?

Deep cross-cultural analysis is necessary for *planning* what is to be taught. However, the complexities of deep cross-cultural analysis may not itself be directly relevant to improving street level tactics and intelligence strategies. That is, deep analysis is necessary to determine the relevant content and to choose illustrative examples, tactics, and strategies that need to be conveyed in the training of police officers, Federal agents, and analysts about the cross-cultural aspects of working Asian organized crime. However, it is equally important that cross-cultural knowledge be structured and communicated in forms appropriate to the complexities of specific crime problems and to the backgrounds, tasking, abilities, and experience of the law enforcement people working Asian organized crime — not academics. Also, in the communication of these Asian assumptions and values, some attention should be paid to the implicit but possibly inaccurate cultural presuppositions that we North Americans hold which in some cases, may hamper our understanding of Asian mindsets and hinder our operations against Asian criminal enterprises. (More points are expanded on in Chapters 23, 24, and 25.)

Question 7: What Are Some Examples of Cross-Cultural Information?

Examples would include skills and knowledge drawn from the following four levels of XC information. (The fourth level would be relevant *only* in planning aspects of XC training programs and/or analyzing special XC problems.)

Level 1: "Do's and Don'ts"

These are well focused, "practical" training materials which can promote interest in the cross-cultural aspects of AC and offer limited crime-relevant insights, tactics, strategies, and "things to look for". Thus, "Do's and Don'ts" constitute a legitimate, but oversimplified and limited, first step. In this book, there are seven chapters of "Do's and Don'ts".

Level 2: Ethnic and Cultural Profiles

This level includes sketches of Asian crime in North America, Asian history, geography, society, marriage, children, death, law and crime, calendars, subgroups, languages, dialects and scripts, names and identity, idioms and attitudes, religions, sexuality, immigration patterns, and holidays. These profiles, and Level 3, help one to understand Asians, their behaviors, and our responses to them.

Level 3: Cultural Mindsets and Paradigms

At this level, information is gathered about cultural traits, time orientation, power distance, identity, "psychology and mental illness", historical and hermeneutic models, (e.g., Vietnamese "village mentality" Chinese guanxi (networking) and Japanese *kata* (the culturally appropriate way things *should* be done), in addition to deeply buried "common sense" assumptions about: permanent self/soul vs. the Buddhist denial of the ontology (satya) of either self or non-self (nir-ātman); attitudes about medicine and "psychotherapy", and Natural Law theory; rebirth and prebirth lifetimes via Karma; human nature vs. Chinese "human-heartedness"; evil and theodicy (defending the goodness of God) vs. the effects of karma; heaven, death, and afterlife vs. Buddhist "afterlife destinies"; origins, finiteness, and neutrality of the universe; shame vs. guilt cultures, "natural" social castes as in India, and the unequal punishments of ancient Chinese social classes vs. the heritage of Anglo-Saxon common law, U.S. egalitarianism, due process, the chain of evidence, and equality before the law.

Level 4: Deep Philosophical Grammars

This level includes complex differences between cultures which strongly influence their "styles" of processing information and their models of the interpretation of everyday experiences, such as monochronic time vs. polychronic time; low-context vs. high-context cultures, space and territoriality; Chinese and Japanese Buddhist "contextualism" (fang bian/hōben): values about coherentist theories of truth; and other Asian epistemologies and ontological foundations illustrated in Sarvāstivāda vs. Sautrāntika Abhidharma, Wang Yang-Ming, Gongsun Long, Nāgārjuna, Confucius, Madhyamika prajñāpti, Han Fei Tzu, Lao Tzu, Lotus Sūtra-upāya; Anglo-European foundations, such as logos, Pythagorean-Stoic-Platonic "hidden ratios/ideas", Anglo-European Natural Law; correspondence theories of truth within Judeo and Graeco/Christian/Anglo-European deductive/axiomatic models in epistemology, ontology, and popular science and technology, as seen in the epistemologies and ontologies of Plato, Aristotle, Euclid, Aquinas, Spinoza, Descartes, Kant, Mach, early Wittgenstein, A. C. Graham, R. Rorty, and G. Lakoff.

Who Are the "Asian" Criminals?

The basic assumption is that although many Asians and Asian-Americans have lived in North America for some time, the cultural traits which make a difference for law enforcement are those of their ethnic homelands. We focus on the Peoples Republic of China (PRC), Vietnam, and other Sinocized countries. This book addresses the following three groups of people: (1) Asians, (2) Asian-Americans, and (3) mainline "North Americans". For the first group, the main focus is upon Chinese and Vietnamese tourists/visitors who hold legitimate passports from another country. (But it is important to remember that much of the XC discussion is also relevant to other Asian groups.) Among the second group, the focus is the same as the first except that these people are American citizens, legal refugees, or Resident Aliens ("green card" holders); members of the upper working class or middle classes; businessmen; and service workers. The focus of the third group, North Americans, is that of various mainline American ethnic groups of law enforcement professionals such as Hispanic-American cops, Afro-American cops and Euro-American cops, of European descent.

I repeat that it is very important to notice that none of the Hispanic-Americans, Afro-Americans, and Caucasian Euro-Americans of middle-European and West-European descent have any more knowledge or special historical or cultural ties to Asians than any of the others. Thus, while there remain cultural differences between the three mainline American cultural groups, Asians are as culturally distant to any one of these mainline American groups as to the other two.

Also, Asian-Americans are not free from XC problems merely because they are Asians. Often, Asian peoples are quite unfamiliar and literally ignorant of other Asian cultures; Korean shopkeepers will know no more about Vietnamese fishermen than do Nebraskans. Many Asians are familiar with only the regional or subcultures of their own immigrant parents. For example, first-generation Chinese rice-paddy farmers do not pass on to their children anything of Chinese city culture. Factory workers' sons know little of upper class Asian culture and probably speak a "low-caste" regional dialect understood by relatively few. Remember that Asian peoples, too, can be extremely ethnocentric, prejudiced, and/or ignorant of other Asian cultures.

In this book, we also focus on two subgroups found in North America and their interactions with law enforcement personnel: (1) Asian members of Asian communities who are either foreign-born or first/second generation who retain many of the cultural characteristics of their family history, and (2) Asian visitors, only a small portion of whom are engaged in Asian-based criminal activities. Asian gang members constitute a special class and problem in that they are usually only partially assimilated, if at all, in either American culture or in the culture of their ethnic heritage. In short, Asian gang bangers are not quite acculturated in either culture although they tend to be more "Americanized" than Asian. While some of the XC aspects of Asians described here will certainly be relevant to Asian gangs, their particular disassociation from *both* mainstream cultures make them a special case for concern, aspects of which are addressed in Chapters 8, 9, and 10.

What Are Some of the Benefits for Police?

The uses of XC knowledge and skills:

- Support a legitimate attitude and confidence about greater predictability and control.
- Reduce uncertainty, misunderstanding, and hostility toward "foreign" citizens.
- Stimulate the creation of new tactics and strategies to combat new AC problems.
- Suggest more accurate explanations for Asian and Asian-American criminal behavior.
- Humanize Asian peoples and reduce the projection of "inscrutability" and foreignness.
- Increase police efficiency, improve departmental "stats", secure promotions, and assist in getting the bad guys.
- Increase the degree of protection and quality of community policing offered to *all* American citizens, Asian and non-Asian.
- Make the job much more interesting for most (but not all) law enforcement personnel working Asian crime.

What Cross-Cultural Data Cannot Do: Planning, Guidelines, Limitations, and Packaging

As noted above in Level 1, the "Do's and Don'ts" are suggestions, XC road maps, XC guidelines — not detailed surveyor's maps nor rules to cover every situation with Asians or within the various Asian-American communities. "Do's and Don'ts" are like jazz (or some Bach fugues) in that every player must improvise around a theme or tune within a framework of chords; nobody repeats the melody more than twice. Thus, XC guidelines for Asian crime will always be incomplete because of changing combinations of the situation, your level of experience, and your personality. However, these guidelines may help police as a first step in learning how to navigate XC communication and apprehend criminals from culturally unfamiliar communities. By acting in ways which thwart the bad XC images some Asians may have about North American police, the Asian communities will benefit, and law enforcement professionals will find their jobs easier, more successful, and more interesting.

Also, let us address a critical point at the outset. The relevance of cross-cultural knowledge and skills is *finite.* A wide-ranging array of cross-cultural knowledge and skills is no magic wand with which to win all law enforcement battles with Asian organized crime. Nor will it solve all our problems of communication and trust between police and mainline society including the various Asian communities. Certainly, XC skills and knowledge will *help* law enforcement professionals both in combating criminals and in helping to reduce police stress levels. In short, if well organized, it will be of considerable help but only in certain contexts, when there is a clear recognition of its relevance and it is appropriately packaged for different uses and different types of law enforcement personnel.

What is meant by "packaging" is the planning, analysis, and distribution of cross-cultural information in an appropriate *form* (book, manual, TV training tape) and pitched at various usable/pragmatic *levels of complexity and direction* appropriate for street cops, detectives, intelligence analysts, and administrative planners, *not* academics as I have tried to do in this book. In short, important XC aspects of culture relevant to and packaged for the scholar usually are *not* relevant nor appropriately packaged for law enforcement people.

For example, the complexity of the cultural roots of Asian mindsets in religion, philosophy, social theory, and law; ideas about rebirth, fate, elite education, classical literature, formal methods of reasoning; and even some aspects of social rank and family behavior are the appropriate objects of the scholar's analyses. Only a part of all that is relevant for law enforcement, and most of it is largely relevant in the planning of training programs and the explanation of special problems. However, for most of those engaged in fighting Asian crime and the planning of in-service training programs, these interesting but complex aspects of culture are usually described in a manner far too abstract, too theoretical, and too far distant from the pragmatic needs of the police officer or intelligence analyst who must investigate the deliberate illegal behavior of Asian criminals. However, exposure to issues in multicultural community policing, hostage negotiation, financial crime, info-wars, alien smuggling, or homicide investigation will make one appreciate the complexities of the issues and the need for the application of a combination of extremely intelligence-intensive *heuristic* skills (seldom taught in universities) which require an amazing breadth of information and the ability to see the crime issues from an amazing variety of scenarios and points of view.

"Heuristics" are skills and knowledge which assist in the expansion of one's knowledge by provocation and by offering new information to stimulate the reader to discover more insights, more connections, and scenarios for him/herself. Thus, not only are such specific kinds of information, skills, and cross-cultural scenarios offered in this book, but also the whole book itself may be considered a heuristic device. This is because, as yet, there simply is no other cross-cultural book for police, analysts, prison guards, or prosecutors similar to this cross-cultural sourcebook. Therefore, this book's uniqueness lies in its being a sourcebook, a heuristic provocation, and stimulus to help law enforcement deal with new, unfamiliar aspects of Asian crime.

To focus on case-relevant materials for most police, the seven "bullet" chapters of this book have been focused on cultural "Do's and Don'ts." These "cookbook" chapters are followed by "basic mindset" chapters and two sizable chapters on ethnic profiles of Chinese and Vietnamese cultures. These different levels and arrangements are attempts to accommodate the fact that different levels and different types of XC information are needed for different problems, tasks, and policing responsibilities. For example, it is one type of XC tactical knowledge to know how to best interview a Theravāda monk to gain the support of Buddhist community; it is quite another type to know the deeper cultural and strategic models of Asian criminal entriprises. The merits of using Standard Telegraphic Code (STC, Chapter 20) is yet another specialized type of training.

For a more complex, but crime-relevant example of the "deeper cultural models" which function as heuristic devices (one type of XC knowledge), analysts have noted that there are significant cultural differences in internal organizational patterns between the La Cosa Nostra/Mafia and the Chinese Triads and Tongs. These cultural differences may help to explain the presence or the absence of certain *styles of organizational leadership and connections.* Asian and Asian-American criminals who are responsible for importing over 50% of the street heroin (90 to 95% pure!) are not always affiliated with Triads or Tongs; rather, they are opportunistic, short-term linkages coordinated for specific enterprises. Many groups are multi-ethnic "hook-up" organizations between Thai, Vietnamese, and other Asians. In short, one major cultural difference is in the organizational models of an Anglo-European, linked, *hierarchical* military chain of command vs. a Chinese networking, *opportunistic,* shifting affiliation, or a guanxi model of organization. (See Chapters 13 and 15 for descriptions of why Triad guanxi relationships are not quite like military "chains of command" as found in the LCN and Mafia.)

In summary, for cops on the street and in the Asian communities, we need such descriptions, but we also need cookbooks; check-off lists of tactics, profiles, mindsets, and comparisons; and general descriptions of strategies compatible with lots of exceptions. We do not need a flood of number-crunching dissertations to justify that police professionalism is "scientific" because it appears quantitative and exhibits lots of numbers. For other police strategies, we need other different kinds of XC data, arranged in various ways for different tasks and tactics. This book is not the last word in fighting Asian crime; however, it is a sizable supplemental word — and one that, with the help of interestered cops and agents, will be improved.

Sources, Methods, Applications: Academic and Law Enforcement

The next few pages will deal with my academic background and opinions about field work regarding Asian crime. Readers who have little interest in methodology or who have little time may wish to skip these few pages and go on to the next section.

The sources of this sourcebook are many, including more than 30 years of the author's own cross-cultural specialization in Asian studies, Asian language training, travel and foreign residency, analyses of intercultural formal logics and epistemologies, comparative philosophy and cultural anthropology, and methods of approaching and using the vast literature concerning XC communication. However, the most important sources, particularly for the "Do's and Don'ts" lists, were the many, many interviews with experienced Asian crime investigators and intelligence analysts in the field; in bars and patrol cars; on the streets; at AC conferences, offices, and restaurants. (The interviews in bars were the best — and the most informative.)

The sequence of my field work can be summarized by the following six questions which guided my inquiries with analysts, gang specialists, detectives, street cops, corrections officers, and prosecutors:

1. What are your local AC problems here and how do you deal with them?
2. What do you see as unique problems with "Asian crime" not found with non-Asian crime?
3. Do you think these particular problems can be overcome? How?
4. What kind of special training (if any) do you wish you had received when you started working AC?
5. How and where did you get what you know about AC tactics?
6. How do you think you could get more of what you perceive you need?

These responses were then categorized and merged with my other research; different types of information were selected; levels of exposition were determined, written, and then tried out on law enforcement audiences at Asian crime conferences.

Furthermore, although I have taken graduate courses and read widely in cultural anthropology, the methodological assumptions of this book about the XC aspects of AC are not those of a social "scientist". I am a comparative epistemologist, an Asian Studies specialist in comparative epistemology, formal logics, cognitive hermeneutics, and philosophical anthropology — in short, an academic Humanist whose research remains within the comparativist Asian Studies circles of the Humanities. There are two good reasons for pointing this out. First, the scholar has an obligation to state who he is and how he is about to analyze something. Second, the reader may be very naive about the study of the interrelationships between criminals and cultures, and may hold the oversimplified view or prejudice that such XC studies somehow belong exclusively to what is popularly called "social science". I disagree with this thesis. The problems are too big and too important to remain narrow in data, epistemology, and comparative methodology. (See Chapter 24.)

Moreover, the range of human knowledge and skills which *could* and *should* be brought to bear on something as complex as the interplay between several culturally distinct groups is enormous. Today, unfortunately, only rather narrow "social science" perspectives seem to be the major (and the only) players in approaching Asian criminal activities. Furthermore, given the complexity of Asian crime problems, it is important to note that these "scientific" players are neither a reflection nor a function of what is needed to get the law enforcement job done. Rather, this common, restricted range of players for analyzing Asian crime is a reflection and function of the presuppositions of what three groups (academic subcultures) habitually think and deem relevant and (unfalsifiably) effective.

These three subcultures are (1) North American intellectual and academic cultures, (2) policy makers within the administrative subcultures of law enforcement, and (3) sub-subcultures of first-line police who reflect the narrow criminal justice training they have received at most universities and community colleges. This training is generally devised by criminologists and sociologists, who are, I remind the reader, academics, not cops. Furthermore, only a minority regularly publish blind-reviewed research. The minority of criminal justice faculty who publish at all tend to be oriented towards the narrower ethnocentric-centric methodologies and sources of North American social sciences — most of which is narrowly and provincially Anglo-European in vision, scope, and depth. Worst, they usually know nothing of Asian cultures. The few who do — Professor Ko-lin Chin and David Kaplan are two good examples — prove the point by their exceptionally distinct scholarship. Therefore, this narrow range of approaches and the limited outlook of the players in combating AC are truly an educational embarrassment and a methodological mistake, for the problems of AC are much wider and more complex than the range of methods and strategies with which we habitually approach them.

However, while this book is analytic, rational, and empirically oriented in its field work and interviews, it is not simply an expository body of scientific field data. It is normative and speculative as well, for the book was written to help cops, and "to help" here means to recommend different approaches to law enforcement strategies and tactics. No doubt, some suggestions here will not be helpful in every case. However, many suggestions *will* be helpful because many suggestions have been verified again and again in the streets of North America. Cops use them! Also, these XC skills and knowledge remain verifiable and falsifiable, two necessary conditions for reliable empirical data about XC data and XC training.

Thus, in applying these crime-related "Do's and Don'ts", the author has kept in mind the modest assumption that in certain respects, Asians are to be approached differently than most North Americans, Afro-Americans, or American-Hispanics. Simply stated, Asian cultures differ significantly and necessitate different approaches. While these "Do's and Don'ts" will focus largely on the Chinese and the Vietnamese, they generally apply to other Asian groups too.

Another objection that ought to be faced head-on is that some critics may feel that the descriptive information here is directed to an idealized "Chinese" or "Vietnamese", not the varieties of actual Asian-Americans in this country who manifest differing degrees of cultural assimilation and changing mindsets. To some extent this is true — but largely trivial in a XC sourcebook. All general descriptions are such "idealized" portraits and such descriptions, as in this sourcebook, do not purport to describe all the varieties and degrees of cultural assimilation that range from the JOB-Chinese ("Just-off-the-boat") to the ABC-Chinese ("American-born-Chinese") to the partially or fully assimilated Asian-American who feels as unconnected in the local Chinatown as does a Norwegian-American from Wisconsin feel towards Oslo.

First, such an exclusive study would be valuable but remains quite foreign of the pragmatic goals of this sourcebook. Second, both surface and deep level cultural traits and habits persist through many generations and are manifested in varying degrees in the behaviors and thoughts of third and fourth generation immigrants' children. Third, a XC sourcebook is a set of guidelines to suggest, not to represent, a definitive description of a semi-assimilated immigrant population such as the half-assimilated generations of Irish living in England — a study of little use to the London and Midlands law enforcement personnel. The latter report that they must work with the limited generalities they have acquired through cultural acquaintance and informal "XC" training.

Therefore, these "do's and don'ts" do hold, in most cases, if you are NOT talking with hard core gang members, incoherent scumbags, or obvious criminal "officials". In general, the "do's and don'ts" hold if you are talking with traditional, Asian-born Asians, first and second generation Asian-American community leaders, mature Asian-American citizens, and Asian foreign visitors. Exceptions to these points are noted and will be obvious.

Some Asians and Asian-Americans May Not Like this Book

Some Asians and Asian-Americans may not like this book, *not* because it is unfair or grossly inaccurate, but because of three general reasons, each of which will tell us something about ourselves or are XC perspectives. First, the book necessarily *generalizes* about Asians — and nobody likes generalizations about themselves. We all know too many exceptions and too many counter-examples to whatever generalizations are asserted about ourselves: "*My* family's not like that" or "*My* friends don't act like that!"

For a personal illustration of this, I refer to the reactions of groups of American undergraduates I taught on an around-the-world teaching trip and in a study-abroad program in England. To help them gain a XC perspective on "foreigners" *and* themselves, I picked an excellent textbook, *American Cultural Patterns: a XC Perspective.*[2] Using this book as a guide with which to agree *or* disagree, I asked the students to look at themselves as representatives of American culture in roughly the same manner as they were looking at and judging all the "foreign English culture" with which they came into daily contact. Few could do it and most of them initially hated this (excellent) book!

However, they learned a tremendous amount about themselves because they were forced to see themselves as foreigners just as they continually observed the "Brits" in whose country they were living and studying. Overseas, *the students* were the foreigners! They were required to justify their perceived differences in cultures by contrasting their perceptions with the descriptions about Americans in the textbook. Of course, the student's perceptions were based on years of experience as Americans, but I required them to justify their disagreements with the (accurate) textbook generalizations. This made them start the hard work of gaining different, multicultural perspectives. Reflecting on their perspectives of foreigners and themselves allowed them to see themselves and their fellow Americans as foreigners see Americans — a difficult task. In short, it is simply difficult and sometimes irritating for Americans, Asian-Americans, and Asians to determine and evaluate without prejudice how each appears to the other. Obviously, some people will refuse to do it.

A second common factor of why some Asians will not feel comfortable with this book is that it generates, for some, a quiet feeling of anxiety that if their various cultures are too well known, the mystery will be gone and knowledge of their cultural patterns might be used to thwart them in business and other social interchange with non-Asians. This point has been made by a Chinese-American lawyer with regard to the widespread Chinese cultural motif of "working through connections" (guanxi).[3]

There is a third factor for why some Asians and Asian-Americans may not like this book. Asian immigrants, now expatriates and no longer active participants in their home culture, often naively see themselves and their original culture through an idealized recollection of their cultural roots. Furthermore, their recollections are often colored by understandable but excessive nostalgia. Often their memories are carefully reduced to a compensatory vision, a silently trimmed picture of what the Asian expatriate thinks he is or was, or how he/she would like his/her homeland to be. Consequently, to survive the resultant tensions of seeing their children so Americanized, the Asian immigrant sometimes paints an inner picture of what he thinks he must be and will brook no criticisms of his vision of his homeland, nor of the vision of himself, of what he thinks he is and was. In the words of Shashi Tharoor, his vision "admits [of] no foreignness."[4] Therefore, some Asians will not be at all comfortable with someone who points out these differences within the vivid context of crime linked to their home culture.

Furthermore, most studies by foreigners about one's own home culture are often seen as too brief and too sweeping to capture the dusty details and sweet smells of recollected everyday life in the home country. At the same time, studies by foreigners seem too brutal, too callous, and oversimplified, incompatible with the warm childhood and neighborhood memories (which we all possess) of "home". These memories are of a homeland which once existed, but now, if one dares to admit it, is gone from all but the memory and can never exist again.

It is a sad fact, as the Abhidharmists of Buddhism saw so clearly, that everything changes and that accurate self-knowledge is at a premium everywhere in the world! (The author is no exception.) As the son of an immigrant Welsh coal-miner who had the guts to try for a better life in a foreign country, the author is well aware that all of us are the descendants of immigrants. (After the last two centuries of wars, most of the Europeans are, too; Americans admit it!)

Finally, we might remember that as with most non-Asian-Americans, Asian-Americans are generally fine, decent people, as idiosyncratic as we are, who are family-oriented, taxpaying, individual citizens who contribute far more to our increasingly diverse country than a few criminal scumbags cost us. And, as with most non-Asian Americans, Asians are good, warm, loyal friends and good, solid neighbors. However, we also do not want to ignore that fact that as with a few non-Asian Americans, a few Asians can be ruthless, cheating, lying bastards. So, in the gritty world of cops, what's new about that?

Culture, Police, and Asian Crime

3

關係

The purpose of this chapter is to tell you what culture is and why it is important for law enforcement professionals.

The Cross-Cultural Context of Asian Crime in America

In his opening statement at the 1991 Senate Hearings on Asian Organized Crime, Senator Sam Nunn stated:[5]

> In our review of the Asian criminal world, we have found not only a culture very different than that with which most Americans are most familiar, but also a culture rich in virtues in loyalty, pride, and honor. Unfortunately, we have seen that those virtues can be used and exploited to protect and insulate Asian organized crime from law enforcement efforts.

Most North Americans know that there are significant cultural differences between Asian and American cultures. Many know that our trade balance with the Pacific Rim is over 40% greater than our trade with Europe. However, while many police see variations among American culture(s) every day, it is generally not well known how these cross-cultural differences have become more important for police. According to Hammer and Weaver,[6]

> Currently, there are 29 million Blacks, 17 million Hispanics, and 5.1 million Asians; a total of 53 million non-white people living the United States at the end of 1995. These people make up 21% of the population and will reach 25% by the year 2000. Projections suggest that in California, whites will drop from 64% to 48% of the State's population by the year 2010, and in the next century, Blacks, Hispanics, and Asians will outnumber Whites in the U.S. Further, since 1946, a total of 2.2 million refugees and 15.2

> million immigrants were admitted to the U.S.... Asia has accounted for the greatest number of immigrants since 1978 and in 1987 accounted for 42.8% of all immigration to the United States.

Thus, we are likely to have a foreign-born population of a record 19.8 million (8%) in 1990, and the Asian population is projected to be 10% of the U.S. population in a mere 57 years.[7] Another current estimate projects that "about 900,000 immigrants will continue to arrive ... during the 1990s. And by the middle of the 21st century ... more than 20% of all Americans will have come to the United States since 1990 or will be the children of those who did."[8] Furthermore, with a 108% rise in the Asian-American population in the last 10 years, including a 135% increase among Vietnamese, many law enforcement people are aware of the expanding Asian populations all too well. Thus, police do not need to be told that the American population they serve, protect, and occasionally investigate is changing radically.

Indicative of this trend is the fact that "there are as many Vangs (from Laos) in the Fresno telephone book as there are Jones."[9] Furthermore, compared to the recent past, today there seem to be more Koreans and Korean-Americans, more Chinese and Chinese-Americans, more Vietnamese and Vietnamese-Americans — and more and more Japanese businessmen. Police are confronted by these Asian-based changes in our population in addition to our expanding mixture of ethnic cultures from across the globe. As for most of us, almost all Asians, here and abroad, pay their taxes, raise their kids, and worry about the future. In short, Asians are honest, hard-working people who contribute to our communities and to our collective future. However, as in any group of humans, there are a few bad guys, and a few of them are Asian bad guys — and it is to them and the cops who must apprehend them that this book is directed.

What Is Culture?

Street cops, special agents, and other law enforcement personnel know from bitter experience that differences in cultural background may create difficulties in their efforts "to serve and to protect". Whether the suspect is a suddenly uncomprehending Cuban, a 38-year-old Iranian "student", a(nother) Nigerian chief's son, a transient Vietnamese (holding a double-drilled ping-pong ball!), or a drunken Welsh coalminer from Cardiff "on hoolidey", cultural differences do count, especially for cops. The point here is that although the law and the police goals remain the same, sometimes the means to them differ as a result of cultural differences.

When cops walk the streets or cruise the neighborhoods in unmarked vehicles, cultural differences count and make a difference. They count because they affect the dynamics between people. For example, both suspects and police officers quite naturally communicate and act out of their own cultural mindsets, their personal and publicly available frameworks of habitual attitudes, the deep values, images, and social explanations with which they shape and make sense of their experiences in the world. Of course, these frameworks include culturally grounded expectations about the law and law enforcement. Furthermore, when these cultural differences are too great or are mutually incompatible, communication and the prediction of behavior breaks down and trouble, hassle, and stress result — for both sides. With these cultural issues in mind, let's take a closer look at "culture".

First, what is "culture" in the context of references to "cultural differences"? When using the word "culture", we are referring to the largely implicit frameworks of shared ideas, beliefs, social expectations, habits of mind, one's mental software.[10] Also, a part of culture is one's assumptions about the physical and mental furniture of one's self, the relationships between body and mind, and the relations and expectations between self and the world. One descriptive metaphor for "culture" is that of a "conceptual-grammar". That is, cultural frameworks function as grammars function. Grammars describe, shape, and mold a language and also act as reference points to which we refer to get bearings on what can be said, what ought to be said, how to say it, and how to come to know what it means. Thus, culture refers to an integrated, fairly coherent, consistent grammar through which we see ourselves and the world. It is a web of practices (symbols, heroes, rituals), ideas of one's "self" and its characteristics (national, ethnic, generational, class, employment, gender), personality and relationships (between self and society, masculinity and femininity, youth and age, control of aggression, the expression of anger and feelings), and core values/norms.[11]

Most of the shaping and molding of both language and a person's culture occurs beneath the surface of the speaker's conscious mind. Languages and ideas are the building-blocks of culture which shape thoughts and thus behavior and are the means through which we recognize and predict behavior. To illustrate, at the first meeting of a university course dealing with cross-cultural issues, I sometimes ask: "Of what is the Golden Gate Bridge made?". Students' usual replies are steel, concrete, iron, paint, stone, etc. However, those accurate answers are also incomplete. They left out *ideas*! That is, the Golden Gate Bridge is made of ideas just as much as it is made of steel and concrete. Likewise, we are who and what we think we are because of our ideas, our ideas of ourselves (the inside), our ideas of what is not ourselves (the outside), *and* our ideas about the relationship between what is supposedly inside us and what is supposedly outside of us.

And where do we get these ideas? We get most of our ideas of what and who we are from what surrounds us, our parents, friends, neighbors. In short, we learn most about what we are from our social environment, which, in turn, is influenced by history and chance. Furthermore, it is from our culture that we get our ideas about what should count as a *good* idea, how to use it, and how to filter our experiences through it — in short, to make sense of the world.

Simply put, as functional adults, everyone generally operates within fairly coherent, consistent sets of ideas. We may call these sets of ideas "mindsets" or "world views". All of us have mindsets by which we try to make sense out of the world. We anticipate what will happen, who and what we are, and what we value by instantaneous reference to deeply buried but largely unconscious frameworks. Because most of our mindsets are buried in habits and what we think we see, we, in fact, only see things which are "damned obvious". We are seldom called upon to re-examine our buried mindsets. In fact, we usually become conscious that we actually have particular mindsets only when two conditions arise: (1) when we are confronted with mindsets that are substantially different, and (2) when it is important to us to understand the different mindsets of others to get what we want.

As I introduce in Chapter 13, our mindsets (or world views) are the cultural sunglasses we all have acquired as we grew up and through which we see the world in colors. Cultural mindsets are like tinted sunglasses. They help us see some things but they filter out other things; the world looks red through red sunglasses. If one reviews these ideas, one can see that if we are functional adults, we know the rules of the game of our culture — who and what we are, what's important, and the way things are done. These are rules of the game that "everyone knows". Roughly speaking, that is culture.

Consider the following two generalizations about compatibilities between cultures: "Compared to the Brazilians, the Vietnamese are very Chinese." "Compared to the Tibetans, Americans are very European." Thus, the contexts of comparisons are crucial if we are comparing Asians with the rest of the peoples of the world. However, we might benefit if we looked at an analogous comparison with an accurate North American comparison, namely, "Canadians are very American." What we do *not* mean here is that the Canadians *are* identical with U.S. citizens. Rather, what we mean is that in comparison with the composite cultural differences we find among the Thais, Brazilians, Kenyans, Mexicans, Icelanders, Indians, and Russians, the Canadians are closer in their general traits with U.S. citizens than with this composite of diverse countries and cultures. Analogously, the Vietnamese are closer in their general traits with the Chinese than with the Brazilians, Kenyans, Mexicans, Icelanders, Indians, or Russians.

Let us turn to a sports analogy to illustrate some XC incompatibilities between cultures, between different mindsets. While playing sports, you just cannot claim that you "caught the puck, passed it to third base, and got a first down." Why? Because you are not playing by the rules of American ice hockey, baseball, or football! You are confusing the rules, vocabulary, and thus the ideas of what is legitimate, expected, and allowed within (and between) hockey, baseball, and American football. Likewise, if you are confronted by two different cultures, the same kind of confusion about the cultural rules of the game may occur. It is then that you need to know three things: (1) the rules of the game of one's own mindset-culture, (2) the rules of the game of the other foreign mindset-culture, and (3) how to appropriately modify your ideas and behavior between mindsets to accomplish what you want to accomplish. This constitutes knowing cross-culture skills and knowledge — the goal of this book. Furthermore, it is important to remember that to understand is not necessarily to agree or recommend.

Whether they be Fukienese Chinese Snakeheads, Hanoi Hustlers, Houston Hard Chargers, or Chicago-Amerasian Jag-Offs, criminals wear cultural sunglasses, mindsets, PAEFs; so do sharp North American cops — and the rest of us. As with sunglasses, culture colors everything we see, much like a cocoon of ideas and expectations — a mindset-driven cocoon wrapped around us and through which we see the world. For law enforcement personnel, culture is a cocoon through which we see crime and judge how to act against it; the cocoons of culture shape what we see and what we expect to see. Therefore, by analogy, the mutual interplay of people involved in intelligence analysis or interrogation or a traffic stop may be confused and biased by the inaccurate projection of one's own cultural grammars on someone whose cultural grammar is different; often this projection is coupled with vast ignorance of the assumptions and effects of Asian culture that may lead to lost opportunities and at the worst, to disaster and danger on the street.

On the one hand, the cocoons of culture make us human, make us predictable and define the social rules of the game found everywhere: how we greet one another, how we exchange favors and obligations, and how we learn to recognize and trust one another. On the other hand, cultures not only make us appear different to others, but different behavioral rules of the game reflect different perceptions of crime. These perceptions, in turn, lead to different perceptions of police tactics within the Asian-American community. However, once, we recognize that there actually *are* cultural differences and that we are able to learn how these Asian mindsets differ from our own, we can then fine-tune our own cultural radars by learning about XC skills. Therefore, when we realize that we are all wearing (cultural) colored sunglasses and that the colors are sometimes very different, we will make *informed* decisions about cultural difference, and get on with our work of catching Asian criminals and protecting the general and culturally diverse public.

To summarize, while it is impossible not to have cultural mindsets, we *can* learn to see other people's cultures and to compare them. The goal is not necessarily to agree or act in accordance with another's mindset, but rather to understand it and predict and act upon the knowledge gained by understanding both sets of mindsets — yours and theirs. Then you can use the appropriate XC skills to achieve your own professional law enforcement goals. Thus, in most instances, police goals remain the same for all personnel. However, sometimes the strategic, tactical, and communicative *means* toward attaining the same police goals differ because of cultural differences in either the target group or the source group, or both.

How Are Cultural Traits Conceived and Used?

We Anglo-Europeans also have a particular tendency to look to external, measurable factors to explain and predict how and why people act, and how and why people succeed in different places. One set of factors usually ignored are those culture-specific sets of cultural traits that persist and are at least necessary conditions for success over centuries, across the world, and under very different social, economic, and geographical circumstances. As Thomas Sowell has argued, these cultural traits persist among broadly identifiable cultures even as they are spread throughout the world because of wars and/or immigration. In our subcultures, we normally point to social, economic, political, and geographical conditions to explain and predict why certain groups prosper. We seldom consider that they may also prosper because of culturally distinct skills and predilections, at what has been called here, "mental software" or habits of mind. While economic and geographical conditions, social and political organization, and the semi-random forces of history are intertwined components of the interplay and intermixture of cultures, the subcultures of Anglo-European academics and social policymakers tend to ignore persistent cultural traits as a significant component in explaining why certain groups succeed in adjusting to their environments in certain repeated ways over many centuries and while scattered throughout the world.

For a relevant example here, the clear commercial successes of the overseas Chinese throughout Asia and the rest of the world exemplify that their combination of certain cultural traits, thrift, hard work, family and Face, guanxi, and economic brotherhoods (hui) contribute mightily to their success. This remains true in spite of the fact that the economic and geographical conditions and the social and political organizations of their adopted countries differ considerably. Several examples follow:

1. "At one time, half the officers in the Malaysian air force were Chinese, and only one-third were Malay — just the reverse of their proportions in the populations of the country."[12]
2. "In the British colony of Hong Kong, Chinese children outperformed the English school children on nonverbal tests, despite the higher socioeconomic level of the English in Hong Kong. The Chinese also outperformed the Malays in Singapore and the Indonesians in Indonesia."[13]
3. Usually differences in the well attested superior Chinese perceptions of spatial conceptions are held to be genetic, but some have urged an alternative explanation: "a course of (explanatory) action equally compatible with purely cultural differences in styles of thinking ... (and based on) different types of abilities and modes of learning ...."[14,15]

In different ways, culture shapes, leads, and colors our perceptions; thus, culture counts!

Cross-Cultural Competency Is Not Just Language Competency

Everyone is familiar with the difficulties of not knowing the language of those with whom you are trying to communicate. Obviously, language is very important. However, many people equate knowing an Asian culture with knowing an Asian language. Not so. Many people are unaware of the equally difficult problems generated by differences in cross-cultural frameworks while communicating with Asians. Most persons who learn a foreign language in a university pick up something of the culture, usually trivial. However, both cross-cultural competency and language competency can be learned and are equally valuable and equally different for law enforcement.

In short, cops on the street in Asian communities do not have to learn an Asian language to learn something useful about Asian culture and to develop *helpful* cross-cultural competency. This also holds true for detectives, gang specialists, intelligence analysts, prison guards, and law enforcement administrators. Happily, we can learn a great deal of knowledge to help us deal with Asian crime without going through the arduous task of studying an Asian language. There are XC aspects of a criminal culture which are relevant for Asian crime but which remain quite distinct from the ability to speak the appropriate foreign language. This generally unrecognized distinction between foreign language training and cross-cultural training is often ignored in planning police training programs. (See Appendix B and C.)

Because language training requires long periods of instruction to reach an appropriate level of competence, one contrast becomes obvious; cross-cultural training can have immediate results in improving community relations, in intelligence analysis and interrogation, and in the recruitment of informants. Furthermore, while both language training and XC training are ideally required, cross-cultural training is less expensive than foreign language training, and with tight budgets cross-cultural training can be distributed to more officers for less money for greater immediate effects!

Police as Cross-Cultural Learners

Underlying the problems of cross-cultural differences and language barriers is the fact of Asian cultural distance from most police officers. Also, a problem is the understandable reluctance of some police officers to *attempt* to bridge that gap. More often than is usually admitted, overworked and understaffed law enforcement units are not only unfamiliar with Asian cultures but they are sometimes hostile to non-mainstream American cultural ways; and this holds true not only for white American police, but for Hispanic-American police and Afro-American police as well. While all officers are faced with problems of high crime and low budgets, some law enforcement officers are understandably reluctant to plunge into the complexities of Asian cultural behaviors. They are reluctant not only because of the added burdens of time and unfamiliar topics, but because of the cultural distance most officers feel between their own mindsets and the mindsets of Asian and Asian-American criminals. Hopefully, this book will help to relieve a few of those burdens.

As is heard so often, there seem to be more and more differences among Asian cultures generating more and more cultural differences about which police must learn; "learn" is the operative word here. It is very clear that some police have become very astute and nimble at dealing with Asians, such as some members of the International Association of Asian Crime Investigators, members of the California Asian Crime Investigators Association, and the DEA, BATF, DoD, CIA, and FBI specialists. However, they have had to make a deliberate effort to learn about Asians and relevant aspects of Asian-American culture; they certainly were not born knowing these things. It is also important to remember that second and third generation Asian-Americans were not born knowing these XC things either.

However, a glance through the membership list of the International Association of Asian Crime Investigators illustrates the Anglo-European roots of most, but certainly not all, of law enforcement personnel.[16] Thus, Americans and most Asians find each other more foreign than familiar within our North American multicultural societies. Furthermore, in their efforts to combat

Asian organized crime, U.S. law enforcement personnel increasingly recognize the specific problems of cultural differences which occur between mainline American police and Asians and Asian-Americans. These cross-cultural differences generate misperceived intentions, offensive behavior, poor communication, and mutual distrust. For police, these XC differences generate increased on-the-job stress and difficult and/or inaccurate intelligence for police at all levels, including reluctance of Asian-born citizens to testify after you have found the perps or the difficulties in tracing Chinese-American names through Interpol or the Royal Hong Kong Police. Similar problems also arise for analysts and administrators in their planning, identification and the interdiction of Asian and Asian-American criminals — for example, the inaccurate projection of LCN and Mafia chain-of-command organizational structures upon Chinese or Vietnamese guanxi networks.

Thus, law enforcement people know that the growing, real problem of crime is often complicated by Asian cultural differences. This is a problem which usually is not addressed except at Asian crime conferences. Moreover, these XC problems are very seldom addressed in the academic world of criminal justice, and they are very seldom reflected in training manuals and in training programs for most law enforcement personnel. Even when there is an observable growth in Asian and Asian-American crime, this growth is NOT reflected in the instruction about XC differences within most law enforcement training programs.

For example, there are many Midwest and Southern states that lack a law enforcement person who can record, identify, and transmit an Asian name correctly. "Correctly" means that the Asian suspect is correctly identified as to his/her correct ethnic and linguistic identity and that the Asian's name can be recorded in the relevant Asian language and codes — such as the Standard Telegraphic Code — so that it can be traced (for example, by the Royal Hong Kong Police or the Japanese National Police). (See Chapter 20 on Standard Telegraphic Code (STC).)

Unfortunately for most police trainers, there is neither a general awareness of the cross-cultural aspects of Asian crime nor is there much known about how to determine what the relevant XC aspects of Asian crime actually are, how to apply them, and how to train police to benefit from using them.

Police as Potential Cross-Cultural Specialists

It would seem to me that among thousands of law enforcement men and women, a great many have a great potential to be cross-cultural specialists. Most police have spent years and much of their energy detecting deception and overt lies, examining all kinds of hunches and all kinds of evidence, "figuring things out", and resolving ugly social situations. Most importantly, many police are especially perceptive and skillful at "reading" people.

It is true, of course, that not all police are so inclined nor skilled. However, the general (noncognitive) skills found in a good interrogator, an analyst-detective, or a clever street cop who knows the people of his/her area suggest that many police share some of the same basic traits, skills, and insights with applied XC academic epistemologically oriented specialists. Usually, cops are better at reading people than most people. Moreover, some Asian investigators have become especially cross-culturally nimble while others are in the process of becoming nimble.

However, one crucial barrier to acquiring XC nimbleness is the ability to become adept at something we *all* find difficult on occasion — self-analysis. Thus, I would argue that law enforcement people, in particular, could become cross-culturally nimble if (and only if) they examine their own personal/cultural habits long enough to compare them with Asian cultures with a view toward understanding, not necessarily agreement. Cross-cultural self-analysis is not as hard as it might appear, but it is not characteristic of most of us. (A starting point was the checklist on p. 6.)

Almost all police have learned to understand and separate the ethnic differences from the personal differences among suspects. Police have always learned to maintain a sense of their own cultural background while becoming more professionally competent in dealing with persons of other cultures.

Finally, remember that an Irishman turned in Vallachi! From Vallachi's Senate testimony about the Italian LCN, America discovered that we *do* have an organized crime problem. Since XC skills and knowledge *can* be learned, XC habits, skills, and knowledge can become a permanent part of the fund of perceptions, insights and conceptual tools police bring to their tough work against Asian criminals.

II

Cultural "Do's and Don'ts"

II

Public Relationships 4

關係

Asian Images of Police

In the eyes of most foreign-born or first generation Asians, Asian police (with the exception of the Japanese or perhaps the Royal Hong Kong Police) are neither greatly respected nor trusted. In much of Asia, law enforcement personnel have received, and sometimes deserved, a lot of very bad press. Asian police are often portrayed as corrupt, cold, brutal, disrespectful, and politically dangerous. Worse, if they were friendly, they were probably looking for bribes, extortion, kickbacks, or political advantages.

Thus, many Asian immigrants assume that corruption is as rampant here as in, say, certain areas of Thailand or China. Many also assume that their lives will be as controlled in America as they were in their home countries and that they will have as little potential for changing their social status or material lifestyles as they did in their Asian homeland. It is also helpful to remember that if they move into the poorer parts of some North American cities, some of these qualities appear to be true.

The modern concept of police professionalism is largely unknown in Asia. Thus, it is usually neither anticipated nor recognized by Asians. However, while many second and third generation Asian-Americans have come to learn that this image is false, many police have reported that this bad image still permeates many Asian-American communities. Hence, as a police officer you will not be trusted or assisted until they get to know you and respect you — until you have earned respect based on their own standards. But even then, while there are exceptions, do not expect to be accepted as a real "insider" in the community.

To Help Asians to Get a Better Image of Cops

To help Asian community members to learn about American culture and the police, try to have available to show in community or refugee centers at least two of a series of 16 videotapes produced for foreigners. These videos are available in many Asian languages, including Vietnamese, Khmer (Cambodia), Lao, Hmong (Laos), Mien (Laos), and Korean. The two videos most relevant for law enforcement are entitled "In a Strange Land: Police and the S.E. Asian Refugee", and "Culture Clash and the Law in America". These are produced by Newcomers to America (P.O. Box 339, Portland, OR, 97201; toll-free phone: 1-800-776-1610; about $60 each.).

Asian Families Come First

Be particularly respectful, courteous, and sensitive to the male elders and the senior female elders even though you may not deal with them directly. Remember that the elder males are the senior members of the family, and the family counts for almost everything among most Asians, particularly, for example, among the internationally active Cantonese, Fujien (Fukinese), Hakka, and Chui Chow Chinese.

Sometimes, the senior male may have given his authority to an elder female, the family matriarch, and she must be treated with *great* respect for she wields great authority. Other social connections of great importance and with strong mutual obligations are those of one's shared home province and home village, dialect, surname name associations (hui), economic "brotherhoods" or "companies" (Wade-Giles transliteration: kongsis, Pinyin transliteration: gongsi), and the more widely known Triads (heaven, earth, and man; Tian di hui: "Heaven and Earth Societies", for which the Standard Telegraphic Code (STC) is 1131 0966 2585; see Glossary and Chapter 20).

In the end, the extended family is the most important source, refuge, and foundation of Asians. The family comes first; a person without a family has no center, no anchor, no core. In almost every case, the (biological) family (and next, the various "brotherhoods" or hui) is more important than politics, nationalism, patriotism, or sexual attraction.

Check with the Amah

The elder Amah, the senior female live-in nanny/servant of the children and the family is privy to much of the family dialogue, arguments, and decisions. If she has been ill-treated and has broken away from the family, she might be a useful source of information.

Know and Be Known

Even though we Americans (as a group), probably desire to be liked more than many other cultural groups, try to cultivate quiet respect rather than the familiar open, optimistic American style of friendliness. Cultivate it over several years!

Funerals and Weddings

Make regular appearances at weddings, funerals (unless it is prohibited), and ethnic public holidays. Gang funerals and weddings are important because some unknown gang members or Triad or local Tong Association members may attend in person (Tong: STC 1016; see Glossary.)

Uniform vs. Plainclothes

In general, plainclothes detectives will find that more Asians will speak with you and you will generally fare better in the business district, except in those situations where a uniformed policeman would visibly intimidate gang members within a mall or in a business. Independent of the accuracy of such a perception, Asians generally perceive plainclothes police as having more power than uniformed police.

Respect and Social Levels

Watch the social levels in the communities by noting levels of respectful behavior — who is overly respectful to whom. Note the depth of the bows; deeper is more respectful. Note the seating arrangements at a private dinner; the host's back is to the entrance and the honored guests opposite the host, farthest from the entrance or to the right of the host. Notice who is offered the special morsel of food by the host. (See Cordell Hart's excellent monograph entitled *Chinese*).

Role-Playing

In general, Chinese do not like to play new roles and become uncomfortable when required to do so. They want some kind of a "script" which defines their roles; with the script they know "what they are supposed to be". In contrast, the Vietnamese, Cambodians, Laos, and Thai role-play quite easily and usually have fun with social role-playing simulations (see Chapter 11).

Body Language

Watch their body language. We may easily read too much into a posture of humbleness and/or smiling self-effacement; smiles can cover embarrassment, anger, scorn, or indifference. The failure of some Asian men to put themselves forward in an aggressive manner is usually what is expected of them and is culturally appropriate. On the other hand, if a police officer displayed the casual American gesture of crossing one's arms in front of one's body, this might easily be judged as insulting by a Hmong, who could think that the officer was showing that he was bored — as this gesture among the Hmong might indicate.

At a traffic stop, an Asian's quiet smiling, downcast eyes, exiting of his car, and his approaching the police car may be confusing or unnerving to American police; however, a mature traditional Asian would most likely be merely showing (unrecognized) respect to the officer. Thus, the outward appearance usually is quite independent of the inner plans or insights of the Asian individual. Moreover, smiles, apparent humbleness, and giving "face" do not always mean very much — what's new?! (See Chapters 13 and 15 for further discussion of "face".)

How Not to Sit

In interviews in a traditional Asian home or business, usually it is best to sit upright (do not slouch or sprawl), feet on the floor, hands together on your lap. If you cross your legs, place one knee over the other and do not let the toe or the bottom of your shoes become pointed towards anyone. Pointing is done with an open hand; neither gestures nor tone of voice should be rude, flamboyant, or loud. Even in your office interviews, keep your body posture fairly straight and do not slouch or put your feet up on the desk, etc.

Yakuza Body Language

By way of contrast, one group which shows body language usually quite different than most Japanese is the Japanese organized crime groups, the Boryokudan, also known as the Yakuza. At the middle and lower organizational levels, Yakazu tend to walk with an arrogant swagger, as if they know they are in charge — and can and will take charge. They scan a room like a cop entering on a raid except that they usually wear expensive, upscale clothes, and some have deliberately retained a fuller, more elaborate hair style. While Japanese organized crime is much less visible than most other Asian organized crime, the older Yakuza are not. The name "Yakuza" (the losers) is derived from the three numbers 8, 9, and 3, a losing hand at the Flower Card game; the name "Boryokudan" means the violent ones. About one fourth of the Boryokudan are ethnically Korean. Generally, Japanese-Koreans are considered as ethnic "outsiders" by most Japanese, even though such Japanese-Korean families may have lived in Japan for several generations. They, too, often tend to exhibit a similar swagger and arrogance. Also, remember that personal honor and giving and receiving "face" are very important, particularly for young Korean men.

Humility

Humility has a high value among traditional Asians. Thus, most Asians tend not to speak of themselves, their families, or their accomplishments. Often, they must be asked to respond to inquiries about their families to which most Americans would deliberately volunteer information to try to establish mutual feelings of friendliness. Also, "small talk" about trivial personal things is sometimes (but only sometimes) awkward for them.

Privacy

Privacy and being alone are usually not values shared by traditional Asians; they are usually part of a large extended family within whose boundaries there is little time or chance to be alone. A youngster sometimes sleeps in the same room as a guest at night so that the guest will not have to be alone.

The Avoidance of Public Confrontation

Tact, the avoidance of criticizing others, and behavior which saves "face" for all concerned are usually admired; brutal frankness or abrupt, rough-shod comments are not. Private, non-public conversations are quite another matter. Sometimes the absence of a private response in a culturally appropriate manner might wrongly be considered a gesture of tacit permission or the lack of objection.

Honor the Elderly

Treat the elderly with great quiet respect and with what many Americans would deem excessive politeness. For example, greet, seat, and serve them first. Open doors for the elderly before opening a door for a woman. In some parts of Asia, the elderly are given seats on a bus seats before a woman. Speak respectfully and maintain eye contact with them even as you use a translator; asking permission from a family elder, even if you have a warrant, may get you types of cooperation you could not get in another way.

Indirectness

Many Asians are much more indirect than most Americans. Among friends or acquaintances, many Asians may suggest that they need help, but they request such help in a very indirect manner. For example, they might suggest that their situation would be improved with a loan or some assistance. However, these needs will be described in such an indirect way as to allow the hearer the choice as to whether he will or can loan money or give assistance, all of which are ways to maintain and give "face" and avoid embarrassment.

"Face"

"Face" (Chinese: mian zi, STC 7240 1311) is roughly similar to our idea of public self respect, that external, socially approved *image* of oneself which must be maintained for the maintenance of one's social identity, personal honor, and public approval (see "Face", Chapters 13 and 15). It is obviously closely related to guanxi. Cord Hart mentioned that all kinds of abuse and evils can be endured if only one's "face", one's respectable social status, is maintained (see Appendix C). For example, do not serve a warrant on a restaurant manager in front of his waiters or staff for it will make him "lose face" (Chinese: diu lian, STC 0637 5245). Consequently, he will do something to regain some "face", usually against your best interests. Thus, respect shown and respect given is very important, even with scumbags. Giving "face" means that you are observing the proprieties (li) of showing respect for position, competency, age, and seniority; not to give "face" when it is proper to do so is to offer an insult. It bears repeating that "face" is *extremely* important with families, adult males, and all victims and witnesses.

Provocation and "Face"

Some young Asian males are heavily stressed because of unemployment, poor English skills, and family poverty. When this stress is coupled with impulsiveness and low tolerance for frustration — the "short fuse syndrome" — their perception that you have violated their sense of "face" can be touched off by almost anything. Unknown provocation by an officer on the street could include a gesture, small action, or a look which (to them) appears provocative. While this is not unknown with all ethnic groups, the violation of "face" is a particularly sensitive issue with some young Asian males, especially Koreans.

Guanxi

This extremely important Chinese idea, guanxi (STC 7070 0190; pronounced "gwaan-shee") refers to one's own and one's optional social networks. Guanxi is a web of benefit-driven relations, not a set of mutually friendly relationships desired for psychological wellbeing. Guanxi refers to an established web of mutually beneficial and obligatory connections between persons for whom there are understood relationships of mutual dependence, mutual obligation, and mutual maintenance of "face"; the origins and maintenance of guanxi connections is usually accomplished through (1) blood relations, (2) one's birth province or village, (3) (especially) shared dialect, (4) one's shared family name associations, (5) Tong associates, or (6) "economic brotherhoods", "named societies" (hui), or "Heaven and Earth Societies" (tian-di-hui, Triads). (These topics are explained in greater detail in Chapters 13 and 15)

All these are instances of guanxi connections for which there are implicit expectations and which, if not met, result in one being cut out of the guanxi chain, causing great loss of "face". Many guanxi relations are started at a very early age through family, friends, schoolmates, and refugee camps. Other guanxi relations are acquired in business as described above. Greater degrees of mutual obligations in guanxi relations are characteristically seen in the mutual obligations which hold between members of the Chinese and Korean Tongs, Triads, and Kongsis ("companies of shared assets") and other brotherhood associations (hui). Guanxi is the basic model of Chinese "mutually beneficial and obligatory connections" in intelligence and economic and social matters. However, guanxi relationships are common among all law-abiding Asian peoples and most guanxi relationships are completely independent of any gang or Triad/Tong affiliations. Understanding guanxi is central to understanding Chinese and many Asian peoples.

For example, analogous to our phrase "I've gotta friend in City Hall" (one's personal web of "friends" and "uncles"), one's guanxi network is crucial to almost all Asians. It is through one's personal connections and the connections of one's connections (one's guanxi) that things get done. In many businesses, 10 to 15% of the budget includes anticipated guanxi expenses. For example, a person with strong guanxi relations among mutual friends almost never refuses a guanxi request; one would lose "face". Thus one tries very strongly to do something as close as possible to the guanxi request.

Chinese criminal guanxi networks differ from LCN networks. The latter exhibits absolute hierarchical relationships during a member's lifetime of exclusive allegiance to those in authority above and below each level, by means of absolute chain-of-command relationships located within exclusive, geographically defined turfdoms. (The following is expanded in Chapter 15) Compared with American expectations of organized crime networks, guanxi networks are wider, bigger, deeper, quicker, more anonymous, and composed of nonvertical, optional links that are not well known. Guanxi relations radiate farther, reflect more sources of assistance, and obligations, reflect a stronger sense of obligation to more people, and exhibit more flexible options for new criminal enterprises and cheaper criminal startup costs.

Street Cops and Guanxi

While you seldom will be part of a large, extensive Asian guanxi, try to become a well known component of the public Asian community, the larger social network. As a cop, become worthy of "being known", one who is well known, respected, and trusted to keep his/her word, the social analogue of American guanxi. Also, if you should find yourself poised to establish some sort of guanxi relation, be sure that you have a fairly good idea of what it means and what may be asked of you. It is at that time that you need to decide whether you would wish to respond appropriately to another's request if a favor has been granted to you; if you do not respond appropriately to another's request in the guanxi chain, you would lose "face" and be cut off and considered as unworthy and unreliable. However, do not expect that most Asians will publicly act or speak against the social norms of their ethnic guanxi groups, especially those with more recent Taiwanese-Fukinese, PRC relations.

Gossip is Good

It is probably better to remain quietly receptive to conversation and allow Asian friends, informants, or suspects to enjoy the worldwide pleasure of gossiping. While Asians may express opinions about themselves and others, ask yourself why they might be willing to breach their normal social behavior to speak critically about their friends to you, the outsider. Visit the coffee shops frequently, or have tea and be an active, analytical *listener*, as you scan the younger customers to see if someone fails to pay for the food — a sign of *possible* extortion.

Beeper/Pager Numbers

Try to get a beeper number which lacks the unlucky numbers 4 or 14. Also try not to change your beeper number; many officers have received helpful calls from criminals who have remembered a favor or at least fair, respectful treatment some years in the past and who now use the old numbers to quietly contact trusted officers once again.

Street Negotiations

Often, informal deals, favors, trades, and "street" negotiations are seldom done in offices but rather over food — usually at the end of a good meal together. What matters most are the relationships and interactions between people; what matters less are law-like expectations, explicit rules, or contracts.

Shake Hands Only with Older Recognized Gang Leaders, Not with Younger Gang Members

If you bring in a gang — usually referred to as "gang bangers" — to the office, shaking hands with those gang bangers at the low end of their social scale within the gang has been characterized as a "round-eyes's way" or the "white man's game", and this contributes to their perception that you do things the awkward way. Let the gang hierarchy remain intact. Save your public courtesies for the ones to whom you need to give "face" and show simple respect. Avoid letting a gang banger assume a close, controlling stance or gesture such as putting his arm around your shoulder. A respectful gesture of leaving is the double-handed handshake. Use it sparingly and with great selectivity — it usually conveys considerable respect and "face".

Intimidate Gang Suspects by Sitting Next to Them

In the coffeehouses or bars, intimidate gang suspects by sitting next to them and making friendly, familiar talk with them. Make others think they might be snitching to police. While sitting with them, look closely at their hair to see if you can see signs of colored "hair dust". This coloring product is sometimes used prior and during a crime; then it is easily dispersed by sticking their head out of a moving car allowing their hair to return to its natural color. Also, when close, discreetly look for recent burn marks or fresh tattoos. (See Chapter 11.)

Foreign Courtesy Terms

Learn something of the geographical and historical background of the Asian people in your district. Explore their general culture, their food and festivals. Learn a few courtesy phrases, for example, learn the simple Chinese words or phrases for thank you (*shay shay*), hello (*nean how ma*), goodbye (*zai jian*), Mister, (*syee-an shung*) after the man's family name, and Madam (*eye-ren* or *new shur*) after the woman's family name. (Obviously, these are transliterated in neither the Pinyin nor Wade Giles systems. Cassette teaching tapes for such courtesy terms are available for under $20.) Let your Asian friends correct your pronunciation. Also, learn to recognize some of the obscene slang imperatives ("F— you!" is *diu nei la* in Cantonese) so that you can pull gang bangers up short if they are cursing you in their Asian language.

Do Not Use Slang, Parables, or "Pop" References

When talking with older Asians, avoid American idioms and allusions to stories or parables common to Western cultures, as some traditional Asians may not know them or their meanings. Some older Asians lead very narrow lives; they neither watch American television nor know much of everyday American slang or pop culture. Many slang references are culture bound and are either difficult to translate into an Asian language or, if they are translated literally, they do not make any sense.

Observe and Balance Paybacks

Be straightforward in your promises and/or suggestions to suspects and community leaders about what they can and cannot expect from or through you. Remember that *all* favors, yours and theirs, must and will be repaid. Paybacks of all kinds are very important — from tea to help with school officials. They have long memories about trust, unfulfilled obligations, and broken promises. Cultivate quiet social relationships with some senior members of the community even though you know some of them may be trying to cultivate you for their own questionable reasons. If respected community members come to trust you and mutual respect is established over time, information will come to you quietly. They, like most of us, do not forget who is reliable and trustworthy. Then it may be through them that you may learn about who is on the fringe of criminal activities, potential sources of informants and witnesses.

Avoid Co-option

If you are becoming friendly with middle or high level "officials", try to prevent them from using your friendship to intimidate or bluff others — or to compromise you. It is a very thin line! Some have used a photograph of themselves and an Asian investigator to convince other Asians that "this policeman is my friend" — that you are "his" man. Another investigator mentioned that (over 10 years ago) about 11 out of several dozen investigators were under investigation by their own law enforcement organizations for (possibly) being "a bit too close" to some of the local Asian community leaders. Most were judged free of any violations. However, it seems that the cultural distance between Asians and *some* North American administrators makes the latter nervous about their subordinates being "too close" with people about whom the administrators know so little. On the other hand, remember that nothing is free with Asians (or anyone else!) and that there is a price to pay for everything — everything done, everything given, and everything owed.

Holidays, Grand Openings, and Surveillance

Learn which Asian holidays traditionally require that all disputes be resolved and for which affectionate respects must be paid to family members, especially the parents and senior uncles, brothers and cousins. For example, the series of celebrations around the New Year (e.g., Vietnamese Tet) are good times to observe who knows whom and to whom special respect is given. Also at the New Year celebration, the red envelopes of "lucky money" (hung bao) are given to children and single men. Also, the presence of a black headed lion in a New Year parade or holiday parade may constitute a symbolic challenge to other gang factions, and the potential for fights increases.

It is during, and just before, these holidays that you may wish to secure telephone taps, organize surveillance teams, and photograph visitors entering residences of senior family members or family name associations, various hui, etc. Suspects who have gone underground will often turn up in person or make telephone contact with their families during Asian holidays. Grand openings of night clubs and restaurants are good times to see who is prominent to whom and who is becoming (or ceasing to be) friendly with whom. Also, it is a good time to secure photographs of groups and of those newly affiliated members.

Questionable Community Translators

If you cannot find a multilingual sworn officer or a licensed court interpreter, be slightly suspicious of those who obviously are eager to translate for you. If you must use community people or a bystander to translate for you, politely insist that they not re-interpret what you have said. Rather, insist that they convey what you have said in the most literal straightforward way. If they resist, quickly say that you will talk with them later about their perceived need to interpret rather than translate. Then, let them explain (and justify) why and what they think they ought to say for you. Also, remember that in some Asian communities, such as the Hmongs, certain people of certain surname-clans cannot be used as translators because of very long-standing feuds and clan disagreements.

Check Whether Bunsen Burners Are On at the Jewelry Store

If you suspect that a Vietnamese jewelry store may be receiving stolen gold jewelry, check over time whether there is always a working bunsen burner with which gold might be quickly melted down into a completely untraceable form.

Asian Newspapers

Subscribe to all Asian newspapers, realizing that there are disreputable, biased ones. Have a reliable ethnic (native) person read and summarize all information, gossip, and announcements and relay his/her suggestions or suspicions of significant passages, that is, the "real" story behind what is found in the newspaper. Include a direct message in the newspapers that your police department wishes to serve the community and list a phone where citizens — without giving their names — may report such nuts-and-bolts problems as prescription fraud, unreported robberies, welfare fraud, rape, unreported gun wounds, (double) extortion, etc.

Take out advertisements or place articles in the Asian-language newspapers for particular cases for which you would like special assistance from the Asian community. They like to read about the crime news and that the police are actually "working on it" — and that they have not been ignored. From these efforts, you may get a phone call with relevant intelligence. Check the newspaper for announcements of upcoming dances, celebrations, or concerts, for these will attract extortion and/or home invasion robberies during the scheduled events. Dances are often a stage for publicly settling old or perceived losses of "face".

Publicize all successful convictions and protective actions in the Asian-language newspapers. It helps to convince other Asians that the law does work and it helps to strengthen police-community relations with leaders of the community. The newspapers are usually very cooperative and are glad to get the details of community problems and their possible solutions.

Asian Public Apologies

If he is raided, occasionally an Asian gambler (often a Korean or a Vietnamese) may make a public apology in the local foreign language newspaper for bringing shame and bad publicity upon the local Asian community. That, in many Asians' eyes, is sufficient to render what he did unobjectionable.

Folk Medicine and Alleged Child Abuse

The physical effects of three fairly widespread practices of Chinese and Southeast Asian folk medicine (see Chapter 14) are sometimes perceived as instances of child abuse. These practices include: (1) the oiled skin of the patient is vigorously rubbed with a silver coin which leaves reddish striations; (2) a small heated glass placed on the skin and allowed to cool causes circular burns; and (3) burning incense moxa (aijiu) is placed on the skin a process (called "moxibustion"), which leaves small red marks and is often used along with acupuncture.[17]

Passport Profiles

Take particular note of the passports of Chinese or Japanese who exhibit multiple one-day trips in and out of Korea, the Philippines, and Los Angeles with quick turnaround. While Japanese organized crime (Yakuza) probably creates more internal problems for Japan than for North America, Yakuza are very active in Hawaii and Los Angeles, especially in regard to the smuggling of guns and "ice" to Japan.

Forged U.S. Visas and Altered Passports

Some of the highest quality fraudulent passports and U.S. visas are manufactured in Paraguay (South America) by criminals probably trained by Taiwanese organized crime members. Other Caribbean and Central and South American sources for which there is a higher probability of illegal documents and/or Chinese alien smuggling are Guatemala, El Salvador, Belize, Honduras, Costa Rica, Panama, Brazil, Bolivia, St. Lucia, Bahamas, and the Dominican Republic.[18]

Passports, Visas, and Claims of Diplomatic Immunity

U.S. Department of State, Diplomatic Security Service:

Office of Investigations (Washington, D.C.)	(202) 663-0110
Passport Fraud Branch (Washington, D.C.)	(202) 663-0379
Visa Fraud Branch (Washington, D.C.)	(202) 663-0338
Rewards for Terrorism Information Program	(202) 429-2207 or 1-800-HEROES1

Office of Protocol and the Office of Foreign Missions: Inquiries at the following numbers should be made when an individual claims (diplomatic) immunity or in any case where the officer has reason to believe that invalid identification is being presented:

U.S. Department of State federal license tags, registrations, or other motor vehicle information: (202) 895-3532

U.S. Department of State driver's license and general licensing information: (202) 895-3521

Diplomatic agents and family members: (202) 647-4570

Embassy administrative and technical, service staff, and families: (202) 647-1405

Consular personnel and families: (202) 647-1404

International organizations: (202) 647-1402

For reporting traffic incidents/accidents, issuance of citations, etc., involving foreign missions personnel: (202) 895-3522

Diplomatic Auto License Plates

The codes of special red, white, and blue auto license plates issued by the U.S. Department of State consist of three parts. From left to right, they are (1) a white letter against a blue background indicating the status of the license holder as "D" for diplomat, "C" for Consul, "S" for staff, or "A" for United Nations Secretariat; (2) a two-lettered country code in blue set against a white background; and (3) a three-lettered unique number which identifies the license holder (for example, "D AF 009"). The Asian country codes are Japan,

AF; South Korea, WD; North Korea, GQ; China (People's Republic of China [mainland]), CY; Singapore, VK; Malaysia, KR; Thailand, VF; Laos, QN; Vietnam, LD; Myanmar (formerly Burma), CV; Philippines, FR. Diplomatic auto plates of United Nations mission autos reflect the opposite sequence described above. That is, the sequence example above would be "009 AF D".

Person-to-Person Relationships

5

關係

Remember: "Taking out Asian crime takes Asian time!"

Attitudes and Applications

By making suggestions about possible person-to-person relations, it is not meant that you should always follow and do everything listed here — except the "don'ts". Avoid them! Simply put, if you are not Asian, you are not Asian, and no one expects you to act as if you were. However, understanding some Asian assumptions behind behavior, using an occasional gesture of recognition of traditional Asian ways of doing things, will help to convey a degree of sympathy, courtesy, and respect between people. Likewise, avoiding unintended cross-cultural blunders will help you feel comfortable in your assignment, help you secure more assistance and cooperation in the Asian community, and help you increase your stats, get the criminals off the streets, and perhaps get a promotion. As always, be skeptical, but try some of these things out. You cannot help but learn the best ways of dealing with Asians *for you.*

Speak Quietly

Don't come on strong! Remain soft-spoken, polite, and respectful towards all, particularly to the elderly and towards all Asian women. Never comment on any female's attractiveness (or the lack of it). Don't wink and don't use a lot of slang. Also, don't tell any sexual jokes; jokes of all kinds are very difficult unless you really know the language and understand the target culture.

Personal Space

It is also important to watch where people draw the line for the "bubble" of personal space. We all have such an unstated set of spatial boundaries around ourselves. If you do not believe this to be so, watch how people arrange their spaces around others on an elevator as other people get on or off! Do not violate the bubbles of personal space of the Asian peoples to whom you are talking; their bubbles may be a different size than your own. Also, ask yourself if you become uncomfortable because they have violated your *own* "space bubble" although you have not really noticed it. Some Asians appear rude, and some Asians *are* rude, pushy, and aggressive. However, some appear to be aggressive when the real reason they appear so is that they have unknowingly violated the boundaries of your bubble of personal space.

Don't Touch

Among straight Asian peoples, never touch anyone except to shake hands in greeting or leaving, usually between males. Certainly do not touch any female, and no friendly slaps on the back! If clear and unmistakably sincere affection is ever developed for you, you will know it. But physical touching would be, in most cases, an uncommon sign and would seldom happen in a public place. Remain polite but do not touch, even when you are trying to be reassuring and supportive. Convey that through the tone and style of your speech.

Spend Time in the Streets

Go into the Asian communities and talk with everyone. Be on the street corners, not in the office. Visit the tea shops, bars, and restaurants — and just listen. As do most of us, Asians will gossip and tell stories about "the other guys". Visit the hospitals and talk with the families of crime victims — a natural time to illustrate your concern, sympathy, and trustworthiness.

Visit the Temples

Visit all the temples, especially during ethnic festivals. Show that you are genuinely interested in what is going on. Watch what happens at the rituals and to whom particular respect is given. Learn a few courtesy words in the appropriate Asian language, and learn something of the culture, history, and Asian geography of the community's origins. They will appreciate such examples of interest and you will find that information from within the Asian community will come to you more often. Also, your Asian responsibilities will become more interesting to you.

Identifying Ethnic Groups

Until you become familiar with a specific ethnic group, you may not be able to tell each ethnic group apart from others; many Asians can. Talk to them; you will learn gradually to pick up the subtle clues. Mix the photographs in your photo book with different ethnic groups known to you. This will help you learn ethnic differences, and it will help prevent the perception that you are discriminating on racial grounds. Remember that Asians do not consider themselves as "Asians"; they think of themselves as members of a given region, dialect group, family name group just as we say that we are from Chicago, the Bay Area, the Bronx, etc. Only to "foreigners" do we say that we are Americans, Canadians, Chinese, or Vietnamese, etc.

Gestures

Learn how to beckon to someone in a way that does not insult them. While most Asians realize that none of your gestures are intended to insult them, such gestures and mannerisms will still irritate them, make them feel uncomfortable, and thwart your efforts to establish good relations. Use your open hand to indicate (point to) someone. To gesture a request that they come towards you, extend your arm, palm *down*, not palm up, and wiggle your fingers towards you. A palm-up gesture can be insulting because that is the way animals are called.

Other Physical "Don'ts"

- Don't pat an Asian child on the head, for you disturb the "power points" (the highest chakra) in the body especially at the cowlick; it is said to be the site of the "soul".
- Don't point with your foot.
- Don't point at the face of another.
- Don't cross your fingers, because it is an obscene gesture.
- Don't snap your fingers at all, even in a gesture which expresses how quickly you are going to do something; it is a rude, irritating gesture to most Asians because it appears, and in most Asian cultures is, insulting.

Business Cards

If possible, business cards should be printed in English on one side and in the appropriate Asian language on the reverse side. Also, business cards and gifts should be given and received with both hands with at least a polite moment taken to carefully read them to show courtesy and respect.

Applause

At a formal gathering such as for a speech, some Asian speakers will return the applause in a polite subdued manner; they are not congratulating themselves. If you are applauded, you may wish to "thank them" for their applause with the modest gesture of hands folded together at chest level. However, if you do not feel comfortable doing it — and many people do not — just acknowledge the applause with a polite smile and a nod.

Spitting

Although it is officially discouraged in mainland China, as in much of east and southeast Asia — even severely punished in squeaky-clean Singapore! — spitting and blowing your nose without a handkerchief is fairly common. The usual reason is that, "It is natural and hygienic because you are merely emptying your body of waste materials."

Greetings

With the Namaste (na-maa-stay) greeting (hands folded together at chest level) practiced so widely in South Asia and Southeast Asia, straightforward eye contact is politely avoided. Sometimes, a slight bow is used too. With formal East Asians (and not all are formal), do not bow too far down, nor repeatedly. A slight bending of the head with a courteous nod will often do. Greetings are first given to anyone older than the guest. Usually greet the oldest male and then greet each person from the oldest to the youngest. Gift giving, particularly at ethnic holidays, is considered a part of good social manners, and (if approved by your superiors) a small token gift will be considered polite. However, watch out for certain colors, customs, etc. (see Chapter 14) This varies greatly from context to context, so be careful. (Note the caution in "Avoid Co-Option" in the previous chapter.)

Polite Topics of Conversation

Ask about their schoolwork or sports when talking to "straight" young people; with the elderly, inquire about their health or the weather. Do not ask businessmen about their wives or expect them to talk about their families in the detailed ways in which most Americans would talk about such things.

Silence

When interrogating, in casual conversations, or especially in serious negotiations, relax when silence occurs. Wait it out. Americans dislike silence and feel a need to talk after approximately 20 seconds; Asians sometimes consider silence an indirect compliment for the listener may be contemplating the speaker's comments. Since Asians often expect silences and are usually more comfortable with silence, just relax.

Privacy

Privacy and the pleasures of being alone usually are not public values shared by traditional Asians. They were often raised as part of a large extended family within whose boundaries there was little chance to be alone. To them, it seems quite natural to want to be with others. Furthermore, in many Asian languages, the words for privacy have a slightly selfish ring, a bad connotation. It usually suggests abandonment of family and friends, cutting off one's self from one's extended family, perhaps for bad reasons. The idea of "privacy" is unknown, for example, in Khmer (Cambodian). Many Asian peoples think that letting an infant or a young child remain alone in a darkened room to "cry herself to sleep" is barbaric. To the Asian it is common sense that they obviously ought to be with someone.

Saying "No"

Remember that in the polite public context of many Asian countries, it is impolite to utter a direct "No!"; it is felt to be rude, and one loses "face" by uttering a blatant, rude "no." Thus, out of courteous concern, many Asians will (in effect) either say "yes" or they will express a negative response in a very roundabout manner: "Yes, how very interesting;" "I will do my best;" "Oh my, I've never heard of that before;" "We'll consider it" — or by a quiet smile, look away, or change the subject without replying to your question or suggestion. All of these can be "no" answers. If it is necessary to say "no" to someone, try to avoid a flat "no!". Be clear, but convey your negative response as tactfully as possible — privately, if possible. On an occasion when they know that you must respond negatively to a request, a social inferior (to you) might be sent around to receive the "no" so that neither of you will lose "face" and you may continue your friendship or (at least) avoid severing your relationship.

Watch Out for the "Yes" Answers

In Chinese, Japanese, Lao, and Vietnamese, a "yes" response in English may only mean that they heard you and/or that they acknowledge to you that they understood what you said. A "yes" answer does not necessarily mean that they agree to the truth of what you said nor that they agree to act in accordance with what you said. It is your responsibility to ask a question which distinguishes between their understanding what you said and their agreement with what you said.

Get Search Warrants, Not Consent to Search

Many foreign-born Asians are unfamiliar with the form of questioning we use in English. They tend to remain very polite to authority figures and thus answer "yes" to most questions. For example, Mrs. Ngo is likely to answer "yes" to a request from police to search. However, a sharp defense attorney can easily make the case that she was unfamiliar with both the American cultural habits and standard forms of English questioning and consequently did not understand your request sufficiently to give informed permission to search. A warrant will bypass that potential problem.

Do Beat Around the Bush

Don't try to hurry any informal questioning. Traditional Asians operate on their ideas of social and conversational timing, not American standards of "efficiency" and "getting to the point". In other words, do beat around the bush! Indirectness may often be the appropriate way of approaching an important, delicate, or touchy topic. Keep cool and watch quietly for clues indicating indirect suggestions or topics just as you hasten for "themes" during the later stages of interrogation. (See Chapter 9.)

Removing Shoes

If you are about to enter the house or apartment of an Asian family, check whether members are wearing slippers or socks without shoes. If so, take off your shoes once you are inside the door. It is one of a number of face-saving gestures of goodwill which you will find helpful and courteous. You will not get anything for having done it, but you will have avoided silently offending them. On the other hand, there may be good reasons for not being caught shoeless during an emergency call. Try, at least, to explain why you cannot remove your shoes in a given situation.

Don't Push Things Around with Your Feet

Avoid moving chairs, tables, closing doors, etc., with your feet. As in many countries, the feet are considered the lowest and dirtiest part of the body and to touch anything with your shoes on is considered rude and offensive and contaminates whatever you touch.

Interviewing Witnesses, Victims, and Monks

6

關係

Address Elders First

In general, foreign-born and first generation Asian peoples are notoriously closed-mouthed and quietly uncooperative with police. Even if they report a crime, expect that they are going to withhold information or ignore information which may throw a bad light on themselves (such as undeclared money) or information they think irrelevant. One way to overcome this is to go through the "cultural chain of command" to the elders. Keep eye contact and respect focused upon the elder male even while using a younger person as a translator.

Witnesses, and sometimes informants, are likely to ask the advice of the family elder(s) before giving any information to the police. Furthermore, it is the extended interdependent family-clan from which most support would be found for any Asian who might have become newly involved in criminal activities either as a victim or as a fugitive. Check visitors to and from the residences of senior members during the holidays to apprehend those family members who might have fled but surface in a family crisis.

Even though you may speak to an elder through a younger member of the family, respectfully address and ask the senior adult male for permission to talk to his family. Through the English speaker(s) of the household, ask the elder to tell you of their specific geographical origins and their dialect; this will enable you to select the correct translator if one is needed in the future. Alternatively, an elder female may be the operational head of the household. With either or both elders, try to establish quiet respect, courteous rapport, and trust as you explain the law and your actions. Explain, if needed, the bail system. Senior family members or the younger people who are close to them should be cultivated. If the senior members of the family trust you, which may take some time to occur, they can be very valuable sources of assistance.

Masks and Fingerprint Identification

After a robbery, and if the robbers wore masks, ask each witness separately and repeatedly if he/she recognized anyone's voice or distinguishing marks. Masks may suggest local perpetrators. Also, very few people can wear a ski mask for 2 to 5 hours within a heated house without taking it off for relief. The same is usually true for gloves, so fingerprints may be present even though the victim stated that the perpetrators wore gloves.

Names and Dialect Identification

After a robbery, ask each witness separately and repeatedly if he/she recognized anyone's voice, regional accent, dialect, or distinguishing marks. Many Asians know or can identify more than two languages or dialects. Remember that many Chinese and some Vietnamese dialects are mutually unintelligible, so to identify a dialect is not necessarily to be able to understand it. For example, Vietnamese Amerasians are more likely to speak the Vietnamese dialect of the North than of the South. Do not assume that the victim is of the same ethnic background as the perps. Remember, quite like ourselves, many Asians cannot recognize proper names in certain Asian languages. They are as foreign to them as they are to us.

Ask Direct and Specific Questions: Information Won't Be Volunteered

One cultural difference is that asking leading questions or raising general topics usually will not generate the wide ranging information police might wish to know. Ask very direct, very specific questions with plenty of details and specific alternatives, e.g., "Were there tattoos in the webs between the (suspects) fingers? How was his hair cut?" (Review Chapter 9, "Interrogating Suspects and Recruiting Informants".)

Interviews with Police Are "Doing Business"

Conduct police interviews with businessmen, witnesses and/or victims, as if it were a business venture. Many Asian may well consider it as another form or necessary evil of "doing business". Sometimes investigators need to put a legal but somewhat heavy arm on an uncooperative family by means of discussing community pressure and/or their potential for loss of "face".

Get the Specific and Cultural History of the Suspect's Extended Family

If you have determined who your victims are historically and culturally, you will make fewer mistakes and will know more about what to ask, and where to find out more information in the community. Ideally, for your intelligence database, secure (if possible) the suspect's dialect, home village, and province; the full range of all members of the family along with the full names and locations of as many cousins as possible (with Chinese, up to the seventh cousin); the major surnames in the village or whether all villagers have the same family name; and a complete record of the suspect's education: when, where, and how. Who paid for what, when, and from whom did the money come? That is, look for guanxi.

Special Family Names

Among some traditional Asians, there may be a second name which accompanies the personal name: the brother-name which is shared by all brothers of a particular married man and wife. Thus, if a suspect claims that another person is his brother, but you determine that they do not share the same second or third name, it is probable that they are not biological brothers. However, of the traditional 400 to 500 Chinese family names (surnames), about 45 Chinese family names constitute about 70% of those names in common use (see Robert Hearn's materials in Appendix B). By securing this information, not only will you have a better database on which to trace connections and apprehend criminals, but you also will stand a better chance of gaining the sincere trust of an Asian family and you will be more likely to gain an "Asian friend" to improve your departmental stats and to increase your ability to protect them (refer to "Asian Friends," in Chapter 7).

Check Beauty Salon Connections

While talking with the wives of victims, find out whether they talked too much, bragged about their business and family successes, or gossiped about others while in the local beauty salon. Then check whether any of the women who work in the salon have suspicious boyfriends who fit a gang banger profile. Check for photographs of bangers who have their hair done there. Many of them love to get the latest hairstyles and be photographed at the salon.

Quietly Check with Dads for Any "Extracurricular Activities"

Take the father or elder males to one side and quietly press them individually as to whether they have recently visited massage parlors or bath houses and may have bragged or gossiped about their own or someone else's financial successes.

Travel Agents

After a home-invasion robbery, ask each witness separately and repeatedly if he/she has contacted a local Vietnamese or Chinese travel agent about a prospective trip back to Vietnam or to another country outside of North America. Travel agents would rightly suspect that the traveler would be carrying gold, jewelry, or cash with him/her to distribute to his/her Asian family or the Asian families of Asian-American friends. A "bent" travel agent might have told a friend who told ... who told ....

Marian Days

If the victims are Vietnamese or other Southeast Asians, check whether the victims had attended the Marian Days festival in Carthage, Missouri, the previous August. This is a religious and ethnic festival held at a Catholic Seminary, usually in early August. About 45,000 to 50,000 Vietnamese and other Southeast Asian people attended in 1992. If the victims did attend, check your information about your suspects with experienced Asian crime investigators who usually attend Marian Days, such as: Detective Rob Harmon, Carthage P.D. (417) 358-2132); Detective Al Lotz, Houston P.D. (713) 584-4846 and beeper: (713) 278-7148; Lt. Jack Willoughby, New Orleans P.D.; or Pat McCarthy, member of the Joint FBI-Chicago P.D. Asian Task Force (beeper: (312) 716-7683).

These Asian crime investigators may be able to help you in the verification of the suspects' names, aliases, changes in appearance, photographs, warrants, gang connections, travel, and other activities. Some of these AC specialists (Lotz, McCarthy, Willoughby, Harmon) regularly attend the Marian Days celebration as leading members of a special Asian investigators team (see Chapter 18 for detailed information on Marian Days). See Figure 1.

Figure 1 Federal and municipal Asian crime investigators mingling with the crowds at the Marian Days festivities. (Photo courtesy of the Carthage Police Department.)

Wives, Concubines, and Mistresses

Do not automatically assume that a male suspect's wife will know any details of his allegedly illegal business just because they are married and/or are good parents. As with many Asians, he may turn over all his earnings to her and she will hold the purse-strings of their apparent household income; from that, she will give him his "spending money". While she may control the family money he gives her, that may well be *all* she knows about his business. The American middle-class arrangement whereby the female spouse knows her husband's business and financial affairs and is a confidant and advisor often does not occur in Asian marriages. Also, as in the U.S. and Canada, this may vary according to social class, education, and whether their home country background was rural or urban (city).

For the Chinese or sometimes the Vietnamese, determine through surveillance or other means whether the senior suspect has a mistress or concubine ("second wife"). If so, particularly find out if she has been dropped or feels treated unfairly; try to turn her. A man or a woman scorned is a good source of sensitive information. Tapping into information from a former mistress or concubine in Hong Kong, Singapore, Taiwan, or mainland China is possible if you have or develop the right connections. Remember that the wife has the kids and the checkbook; a former mistress or a concubine may have little.

Threats of Family Gravesite Desecration in Asia

With the gradual implementation of instant satellite telephone and electronic communication throughout Asia during the last two decades, this particular way of intimidating witnesses has become more frequent. The threat of vengeful desecration of the family grave sites in the Asian homeland is a very real and very powerful intimidation technique. It is particularly effective with Vietnamese, overseas Chinese, and Koreans. If possible, get the statements of Vietnamese home invasion robbery victims regarding any identifying marks, etc. of the criminals on videotape before their anger subsides and they start worrying about revenge and are subject to family and neighborhood pressures to remain silent.

Do the Victims Understand the Bail System?

Try to determine whether the family or some of the key elders understand the U.S. and Canadian court systems and bail procedures, in particular. The general model of investigations in Chinese (and thus in Vietnamese) classical times was that wrongdoers would be reported to the Court or directly to the District Magistrate, who would then investigate thoroughly and pull the criminals in to the District Magistrate's "Court" for sentencing or immediate punishment. There was no attempt to bring the accused before his accusers or consider the Anglo-European legalities of due process. Thus, many first generation Asians do not understand North American common law procedures, nor do they have any idea of their own or the criminal's legal options. If they see the alleged criminals back on the streets in a few days, they wrongly conclude that they have bribed their way out and are thus free from punishment. They conclude that corruption is widespread, and crimes against them go unpunished here. Explain that if they are to be protected by the U.S. system of justice, that they must cooperate (at least to a greater degree) with the procedures which will protect them.

In other words, explain why they need to understand and play their part in the system if they are to be helped by the U.S. and Canadian police and judicial systems. Many first generation Asians, unfamiliar and suspicious of the system, become courteously and quietly reluctant to cooperate with American law enforcement for the reasons noted above. However, explanations will have the desired effect only to the degree to which you have earned their trust and have good guanxi.

Hoarding Cash at Home

Many traditional Asians try to avoid the "paper trails" of a bank and deal locally in cash. Try to convince Asian-Americans that the all too common practice of hoarding cash in the house is dangerous and that there are better ways of protecting themselves. One way is to have a secret signal switch built into a lamp or appliance that will alert a trusted neighbor that there is trouble in their home. Thus, police can be called in an emergency, even during a home-invasion robbery.

Greeting Monks, Religious Leaders, and Family Elders

Monks, religious leaders, and respected elders usually have great social status among many Asians. You will usually recognize them by their yellow, maroon, or grey monastic robes (without hoods); their shaved heads; and the respectful behavior of others around them. If they learn to respect you and you have done nothing major to silently offend them or their religious precepts, they and their devotees will often become quite helpful to you. Theoretically, in Theravāda Buddhism, the social status of any monk is higher than that of any layman. Thus, in a traditional setting, expect that the Buddhist monks will be seated at a higher (physical) level than a visitor. Polite, respectful intentions are important here; seeing these, they will usually ignore any unintended XC goofs. Try to do your best and then relax. Remember that they are members of an ethnic culture first and members of a religious order second. Religion is an option for any person, but culture is not.

Only if you feel comfortable with it, learn to greet them with the gesture of palms closed, pointing almost upward, held before the chest. Nod or bow slightly, but do not bow down too far. Do not stand over them or point your finger at them while talking. Go easy on direct eye contact. Be respectful and speak quietly, giving attention to the elders. When interviewing monks, do not try to "get right to the point". Expect to exchange a few pleasantries before anyone gently turns attention toward the criminal issues at hand. If tea is offered, accept it with thanks and drink *some* of it — even if you do not like it. Also, do not ever directly offer a donation of money to a Theravāda monk, for he cannot touch it; offer it through a layman.

Use Quiet Manners with Unfamiliar Religious Objects

Let's assume that you are searching a private home with a warrant and are placing the contents of shelves and drawers on the floor in the middle of the room for later inspection. If you come upon a Buddhist rosary (which is not much different than a Catholic rosary), a Buddha image, old photos, or small castings shaped like a tiny cathedral window with the Buddha image or other apparent religious objects, let the Asians see you carefully set these religious objects to one side so that they are not mixed with (and thus "contaminated" by) other nonsacred objects. When standing near them, do not directly turn your back on a religious Buddha image or an Asian yellow- or red-robed priest, monk, or (especially) a Theravāda monk. Do not directly turn your back on what appears to be an altar, even though there may be "only" a book, a scroll, or some flowers or fruit on it. Such religious objects may be found in either temples or in private homes.

For example, one popular Buddhist "god" often seen in Chinese circles is the jolly, laughing, carefree, fat-bellied Buddha, carrying a sack and often surrounded by happy children crawling all over him. In about 1000 A.D. that form became a popular version of the future Buddha, Maitreya. With sloppy robes hanging half off his round shoulders, his fat chest and belly exposed, he expressed a carefree attitude that all the world was illusion and that happiness and a compassionate awareness of the moment (tathatā) were a good, popular path (mārga) to "salvation", given one's present karmic endowments. He is revered by the devoted, and while he represents naiveté and humor, he is certainly not a joke — and should not be treated as one. As a general example, do not put a *Playboy* magazine next to a print of Gotāma ŚākyaMuni , the historical Buddha, or a Hong Kong poster of Maitreya, the future Buddha of Mahāyāna Buddhism (Fo da chen, STC 0154 1129 0042) next to a *Hustler* magazine.

Use an Interpreter with a Monk or Religious Leader

Unless a monk is fluent in English, using an interpreter will give (both) Asian monks and you time to think of suitable replies to demonstrate civility and cooperation. Initially, their replies will be what they think you want to hear and what would be an appropriate response for someone of their position to say. Wait it out, explain the situation and the law, and tell them what you request of them. They will usually cooperate. In short, speak softly and give them great respect and great "face" (see Chapter 12 on "face").

7 Witnesses and Some Cross-Cultural Aspects of Trials

關係

"But Asians Won't Testify"

From the view of many members of many Asian-American communities, testifying in court constitutes an act of either bravery or foolhardiness. This remains a real problem for police and prosecutors. Usually, with some local businessmen, offering money will not help, and it may insult them. However, friendship — Asian friendship — might do it.

Be a Long-Term Friend

If you want a witness to testify, become their friend — an Asian friend. Then they *may* testify because you have become part of their "network of friends" (guanxi) (see "Guanxi", Chapter 15) This Asian sense of friendship means that you will be obligated to do more than you might with an "American friendship". You will be expected to advise them regarding such things as school enrollment, utility connections, paying bills, traffic fines, and licenses and to offer general advice and family assistance of various (legal) kinds. Of course, they will do comparable things for you, and testifying may be one of them.

Asian Friendship

In short, Asian friendship compels one to do a wider range of things for a friend than most mainline Americans are accustomed to. Furthermore, not to help a friend, a guanxi friend, is not only to lose "face" but also shows that you are not a person to be trusted, someone whose word cannot be counted upon. If an Asian-American agrees to testify, make certain that an Asian understands what he/she will need to do if he/she becomes a witness. Try to relieve their apprehensions or fears of revenge from the suspects — no small job! Arrange some family or larger Asian community support if possible. Take time to protect them! Also, incorporate their cousins and uncles and aunts in the circle of protective friends who will keep tabs on them.

Home Protection Before Trial

While awaiting trial, your Asian witnesses will certainly be receiving intimidating phone calls telling them to withdraw. Protect them. Phone them at least once a day to reassure them. Get them a pager/beeper with their own coded number. Have a marked and an unmarked patrol car check their homes from time to time, especially at night. Arrange signals of danger with window shades or house lights.

Don't Make Witnesses Lose "Face"

A rare action that has been done, but that should be avoided at all costs, unless *absolutely* necessary, is to put witnesses under a witness bond or even keep them in a county jail for their safety until trial. When this is done, the witnesses are shamed and terribly embarrassed. They will lose "face" to an unbelievable extent within the community. On the days your witnesses appear for trial, escort them to and from their cars and maintain good rapport with the friends and relatives who accompany them. And stay in touch!

Protect Witnesses from Gangs

During the trial in which a witness is expected to testify, keep the witnesses and family in an isolated room away from the hallways around the courtroom. Often, as witnesses are waiting to testify, gang members or other hostile Asians will try to intimidate them by uttering slang threats in their native language, using threatening hand signals, or just by silently staring at them.

Subpoena Blanks

It has been suggested to keep subpoena blanks on hand for the following reasons. Check with your superiors to determine if these scenarios are legally justifiable. After determining whether the judge would want to make gang members exit the court room, one could use the blanks to serve subpoenas on the gang members to become state witnesses. Then the District Attorney may introduce a motion to the judge to exclude them from the court. After removing your witnesses from the glare of gang members by legally excluding the latter from court, you may be able to get rid of the gang members altogether by taking Polaroid photographs of them for your photo book. As is well known, they do not like to be photographed by police and often leave after such actions.

Then, check the gang member sheets for identification, priors, tickets, etc. If one finds that they are, for example, illegally parked or in violation of *some* legality, try to match their photographs with any out-of-state license plates. Do this especially if they fit the profile of wearing "new-wave" style clothing and driving fairly new, Japanese sports cars; tattoos do not always mean gang affiliation. Check the trunks of their cars for duct tape, luggage tags, hotel receipts, photographs or tickets of any kind. If you verify this profile, check these suspects very closely to see if they are wanted elsewhere. As noted in Chapters 8, 9, and 20, check their names in all possible combinations of their personal, middle, and family (surname) names. Ask them if they speak Vietnamese, Khmer, Thai, or a particular dialect of Chinese. Do not ask them for their "first" or "last" name, for that assumes our name order. It is better to ask Asians for their family, personal name, a "milk" name, and a nickname.

Avoid Loudmouthed Clerks or Reporters

Within the courtroom, try to avoid loudmouthed court clerks or reporters who yell at Asian witnesses to repeat the spelling of their (unfamiliar) names, especially when the defendants and the defense lawyers make a show of copying down their addresses. Also, try to avoid crude judges and court personnel, and always be on the lookout for possible gang intimidation.

Use the District Attorney's Explanatory Time for Relevant Cross-Cultural Topics

With any Asian-American crime, encourage and assist the District Attorney in using his explanatory time during opening arguments to discuss the relevant aspects of Asian culture, dialects, immigration history, and the relevance (if any) of special holidays, family, or Asian social obligations. Also take time to explain any uses of the Standard Telegraphic Code (STC) for Asian names and such "odd" things (to us) as Chinese same-surname villages where everyone has the same family name. Explain that the far-reaching guanxi connections may indeed mean that distant relatives throughout the world may assist unknown persons "merely" because they share the same village lineage, dialect, family names, or are a "friend of a friend of a friend of a friend ... "; that is guanxi in action.

Point out features that distinguish gang cases from non-gang cases — witness intimidation, threats of retaliation and "paybacks" and non-cooperation with police. To be effective with a judge and/or jury, the prosecutor should translate the nuances and small details of the gang subcullture and behavior to counter their "common sense" interpretations of "these clean-cut gang boys." For example, note that many "floating" Southeast Asian gangs have no permanent leader and actually shift leadership according to what is functionally needed for the next crime. Also, note their differences in motivation and intimidation, and their core values such as group loyalty, brotherhood, and inner-group discipline. Explain tattoos and gang symbols and paraphernalia as evidence of aiding and abetting; the effects of this information are important in that the evidential impact — the psychological effects in strenghtening the impact of the prosecutor's knowledge and understanding of gangs towards the jury — is very great. Most judges and juries tend to admire and trust the prosecutor's charges and the testimony of police who have obviously understood and "figured out" gang subcultures, symbols, motivations, midsets, and affiliations.

Educate the Jury About Asian Names

Plan to assist and educate the jury about Asian names. Most mainline Americans can follow complex testimony about Asians more easily if the Asian person's "American" name is used rather then his/her Asian name. Therefore, as you brief or question the witnesses before trial or at cross examination, be sure that you get their "American" names (they willl have one or two).

Use Posterboards

As you prepare for, and during, the trial, construct large posterboards that illustrate the various relationships between the Asian defendants and witnesses. Be sure to describe and use their American names along with their Asian names. However, as a general rule, use the American names in describing gang/Tong/Triad/hui activities and relationships. These "American names" will help the jury and judge to follow the testimony. Ease of comprehension about a "foreign culture" and name recognition are most important here.

Suspect's Appearances

While suspects often change their appearance during obvious surveillance, defense attorneys will sometimes arrange for defendants to change their clothes, hair styles, and seating positions in the courtroom to confuse the witnesses on cross examination. Take closeup color Polaroid photographs of defense witnesses to detect changes in hair color and haircuts. Some of the newer (and smarter) gang members have learned that it is to their profit to appear clean cut and not to exhibit the "new wave" punk styles of clothing and haircuts. Some of the smarter, younger gang members have learned the advantage of not appearing as bangers at all and may exhibit a very preppy or nondescript style of dress and demeanor. Take time to carefully identify the suspect before the trial begins so that there will be no hesitation in identifying him/her. Remember that to some Asians, all Caucasians or all African-Americans "look alike"!

Photograph Their Ears

Get their ears in all photographs because the ears are a very distinctive means of identification and can seldom be altered. Most people in the world know of at least a few other ethnic groups who "all look the same to me!". Thus, photographs may help mainline Americans to keep track of ethnically unfamiliar suspects during trial.

Explain the Uses of Standard Telegraphic Code for Chinese Names

Sometimes evidence is entered in the trial which involves the tracing and identification of Chinese or Japanese names. If your court opponents know that you (or anyone else in your department) do not know these written languages, you might anticipate a hostile question about the accuracy of your identification procedure. If STC (Standard Telegraphic Code; see Chapter 20) was used to trace names, prepare a large posterboard for the jury to illustrate and explain how each of the Chinese and Japanese characters (ideograms) of the names is matched with simple coded numbers. This posterboard would answer the hostile question and reassure the jury that there is a fairly simple procedure (in theory) for tracing these names, even though they are written in a way totally foreign to most jury members.

Home Protection after the Trial

After the trial, call witnesses every day and night for a few days and then several times per week during the subsequent weeks. Keep the "network" going. They may not become explicit informants, but their quiet help or advice about community relations or specific persons may become very useful. Keep your guanxi going; you may need these people in the future.

Suspect's Records and Affiliations

8

關係

Know the Suspect's Ethnic Background

When charging a suspect, make sure that you have accurate knowledge of the nationality, ethnic group, or dialect group to which the he or she belongs. For example, an ethnic Chinese who was born and lived in Vietnam may or may not claim that he is Vietnamese — for his own reasons. Consequently, you might request the wrong translator, draw inaccurate conclusions, or fail to trace him and his connections in several data bases.

Records and Standard Telegraphic Code

For identification purposes, try *not* to rely solely on the suspect's driver's license or the way he/she spells his/her name in English. Run any inquiries at least three times using *each* of the names as a possible surname. Use STC (Standard Telegraphic Code) to record and trace Chinese and Japanese names. STC is used by the DEA, FBI, FinCEN, Interpol, Royal Hong Kong Police, and Japanese National Police and is found on Hong Kong passports. Korean and Vietnamese names are written in different alphabets with special diacritical marks to denote particular sounds or tones in pronunciation.

Get Three Handwriting Samples of the Suspect's Name in Chinese, Japanese, or Korean Characters

Have the Chinese or Chinese-American, Japanese-American or Korean-American suspects write their full names slowly, carefully, and without sloppy handwriting. Ask them to write down their nicknames and the names of their parents. Do this even if the suspect is (or claims to be) a Viet-Ching, a Vietnamese of Chinese family background; they usually will know the Chinese characters for their family name. Do your best to transcribe the sounds of foreign "nicknames", but do not expect much precision, for nicknames represent a difficult problem in written identification (see Chapter 20). Give the suspect the STC book and ask him to find and show you his/her surname and personal names, etc. in the STC book. Then, in all communication about the suspects, carefully indicate which STC number is the family name or surname, etc. (see Chapter 20 on "Standard Telegraphic Code").

Photo Books

With the permission of their superiors, some investigators let gang members look through the police photo book while they listen to comments about the viewer's enemies and acquaintances. In conversation, the gang members can be tricked into revealing names, aliases, nicknames, dates, "signature" methods of operation (MOs), and procedures characteristic of other gang members. Do not confine your photos solely to Asians or Asian-Americans.

Since fewer gang-related felonies are solved with physical evidence or trace substances than with confessions or photograph identification, your photo book is extremely important. Many times, photographs are the single most important link among crimes committed in different jurisdictions. Copy or secure all photographs obtained in searches of gang motel rooms, apartments, and autos. Check the *IAACI Newsletter* for wanted photographs.

Check Local Hair Salons for Photos

Check local hair salons for photographs of gang members for your photo book. Many gang members seem to enjoy getting the latest haircuts and happily agree to have "in-house" photographs taken of their newest haircuts. As noted, be sure that you get the *ear* in the side photo. The individual's ear is as distinctive as any other part of the head and is easily identified and seldom altered.

Gang Mobility

Expect extreme mobility on the part of organized crime or smaller semi-organized criminal groups. Contrary to most other North American criminals, Asian gang members tend to travel to areas where their fingerprints or photographs are not on file. They travel enormous distances to commit crimes, especially the Chinese, Vietnamese, and Cambodians.

Vietnamese Community "Safe Houses"

Many Asian and Vietnamese youths (and middle-aged men) who newly arrive are (usually) immediately taken into the community and, in effect, are given functional "safe houses". This is done out of a long tradition of hospitality towards kinsmen, distrust of the police, harboring fugitives during the long extended wars with the French and the Americans, and a sense that they are all "strangers in a strange land". As a result, for example, some very law-abiding, family-oriented Vietnamese may feel a special sense of obligation toward any respectful-appearing, fellow Vietnamese. The young recognize the clues of their own subculture and, as is common in the various youth subcultures of North America, "like knows like"; thus, they are given help and a new place to "crash" — a navya-saranam ("a new refuge").

Telephone Record Links

Telephone records of Asian youths are very important for link analyses. Many Asian criminals remain connected to each other by very frequent phone conversations, domestic and foreign. Take copies (where possible) of personal telephone records or small personal "vest pocket" number books. They may yield not only numbers but a way to decipher the nicknames and slang so widely used.

Check Motel Phone Books

In searching the former motel rooms of gangs, check the phone books for common Vietnamese names such as "Nguyen" and "Tran" to determine if any Asian names and businesses have been circled or otherwise marked.

Check Home Country and Regional Connections

Telephone linkages are sometimes crucial in determining narcotic and home invasion connections. For example, Hong Kong and Singapore may be linked by two Cantonese-Yue speakers: dialect and slang links between Hakka speakers (Hawaii/Hong Kong) or Chaozhou (Thai: Chin Taechiu) speakers (Bangkok/Hong Kong/Shantou in southern Fujian).

Check Refugee and/or Dialect Connections

If possible, determine if the suspects were processed through a particular refugee camp where they might have met someone else whom you know but have no (other) evidence with which to presume a connection. See if they share a dialect connection with some other person you might think is connected to the suspects. The networks developed in refugee camps are often the basis for later gang activity. Such information, coupled with a telephone record analysis, may help you to estimate that the interstate (or foreign) connections are between those who spent time together in the same refugee camp(s). When appropriate, check with school security personnel, a good source of detailed information about new addresses and relatives.

Women's Married Names

Check marriage relations, for some Asian women often keep their own family name and use it. Thus, husbands and wives do not necessarily use the same "last" name except in formal social situations.

Aliases May Be Legitimate

Do not automatically assume that, because the record of an Asian-American citizen has several aliases, he is necessarily "playing games" to avoid identification. Rather, he/she may have several different legitimate additional names — even if different than on their passports. For example, every Thai citizen, whether he is Chinese or of another non-Thai descent, must have a Thai official name for his passport. His friends call him by another local slang name; his family, another name. Also, he may have included or omitted his birthplace in writing his name.

"INS" Names

Moreover, an immigration (INS) official may have recorded an Asian immigrant's name inaccurately at his first entry to America. For example, when a Customs agent did not hear the "L" in the Thai name "Lim", the agent recorded the name as "Im". All of these different names might be used on different occasions without necessarily attempting to mislead anyone. It is one of our cultural characteristics that most of us have fairly simple three-part names. While several aliases might correctly alert police to project suspicion toward the Euro-Americans or African-Americans who have several aliases, warranted suspicion for those reasons alone is initially less plausible with most Asians — but far from impossible.

Check School and Refugee Organization Connections

When appropriate, check with the school security personnel and janitors, good sources of detailed information. For other information, begin with local service organizations and then check with national organizations — for example, the Southeast Asian Refugee Studies for their newsletter (University of Minnesota, Center for Urban and Regional Affairs, 330 Hubert H. Humphrey Center, 301 19th Ave. South, Minneapolis, Minnesota 55455). For their publications, call (612) 625-5535. For other typical examples, Jim Delany, Catholic Family Center, Rochester, New York, (716) 546-7220, and Stephen Cottrell, Box 9733, 75 Morgan Avenue, Mississippi State University, Mississippi 39762, are widely experienced both in Southeast Asian ways and in information about other relief services for Asians refugees.

Legal Ages

If you find that an Asian suspect has changed his legal age to an older age or has petitioned to do so, once again he may not be "playing games". At resettlement camps, many parents gave younger ages for their children in order to ensure that they would be able to receive more formal education. Thus, there are some juveniles who are, as some officers suspect, 4 to 6 years older than their school identification cards indicate.

Use INS Agents

Sometimes, the I-94 and/or the Resident Alien ("green") Card are helpful in identification. Check your local INS agent for help. They have wide legal powers that make extensive legal searches possible. After discussing these powers with INS agents, you might find it extremely useful to have an agent accompany you on the search.

Victim's Profiles

In home invasion robberies, interrogate the suspects closely to find out what attracted them to the victims. Check the victims closely to find out what made them attractive to the suspects. Often the home invasion victims can supply probable candidates even if the criminals tried to conceal their ethnic and personal identities. Look very closely at those close to the victims, including relatives, girlfriends or boyfriends (and their friends), or the victim's children. From looking at these clues, you may find other connections: whether an "inside" person set them up or whether the burglary was planned through a gang connection or a travel agent. Determine whether one victim was treated less viciously and given more "face" than other victims and thus could be a possible link to the criminals. Examples of what attracts gang members are gambling debts; flaunting of expensive jewelry, autos, or Rolex watches; a reputation for wealth; an owner's well known suspicion of banks; a new employee from out-of-state who noted the owner's schedule, entrance locks, and other safety precautions of the owner's home or business.

Interrogating Suspects and Recruiting Informants

9

關係

Are There Any Significant Differences?

It has been estimated that physical evidence is "only about 5 to 10% of what is normally offered in testimony in a judicial setting. Consequently, the remaining 90 to 95% concerns itself with conversation … "[19] The general question addressed here is whether there are any relevant cultural differences in mutual conversations between Asians and mainline North Americans (Caucasians, Hispanics, and Afro-Americans) that are of particular relevance to criminal interrogation, such that some details of the interrogation process should be modified in light of relevant XC knowledge and skills. Thus, if cultural differences sometimes change the "rules of the game" in discourse between some Asians and non-Asians, these differences may be of relevance for interrogating Asian suspects.

Generally, there *are* XC aspects relevant to interrogation. Whether these XC features are crucial, modestly important, or trivial remains an open question. Ultimately, the answer to this question will be decided by the empirical data and the pragmatic values of experienced interrogators. However, some nontypical information, in particular, characteristics relevant to specific Asian groups, are useful to know. Examples include the common marking of extortion money at holidays (red envelopes), eye contact, refugee background, language abilities and preferred dialects, customs pertaining to marriage and children, coming-of-age customs, body language between sexes and between parents, the extended family and children, and some knowledge of and insight into the general ideas of "human nature" and religion particular to a specific Asian group.

The general model of interrogation is assumed here to be the John E. Reid method as described in *Criminal Interrogation and Confession*, by Fred E. Imbau, John E. Reid, and Joseph P. Buckley and widely taught by Joseph Buckley and his associates.[20a]

Suggested "Do's and Don'ts"

Separate Asian Suspects Immediately

Do not allow them to talk to each other from the moment you take custody of them. It is probable that you may not know the language or their dialect and you may need to prevent them from setting up their cover stories and their backups. While all suspects may try to do this, the Asian situation is particularly important. Because you cannot understand them, they can say things which would be admissible as evidence against them which they would never say if they were speaking English. Separating them from each other saves you from having to work to disprove their phony claims at a later time.

Videotape and Record All Interviews

Videotape and/or record all interviews and/or interrogations. Not only may there be crucial evidence to verify their treatment during interrogation, but tapes will allow others to retranslate and interpret important idiomatic foreign words or phrases.

Interrogation with Asians Takes Time!

Start interrogation over an extended period of time and remain patient. Interrogating Asians takes time — and more time! Break in the middle to let the suspects "stew". (If you want to stir the "stew" a little more, use the unlucky numbers 4 and 14 in your contacts with them.) However, expect that this interrogation usually will take longer than with many non-Asians.

Give "Face"

After starting the interrogation, back off for a moment or two to give "face" and space. If possible, allow every suspect to keep "face" to *some* degree, even when you catch a gang member in a lie. "Face" is that socially approved image of oneself one shows to others which must be maintained for social approval, social identity, and self-respect. If possible (and it often is not), try to avoid anyone associated with the suspect from losing "face" by being a known associate of the suspect. As in Japan, some witnesses will avoid being seen publicly talking to the police. Thus, try to keep some interviews with respectable nonsuspects as private as possible. Respect shown and respect given is *very* important and should be maintained; the threat of its loss and shame on the family is one good type of leverage for police recruitment of informers. Also, talk of honor, family, disgrace, and mother may (and only may) touch the proper emotional buttons.

Your Invasion of the Boundaries of His Personal or Intimate Zone May Be Different Than with a Non-Asian

After having established a relaxed rapport, and as you slowly move into his personal zone (1.5 to 4 feet), you may find that his reactions to your "invasion" are not the same as with other non-mainline North American ethnic groups. You may have to get closer to get to him, but always maintain the rapport which is necessary to avoid the suspect's perception that the interrogator's increasing closeness is hostile and aggressive rather than emphatic and friendly.

Don't Allow "Asian" Sitting Positions

Don't allow the Asian suspect to sit with his legs folded under him (the so-called "lotus" position) or to squat on the floor. Sitting in the chair will keep both of you at the same eye level; he will not easily be able to turn around to communicate with or intimidate a translator. You will be better able to "mirror" his body posture and he will more likely "mirror" your body posture — feet flat on the floor, open legs, upper body leaning forward, elbows on knees, open palms, head down, head held in his hands, the whole body inclined towards the "confessional" posture.

Alien Registration Numbers

To positively identify alien residents, get their alien registration number if possible; some may have more than one. Check with an INS agent you can trust to tell you about how to get such information and who will keep you abreast of the current requirements of legal aliens.

Courtesy Beverages

While one ought always to serve a beverage to a guest, a witness, or informant, one might also wish to do so for a suspect whether he is in a sullen stupor or waiting to talk. Do not merely ask if he would like a beverage, for he will likely decline. Just do it. He may not touch it but may be pleased that you have treated him courteously, shown respect, and given him "face".

Listen for Asian Clues for Interrogation Themes

During the non-accusatory first interview (Reid method) prior to the actual interrogation, listen to the denials carefully for topics and themes that indicate his/her important values. For example:

"I would not shame my family."
"But I could not have done that, he's a friend and I have special obligations to help him."
"They were the only Vietnamese from my father's village."
"He is named Wang, too."
"My brother is very religious." (upāsikā , chu-shih)

Family surname associations or family connections to a given village or area are good sources of interrogation themes. In effect, the suspect may be telling you which cultural buttons are important enough for you to use.

Keep Cool and Don't Get Angry

If you are dealing with traditional Asians, in contrast to Asian-American gang members, losing your temper will cause traditional Asians to believe that you are untrustworthy and dangerous and that your suggestions or "deals" are not to be trusted. Unless you are in the middle of playing some version of "good cop, bad cop", do not allow any anger to show; psychological pressure, empathy, and gamesmanship are probably more efficient. However, such gamesmanship does presuppose similar cultural backgrounds and you will need to know enough about the Asian subjects particular cultural background to sympathize in a knowledgeable way. Thus, cultural background is a necessary condition for establishing sufficient rapport with the suspects to draw a voluntary confession from them.

Use the Threat of Loss of "Face"

Let the gang banger talk about his family and noncriminal friends. To pressure him into turning, one possible theme is loss of "face". Describe the potential courtroom scene that would occur if the suspect goes to trial; recount the details as the prosecutor describes his criminal activities and associates for all to hear. Then describe the subsequent loss of "face" that his family and family friends would experience.

The Threat of Loss of "Face" with Female Gang Members Is Weaker

With respect to the all-too common double standard in the treatment of women, Asians often will condemn sexual activities in women but not in men. Thus, a female gang member already will have lost most if not all of the "face" she is capable of losing by virtue of running with a gang. Often their disgrace is too great to accommodate any ongoing family relationships.

If Possible, Let Your Actions Contrast with Other Police

Where possible, use contrasts with other police in your dealings with gang bangers to enhance your image, making you the good guy. If other police are habitually rough on gang bangers at traffic stops, in malls, etc. contrast your more respectful responses with other law enforcement actions. Examples include not embarrassing them too greatly, not pulling their shirts back in certain public places to check for needle marks or gang tattoos, lifting T-shirts but not half-stripping them publicly. By these contrasts you may enhance your image and find that they may be more willing to talk to you about other gang bangers than to other officers.

Don't Hurry

To repeat this important point, do not hurry the interrogation. Traditional Asians operate under their own norms of social and conversational timing, not by such American standards as "efficiency", "honest directness", or "getting to the point". Therefore, *do* "beat around the bush"! Indirectness often may be the appropriate way of approaching an important, delicate or touchy topic. After raising a topic or making a point, wait in comfortable silence for awhile. This is often the way many Asians "question" one another, indirectly presenting an opportunity for a response or discussion of a general but relevant topic. They may respond to police in this manner. If not, walk away from the interrogation room and let the suspect think about it for awhile.

Eye Contact

As with many Hispanics, many Asians will avoid direct eye contact for sustained periods unless they wish to challenge or try to intimidate you. Looking down or away usually would be the more expected mannerism when confronted by a person with authority. There is an often-told story of the Anglo teacher who snapped, "Look at me when I'm talking to you!", not realizing that the Hispanic pupils *were* being respectful; they were avoiding the disrespectful alternative of staring into her eyes. In their Hispanic culture, direct staring, however bland, would have been considered a challenging affront to the teacher. On occasion, this occurs with some Asians, too.

Try a Third Party for Negotiations and Saving "Face"

If you fail to establish sufficient rapport to generate a confession, try an integrated approach with a partner who can act as a "cut-out" or third party. Using a third party for marriage or property disputes and political negotiation is much more common in Asia than in North America. The third party can be someone with whom the suspect can sympathize and negotiate a confession while maintaining "face" and social dignity.

Reading the Suspect's Social Troubles with English

Using the John E. Reid method of interviewing and interrogating (see Glossary), one may wish to keep some of the following remarks in mind while interrogating Asians. First, these general remarks are not meant to suggest that most of the Reid method of interrogation cannot be used with marginal speakers of English. However, these remarks do suggest that most of the Reid method assumes and is dependent on the suspect being able to express himself and the interrogator being able to recognize some fairly subtle differences in the uses of the English language. Second, these remarks do not refer solely to the suspect's degree of fluency in English; they refer to the built-in uses of language to convey subtle shadings of social and personal meanings that would be revealing to the interrogator's "reading" of the suspect's manner. This may include assessment of the suspect's potential for an imminent confession, more theme-oriented talk, or "stone-walling". While pacing the speed of your talking and choosing the appropriate themes, level, and type of vocabulary, do not mispronounce English words or phrases to match his/her social or criminal troubles. Minimize your use of Asian words unless you are fairly fluent. Don't distract him or give him anything about which to feel superior.

Manipulation of Status Words

English doesn't have many words, such as pronouns, that indicate superior vs. inferior social positions. Under conditions of stress, fear, and/or the wish to send signals of potential subordination, the absence of these distinctions in English may make communication difficult for a speaker of a language in which these ways of conveying distinctions of power and subordination are understood and are commonly used. In other words, it is difficult to convey respect and a willingness to cooperate when one is used to doing this by the structure of one's language. For example, in English we have only one word for the singular and the plural second person pronoun "you". On the other hand, the Chinese, Vietnamese, Korean, and many South-Asian languages, as well as German and French, have various ways to indicate social relationships such as degrees of intimacy or the social superior or inferior status of the speaker towards the recipient of the speaker. The Japanese language has many such words which designate social hierarchy and contextual distinctions indicating levels of superiority and status.

Be Suspicious of "Yes" Answers

In Chinese and Japanese in particular, a "yes" response in English usually does not mean that they are saying "yes" to the content of the proposition (or sentence or question) asked. Court cases have been lost because the "yes" in the confession or disposition was culturally ambiguous and thus the alleged admission of guilt was not established in court. As noted before, it is probable that such a "yes" means only that they heard you and that they acknowledge to you that they understood what you said. However, it is *not* necessarily the case that they agree to the truth of what you said nor that they agree to act in accordance with what you said. Hence, it is the interrogator's responsibility to ask a question which distinguishes between understanding and agreement.

To make that distinction, it is the interrogator's responsibility to ask specific questions. The suspect seldom will volunteer information that is not pinpointed specifically. It is suggested that one always ask Question 1 and either or both questions 2 and 3.

1. Did you hear and understand what I said?
2. Is what I said to you true? What I said to you, is it true?
3. Do you agree to do what I asked you to do?

Do not ask general question such as "Did you have a gun?". This is too easy to deny. Rather, ask specific questions such as "Where did you hide your gun?". However, once they do start talking, shut up and let them roll. Do not interrupt them with questions about details which can be followed up later. Listen, listen, and listen, even when they struggle with English. Also, listen to what they do *not* talk about and then re-interview them later about what they omitted or conspicuously avoided mentioning.

Flatter with Food

The availability of Asian food is a more important piece of psychological-social leverage to most Asians than most Americans imagine. Therefore, when interrogating an Asian suspect, order the appropriate Asian food for a carryout lunch or dinner. Let him pick his favorite restaurant and specify his favorite dish. You place the order in English and convey nothing in his native language. This gives the suspect "face". He will not forget it and it costs you nothing. Finally, eat (his food) with the suspect; let him talk about it and what he likes. This may take you around to more relevant gossip about other criminal activities or gangs in the area where he lives.

Moreover, for many older, traditional Asian criminals, one of the worst aspects of prison is the "terrible food". This means that they cannot get good

Asian food, prepared correctly and with the appropriate sauces — or even good rice or vegetables. Surprisingly, it has been a bargaining point in turning a few Asian criminals. Two Asian felons, so I was told by a Federal investigator, not only released crucial information, but chose to finish a somewhat longer sentence in a Hong Kong prison rather than serve out a much shorter sentence here in what was to them, a gastronomic wasteland. On the other hand, other Vietnamese claimed that they would rather do twice the time in an American prison than half the time in a Vietnamese prison. Obviously, the individual suspect's circumstances and experience are crucial factors that police may use as leverage.

Use Hospital Visitors

If the suspect is hospitalized, play on the sympathies and/or the desire for revenge on the part of the traditional family or friends. To him, emphasize his losing "face", his position in either the family or the gang, his reputation, and other shame factors external to him. Visit the family often at the hospital and watch who is really the Senior, not necessarily the one whose English is best. You can be certain that they are watching you to see if they can use you for their own ends. These contacts can be useful even if an individual flees to lay low for awhile; Asians, too, have long memories.

Telephone Records

Many Asian criminals remain connected to each other by very frequent phone conversations, domestic and foreign. It is one common way that they maintain their guanxi (connections).Take copies (where possible) of personal telephone records or small personal "vest pocket" number books. They may yield not only numbers but a way to decipher the nicknames that are widely used. Photograph and copy all ledger and telephone books, all INS cards and numbers and all I-20s Visa documents attached to foreign or U.S. passports. Check for the expiration dates of all "official" documents including Residence Alien Cards ("green" cards) and other foreign appearing documents. (Do not remove attachments if they are stapled to the passport.) Next, contact someone who knows how to use the Standard Telegraphic Code (STC, or Chinese Telegraphic Code) and the *Sino Surname Syllabary* for Chinese, Japanese, or Korean names. (See Chapter 20 for STC and names.)

Get Address of the Suspect's Mother

The investigator would wish to distinguish a suspect's "official address" from his real address. For Chinese informers, suspects, or witnesses, it may be advisable to get the mother's address rather than, say, the Tong address or his girlfriend's apartment. His mother will be the suspect's central and trusted source of communication with the all-important extended family. With the mother's address, police have the possibility of threatening to bring questions or even shame on the extended family and bringing about a suspect's devastating loss of "face".

Assumptions of Reid Interrogation Across Cultures

Since the goal of legal interrogation is to get a guilty, nonpsychopathic, Asian or Asian-American suspect to *voluntarily* confess, a slight knowledge of Asian culture may help. Obviously, many interrogators have learned to value and apply these particular points of emotional, social, and cultural empathy by themselves. The specific interrogation method assumed here is the widely taught John E. Reid method of interviewing and interrogation.[20a,b] A major goal of many interrogation approaches is to create a receptive psychological relationship between suspect and interrogator ("a sympathetic and understanding attitude", Reid: Step 2.D) by illustrating that you (the interrogator) "understand" his particular social situation as an Asian. In short, with your "understanding", he may finally become awash in feelings of frustration, desperation, and righteous trust in you — his "buddy" who really understands him. By picking the culturally correct investigation theme he will be able to reduce his anxiety by "getting it off his chest" and confess.

It is also obvious that many of these particular tactics and strategies of interrogation are not confined to Asian suspects/defendants. However, relevant cross-cultural factors consist of detailed knowledge of Asian and Asian-American cultures which can be used to increase the probability of confession. To promote empathy, sympathy, and the "you're his best buddy syndrome", and to be effective and "real" to the Asian defendant, you must speak to him in such a way as to illustrate that you know and empathize with some of the real issues and everyday pressures of Asian and Asian-American cultures: job discrimination, social discrimination, and the double-bind pressures of two competing cultures. Certainly, you can scam him about your evidence,[21] but you must do so within a cultural context that is appropriate in his/her multicultural daily life.

The Asian-American Suspect's Cultural Double-Bind

The Asian-American gang member is pulled in two, competing cultural directions, Asian and Canadian or American. To imagine how it feels to wrestle with the barriers of living within a society whose boundaries and language you do not know well, you need to know about the suspect's competing cultures — here and in the Asian home-country. One competing culture is comprised of the family values and lifestyles of the Asian home country, probably exaggerated by the homesickness of his hard-working parents. The other competing culture is the attraction and cultural pull of the "MTV–Al Bundy–heavy metal–new wave–L.A. Law–Every-man-for-himself" syndrome to which many young, unskilled Asians in their teens, 20s, and early 30s feel strongly attracted. Each of these cultural forces would be pulling the Asian-American in different, culturally incompatible directions. The double-bind is that embracing *either* of these cultural directions will inevitably bring severe, upsetting criticism upon the suspect. Imagine the following themes:

> "If you were trying to be successful in school, or liked to party, your parents and their friends would say you were too Americanized … weren't Asian … losing your sense of who you really are …. and if you stayed away from all that, they'd say you were too Asian and that you weren't trying to fit in and make it here like your parents … working two jobs each … not really learning how to get along here …"

Thus, it is an advantage to the interrogator to learn where the main issues of discrimination and cultural maladjustment are most likely to be experienced in an Asian-American suspect's life in order to know which cultural buttons to push. Use those hot button issues and problems as themes to express your empathy, to gain rapport and trust during interrogation. Last, armed with sufficient XC knowledge, and the right theme you will be able to offer the suspect selfserving excuses that will, in his eyes, allow him to admit guilt for reasons which are plausible and sufficiently selfserving in his own psychologically overstressed mind (Reid: Steps 7 and 8). If, on the other hand, you push the wrong cultural buttons, you will alienate the Asian suspect, and the interrogation sequence — from your statement of strong evidence that he is guilty (Step (1) to the point of giving him an excuse to reduce his over-stressed choices — will cease.

Interrelations and the Need for Cultural Knowledge

Our recognition of the differences between cultures and the differences in linguistic competency suggest that we should note some general prerequisites for interrogation of most traditional Asians, namely, what the interrogators should know beforehand and what difficulties they should anticipate. First, we should be aware of how difficult it is for an Asian suspect to express the verbal and non-verbal clues we depend upon as interrogators. Second, we should be aware of how difficult it is for a North American interrogator to recognize and accurately access the subtle XC verbal and non-verbal clues and nuances in the shifting mutual relationships between speaker and listener. In the following 12 points, I shall suggest some important relationships, methodological assumptions, and areas for discussion.

1. Ideally, the interrogator should have adequate cross-cultural knowledge to recognize and understand something of the verbal nuances or shadings of meaning in the suspect's speech and/or nonverbal behavior, such as whether he is having trouble with English, weakening in his resolve to deny guilt or is just tired; perhaps he is being subtly pressured by the translator, fearful, or obsessed by his external obligations to family, gang, guanxi friends, etc.
2. Ideally, the interrogator should know enough about the Asian suspect's culture to avoid projecting the interrogator's own cultural assumptions and interpreting the suspect's speech as if it arose from within a North American cultural context. An example would include the interrogator's knowledge of Asian problems regarding racial discrimination, family and guanxi obligations, and the habitual use of physical vocabulary to describe and conceptualize mental disorders.
3. Ideally, the interrogator of an Asian suspect should have sufficient cross-cultural knowledge of the verbal shadings in both the suspect's specific Asian dialect and his attempted English to recognize when the suspect is trying to project subtle changes in his attitude while trying to maintain "face". An example would include certain verbal markers of the suspect's softening of his refusal to admit guilt. This would require an interpretation of the suspect's choice of language and nonverbal behavior that would provide the foundations for the interrogator's accurate, emphatic " … awareness of the listener's attitude" and of a potential "weakening of [the suspect's] denials" (Reid: Step 3).
4. The interrogator should have the ability to recognize, be aware of, and accurately assess the fitness (or the lack of it) between the following relationships; namely, the accuracy and the "fit" or appropriateness of the interrogator's understanding of the suspect's cultural mindset, upon which the interrogator's choices of themes and subsequent question will be based, and the ability to choose appropriate cultural vocabulary and examples when formulating the "Alternative Question" (Reid: Steps 7 and 8).
5. "Focuses on the fitness" or cultural appropriateness between the suspect's vocabulary and verbal and nonverbal behavior and the interrogator's appropriate and relevant understanding and actions based the interrogator's cross-cultural knowledge of the suspect's mindset.
6. With a base of accurate cross-cultural knowledge, the interrogator can choose an appropriate and fitting theme to shape his formulation and

use of the "Alternative Question" in order to provoke an admission of guilt.

7. The interrogator should know how to use the potential ambiguity of asking the "Alternative Question" (Reid: Steps 7 and 8) in a culturally appropriate way, that is, by choosing a culturally appropriate theme expressed in culturally appropriate vocabulary.
8. An example of an "Alternative Question" is "Jian, did you take the money to honor your guanxi obligations and help keep 'face' for your family or did you take the money to play Pai Gow?" (Pai Gow is a Chinese card game.) In this example, the culturally appropriate theme is that of guanxi-social obligations vs. gambling.
9. This "Alternative Question" deliberately uses a flaw in logical reasoning called "the fallacy (flaw) of a logically complex question" — building a false assumption into your question. An example of a logically complex question would be to ask an unmarried man: "Have you stopped beating your wife yet?". Either a "yes" or a "no" answer would be an admission that he has a wife, which is a false assumption built into the question.
10. Analogously, both alternative sides of the "Alternative Question" (Reid: Steps 7 and 8) to Jian (above) *presuppose* the suspect's guilt to which either of his responses constitutes a legal legally binding admission of guilt.
11. It is taken for granted that in answering the "Alternative Question", the suspect is aware of the logically complex nature of this question which assumes his guilt for both affirmative and negative responses.
12. The net effect of an interrogator's cross-cultural skills and knowledge will be demonstrated in the particular choices of both the theme and the expressions and examples associated with the theme. All must fit with — be culturally appropriate to — the suspect's values (gambling, guanxi, family, "face") and activities (a love for gambling).

Thus, the "Alternative Question" must be chosen on the basis of culturally accurate and appropriate knowledge and it must be expressed in a culturally appropriate form that fits the suspect's cultural background. If the question is culturally appropriate and plausible to the Asian suspect, then it may be a culturally plausible way to "excuse himself". By means of his answer to the "Alternative Question", the Asian suspect may reduce the anxiety generated by the crime and during the interrogation, and the interrogator will secure his legal confession. Therefore, it is particularly important to know about the suspect's claims of discrimination or perceived discrimination, family home life, community life, feelings of solidity, family history and religious affiliations, cultural attitudes about mental illness, his/her guanxi members, and his/her economic hardships and obligations. Knowing something of the family's cultural background will let you make a better case and choose better "themes" within the general framework of the Reid or other similar method of interrogation. Finally, we should remember that such a confession would undergo the careful scrutiny of the defense attorney regarding the suspect's explicit awareness of all these points to avoid the charge of cultural ambiguity sufficient to destroy the prosecutor's case. One such ambiguity is illustrated next.

Interrogating Home-Invasion Robbery Suspects

The materials in this chapter should be considered in conjunction with the analyses of Chinese mindset in Chapter 13, Major Components of Chinese Mindsets. Within this section, a series of successful police tactics will be described for optional use. **However, once again, do not adopt any of these tactics if any of these descriptions appear to you to violate lawful statutes or agency or departmental policies.** For example, let one Asian-American defendant think that the other ones are turning. Plant seeds of doubt by taking the silent but hard-nosed suspect to the doorway of one of the "soft" suspects and ask: "Is this who you're talking about? Him? OK!", and whisk him away before either has a chance to speak.

About Interpreters

With thanks to Lt. Jack Willoughby (New Orleans P.D., a.k.a. "WoFat"), the following paraphrase constitutes additional excellent advice regarding the use of interpreters:

> "Keep your interpreter behind the suspect and out of the line of any possible communication or intimidation through facial expressions, body language, or hand signals in the direction of either the suspect or the interpreter. Advise the interpreter that you will be recording the interview and that you will be getting another native speaker to double-check his work. Make it understood that this is not because you do not trust him, only that this is standard procedure so the translation will stand in court under challenges from the defense attorney and the interpreter used by the defense."

Think Like an Asian-American Defense Attorney

Take your time writing your report. Think like an Asian-American defense attorney who will scrutinize it carefully. Pay particular attention to those Asian aspects of the case which are fuzzy, obscure, or could be challenged on the basis of cultural ignorance or racial prejudices, many of which may be more obvious to an Asian-American than to a non-Asian-American. Check whether there any potential foreign language problems or inaccuracies in regard to specific words, technical terms, styles of speech such as questions, dialect differences between police interpreter and suspect, or other aspects of cross-cultural understanding. Double-check your report and then let your partner check it. Also, review it carefully before the trial and talk with the prosecutors to prepare for all possible challenges to your notes.

Recruiting Informants

While it is hard to overcome cultural barriers, it can be done with friendliness, attention to some XC details, and small modifications in one's behavior and language and sometimes, *money.* Equally important is an officer's internal commitment to develop and deserve the trust and support of admirable members of the community — decent, hardworking, family-oriented solid Asian people — who have, as do we all, their own justifiable and unjustifiable agendas and hidden goals; to them, money may be an insult. Also in need of an officer's implicit external commitment and long-range support are a variety of "scumbags" with whom you must develop trust and give rewards. Although some businessmen will refuse money and may even feel insulted by your offer of it, others will not only take it but will try to negotiate more. With the latter group, introduce small amounts of money only after you have made them produce something for it; many will start whoring for it by exaggerating information. Many people in between well-to-do businessmen and street bums will accept money only after you have offered a "face"-saving reason in a quiet discussion during which they have come to feel comfortable with the private arrangement. In general:

- Be in the streets and the temples and visit the shops and important community locations regularly, especially during Asian holidays.
- Know some Asian phrases, history, and foods — maybe some of the popular (and legal) card games.
- Do favors and develop networks (guanxi). Roll over some of the minor street bangers and make them obligated to you. Then lean on them (only verbally, of course).
- Develop informers from gang members' ex-girlfriends, bar-waitresses, and Asian families at hospitals and in welfare offices; they can guide you to others who might know what you need to know.
- Even professionally educated Asian-Americans, e.g., immigration lawyers and physicians, can become hooked into positions that make them vulnerable to extortion and blackmail. Because those situations could pose great danger to their "face" and/or social standing both in the

community and to their families, their recruitment as informers becomes possible.
- It is important to praise your informants. Exaggerate their helpfulness to you and many will work even harder for you. Praise is cheaper than dollars!
- Visit convicted criminals in prison to develop them as quiet informants.Use trips to and from prison with them as opportunities to offer them "good food" to help soften their attitudes about cooperating with you; even if the "good food" is only "fast-food", it will be a very welcome change from prison food.

An example of a possible sequence in recruiting an informant follows. Invite the suspect to come in and talk to you voluntarily, giving him the reason that "what I'm going to tell you will make you make the most important decision of your life." Tell him that you know everything about him and you know he is going to get the maximum Federal time — "Yeah, we've got enough for a RICO indictment." Refuse to talk to him with a lawyer or a relative, but verbally hammer on him the bogus (or legitimate) details of his imminent conviction. Wait patiently until he volunteers to come to talk with you; let him pick the location so he feels comfortable with just the two of you. Then confront him with a semi-bogus case based on the assumption that you have been following him for some time. Use convincing small details of phony surveillance, street details, locations of hangouts, gossip about his girlfriend or friends, and other details of street intelligence, all of which are "on paper" in the big file folder "we've got on you." Then feed him the pitch to bend him, to make him into an informant: "I can try to help keep you out of jail if you cooperate with me — all in confidence (secret) of course. I can't promise that you won't go to jail, but I can try very hard to help you, if you cooperate with me." It's legal, and it may work.

The names of Asian gangs change constantly, in contrast to many Hispanic and Afro-American gangs where the names and turf battles remain fairly constant. Perhaps the word "groups" rather than "gangs" is more appropriate. The charting of gang names is time consuming and with the constant shifts and dissolution of Asian youth gangs, the efforts of law enforcement intelligence personnel may be misdirected. Some police have argued that since the guanxi relations and memberships are constantly changing, the mapping of gang labels may be less productive than many assume.

With people who fit the conditions just described, Asians and Asian-Americans are no harder nor any easier to recruit as informants than any one else. Moreover, they live in small communities where everyone knows everyone else's business. Furthermore, they love to gossip about each other to a third person. However, you must mix well and often at *all* levels of the communities to become an "Asian friend".

Interrogation and McCarthy's "Gang Crime Magic"

This subsection has two major goals, namely, to describe some imaginative tactics in interrogation and to describe the importance of knowing something of the cultural background of an Asian suspect to establish some degree of rapport and understanding. The following section is the author's summary of some "gang crime magic" described by a veteran Asian gang interrogator, Gang Specialist Pat McCarthy, Chicago Police Department, who has been detailed to the International Organized Crime Task Force, a joint task force with the FBI, Chicago P.D., and the Illinois State Police. This description should not be taken as either a recommendation nor an endorsement of the tactics used by any of the organizations noted above. The system of interrogation presupposed here is that of the John E. Reid Method of Interviewing and Interrogation.

The thrust of these tactics is that you may wish to legally *scam* the suspect, that is, lie to him *legally.* The goal is not to promise what is illegal, but to scam him into thinking that you have "overwhelmingly accurate specialized tests" that will confirm your assertions that you *already* have sufficient evidence to convict him. After meeting with the suspect in the streets, let him think about this for awhile. If he is not quite convinced, you should use your imagination and try some of the following examples of Pat McCarthy's "gang crime magic". Once again, this description should be taken neither as a recommendation nor an endorsement of these tactics by any of the law enforcement organizations noted above.

You are going to lie to him (the suspect). You can, quite legally, based on the precedent established in *Frazier* v. *Cupp*; 394, U.S., 731 (1969). (If in doubt, have your legal department check this claim and act accordingly.)

Invite the suspect to *voluntarily* visit you in your office. Repeat the previous sequences about your evidence and the certainty of his conviction. Then state that you have some special techniques that will give convincing forensic evidence of his guilt. And that it is to his advantage to know that you are going to show him that he is truly going to jail.

The magic begins. With his permission (*"I ain't got nothing to hide!"*) carefully take sample scrapings from under his fingernails and wrap them in a clean white sheet of "evidence paper for the lab". Tell him that this is a new test that verifies he has been around firearms in the last 6 months. Again, with his permission (*"Sure, I told you, I ain't got nothing to hide!"*) fluff up his hair and take a few samples of loose hairs onto a clean white sheet of the "evidence paper for the lab", explaining that it will determine whether he has been around firearms in the last 6 months. Rub skin lotion over his wrist and the top of his hand and then gently scrape some off onto "a clean white sheet of evidence paper for the lab". With a couple of really low-level rocket scientists, outlines of their bare feet were made to "corroborate blood pressure changes that go along with exposure to the nitrates in gunpowder." When the taking of "evidence" is completed, have a partner pop in to announce with a very straight face that "the Fed tester just flew in and will have the lab set up in 20 minutes." Take the "evidence" out of the interrogation room and have a coffee. After your break, return to inform the suspect that the tests show, along with the other information you have, that he will certainly be judged guilty.

At this point, you may want to tell the suspect that you would really prefer to "rehabilitate" him and have him work for you rather than go to jail. Then secure more information for your own personal "understanding" about the suspect to enable you to choose the appropriate Reid method themes (Steps 7 and 8). Then, offer the suspect a choice between "Alternative Questions", both of which constitute legal admissions of guilt — e.g., "Jian, did you take the money to honor your guanxi obligations and help keep 'face' for your family or did you take the money to play Pai Gow?" Sympathize with the suspect to reduce his anxiety and feeling that you are an adversary. Deny his denials and keep pushing the themes as you keep him talking to you prior to getting him to finally admit his guilt.

The interrogator continues: "Yeah, the bastard probably deserved it … I understand how you felt," and "Sure, you were just doing your friends a favor, weren't you? Sure, I know. Something just like that happened in my family too. My brother-in-law got himself … and he tried to protect my sister.… " Then you fine-tune the quiet shift in your pitch: "But I'd really like to see you rehabilitated, not convicted. You'd like to be rehabilitated, wouldn't you? And you have the opportunity to tell your side of it to the judge. After all, we've got all the evidence — the fingernails, the hair samples, the lotion, the bulges in your feet — so you can tell me your side and we will try to help the judge act to rehabilitate you. You'd like that, wouldn't you?" Then move in closer and use the "touch", etc. (Reid: Steps 7, 8 and 9).

At the risk of irritating the reader, I repeat the point that it is an advantage to know something of the culture of the Asian or Asian-American suspect. Since the central goal is to get the Asian suspect to confess *voluntarily*, a slight knowledge of Asian culture helps. For example, one means to get a voluntary confession is for you to create a psychological climate by illustrating that you "understand" his particular social situation as an Asian. With your "understanding", he may finally become awash in such feelings of frustration, desperation, and righteous trust in you — his "buddy" who really understands him — that he will be able to reduce his anxiety by "getting it off his chest".

It is also obvious that many of these strategies of interrogation are not confined to Asian suspects/defendants. However, the cultural points that are relevant to Asian or Asian-American culture should be known and used with accurate detail. Certainly, you can lie to him about your evidence,[22] but do so within a cultural context which sounds believable to him and appropriate in his/her multicultural day-to-day life. For the Asian-American suspect who is guilty of a criminal offense, it will be the combination of your allegedly anxiety-increasing evidence, your culturally astute sympathy, and use of "Alternative Questions" (question-begging alternatives wrapped in culturally appropriate themes) that will give him an excuse to confess to reduce his anxiety. But remember, more of the shame-sensitive anxiety of most Asians comes from factors external to them than would be the case with more inner-directed, internalized, guilt-sensitive North Americans. (See "Mindsets", Chapter 12.)

Therefore, to imagine how it feels to wrestle with the barriers of living day-to-day within a society whose language you do not know very well, you need to know about the suspect's ethnic culture — here and in the Asian home-country. Some special cross-cultural buttons are illustrated below using a hypothetical young Asian-American suspect:

> "Yeah, we understand the language barrier. What a downer. At your age its hard to really pick up the language the way the younger kids do! Yeah, then the job discrimination … the way they look down at you … Yeah, they call you 'flat nose'! Yeah, I understand … and your parents have to work at crap jobs … never home...working at jobs they'd never have had to do in X … And its hard to be a good Buddhist here too.. You got any Buddha images? Or Buddhist rosaries? How about your mother? Does she have any? Your brothers got any tattoos for protection? That old-fashioned stuff doesn't work too well here, does it? … Even though you're respectful and try to do what your Dad says … Yeah … sure, I understand. Like if you're trying to do good in school or you like to party, they say you're too Americanized … and if you stay away from all that, they say you aren't trying to make it here like they are… working two jobs and all… Yeah, it's tough."

In short, learn where the main issues of discrimination and cultural maladjustment are most likely to be experienced in an Asian-American suspect's life. In most cases, there will be plenty of candidates for possible areas of XC stress and trouble. Use those issues and problems to express your empathy to gain the rapport and trust during interrogation; listen for XC information with which to develop themes and gain excuses that will, in his eyes, allow him to admit guilt for reasons which are plausible and sufficiently self-serving to his own psychologically overstressed mind (Reid: Steps 7 and 8). If, on the other hand, you "push the wrong cultural buttons", you will alienate the Asian suspect.

Asian Youth Gangs 10

關係

Only a portion of the aspects of Asian cultures described in the preceding chapters applies to the subcultures of North American gangs. However, because the members of Asian gangs usually have not been successful in integrating themselves into either their home country culture or the mainline cultures of this country, it is difficult to describe their subcultures as either "Asian" or "North American". Thus, in large part, the information in this chapter may provide some useful information about groups that remain tangential to the interaction between mainline Asian and North American cultures but tend to favor the latter.[23] See Figures 2 and 3.

What Is a Gang and Who Are Its Members?

The comments here refer to groups who range in age from those barely into their teens to those approaching their middle 20s (the average age is 16 yrs). Japanese gangs are not included here, not because they have no youth gangs, but because Japanese gangs are largely absent from criminal activities in North America that are so commonly associated with young criminals of Vietnamese, Chinese, Korean, and Southeast Asian descent. For example, the largest population of Vietnamese outside of Vietnam can be found in Orange County, California, where over 140,000 Vietnamese have settled since 1975.

Definition of a Gang

A gang is a group of recently associated individuals who have identifiable internal leadership and organize and identify with or claim control over a specific territory and/or engage in criminal and/or violent behavior.

Figure 2 Vietnamese-American gang members. (Courtesy of Investigator Al Lotz, Houston P.D.)

Why Do Some Youths Become Gang Members?

Some or all of the gang members exhibit some or all of the following characteristics:

- They grow up within or near a gang subculture.
- They exhibit substantial educational deficiencies; they speak English poorly, are poorly educated, and have few qualifications for most jobs.
- They exhibit serious socio-economic deficiencies which means that they are poor and were raised in poor families.
- They have been exposed to and have participated in racism and cross-cultural discord and violence.
- They find substantial ego-fulfillment, prestige, psychological security, and sexual opportunities in gangs.
- They lack adequate consistent parental guidance.

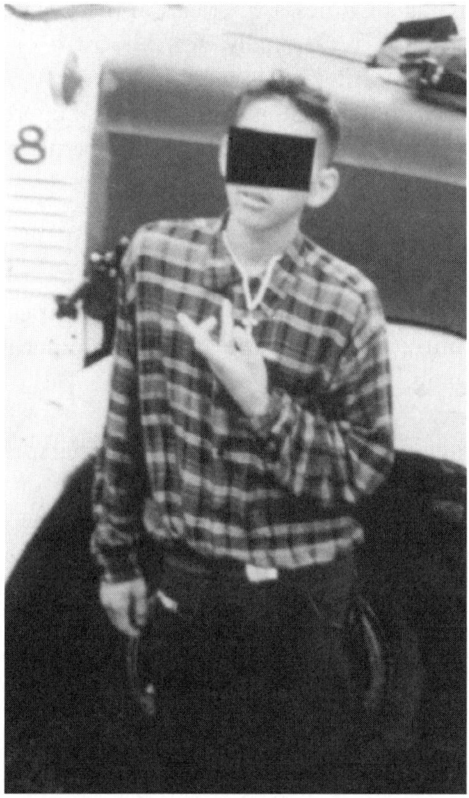

Figure 3 Vietnamese-American gang member throwing hand signs. (Courtesy of Investigator Al Lotz, Houston P.D.)

Conversion to gang membership may occur in as little as two or three days. Intimidation and heavy obligations are induced in new members very quickly and, often, brutally. At the same time, deep bonding techniques are brought to bear on the new member to make him feel that he has been brought into a new family where he is protected and to whom he exclusively owes his allegiance, his intelligence, and his muscle.

Are Gangs Largely of a Single Ethnic Type?

They often are of mixed ethnic groups of Southeast Asians when they are early teenage gang members, as in the "Rainbow Junior Gangs", but as they enter their late teenage years, they tend to shift to membership by similar ethnic background. A number of Chinese-Vietnamese Americans (Viet-Ching) have elected to change their legal names to the Chinese form, or to the Chinese-American spelling. In spite of several generations of family residency in southeast Asia, some Viet-Ching Americans conclude that there are advantages in being a Chinese-American in the United States over being a Vietnamese-American. Occasionally, some Korean or Vietnamese gang members have teamed up with Chinese gangs; on even rarer occasions, a single white male has entered an Asian gang and, at arrest or apprehension, is usually the "fall guy", the member all others identify as the perpetrator of the crime.

Levels of Adherence to a Gang

Gang members and those who appear to be related to gangs can adhere to four levels of commitment of the gang and to any other implicit or explicit affiliations of the gang.

1. *Hard-core gang members:* These are the essential members of the gang, without whom there would be no gang.
2. *Affiliates:* These are former gang members or others who drift in and out of the gang's activities but are known and accepted by the hard-core members.
3. *Peripherals:* These are pseudo-members who are at the edges of the gang but are not really accepted in any serious way by the hard-core members.
4. *Wannabees:* These are those who may appear to be gang members to outsiders by virtue of their dress and body language, but, in fact, are not.

Documentation for Identifying Gang Membership

- He/she admits gang membership.
- He/she is consistently observed to associate with known gang members over a period of time.
- He (seldom she) exhibits gang tattoos. Here, one must be cautious for many tattoos are not gang-specific and some widely observed tattoos are regional or ethnic symbols not related to criminal activities. For example, clipper ship tattoos express the general idea of freedom and do not denote gang membership.
- He/she exhibits gang paraphernalia.

Gangs as Surrogate "Families"

Gangs often serve as a surrogate family to some Asian-Americans or Asian-Canadians who enter North America too old to become acculturated and develop good language skills. Often Vietnamese and Chinese gang members feel torn in two competing directions: the powerful pull of Asian family culture and the all-pervasive American TV and/or gang cultures of their high schools. Many Vietnamese-American gangs planning home invasions are known for their integrated, careful organization (who does what to whom is decided beforehand) and sophisticated strategies (carefully placed backup cars, lookouts, and backup plans). In contrast, their personal lives often tend to be chaotic, violent, revengeful, dangerous, anecdotal, nomadic, and "floating" towards few long range goals. However, the gang becomes a personal escape from social tension, racial discrimination and potential loss of "face" within the family and community. Also, gang members tend to develop a mindset which enables them to live completely in the present, with little thought for their future or past — a floating existence focused on the present with few expectations for anything but prision or death. Also, the gang reconstructs some features of the hierarchical Vietnamese family: women clean and cook, and the leader (quasi-father) guarantees distribution of "family" resources and the booty from invasions. Some family features not reconstructed in the gang are any moral, societal restrictions or ethical obligations towards people outside the gang. Gang life is a naive, short-sighted teenager's "kicked-back" paradise: hanging out all day with friends who totally support one another even with their lives, no restrictions, no hours, no school, status, avaliable sex, shared money, and access to drugs. Moreover, many members of the Asian communities are fearful, closed-mouthed, and embarrassed by gangs, but most remain very reluctant to cooperate with police and/or act as witnesses at trial. From the viewpoint of gang members, their primary enemies are other gang members; police are secondary enemies and the ethnic communities are a source of safe houses, connections, new recruits, and monied victims.

In general, Asian gangs resemble Latin/Hispanic gangs more than Black gangs in that that the latter focus primarily on the individual aquisition of money, while Latin/Hispanic gangs and Asian gangs tend to be more focused on the group. Compared to other gangs, Vietnamese gangs are less focused on securing and maintaining their own turf. Their physical focus centers around coffee houses, a temporary series of transient coffee houses which they share with Vietnamese businessmen and other members of the Southeast Asian communities. While they use marijuana and some crack cocaine, they are not tied to one physical area to sell drugs in the way that some Hispanic and Black gangs establish and defend their turfdoms. Being extremely mobile, living in and out of motels or apartments, with little or no physical or long-term continuity to their lives, Asian gang members focus on their "gang families" rather than on their biological families. Consequently, they have little or no conscience regarding the feelings or the rights of others. (See "Village Mentality", Chapter 18.)

Signs and Stages in the Development of New Gangs

- Increased presence of grafitti and painted gang initials
- Increased school disturbances during covert gang recruiting
- Indications that gangs are outlining their "turf" within or between high schools
- Increased phone calls to police from malls, skating rinks and pool halls
- Increased phone calls to police about drugs being sold in formerly drug-free neighhborhoods
- Increases in disturbance and "party" calls to police
- Increases in auto theft and hijackings
- Increases in calls to police about domestic and public fights and shooting confrontations over gang "turf"

Often, smaller police departments and community organizations underestimate the sophistication of gangs, some of which have recently developed strong, well-organized regional connections including "get out the vote" social improvement organizations and Political Action Committees(PACs) which can legally receive political contributions of money. Also, many gang members know of the 1st degree enhancement law which increases the severity of conviction, that is, more years in prison if certain gang conditions are present at the crime. Therefore, there is a tendency among some knowlegable gang members to deny their gang membership and show fewer "colors" or gang hand signs. Last, remember that in some gangs, the signs, symbols, colors, and grafitti may change frequently.

Some terminology for Chinese-American and some Vietnamese-American street gangs are:

Dai-low-dai "Super Big Brother" (Super Boss)
Dai-low "Big Brother" (Boss)
Dai-ma "Big Horse" (Middle Boss)
Sai-low "Little Horse" (Soldiers)

Gang crimes are interrelated, but the division of labor among police departments isolates street police and diminishes communication with gang specialists about these illegal interrelationships. Many gangs have little consistent organizational structure. Leadership is flexible and may often change as they execute different robberies in different locations. However, there is little independent activity across the gangs. For example, the Dai-lows may direct fighting among themselves, but occasionally the Dai-lows cooperate and/or work together with other drug handlers, sometimes from rival gangs or other ethnic groups.

Most Asian gang members photograph themselves very often as if to prove to themselves that they actually do have a family. Get those photographs for your photo book when you can! Members of Asian often tend to blend in visually with the local dress styles and do not flag their colors, etc. as much as Hispanic, Black, or White gangs do. Some gang members have dressed as preppy college students for a burglary. Members of most gangs which have been cohesive over some time are extremely careful to share whatever they have with other members of their "families", even so far as to save a portion of the remaining potato chips for a member who stepped out briefly.

Home-Invasion Robbery Victim's Profile

The following is the author's modification of a profile Officers Philip Hannum and Al Lotz have used to describe a potential home-invasion robbery victim who is (usually) a mature Vietnamese or Chinese perceived to:

- Own or operate a successful business
- Possess great wealth
- Avoid using a bank but hides his wealth in or around his home
- Fear reporting a home robbery because of the threat of revenge or possible welfare or financial fraud
- Be "culturally prepared to relate his victimization to fate, spirits, or religious reasons instead of greed and opportunity [of others]"[24]
- Have an "insider" present or near who has helped to plan or at least inform the criminals about crucial details of the victims and/or the crime site
- Be a victim, two thirds of whom will not report the crimes inflicted upon them

Organizational Models and "Pickup" Gangs

Sometimes, Chinese gangs use the Triads as models of organization; the Vietnamese do not. Thus, although Vietnamese "pickup" home-invasion gangs are often very well organized (however temporary), they do not fit the traditional model of "Organized Crime" as found in the Mafia or the La Cosa Nostra. Vietnamese home-invasion gangs are usually "pickup" gangs. Burglaries are often planned at great distances and several members will travel long distances, picking up and replacing some members and then changing personnel as they move along, robbing in different places as their financial needs dictate and their intelligence information promises lucrative victims. Except for the Jamaicans, these Vietnamese "pickup" gangs are probably some of the most vicious gangs operative today.

Caucasian "Throw-Away" Gang Members

On occasion, Vietnamese youth gangs will allow a white male to join and run with the gang for awhile. However, as soon as the gang is apprehended or even challenged, they usually will all point the finger of blame at the Caucasian youth and he becomes just another "throw-away" member.

On the "Toughness" of Asian Gang Members

In interviewing investigators, I have observed two modes of thought about the "toughness" and resistance to interrogation. First, there is the point of view that some or most older suspects whose background includes experiences as "boat people" or a quasi-military life are almost impervious to intimidation and the threats of prison. It is said that they have experienced or suffered so much that there is little police can threaten or suggest that will disturb their stoical attitudes. This attitude has been paraphrased as, "After what these people have been through, nothing you can do will be more frightening."

The second point of view is based on the experiences of many officers who have found a "softening" of the former "tough" attitudes among second generation, North American-born gang members or older Asian-born members who have become accustomed to the greater degree of material comfort and social freedom found in North America. These gang members, it is held, are quite strongly affected by the loss of freedom and the traumas of prison existence. These gang members may be as open to "rolling over" as anyone else. This interviewer has not found a predominance of evidence to support the predominance of either point of view. In short, as far as the possibility of Asians vs. non-Asians being turned, the old answer holds: "Some will and some won't!"

Numbers, Gambling, Tattoos, Food, and Regionalisms

11

關係

Some Cross-Cultural Crime-Related Aspects of Numbers

There is a whole range of special Chinese Triad and Japanese Yakuza uses of numbers to denote offices and relationships within their criminal organizations. These can be found in FBI and other federal publications; others can be found by looking at the reading list supplied at the end of Chapters 13 and 17.

Number 8: Eight is a lucky, auspicious number; multiples of eight are often enclosed in red envelopes as "lucky money" to be distributed during holidays or at store openings.

Number 4: Among speakers of the Chinese dialects of Mandarin and Hakka, the number 4 is unlucky and is avoided in license plates, floor numbers, and phone numbers, etc. Four is avoided because it is similar in sound to the word for death. In Hong Kong, however, the Cantonese pronunciation of 4 is not as close to the Mandarin or Hakka pronunciation for the word for death, and the prohibition against its use is seldom found. However, counter-examples occur. One wealthy non-typical Chinese used "4444" On the license plate of his Rolls-Royce as a way, so his chauffeur stated, to indicate that "he did not give a damn about tradition, or luck, or about anything!".

Number 108: The numbers 108, 1080, or 1008 are Triad numbers. For example, a gang member may politely request a donation from an Asian merchant to help offset the "medical expenses" of a friend. He says: "Yeah, could you help us with $108? We're trying to help him pay a hospital bill of $1008." And so the extortion begins, based on cultural lore largely unknown to most non-Asian cops. Triad and street gang folklore has it that in the middle of the 17th century, 108 Chinese Buddhist monks attempted (in vain) to defend the Shaolin Buddhist monastery. Only five survived and those five formed the basis of the five earliest Triads. Hence, the use of a multiple of 108 in the gang member's request to a Chinese merchant suggests a Triad connection on the part of the speaker. As a result of the widespread fear of the Triads among most Chinese outside of the People's Republic of China, this indirect reference to a Triad increases the level of intimidation.

Numbers 5 and 3 (a death threat): An East coast federal law enforcement officer recently received a letter, so I was told, containing two regular playing cards — 5 and 3. While this incident was probably a "setup" on the part of one criminal against a rival, consensus has it that this was intended to be a death threat. Apparently, in Vietnamese 5 means "revenge" and 3 means "taking a chance". Also, these two joined numbers apparently have a composite meaning in Cantonese. Cantonese is a dialect of southeastern China, in modern Guangdong province, spoken by many of the earliest Chinese in North America and sometimes spoken by Viet-Ching — Vietnamese who are ethnic Chinese. In Cantonese, the very slow pronunciation of 5 and 3 approximates the phrase "not living". Thus, together, 5 and 3 constitute a very intimidating message.

Dropping the First Number of a Triad Identification Number: The identifying number of a Triad usually consists of three numbers. For example, in Malaysia, a Triad had split off and formed a new independent branch. Consequently, the first number (1) was dropped indicating that it was a new branch of the old 108 — as in 108 becoming the 08. However, there was usually a character meaning "new" or "little" added to the 08 to indicate that it was the "new (offshoot) 08"; this, of course, brought the number of characters back to three once again. Thus, it seems reasonable to draw the conclusion that when such a Triad number is represented *without* the leading number but *with* the remaining two numbers, the triad has spun-off a new independent branch usually made up of the some members of the old Triad.

Inspector John McKenna (San Francisco P.D., Retired) noted a range of other aspects of Chinese numerology and superstitions:[25]

> House numbers may be part of mix. Here in the West the number 7 is thought to be lucky and the number 13 unlucky. The Chinese are rather so-so about 7 but wild about 13 because it is the number of lunar months in the year and is significant in the Buddhist religion. The number 9, when

written in the Western way, resembles the Chinese character for "long life", so having 9 in your house number is a good thing; 88 is also preferred, resembling the Chinese character for "double happiness".

All of this again brings us to numerology, a Chinese science happily exploited by the Cantonese whose multi-toned dialect is a punster's playground. Each number's sound is akin to another word's character. That way you will not find a 4th floor in some buildings as the number 4 can be ascribed or associated with "death". A major (Asian) television station never had a 4th or 14th birthday. On the other hand, 8 is a favorite, as it sounds like "prosperity". Prosperity of course is the life blood of Hong Kong. The magical date of 8-8-1988 was so propitious that the staid chairman of the, then under construction, Bank of China allowed the workers to plan celebratory events.[26]

If you are lucky, you might (for a fee) get a telephone number replete with 8s. The licensing authorities hold back for the highest bidder vehicle licenses rich with the number 8. Three (sounds like life) and 9 (akin to eternity) are additional numbers [that] bring joy to their holders. Many shops and restaurants have highly coveted street numbers to bring joy and contentment.[27]

Gambling

If you find that there are many cars parked outside of Asian-American restaurants after business hours, the probability is greater that there is Asian-only, illegal gambling occurring. If there is illicit Asian gambling in your area, in a social, legal setting, learn some of Asian gambling games such as 20 Point Mah Jong, Chinese 7 Card Poker, or the Korean card game Wah-To. This would establish professional credibility, personal rapport, and cultural cordiality. It also would allow you — with the help of a translator — to explain the posted or written house rules of illicit gambling to a jury. In addition, it would enable you to establish that there is actual commercial gambling going on, not just mere social gambling, and that such activities may be subject to prosecution and/or forfeiture.

An excellent 33-page pamphlet on Asian gambling titled *Asian Games* can be secured from Dale Zlock, Special Agent (Enforcement), Washington State Gambling Commission, Tacoma Mall Office Bldg., 4301 S. Pine, Suite 307, Tacoma, WA 98409, (206) 438-7688. From Dale Zlock's pamphlet the following are typical games associated with cultural groups: (Chinese) Pai-gow, Pai-gow poker, 13 card Poker, Mah-Jhong; (Vietnamese) Bai Tu Sac, 13 card Poker, Pai-gow, Pai-gow Poker; (Cambodian) Apong (a dice game), Blackjack, Poker; (Laotian) Numbers, playing the Thai lottery; (Korean) Hanafuda cards (20 card and Go-Stop); (Japanese) Hanafuda cards, Baccarat, and Las Vegas casino games.

Elders and Minor Children in Gambling Houses

If you are about to raid a gambling house, at a home in which people live, be prepared to relocate elders and minor children while the premises are being searched; they are not excluded during the gambling. Do not assume that an elder sitting quietly in a gambling room would have no access to nor interest in obscuring a firearm in her/his vicinity. Grandma's cushion might be covering an Uzi! Photograph and copy all ledger and telephone books, all INS cards and numbers, and all I-20s visa documents attached to foreign or U.S. passports. Check for the expiration dates of all "official" documents including Resident Alien Cards ("green" cards) and other foreign appearing documents. (Do not remove attacments if they are stapled to the passport.)

Figure 4 Old men, a "Batchelor Society," gamble in a public square in California. (Courtesy of Sgt. Tom Perdue, San Francisco P.D.)

Tattoos and Slang

Photograph all tattoos and compare them with known gang or Triad symbols, knowing that fashions in tattoos change constantly. Look especially at the individual who is wearing long sleeves when everyone else is wearing short-sleeved shirts. Animal and sailing ship tattoos are fairly popular but do not mean that the owner is a gang member. Straight-line cuts are to show toughness — the more cuts the tougher and/or higher the gang rank. A burned cross indicates toughness. These burns are then flaunted to intimidate others. Tattooed initials found almost anywhere on the body are usually of the name of their gang and these initials may be discovered on and within clothing, shoes, hats, caps, and other new wave or punk accessories (see Figures 5 to 9). As gang membership may shift constantly, so may the meanings and the enormous variety of tattoos shift. Furthermore, except for purposes of identifying individuals, the tracking of gang tattoos and their meanings (if any) is enormously time consuming and may not indicate a relationship. An excellent survey of California gang tattoos may be found in *Asian Gang Activity,* 4th ed., 1994, by Michael L. Martin, Asian Service Unit, Gang Suppression Unit, Garden Grove Police Department, pp. 23–50 (*Confidential: for Law Enforcement Personnel Only*). Also see Chapter 18 in this book.

In general, the two most famous organized crime groups where tattoos do designate membership are the Japanese tattooed Boryukadan (Yakuza) and the Koreans (see Figures 10 to 12). The tattoos of Koreans tend to explicitly display Mahāyāna Buddhist themes, such as Bodhisattvas (savior gods), and fierce-looking temple guardians; Korean tattoos are usually more violent than the Japanese or Chinese tattoos.

Groups of tattoos or burned dots on the hands, arms, or elsewhere do not *necessarily* indicate gang membership. However, they do connote (at least) receptivity to gang-like behavior against society. Tattoos may suggest weak gang affiliation, perhaps as a peripheral who is at the edges of the gang but who is not really accepted in any serious way by the hard-core members.

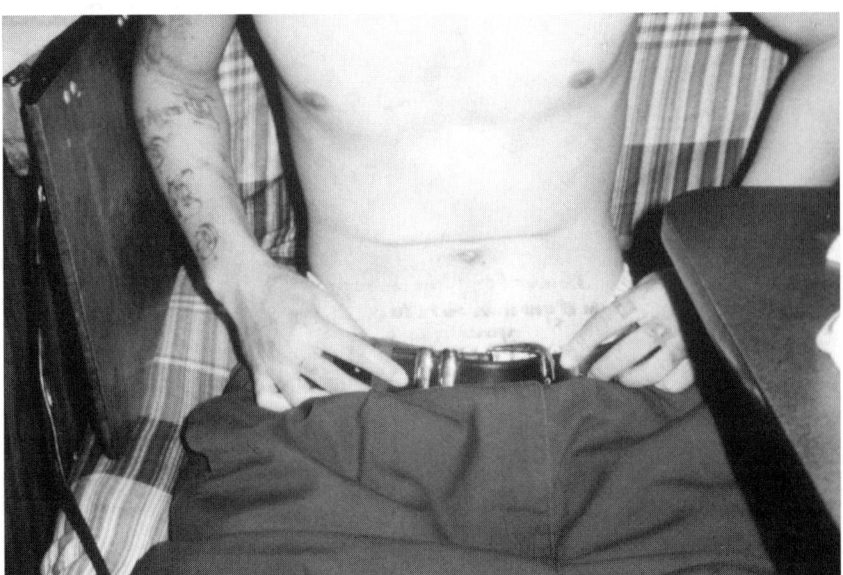

Figure 5 Vietnamese gang member's tattoos. (Courtesy of Investigator Al Lotz, Houston P.D.)

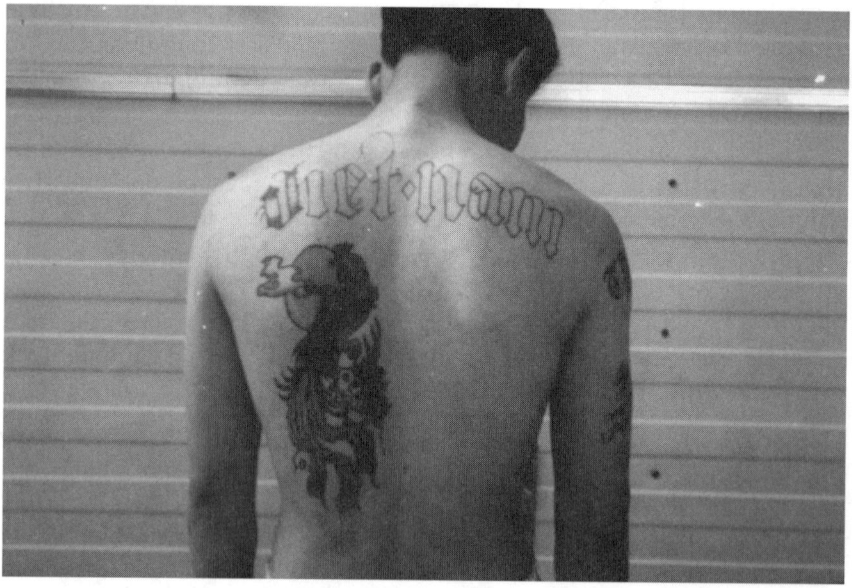

Figure 6 Vietnamese gang member's tattoos. (Courtesy of Investigator Al Lotz, Houston P.D.)

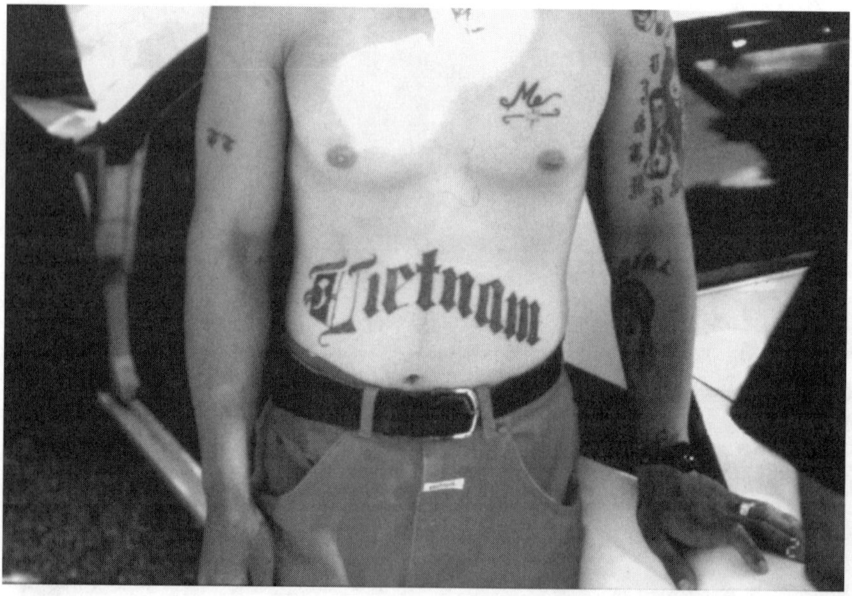

Figure 7 Vietnamese gang member's tattoos. (Courtesy of Investigator Al Lotz, Houston P.D.)

Figure 8 Vietnamese gang member's tattoos. (Courtesy of Lt. Jack Willoughby, New Orleans P.D.)

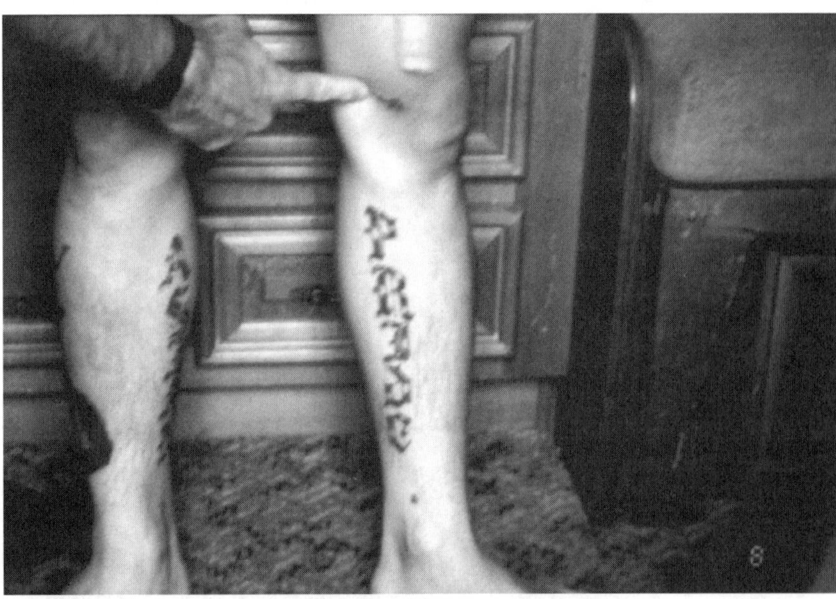

Figure 9 Vietnamese gang member's tattoos. (Courtesy of Lt. Jack Willoughby, New Orleans P.D.)

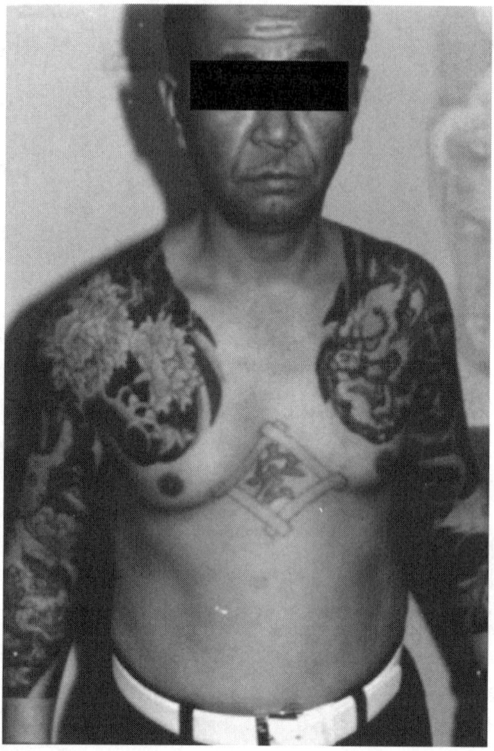

Figure 10 Japanese Boryukadan tattoos. (Courtesy of Investigator Al Lotz, Houston P.D.)

Figure 11 Japanese Boryukadan tattoos. (Courtesy of Investigator Al Lotz, Houston P.D.)

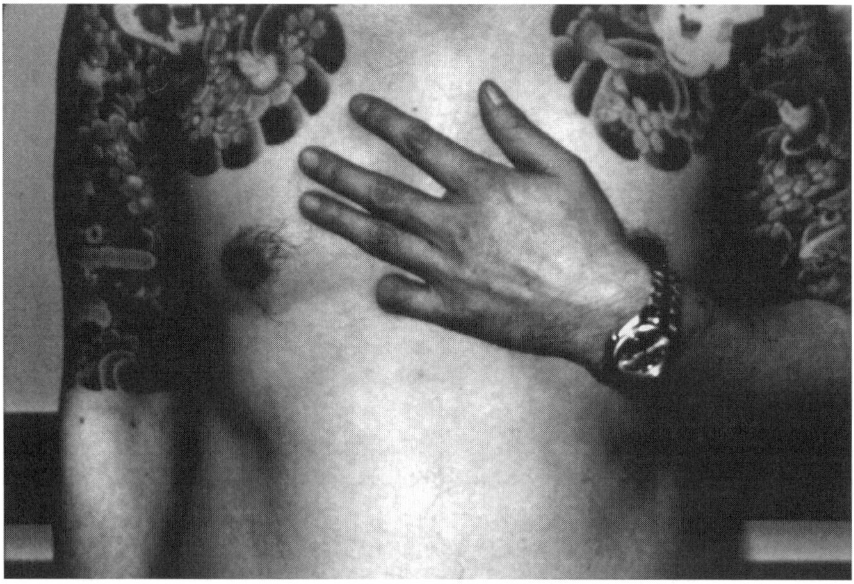

Figure 12 Japanese Boryukadan tattoos and partially missing finger. (Courtesy of Investigator Al Lotz, Houston P.D.)

Or a tattoo may indicate that he/she is a "wannabee" who may appear to be a gang member to outsiders but, in fact, is not (see Chapter 11)

For example, a "TTTT" or a "TTTTT" tattoo does not necessarily mean that the individual has spent time in prison, although prison *may* have been the origins of these "T" tattoos. Four or five "T" tattoos are usually thought to mean money (Tein), prison (Tu), love (Tinh), crime (Toi), and revenge (Thu). One burned or tattooed dot on the arms or hands is usually thought to mean "my lonely life" or that the tattooed person is possibly "available" for gang recruitment. Three dots on the hands, arms, or almost any part of the body mean "my crazy life" (Toi O Gica).

Five dots on the hands, arms, or on almost any parts of the body mean "a group of tight (good, brother-like) friends" — Tu (for), Gai (group), De (brother), Huynh (friends), Hai (beach). Some will claim that the four outer dots indicate north, south, east, and west and that the wearer is standing in the middle. This is paraphrased into something like "I've got friends everyplace in the world."

When the tattoos are in words, have them translated by a native speaker who really knows the common street language, realizing that many of the words may be the street slang of Asian Yahoos, not Asian rocket scientists. In one case, great amounts of time, anguish, and discussions about using anti-terrorist SWAT teams, etc. were spent in reaction to words heard on a Cantonese language wiretap before someone figured out that "shooting down the airplane" merely meant male masturbation. Thus, some tattoos may help to determine gang affiliations and geographical origins; on the other hand, some tattoos are merely comments on the supposed marvels of the owner's reproductive machinery.

Food and Eating

Learn to eat (and never refuse to try) some local Asian ethnic foods. Restaurant owners are great sources of intelligence — even if they may want to use your "friendship" for their own purposes (see Chapters 13 and 15). Many North Americans eat a wide range of "ethnic" foods: Chinese, French, German, Mexican, Thai, etc. Most unfamiliar Asian foods are not much different than Mexican food is from German food; nor is Greek food much different from Chinese food. Furthermore, Korean kimchi is no more offensive to some Americans than is cheese to some Asians. If you are not into ethnic foods now, give it a try.

Although people and contexts vary enormously, a few suggestions for dining with Chinese and many other east and southeast Asians might be helpful:

"Do's"

- Do follow what others are doing, but don't be afraid to make a mistake with unfamiliar utensils or sauces.
- Do enjoy the food, for it is usually tasty, interesting, and occasionally subtle and has been chosen carefully.
- Do wait for the host to serve you with his special "serving" chopsticks
- Do have a quiet sense of humor.
- Do wait to begin eating or drinking tea until the host begins.
- Do put food you don't want to the side after poking it around politely
- Do put bones to the side along your dish/plate.
- Do bite off portions of a large piece of meat while holding it in your chopsticks.
- Do offer toasts to your host with a gesture of eye contact, a raised glass, and whatever words you choose.
- Do lift your dish up to your mouth and shovel the food in with your chopsticks.
- Do allow yourself to slurp a little as you suck in a long, slippery noodle (without splashing).
- Do politely cover your mouth if you use the often served toothpicks at the end of the meal.
- Do after thanking the host/hostess, say a polite goodbye to, first the elderly, then the rest of the guests with husbands first.

"Don'ts"

- Don't protest where the host seats you, for position implies social rank or honor, and that matters.
- Don't refuse food; try some, then push it to one side and ignore it, if you do not want it.
- Don't take food from the large bowl with your own chopsticks, particularly the ends with which you have eaten.
- Don't suck on your chopsticks.
- Don't stick your chopsticks upright in your rice bowl, for it is bad luck and is similar to an offering for the dead.
- Don't fail to signal that you have finished by aligning your chopsticks together across your dish.

Accepting Free Asian Meals

Different departments and agencies have different policies about accepting small tokens or favors such as lunch. In general, of course, you should follow your department's policy. However, in general, most police I have interviewed about this have suggested to me that if you are on the street all the time, insist on paying for your food most of the time, even your pot of tea. Asian merchants may think it is part of the cost of doing business, but it is probable that they will want a "special favor" sometime, and … !

Among the Chinese, however, most Hakka, Cantonese, and all Fukinese/Taiwanese restaurant owners offer explicit hospitality. To refuse their hospitality would make them lose considerable "face". Talk this over with your superiors and work something out that allows you to CYA. On the other hand, if you are invited for a special dinner (say, a celebration or wedding), accept and enjoy the great food. If you are worried about the hot spices, drink a glass of half-and-half cream before and tell them that you have a stomach condition.

Regionalisms, Anti-Stereotypes, and Role-Playing

The countries of Japan, China, Vietnam, Korea, Taiwan, and Singapore all share the cultural backgrounds of Confucianism and Buddhism. They do not share a common language, although Japan uses many Chinese word-characters that are called "kanji" in Japanese; the meanings sometimes vary.

Chinese, Vietnamese, Laotian, and Thai are tonal languages where a difference in tone distinguishes a difference in meaning of the "same" word-character. In contrast, Lao and Vietnamese are both alphabetic and tonal languages; Cambodian (Khmer) is an alphabetic language but not a tonal language. Furthermore, many Northern Chinese do not eat nearly as much rice as their countrymen in the South; many Northern foods are wheat based, not rice-based.

Among many of the 26 provinces of China, there are mutually unintelligible dialects. Furthermore, even among some regional dialects, not all speakers can speak intelligibly to one another or mutually understand each other. As noted, they can all read the same Chinese characters and get the same meaning; only the pronunciations may differ. (See Appendix B.)

Role-Playing

In public situations, Chinese prefer to follow the public role assigned them by society; that is, Chinese do not like to "role-play", to play new roles. They do not like to get "out of character". Usually, they tend to follow the public social script of who they are and how they should act towards others. On the other hand, Americans are fairly good at role-playing, as are the Vietnamese, Cambodians, Laotians, and Thai who role-play quite easily. In general, Chinese and Japanese want a publicly sanctioned, widely understood social "script" (Japanese: Kata) which generally allows them to know who does what, when, how, and to whom. This publicly described script defines their roles and they wish to stick to it. With the script, Chinese know who they are supposed to be, and thus what they are supposed to do, to have, and how to respond in role. Sources of these roles are family, family name associations, dialect, regional lineage, and village educational connections; this generally holds true even if they are the third or fourth generation overseas Chinese and have never seen their "homeland".

By contrast, individual Chinese are perceived by many experienced Americans and others, as always role-playing, always "in role", never "off duty" or "off camera". Thus, they are perceived as socially correct and formally friendly but basically emotionless, impersonal people who never reveal having a "real self". This, of course, is not an accurate description of the inner life of a Chinese person, but their mode of personal interaction sometimes generates this reaction. This reaction is particularly acute for Americans for whom the flaunting of one's unique personal self is of primary importance even in social interaction.

III

Mindsets, Profiles, and Religions

Contrasting Chinese and American Mindsets 12

關係

An Introduction to Mindsets

In this chapter, we enter the slippery world of cross-cultural generalizations about ethnic mindsets. While it is clearly relevant, it is also a more difficult field and open to more counter-examples and criticisms. The XC traits described here are clearly based on considerable consensus, reflection, and my specialized education in Asian studies, Asian residency, and published comparative research. The generalizations stated here as mindsets — which are not refuted by a few true counter-examples — will remain controversial to some and sensitive to a few. However, these generalizations are empirically verifiable and falsifiable (in theory if not always in field practice) and I remain receptive to civil debate if serious doubts arise.[28]

Furthermore, the strength of particular features of Chinese mindsets may vary considerably between overseas Chinese such as those of Hong Kong, Singapore, or Taiwan. Other variants in the strength of particular mindsets may also be found in countries with economically significant Chinese populations such as Malaysia, Indonesia, Thailand, etc. As with India and Indians, and Ireland and the Irish, sometimes the overseas ethnic groups display stronger or different aspects of their ethnic mindset than are found in the homeland. As noted at the beginning of the book, both the "Do's and Don'ts" and the mindsets are suggested guidelines, XC road maps, not detailed surveyor's maps, nor are they manuals that will explain every situation with Asians or within the various Asian-American communities. Try these mindsets and see if they help you to understand your situation. Most will fit to some degree, but not all.

Cultural mindsets are culture-specific world views. The author's choice is to call world views "publicly available explanatory frameworks" (PAEF). PAEFs are collective visions of one's self and one's view of the world particular to relatively discrete cultural groups. Moreover, PAEFs are what is publicly available in one's culture. The content and style of culture which is public, available, and known by everyone in that culture is not the same across the world. Various Asian PAEFs are obviously not publicly available in many parts of the U.S., Zaire, Mexico, or Śrī Lanka. Ethnic groups are isolatable by general culture, language, and/or historical or religious continuity, plus a combination of either or both culture or language. Simply put, as functional adults, everyone operates with and within fairly coherent, consistent frameworks of ideas by means of which we matured and learned adult "rules of the game". All of us have implicit mindsets by means of which we become conscious of ourselves and with which we try to understand the past, function in the present, anticipate the future, and try to make sense of the world. Obviously, most of the components of our mindsets are seldom made explicit; we learn about these mindsets in the same unconscious way we learn our first language, by unconscious immersion. Furthermore, by the time we become old enough to think to ask, we find that there is no need to ask. The rules of the game are *obvious* "common sense".

Mindsets are of two types. First, there are belief components and there are second, models, or exemplars, for processing information. The first consists of quasi-factual assumptions and normative expectations, such as individual thoughts and cosmic ideas of self, origins, death, publicly legitimate purposes and goals, one's social obligations, interpretations of history, prospects for the future, children, uses of the past, war, sex, etc. The second type of mindset may be termed "habits of mind" or "mental software". These are public, tacitly understood, theory-laden, and culture-bound styles of processing information by which evidence and experience are selected, organized, processed, evaluated, and reconciled. They are cohesive *systems of applying* the "rules-of-the-game" rather than the tactics of playing the game.

In a discussion of Chinese mindsets, Cordell Hart offered another illustrative example of the use of an unrecognized component of a mindset, a "habit of the mind". For example, when a Chinese person uses a particular cultural model (guanxi) when responding to an inquiry about guanxi ("networking or connections") without ever recognizing that he is using that particular cultural model. Mr. Hart's example was a response to his inquiries about "connections/networking" (guanxi) when the Chinese person stated that he never practices it — but he offered to check the matter out with certain of his colleagues on the [police] force who all spoke [X dialect] and were members of his police academy class; he could trust them to be candid.

That is, the Chinese fellow claimed not to use guanxi while processing information and choosing a course of action in a guanxi manner! That is a "habit of the mind" and is a component of a mindset. (There is more on guanxi in Chapter 15 and in Cordell Hart's essay in Appendix C.)

When the expectations and behaviors compatible with and appropriate for these mindsets differ between persons of widely different cultural backgrounds, there occur cross-cultural incompatibilities, behavioral anomalies. Commonly known XC anomalies are eye contact behaviors and expectations about time frames regarding promptness and being "on time", personal space, and touching. As many know, the foundations of anomalous beliefs or attitudes are more difficult to identify and analyze.

Cordell Hart's guanxi example illustrates:

1. A typical mindset-dependent component
2. That the culture dictates its use, rather than the individual for whom it is usually "obvious common sense"
3. Its use is usually *unrecognized* by those who use it
4. A comparative analysis is often helpful to define the parts and cultural boundaries of the idea
5. A comparative analysis is often helpful to define the proper cultural-social context of its appropriate use
6. A comparative analysis is often helpful to determine the behavioral implications of its cross-cultural contrasts within several cultures
7. Comparative analysis is often helpful to justify claims of understanding and courses of behavior between cultures

The mindset that has had a major influence in all of Asia is the traditional historically sanctioned Chinese mindset, the heritage of the modern People's Republic of China (PRC). It is well known that the Chinese tradition has strongly influenced and shaped the thoughts and cultures of Japan, Taiwan, Vietnam, Singapore, Hong Kong, and the two Koreas. Thus, these countries will be called "Sinocized" countries. It is granted that some contemporary aspects of the culture of the PRC differ strongly from the cultures found in Taiwan, Singapore, and Hong Kong. However, the cultural history of mainland China — Zhong Guo, "Middle Kingdom" — the PRC, constitutes the origins and historical *core* of the varied traditions of Chinese culture scattered throughout the world. Thus, we shall focus on the PRC with some qualifications about differences in other Sinocized countries. A brief description of Taiwan, Singapore, and Hong Kong will follow that of the PRC in Chapter 14.

We shall describe general Chinese mindset, and contrast them with American mindset by focusing on their general cultural traits. Traits are accurate generalizations that include facts, attitudes, values, and general tendencies of most of the influential groups of these two cultures. For example, I have modified a fundamental contrast stated by a very experienced, trilingual Federal intelligence officer:[29]

> The general American cliché says: "Be true to thine own self."
> The American person says: "Be true to thine own self and to the expectations of one's neighborhood associates."
> The Chinese person says: "Be true to the expectations of thine own extended family and one's guanxi."
> The Japanese person says: "Be true to the expectations of thine own fellow workers."

While there is rhetorical license exercised here, there is also more than a grain of truth about individualism and collectivism — the emphasis on either the single person or the group. Thus, there is a fundamental cultural difference between most aspects of American and Chinese mindsets: American individualism vs. Chinese family-bounded collectivism. In contrast to those two is Japanese collectivism where the expectations of the group lie not in the family but the Japanese's relations with his work mates and his membership in voluntary social associations. The importance of these contrasts for law enforcement are in the ideas and boundaries of what we Americans assume to be deception, lying, and truth-telling vs. rhetorical "white lies", and in our cultural expectations about "face", honor, trust, and obligations. Also, our ideas of "truth" can be found in our implicit *models* of how we determine what is "true" — theories of truth such as correspondence, coherence, and pragmatic theories. Also buried in our mindsets are our values about the limitations and necessary social and cultural conditions of truth-telling. As a result, surface and deep cultural mindsets strongly but silently influence our values about the "limitations and culturally necessary conditions of truth-telling". Therefore, unpacking these ideas for analysis will require that we examine an outline of some basic contrasts between the Chinese traditions and the North American cultural traditions of the U.S.A. (I am not prepared to judge my friends, the Canadians.)

The Importance and Limitations of Cultural Generalities

It is important to understand that the purpose and justification of this chapter is pedagogical. It is to facilitate the organization and assimilation of new comparative information by going from the familiar (U.S.A.) to the unfamiliar (PRC) by means of cross-cultural generalities. Four basic ideas are assumed:

1. By first describing our more familiar American culture, we can more easily gain a perspective on ourselves before we compare the less familiar aspects of Chinese and Vietnamese cultures.
2. In general, the most important cultural factors that influenced Vietnam came from China, not France. An understanding of these aspects of Chinese culture will more easily allow us to understand more (but not all) of Vietnamese cultures.
3. Vietnamese and Chinese cultures are not identical. For example, when we compare Britain and the U.S.A., we see many shared aspects between the two cultures, but we do not assume that Britain and the U.S.A. are identical. Likewise, we know that Vietnam and China possess many significant cultural differences and that they have been involved in major historical, political, and social conflicts.
4. By working Asian crime, the law enforcement reader will continue to learn more about Asian and North American cultural differences, and in time he/she will come to see these generalities for what they are, general teaching aids and introductory materials to be taken with the proverbial "grain of (conceptual) salt".

Finally, the following generalizations were written over many years of teaching for a variety of readers with different levels of education and with a variety of interests. Thus, the range of complexity and vocabulary will be slightly greater than with the preceding cross-cultural do's and don'ts. Read what interests you and ignore the rest. Then, check them against what you find in the streets and in the Courts.

Comparative Mindsets: Society, Self, Values, Epistemic Models, Religion, and World Views

We will focus first on the following generalities, which are factual and normative (value) traits or features observed in the Chinese traditions and in the Anglo-European traditions of North America as observed in the U.S.A. These contrasting features are arranged into three categories: Society (1–11); Self (12–21); Values, Epistemic Models, Religion, and World Views (22–27). In each of the 27 numbered paragraphs, there is a paragraph about Americans; within the same paragraph, a generality about Chinese will follow *in italics.* All are truncated generalities; numbers 22 to 27 are conceptually complex.

Society

1. The U.S.A. is geographically large with ample natural resources, a relatively small population, and a high standard of living; its prime values are democracy defined in terms of personal freedom, economic free markets, geographical mobility, economic power, self-reliance, legally codified maximum individual choice, minimum government intrusion, and a comparatively great degree of social egalitarianism. This is usually coupled with an absence of its own historical awareness and (apparent) ever-expanding geographical and economic horizons. With only one civil war during its 300 years as an economic entity, freedom is popularly considered of primary importance, as are the universally desirable values of independence, individual autonomy, privacy, and independence from intrusion as long as one does not restrict other's freedoms. Coupled with this idea of freedom, is the belief that economic, political, and social and (multi) cultural freedoms are interconnected and the development of one will always lead to the development of the others. Usually unnoticed are the quiet American traditions of effective cultural frameworks encompassing our legal systems and such cultural mores as civil disagreement and dissent, governmental checks and balances, rule of law, respect for facts vs. norms, and the presumptions of political stability and good faith argumentation.

The PRC is a geographically large nation (slightly bigger than the U.S.A.); most Chinese live in a relatively small fertile area, thus reflecting the presumed need for strong centralized governmental control, emphasizing primary importance of social stability and order, clear social ranking, and cooperation rather than social mobility and personal freedom. This is a historically sanctioned, near-static, multi-ranked society with a low standard of living in which most people remain illiterate, poor, and with fewer opportunities for education, economic potential, individual choice, or social mobility. Chinese worldviews are permeated with close memories of the humiliating carving of absolute spheres of influence within China by the colonial powers, the forcible introduction of heroin by the British in the last century, the Taiping Rebellion, the collapse of the Manchu dynasty, the long and brutal Japanese aggression of the second World War, the civil wars between warlords prior to 1948, the devastating struggles between the Nationalists of Chaing Kai-shek and the Communists of Mao Zedong, the hope of the Communist Revolution, and the brutal chaos of the Cultural Revolution. In the 1990s, simultaneous with the diminished role of political ideology and centralized government control, there is tremendous growth in rampant entrepreneurship; small, flexible family-bounded businesses; stock speculation; and inflation. The extended family, dialect, native-village associations, and, above all, social stability, remain the foundations of primary values.

2. The U.S.A. is unified by a single language coupled with generally mutually understood dialects. It allows and supports mass education at all levels resulting in about 35 to 40% participation in university-level education but with increasing socially ranked elitism. Widespread education resulted in immigrants' eventually gaining a new "American" identity and a sense of social and legal equality (egalitarianism) during three centuries of enormous voluntary immigration into the U.S. While a strong public emphasis has been placed upon the freedom of choice and the importance of the individual, Americans, like the Germans and Japanese, have also dampened the extremes of rampant individualism by generating and joining a large variety of intermediate institutions such as church groups, book clubs, private schools, hospital guilds, fraternal organizations, and citizens' associations, all of which help to promote social trust between individuals and build the necessary spirit of cooperation and critical civility. These institutions presuppose and strengthen " … a moral community … an unwritten set of moral rules that serve as the basis of social trust"[30] and provide a forum for organized legal dissent against excessive government control; critical, cooperative social action; and development of large, private corporations that transcend the boundaries of family and/or workplace.

The PRC is unified by the written language, but hampered by a series of mutually unintelligible spoken dialects. Higher education is available to a very small percentage of the population; a uniform elitist education remains the basis for the selection of government personnel. An historically sanctioned absence of voluntary immigration into China has helped to prevent legal equality or universal equality (egalitarianism) between social classes. Because of the central place of the extended family, guanxi relations based on kinship, dialect, native-village, and surname associations and the absence of a tradition of intermediate institutions between the State and the family-bounded individual, China, like Italy and France, has emphasized organizations where person-to-person trust and voluntary institutional relationships are limited to those between family, dialect, native-village, surname associations, and guanxi members. Largely excluded are unwritten nationwide moral rules or developed legal traditions that serve as the basis for organized legal dissent against excessive government control and social criticism coupled with cooperative social action. Still lacking are an established tradition of property rights and commericial law. The family-kinship structures at the top of most large Chinese businesses speak to the Chinese cultural reluctance to develop large, hierarchical corporations (as in Germany, Japan, and the U.S.) where professional managerial relations transcend the boundaries of family, guanxi, and/or workplace. For almost all traditional Chinese, the extended family and strong guanxi membership constitute the limits of common social trust and personal obligations.

3. The U.S.A. has a historically sanctioned 200 years of a large voluntary immigration from Europe, but not Asia. There was involuntary importation of Africans whose present culture is far more Anglo-European than traditional "African" and is mixed within a tension-filled but constant sense of strident populist ethnocentrism juxtaposed with constant everyday ethnic assimilation, cultural redefinition, and ethnic re-assertion by later generations. Among many Americans there is moderate interest in other cultures and the integration of other cultural perspectives. Social interactions among *individuals* of these groups are relatively smooth compared with the considerable contemporary tension among and between politically active groups of Hispanics, Afro-Americans, and Anglo-Europeans.

The PRC has experienced a general absence of voluntary immigration resulting in an insular, ethnocentric, and quietly hostile avoidance of non-Chinese perspectives in culture and a strong suspicion of foreign ideas and practices. Ethical values and politics are coupled with a class-ridden suspicion and occasional rejection of excellent Chinese technological developments, such as the 15th century Chinese trading fleets of over 300 ships which included huge 400-ft ships with crews totaling over 28,000 sailors. Ranging throughout the Indian Ocean and the China Sea, these fleets surpassed anything the rest of the world had developed at that time.

4. In the U.S.A., because of its immense immigration and its historically sanctioned re-definition of the cultural identity of the individual coupled with the Judaic-Christian-Hellenic-Renaissance emphasis upon the uniqueness of individuals and their free choices — freedom-to and freedom-from are emphasized as primary values. Less emphasized in public are the necessary or contingent responsibilities of free choices or a lack of constraints which are concomitant with the exercise of personal freedoms.

In the PRC, due to the immense influence of Confucian and Legalist elite governmental structures, a historically sanctioned emphasis was placed upon the outwardly directed obligations of individuals and their concomitant ranked social and ethical responsibilities (guanxi), not upon individualistic, personal free choices. This was coupled with a ambivalent suspicion of national government and national authority due to aspects of the previously mentioned traumas of the exploitation of China and wars of the last 150 years. There is a centuries-old emphasis upon frugality, work, maturity (rather than youth), family-controlled businesses, and the long-range welfare of the extended family. Also important is a sense of ethnic identity coupled with the hope to raise China to its former position of respect and (probable) economic power and intellectual and aesthetic prestige. In the 1990s, this emphasis upon national identity has been temporarily eclipsed by the sudden lessening of governmental controls, greater degrees of personal, and economic and entrepreneurial freedoms resulting in the contemporary frantic drive to make money. However, China is no longer a sleeping giant; it is fully awake and active.

5. In the U.S.A., there is great emphasis upon youth rather than age, upon social mobility, public quasi-religious morality, technological entrepreneurship, a plastic-moneyed society with reduced preference for personal savings and a historically multi-leveled society with enormous possibilities for social mobility. Compared with Europe, the gap between the small segment of the population who owns the top 50% of the wealth is increasing in the U.S., while at the end of the 20th century, the U.S. is undergoing its third and largest influx of illegal immigrant populations with the result that intra-ethnic tensions are increasing.

In the PRC, there is a relatively new emphasis on strident economic entrepreneurship and private ownership coupled with an older, established, tension-filled, historically sanctioned absence of social or legal equality, egalitarianism between social classes, or a strict legalistic interpretation of universal basic principles; there is an emphasis upon stability, group orientation where age and maturity and guanxi obligations and responsibilities rather than youth and novelty are favored. This prideful sense of homogeneous PRC ethnicity (everybody is Chinese, Han) is challenged (if not temporarily eclipsed) by a contemporary sense of partial social alienation, international ambiguity, and intellectual marginality which, in turn, is challenged by the drive, successes, and international skills of the 55 million overseas Chinese whose re-definition of what it is to be Chinese is intense, sophisticated, and internationally astute. No longer will Chinese language skills and residency in the PRC function as sufficient grounds to be deemed "Chinese". Often confused by Chinese and by non-Chinese commentators is the distinction between (1) "westernization" about which many residents of the PRC, Taiwan, Singapore, and Hong Kong and overseas Chinese and other Asians have great reservations and/or criticisms, versus (2) "modernization" about which fewer Asians have reservations and/or criticisms. Taken as a whole, Japanese feel that they have wrestled with both problems and have brought them to a very successful, comfortable resolution. Obviously, the PRC Chinese have not; various overseas Chinese are still working it out.

6. In the U.S.A., efficiency and technological (job) competency are important cultural values. Quantified units of time are considered as valuable commodities. In communication, directness, straightforwardness, measurable facts, and a relative lack of emphasis on rhetorical tact and saving "face" are valued. In general, Americans exhibit a great receptivity to new technology; one's identity as a professionally or technologically competent person may initially override questions of character. The world is generally considered a fairly predictable place and one should take remedial action when contrary events occur, thus illustrating the American optimistic view that there must always be "some" remedy for human problems.

In the PRC, the view of time as a quantified commodity is largely lacking in traditional Chinese society. In communication, indirectness, inquiries through a neutral third party, long-term trust, rhetorical tact, and saving "face" are valued; in general, higher levels of traditional Chinese elites have displayed little receptivity to new technology, whereas the worker levels and contemporary Chinese manifest a shifting ambivalence toward new technology as it has been intermittently viewed as "contaminating" because of unwelcome connotations of Western social morals and political values. Technological competency is thought to be secondary to being the right sort of person in regard to values, style, and manners coupled with good guanxi. The world is viewed as an unpredictable place; strange unforeseen things could happen, and, quite often, do happen. The world is full of random and semi-random events, and one should not assume that one should take remedial action when contrary events occur. To "hunker down", persevere, and endure may be the only predictable option.

7. In the U.S.A., Americans view the "gray area" between crime and sharp business practice as problematic but rely on legal interpretations of Anglo-European civil and criminal law which utilizes (presumed) universal, semi-deductive inferences from basic principles and precedent-setting cases to distinguish between crime and legitimate business. For all the contemporary strains on and criticisms about the American legal system, it is generally effective and constitutes a pervasive symbol of social and political stability, the centuries-old mores of the rule of law vs. force applied within a 200-year history of economic expansion and social opportunity. The legalistic implementation of established norms are meshed with the cultural mores that sustain it and guarantee a national culturally sanctioned legal framework within which political, economic, and social tensions can be debated, modified, and brought to a pragmatic resolution. The sharp rise of local youth gangs throughout all major cities and in most large towns and the increased visibility of international organized crime has brought the fear of being a crime victim to a new height in public values.

In the PRC, that which Americans view as problematic gray areas between crime and sharp business practices are viewed by the Chinese, who are more "tolerant", as merely good business entrepreneurship to supply desired goods and services between trusted guanxi "friends". They have not historically appealed to legal interpretations of criminal law to distinguish between the two. The diminution of strict legal interpretations occurs because of the interplay of "face", mutual guanxi, public deeply rooted public custom, and the balancing functions of "face" and social obligations. The (formal) legal system, by international Anglo-European standards, is comparatively immature and underdeveloped, and does not display in practice the egalitarian opportunity for the implementation of established norms intertwined with the cultural mores that sustain it;

thus, in the PRC, there is not a guaranteed national, culturally sanctioned social and intellectual tradition, a generations-old established framework within which political, economic, and social tensions can be debated, modified, and brought to a pragmatic resolution. The relatively small but publicly visible increases in local and organized crime have added to the sense of a "moral emptiness" regarding the future direction of the country.

8. The U.S.A. is a low-context culture where social relationships, knowledge, and business expectations are to be "spelled out" explicitly between people, where universal, egalitarian legal contracts and legalistic, adversarial approaches and solutions are the norm. Tension exists between egalitarianism and earned meritorious social rank. The guides and possibilities for living remain in the future rather than within the "lessons" of the past. Traditionally and comparatively, North Americans are largely middle-class in a society where over 60% of those whose incomes are defined as at the poverty level have automobiles and, by global standards, live a fairly comfortable standard of living and still harbor semi-realistic dreams of entering the upper middle classes with higher probability of achievement than many other places in the world. Public expectations about what is due an individual by society is justified by virtue of formal principle-based entitlements based on legal rulings which are applicable to all citizens.

China is a high-context culture where relationships, knowledge, and expectations are well known ("the way things are done", as in Japanese "Kata") and people are usually "in the know". Social relations and stable person-to-person expectations between relations of "face" and guanxi need not be "spelled out" to everyone in the legalistic style of Anglo-Europeans. The Chinese are oriented to the past in that the lessons of the past are thought to be the best general guides for the future. Because of such disasters as the Cultural Revolution, Chinese are far less tolerant of degrees of civil unrest and social disruptions which seem to border on social chaos than are most North Americans. Public expectations about what is due an individual by society is justified by virtue of nonformal nonentitlements based on family and guanxi (but unequal) person-to-person relationships within a high-context culture rather than on legal rulings and formal entitlements applicable to all citizens. Chinese guanxi reflects more sources of assistance and obligations, more types and degrees of nonlegalistic nonentitlement connections of obligations, because it embraces more sources than most Americans would choose, cultivate, maintain, or embrace by virtue of mainline American culture. Chinese guanxi also reflects a series of person-to-person obligations and situational ethics as defined by social context and not by legally defined social entitlements, because it embraces more cultural, legal, and economic sources than most North Americans would expect or tolerate.

9. In the U.S.A., the second most religious society in the world (India is first), is prone to religious enthusiasms where nationalism (Manifest Destiny) and history (New Covenant) are held to be ultimately religious in both structure and goals. These normative goals are accompanied with a sanctioned monolinguistic, semijingoistic ethnocentrism which aggressively asserts that the U.S.A. still has a Manifest Destiny in the 1990s. Most of these American assumptions have been projected upon China or have motivated and shaped many of the rather exotic and factually inaccurate views about China as either the (other) Evil Empire of "Red China" or as the weak but sleeping giant to which we should extend our Christian, benevolent, technologically astute desire to show them the way to the one true path of American-style capitalism — or, as in the 1960s, the image was of the brave champion of the economically oppressed and the colonialized third world. All of these views were American projections and failed to reflect the facts of internal Chinese life about which there was little information until President Nixon, Dr. Kissinger, Mao Zedong, and Zhou Enlai (with implicit pressures from the Soviet Union) changed the rules of Chinese-American dialogue. The U.S. Constitution was founded on assumed universal, normative, social, and political principles of John Locke and the West European rationalism, the "Rights of Man", all of which assume worldwide validity, rule-governed legal systems. The American view of freedom is manifested in the tendency of Americans to be *simultaneously* fiercely independent *and* enthusiastic "joiners" within a variety of intermediate voluntary associations.

Comparatively, China is a historically sanctioned, quasi-naturalistic, non-monotheistic society, permeated by house, local, earth, and city deities. Chinese have been periodically indifferent to religious enthusiasms and/or apocalyptic views of the future, although severe secular exceptions to the contrary have occurred and have focused on charismatic political figures, e.g., Kong fu zi (Confucius), Prince Kung, Mao. Despite contemporary official recognition of cultural diversity, but with little public receptivity or interest in it, there is a historically sanctioned ambivalence to integrate non-Chinese ideas and perspectives into either the theory or practice of Chinese society. Exceptions occurred when some Chinese central planners predicted that the introduction of a few selected Western capitalistic and technological practices could be done without changing society and that the Chinese cultural core could be maintained by following the (dubious) maxim of the 19th century "modernizer" Zhang Zhi-dong: "Chinese learning for essential things, and Western learning for practical things." The basis of contemporary Chinese legal and political frameworks are not founded on assumed universal, normative, social, and political principles nor of West European rationalism, the "Rights of Man", or Natural Law, but on Marxist-Maoist principles now in practical limbo and in the process of revision, none of which assumes an American-style view of freedom or social structure.

Today, confusion remains between "Westernization" and "Modernization", for many disagreeable aspects of the former are confused with the widely experienced disagreeable aspects of "Modernization"; while some public attention is addressing spiritual or religious values today, there remains a self-described "emptiness" in the public realm of "ultimate" values.

10. Traditionally, Americans have supported education as a major pathway for the English-speaking descendants of immigrants to prosper; however, the U.S. remains the only major country among the industrialized nations to chose *not* to have a centralized "ministry of education" to set national standards and minimum curriculum and to direct the development and course of national education; rather, Americans have preferred local control and local or state financial support, thus resulting in great variance in quality and types of support for all levels of education. In educational skills, Americans prize flexibility, creativity, a well-rounded education, and pragmatic problem-solving skills coupled with much greater emphasis upon the effects of the student's "natural" ability rather than upon the effects of a student's tutored efforts, hard work, and long-term diligence. Of particular contrast with many Asian educational systems is the XC contrast that American students are strongly encouraged to "agree to disagree", "to stand on their own" and argue for individual opinions, to stand up for the individualistic underdog who may oppose mainline opinion, and to argue with authority. Americans spend almost the *least* amount of actual instruction time in the classroom of any of the modern industrialized nations; the competition for entrance into a variety of university or post-high school level education is not too intense except at the highest level universities. About 35 to 40% of Americans achieve some level of "higher" education.

In centralized education systems such as those of the PRC, Taiwan, Singapore, and Hong Kong, Chinese prize memorization, diligence, and homework, group discipline, achievement, and respect for authority. They emphasize quantitative knowledge and spatial-oriented skills coupled with many more hours in actual classroom instruction than Americans. They usually do not learn to "agree to disagree" and to argue for individual opinions, but rather to be respectfully subservient to collectivist opinion. The competition for entrance into a variety of university or post-high school level educational slots is very intense even for the lower-level universities. In PRC, only about 4 to 5% achieve some level of "higher" education. The Chinese generally favor the U.S.A. (followed by Canada) for postgraduate study, not only because of the high quality of education but also because of the generally liberal availability of research fellowships, teaching assistantships, and lack of supervision or inquiries by the INS or the Foreign Student Advisor about their residences, guanxi activities, travel, or gathering of technological and public domain intelligence data. As many governments have long known, a graduate student visa is a relatively easy way to legally penetrate the U.S. and establish networks (guanxi) for monitoring, spotting, assessing, pitching, running, and terminating "significant" personnel — assets — North American or Asian.

11. Coupled with an underground tradition of pornography, the depiction of the female nude body as sexually stimulating and/or as an aesthetic object has been a constant, important element in the modern or ancient Greco-Roman and Anglo-European artistic tradition.

The depiction of the whole female nude body as sexually stimulating and/or as an aesthetic object has been largely absent in the Chinese artistic tradition, whereas the traditional footbinding, subtleties of gesture, indirect allusions to sexual situations are common. Thus, except for a small recent underground tradition of pornography, female nudity has played almost no role in Chinese art in contrast with the ancient Greco-Roman and modern Anglo-European traditions or those of India.

Self

12. In the U.S.A., one's actions and judgments of others are based on one's earned social status, usually based on one's own ideals or employment. Emphases are on ideas of personal fairness, potential and actual male-female pairing relationship and the various qualities of "self".

In the PRC, one's actions, judgments of others, and public relationships are based on one's role/status in society which is usually based on the social status of one's parents and "face" and guanxi relations. Emphasis on self usually arises only in the context of collectivist group dynamics; however, with ideological drift increasing inside and outside of the PRC, there remains great pressure to assert entrepreneurial leadership within contemporary ideas of family-bounded collectivism and the present economic free-for-all. Thus, there are great transitional pressures on the image of the individual within the increasing international aspects of China's changing contemporary society and among the varieties of overseas Chinese.

13. In the U.S.A., individuality is prized, where one's idiosyncratic qualities, interests, and personal goals are of primary importance and are a source of great personal and family pride and public attention. Also prized are absolute truth-telling, individuality, competition, organized sports, and new approaches. Also thought to be generally good are personal innovation and new skills outside one's present social role and opportunities for pre-university or vocational orientations that generally affirm the general political and moral idea that all persons are equal of worth. However, this egalitarianism is not implemented in practice.

In the PRC, harmony, duty, the collective obligations and goals of family, "face", guanxi, and public reticence about personal and family business are most highly valued. There is great emphasis on early discipline, modesty, the dampening of aggressiveness and sexuality, and strong avoidance of public confrontation. They reject the American style of telling the truth regardless of the consequences without regard to the effects of loss of "face" and public shame, as they also reject prohibitions against "white lies" for social harmony and interpersonal comfort. Except for public legal and political definitions, most Chinese, in actual practice, do not consider all persons equal.

14. In the U.S.A., the individual self is one, unique, and the product of one's heredity and experience or has a God-generated identity which did not exist before this earthly life. From the latter religious perspective, one's self has a personal destiny transcending this life and consists of a single personal unchanging identity maintained in an ethically earned, infinite afterlife or in an afterlife bestowed by the "infinite, unknowable Grace of God", a nonempirical, unfalsifiable claim.

In regard to traditional PRC folk beliefs, the Chinese hold that there are two functional aspects of the "soul" or "self", both of which reside in the person. The "po" is the life-giving animal force of the individual, which at death lingers around the grave site and, if not properly honored in appropriate rituals, may become malevolent and cause trouble for the family while it slowly loses its personal ties and recognition of the members of the extended family. The second functional aspect of the soul, the "hun", is the basis of the individual personality and usually remains benevolent to the remaining family as long as they continue to honor it appropriately and make the correct sacrificial offerings to it, without which it may become hungry and resort to stealing from other grave sites. In this form, the "hun" can be manipulated by sorcerers for evil ends or it may become deified. Since the "hun" does not inhabit the body until one month after actual birth, this supports speculation that this is why, in part, abortion has been more widely accepted in China.

15. In the U.S.A., the distinction between body-emotion-feelings vs. mind-rational-thinking are traditional, historically influenced, PAEF ("publicly available explanatory framework") categories. While explicit appeals to one's emotions and feelings are not always quickly admitted or admired, such appeals are common public justifications for decisions, actions, and public emotional displays. Emotional and psychological stress which is not under one's control often can be resolved or diminished by means of subjective discussions with public medical professionals trained in talk-as-therapy, where intimate private and/or family details are expected to be voiced.

In the PRC, emotions should be kept under voluntary self-control, and appeals to one's emotions are neither common nor acceptable public justifications for personal decisions or policy. The ability to swallow one's anger is a virtue, mental illness is thought to reflect poor self-discipline, and weak willpower and is considered disgraceful to the family or clan. Emotional stress, for which there are no traditional diagnostic categories or psychotherapeutic treatments, is experienced, understood, and treated as biophysical, not psychological, illnesses. Psychotherapeutic discussions with medical professionals to resolve stressful emotional conflicts are both unknown and forbidden to prevent loss of "face" and to protect the family from shame. Mental illness and psychotherapy are unknown as medical categories and such potential behavior must be handled within the family/clan to prevent social disgrace and to protect intimate knowledge of family affairs from outsiders. There is no tradition of discussions with public medical professionals trained in talk-as-therapy where intimate private and/or family details are expected to be voiced.

16. In the U.S.A., the goals of the person and the nuclear family usually take priority over any goals of the extended family, clan, or geographical or dialect group. A fragmented sense of one's short-term social, ethnic, or political history is coupled with a somewhat greater tendency to exaggerate personal qualities at success and to deny personal responsibilities for failure.

Extremely important in the PRC are the hierarchy and collectivism of one's network of mutual support, connections, and obligations (guanxi) and one's personal dependence and strong interdependence on others — family, clan, lifelong friends, guanxi members. Compared to Americans, there is often strong loyalty to those of one's village or county birthplace, surname, dialect, and secondary schools. Also common is a quiet, acute awareness of China's long, proud ethnic history, its actual and perceived accomplishments, and its mistreatment in the international political arena during the last 150 years. Also common in public discussions is a tendency to discount personal qualities at success while diminishing personal blame at failure.

17. In the U.S.A., one's fulfillment lies in attaining goals discovered by first focusing within one's self and then acting externally in accordance with these subjective values, supposedly independent of public social goals. One's worthiness is held to be independent of one's social traits or social background and can be found by searching for authentic inner values of independence from and nondependence on other people concomitant with a very strong ambivalence toward the values of American social institutions. Americans value self-reliance, where psychological support is expected from within and material support results from one's own actions. Also, Americans feel that they have more control over their lives and less external pressures on their personal choices than do most Chinese.

In the PRC, one should align one's self with and subject one's self to duties one has toward extended family and guanxi members by means of focused self-discipline and an outward-directed, ever-scanning, finely tuned, interpersonal social radar. One's actions, judgments of others, and public relationships are based on one's role/status in society, which is usually based on the social status of one's parents. Comparatively, Chinese feel that they have less control over their lives and more external pressures on their personal choices than do most Americans.

18. Chinese are perceived by Americans, as always role-playing, always "in role", never "off duty" or "off camera", emotionless, having a "flat" public persona, never revealing a "real self"; always requiring a "script". In unfamiliar situations, they require knowledge of everyone's social rank with which to judge how to respond "appropriately" and thus avoid an interpersonal, unstructured jumble of relations between persons. Americans reveal personal information about themselves as a tactic for showing that they are open, friendly, and trusting.

Contrastingly, Americans are perceived by Chinese as overemotional, sloppily spontaneous, self-indulgent, unpredictable, lacking both a stable sense of place and personal integrity, and ignorant of the "obvious" Chinese need to know another's precise social role in order to act appropriately towards that role rather than that person. The technical and scientific prowess of "Westerners" is acknowledged, while at the same time the apparent moral and drug-related "decadence" and loss of warm clan and guanxi relationships are points of criticism against North Americans. Before Chinese become genuinely friendly and trusting, they tend not to reveal personal information about themselves (in far fewer cases than an American) until trust has been established over time and the danger of interpersonal vulnerability within their highly closed society has passed.

19. In the U.S.A., having a child is an option, not a necessity. When a child born, it is only a nuclear family event (Mom, Pop, the kids and perhaps, the grandparents); a child is an optional choice to contribute to the population as one's parents did, but to one's parents, one is only partially obliged to honor, support, and/or imitate in one's own life. Living with one's parents is an uncommon option.

In the PRC, a male child is preferred but the birth of a child is considered a singular event within a social compact, an endless chain of human families to which one should contribute as did one's parents. To one's parents, one owes harmony, "face", health, and the deft balancing of filial and guanxi obligations and is obliged to honor and support — within one's household. From a global perspective, the present PRC one-child policy has resulted in a relative increase in coerced abortions, the rural practice of female infanticide, a small preponderance of female orphans, and an uncertain future of filial support with the extended family; however, China is the only major country to have justified and implemented its population control program with a greater degree of apparent success than India, for example.

20. The U.S.A. has a poor record in using and teaching foreign languages, a dim awareness of differing cross-cultural perceptions, and a checkered record in attempts to adjust and prosper in business relations within diverse countries and non-European language/ethnic cultures.

In the PRC, while the teaching of foreign languages and foreign cultures except English is pragmatically minimal, there is a consistent absence of any perceptive awareness of how different cultures are perceived internally; however, the overseas Chinese have exhibited an uncommon ability to adjust and prosper in business relations when they choose to live relatively socially isolated lives while doing lucrative business within diverse countries and ethnic cultures.

21. Americans are usually responsive to a stranger's need for help in an accident and to collective distress in natural disasters. The idea of a collective good and the remnants of the egalitarian early American "ideal of helping equals" is correlated with an American assumption of an infinite good, unlimited resources, a positive, expanding future, and the absence of a particular basic suspicion of strangers as found in parts of Asia and Africa.

Chinese usually deliberately ignore and remain unresponsive to a stranger's need for help in an accident. The suspicion of strangers correlates with the ideas of village mentality found in the Vietnamese and the Chinese and stands in contrast to the Asian peasant's idea of a limited good in which all peoples in an area are in competition for a limited finite amount of resources and wealth, which makes them suspicious of all others except those related by extended family, dialect, surname, birthplace, or other close guanxi ties.

Values, Epistemic Models, Religion, and World Views

22. In the U.S., truth and falsehood tend to be viewed as mutually exclusive, either/or alternatives (strong disjunctions) where the affirmation of one alternative necessitates the denial of the other. One should tell the truth by judging how it corresponds to and how it fits in with what one knows to be the case by personal reflection upon one's own experience, personal history, and what is technologically and culturally sustainable. The underlying model of truth is that metaphorical model of a god's-eye view which holds that truth is that

which *corresponds* (as in Aristotle's *Metaphysics*, 1051, b 3[31]) to a true statement if seen from such an ultimate perspective (the god's-eye view). While an occasional "white lie" for social or emotional reasons is tolerated, not telling the truth in almost every situation is severely prohibited in American society. Public truth-telling is generally thought extremely important from childhood through old age even when, in particular situations, a failure of truth-telling brings shame to the nuclear family or other groups or causes guilt in the individual.

Chinese have demonstrated lesser degrees of behavioral changes when "bending reality" and telling "white lies" than Caucasian Canadians; one should temper what one states as factually true or normatively acceptable by weighing the consequences to one's family, "face" and the continued harmonious welfare of one's family, clan, guanxi, dialect-group (pang), economic brotherhood, and lineage associations (huiguan). The underlying model of truth is a metaphorical model not of an Anglo-European god's-eye view, but of a coherent-pragmatic model of truth which holds that truth is that which is consistent, coheres, is workable, and "fits" the primary ***normative needs*** *within the social framework being used. While not telling the truth in almost all situations is, of course, prohibited in Chinese society, context-restricted deception (intentional non-truth-telling) is generally thought more acceptable than causing loss of "face" to others and/or bringing shame or loss of "face" to the family or other groups through one's failure to honor a variety of obligations between family, friends, guanxi, family name associations (pang), guild groups, companies, and various hui (of which Triads are one type).*

23. In the U.S.A., a general comparative model of epistemic relations (various ways of knowing and justifying reliable information) would include the Anglo-European act/actor distinction; the value placed on innovation, contrasts, and ambivalent change. An evaluation of social relationships would indicate a contrast between a low-context culture (U.S.A.) where a context-neutral idea of independent "truth" is crucial and social relationships and person-to-person rules of the game need be made explicit vs. a high-context culture (PRC, Japan, Korea) where the social rules of the game are generally known and the maintenance of collectivist values and social obligations is of the highest importance rather than a context-neutral one.

Important Chinese epistemic models of "truth" and self are the nonpropositional relationships between a nondualistic sense of personal self split by the demands of "face" reinforced by collectivism, group-benefit-driven guanxi, hui obligation, and a severe predilection for analogical thinking, social stability, intellectual continuity, and overt synthesis (which may include quietly hidden innovation). Also important is multi-associational thinking, which includes a preference for the evaluation of intellectual and social relationships over longer time periods than most Americans. Whatever is "new" is not automatically considered obviously good as it is in the U.S. Equally important Chinese epistemic models are an assumed sensory-based flux of discrete sensations, the reliability of which is evaluated by a culturally pervasive predilection for a generalized coherence and/or implicit pragmatic theory of truth; thus, the appropriateness of an action is seen to depend upon human environments and strategic needs rather than on moral absolutes (the god's-eye view), for, as the Chinese justification assumes, as both environments and human needs change, the formulations of normative reasons (what ought to be done) should also be modified to maximize the welfare of the individual in a family, their long-term values, and those groups to whom the individual has guanxi obligations.

24. In the U.S.A., the most widely held PAEF is the Judeo-Christian view that the benevolent universe was causally created by a single (uncaused) agent-deity who exercises a personal paternalistic relationship with individuals whose collective development as moral agents is a prerequisite for the attainment of the goals inherent in the religious framework of creation. Personal destiny transcends this life, but a single, personal, unchanging identity is maintained in an infinite afterlife. The quality of one's destiny is a function of the rewards of moral development in this life or a function of the unknowable, evidence-free, nonhuman choices of an anthropomorphic vision of the God of the Judeo-Christian-Islamic religious traditions. The contrasting, incompatible Hindu-Buddhist-Jaina concept of Karma is absent in Anglo-European traditions.

In the Chinese tradition, fundamental values and expressions of "ultimate truths" are usually focused within the contexts of ethics and social and political speculation and less so in metaphysics, ontology, or the public systemic aspects of religion. Within the naturalistic amoral but harmonious cosmic order there is neither the mainstream idea of an intentional creation by an agent-deity nor any ultimate cosmic purpose (as in the popular Christian tradition) to which one's ethical development as a moral agent is either relevant or a necessary condition for the unfolding of human history. While there is a wealth of anthropomorphic gods and godlings in Chinese religious practices, there is no monotheistic focal point of a single all-powerful, all-benevolent, all-knowing creator God found the Judeo-Christian-Islamic traditions. Within the amoral naturalistic but harmonious cosmic order, there are observed historical macro-models of value which may guide human society (e.g., Dao), but to which one's idiosyncratic traits and moral development are usually comically irrelevant. Present deeds of non-Buddhist Chinese have an unknown effect on any possible afterlife, and after death one's diminishing personal identity retains its family-clan ritual relationships in a vaguely fading afterlife about which family ceremonies for the dead are necessary to protect and support the multi-generational family lineage (compare the Buddhist view, No. 26). The contrasting, incompatible Judeo-Christian-Islamic concept of aseity (that God is un-caused) is absent.

25. It is debatable whether the force of North American Judeo-Christian (JC) religious thought and ethics has somewhat diminished in the last half of this century with the growth of a variety of nonreligious, semi-scientific, secular world views, but this JC tradition has strongly influenced America's egalitarian and social values. There has been an extensive tradition of a theoretical, formalistic, and practical appeal to transcendental values or truths and/or to egalitarian, universal values, or Natural Law theoretically applicable to all people. The religiously based model of universal ethical values and its quasi-legalistic appeals to universal laws and "absolute truths" (the "God's-eye" view) are also manifested in secular thought, such as: the U.S. Constitution, the U.S. Bill of Rights; the abortion controversies; the "infinite possibilities of redefining ones self" found in our silently lingering pioneer myths; our dualistic, over-simplified, good versus evil "John Wayne-High Noon Cowboy" mythologies; our love of personal freedom; independence; social egalitarianism; a multitude of private social associations; geographical mobility; baseball; and the (often untranslatable) British idea of "fair play" and the innocence of childhood.

In the PRC, universal "human rights" are neither Chinese (Han) in character nor considered an inherent part of the structure of the universe. While there is no religiously or secularized theory isomorphic with Natural Law, interpretations of the Confucian or Neo-Confucian traditions support the values and needs of the masses. While there is less emphasis on the transcendental, quasi-religious aspects in Chinese thought and practice than in the Indian Hindu or American Christian traditions, the (Chinese) transcendental but nonanthropomorphic values were manifested in the ranked hierarchies of Chinese political and social institutions. Whatever transcendental emphasis there was in China was neither found in nor strongly directed to the individual as in the Anglo-European social and religious thought and institutions of the last 400 years. The philosophical foundations of maintaining national prosperity and social order are based on models from the Confucian, Daoist, Neo-Confucian, and Legalist traditions. Due to the immense influence of Confucian and Legalist elite governmental structures, a historically sanctioned emphasis was placed upon the outwardly directed obligations of individuals and their concomitant ranked social responsibilities, not toward individualistic, personal free choices. Today, with the rapid expansion of rampant entrepreneurship among the younger businessmen in the areas of Guangdon, Shanghai, and Fujian, the conservative emphasis has been partially replaced here by a fervent drive simply to make money and indulge in the luxuries money can buy; this will change.

26. In the U.S.A., a degree of increasing secularism during the last half of this century has somewhat diminished the popular dualistic heresy (Manicheaism) of God vs. Satan and with it some of the latter's popularity and his all-purpose use for theodicy and explaining random death and apparent undeserved evil; however, a semi-public ethical and religious dualism still manifests itself in our American future orientation, our social egalitarianism, our belief that historical progress is inevitable, that good/evil and the theological divisions within and between religious traditions are ethically and socially important and "natural."

In the Chinese traditions, there have been no extensive traditions of appealing to transcendental values or absolute truths applicable to all people independent of social status coupled with a morally demanding God of aseity. Fundamental values and the expressions of ultimate truths are usually focused in associated and analogical reasoning within the context of ethics, history, and social or political speculation and, to a lesser extent, in Daoism and Buddhism. While there is a wealth of anthropomorphic gods and godlings in Chinese religious practices, there is no monotheistic focal point of a single all-powerful, all-benevolent, all-knowing creator God as found in the JC traditions. Present deeds for non-Buddhist Chinese have an unknown effect on any possible afterlife and after death, one's diminishing personal identity retains its family-clan ritual relationships in a vaguely fading afterlife about which family ceremonies to honor and feed the dead are necessary to honor, protect, and support the multigenerational family lineage.

Mahāyāna Buddhists: Through karma, the unfalsifiable normative laws of cause and effect and all intentional physical or mental actions automatically generate good or bad effects, the results of which may appear instantly or may not appear for years or even lifetimes later; however, retribution for bad deeds is inescapable. Present and past deeds cause individual human destinies to transcend each physical death by karmically generating an almost infinite series of lifetimes which appear in various forms such as humans, animals, minor deities, etc., none of whom/which presuppose any eternal, personal identity or "soul"; however, the generation of karmic merit (puṅya) through ethical and religious actions may compensate for bad karma and may generate better forms of rebirth, as in the Heavens of the Bodhisattvas Kuan-yin or Amitābha. For those very few at the highest levels of religious development, there may be karmic movement toward an optional but future release from karmic rebirth, often referred to by the prajñāpti/upāya term of "Nirvāṇa." Therefore, social and religious progress for Buddhist monotheists, polytheists, and atheists is always theoretically possible within appropriate levels of practice and understanding, the ethical and intellectual complexity of which remains a function of both one's karmic endowment and one's karmic capacity. This potential religious progress is dependent on one's level of karmic attainment which, at one's ethical best or worst, is pragmatically equivalent to how one intentionally chooses to act. Thus, within Chinese religious frameworks, piety, morality, devotion, ethics, and the all-important values of the family and the state are practiced, supported, abused, encouraged, ignored, loved, questioned, and revered — much as is true for Christianity, Judaism, Islam, Hinduism, Jainism, Shintoism, and the rest of the world.

27. The rise of the Protestant/Reformation view of a personal unmediated relationship to God and/or the economic and social shifts in philosophical and religious opinion since Descartes/Cartesian dualism provided the license to challenge all authority, secular or religious. Influential West European historical models of processing knowledge are deductive, axiomatic, geometric, mathematical, rational, analytic, adversarial, hidden-ratio-driven, and in axiomatic measurable units as in the style and methods of Pythagoras, Plato, Aristotle, Euclid, Archimedes, Galileo Spinoza, Descartes, Bach, Newton, Kant, Hegel, and early Wittgenstein.

In the Chinese traditions, religious practitioners and sacred rituals certainly existed, but they lacked an independent social position and were almost completely integrated, but ignored, in the secular social structure. Thus, challenges to authority embedded the individual more tightly into the nontranscendental, secular, ranked Confucianized world view. While Chinese technology was perhaps the world's highest for some centuries, Anglo-European styles of scientific knowledge did not arise, and influential historical models of knowledge were neither deductive nor mathematical, but instead were correlative, rather than causal, associational, analogy-driven patterns of complementary polarities and unities, macro/micro-modeled correspondences, e.g., alchemy, Book of Changes (I-Ching), folk medicine, family lineage charts, and models of organizing knowledge such as family lineage charts, guanxi, fang-bian, and dialect associations linkages.

Thus, some of the basic mindsets of North Americans and some of the major mindsets of the Chinese and Vietnamese are often similar and compatible. However, some of the major mindsets of the North Americans and some of the major mindsets of the Chinese and Vietnamese traditions are significantly *different at a fundamental level* and some are *partially incompatible* — ideologically, logically, morally, religiously, and/or politically. These differences have implications in the behavior of Asian and Asian-American criminals.

Major Components of Chinese Mindsets

13

關係

Attitudes About Police Authority vs. the Community

The traditional Asian public attitude towards authority is, usually, to "show respect but keep your distance".[31] Certainly no police officer should expect to find most Asian-born parents or first-generation children extending the kind of automatic trust toward the police that we still find in many smaller North American towns and cities. Although there have been very strong autocratic governments in most Asian countries for many centuries, Asians are no more (or less) suspicious of political power than we are. However, Asians are, in general, more accustomed to autocratic government than are West Europeans, who, for the most part, have exhibited a somewhat greater degree of internal criticism and a greater emphasis on grounding law and ethics on universal principles applicable to all, as noted in Chapter 12.

As noted in Chapter 4, in the eyes of most foreign-born or first generation Asians, Asian police (with the exception of those of Japan or perhaps Korea and Singapore) are neither respected nor trusted. Also, Asian experiences with the sometimes corrupt police of their home countries have led many naive Asians to expect that the American police are also corrupt, unhelpful to the common citizen, and untrustworthy in general. This is not unknown among Americans, but Asian-American distrust is coupled with an insular emphasis upon family, social "face," the barriers of language, often ignorance of North American social custom, and the very real threat of revenge of the Chinese Triad, the Japanese Boryokudan (Yakuza), or Vietnamese gangs. All those factors, plus their misunderstanding, ignorance, or mistrust of our bail and legal system, do not lead most first generation-Asians to view police authority or any American authority in a sympathetic, trustful manner.

It is important to note that most Asians feel very uncomfortable going outside the Asian community to ask for help in solving internal problems. To appeal to local or national government agencies for help is not only a near disgrace, but often it is felt to be close to a betrayal of group/clan loyalty. As a result, for almost all foreign-born and first generation Asians and Asian-Americans, one just does not go outside one's ethnic community to solve internal social and more intimate problems, such as mental illness, child abuse, or domestic violence. The circle is kept as tight as possible and remains as close as possible within the family, clan, or region/village of origin or even within groups who speak a particular dialect. While this attitude is not unknown in North America, it is more deeply held by most Asian-born Asian-Americans and many first and second generation Asian-Americans.

The general Chinese and Vietnamese "rules of the game" of social cohesion and communal self-preservation are no more explicit than are the clear reflections of laws or rules of any other ethnic group. However, social patterns here reflect the home culture. Consider these three general but clear preferences of the Chinese as mentioned in Chapter 12:

1. One should align oneself with and subject oneself to duties one has toward family and guanxi members by means of focused self-discipline and an outward-directed, ever-scanning, finely tuned, interpersonal social radar.
2. High-context culture where relationships, knowledge and expectations are well known and need not be spelled out to everyone, as in Japanese Kata (the way things are done) (see Chapter 13).
3. The fulfillment of one's life lies in learning to cooperate and exhibit the social values that are largely external to a person.

These patterns of normative ideas about how one should focus one's life constitute quietly understood rules that govern proper public behavior; these rules, in turn, suggest strategies which are self-preserving for the community. For most traditional families, the outer boundaries of one's extended family and guanxi are the limits of social trust.

However, in comparison with Anglo-European and American cultures, in the Chinese tradition there are relatively few appeals to common law or any universal, rule-like legal principles to justify either the rule of law or the controversial actions of individuals to which people habitually appeal. Moreover, the lack of a well defined systems of commercial and international law plus the preference for limiting decision-making positions in business to family and kin inhibit the Chinese (but not the Japanese) from developing a range of large corporations in the international marketplace. Likewise, there is little emphasis on individual rights except as members of a group, clan, guanxi, or hui where external sources define internal stereotypes and attitudes. Often, there are only implicit referrals to strategies, "communally self-preserving" goals, or group collectivism which requires that everyone be "in the know" (a high-context culture). As in most cultures, to some degree, mutually understood, high-context contexts, and customs are presumed by means of social custom and well known examples and require ranked strategies and tactics for behavior. Generally absent in traditional Chinese societies were grassroots actions motivated by appeals to universal, legalistic principles or content-neutral laws applicable to *all* citizens. Such high-context Asian cultures require pragmatic behavioral strategies and tactics be understood which distinguish social rank, education, birth, class, and preservation of collectivist family and guanxi goals.

However, in understanding a society foreign to the North American observer, an understanding of the (traditional) justification of foreign customs and values requires an expanded awareness of one's own cultural assumptions as well as foreign cultural values. The latter usually are quite different than we have assumed; as a result, this process of XC understanding at a deeper level often requires considerable effort. This is particularly so when foreign customs and values are contrasted with and reflected in deep cultural mindsets, such as the cultural software of the North American tradition of common law, Natural Law and the "habits of mind" rooted in the Judeo-Christian (JC), Hellenistic, Anglo-European (AE) traditions.

For an example of how the foundations of law may differ, in the Anglo-European traditions one basic presupposition commonly used to attempt to justify values and laws is JC Natural Law theory. This Anglo-European foundation for law and ethics holds that there are implicit principles built into the natural world which we can discover by rational analysis. For example, the Anglo-European view of the universe is one created with a built-in purpose, created by a single god who is a world-creator god. By contrast, a Buddhist Bodhisattva is not a world-creator god. Thus, this represents one deep-level incompatibility. Built into the Anglo-European view of Natural Law is the assumption that there are natural paths of development for each living organism (including humans), and by following these natural paths of development each organism seeks to preserve itself and its offspring. Humans, too, seek these built-in goals; thus, self-preservation, social cooperation, and mutual protection (and, thus, law enforcement) are "natural" values built into human relationships and into the natural world, as well.

Obviously, there is no sense of this Anglo-European Natural Law within the deep background of most Asian cultures. However, this is not to say that there is nothing somewhat analogous to Natural Law in the various philosophical-religious backgrounds of Asians such as the Chinese Dao (Tao) or Hindu and Buddhist karma. It is to say that both the cultural grammar and the content of such analogies to the JC Natural Law theory are considerably different, unequal and incompatible at a deep level of analysis; thus, the Asian foundations of law and law enforcement are quite different. Finally, these cultural differences which are assumed, unknown, or ignored in the deep grammars of everyday strategies of living in Asian high-context cultures and/or American low-context cultures.

Chinese Shame Culture vs. American Guilt Culture

Another important cultural difference follows. Within a shame culture, such as that of the Chinese, there is a greater tendency to act in accordance with one's external obligations to others and less of a tendency to act in accordance with one's own personal goals. Conversely, within a guilt culture, as for the Americans, there is a greater tendency to act in accordance with one's own internalized personal goals and less of a tendency to act in accordance with one's externalized obligations to others.

While there are degrees of evidence concerning why one feels *shamed*, the location of the evidence to justify the answer to the question of whether one feels shamed remains external to the person. While there are degrees of evidence concerning *why* a person feels *guilt*, the locus of the evidence to answer the question of whether one feels *guilt* remains internal or within the suspect's personal feelings. Thus, the standards and of evidence of shame are usually external to the suspect and the standards and sources of evidence of guilt are usually internal to the suspect.

Overall, shame is stronger than guilt because the suspect who has been shaped by a guilt culture can, to a considerable extent, suppress and control the effects of inner feelings of guilt, whereas the suspect who is shaped by a shame culture cannot, to as great an extent, suppress the multitude of emotional effects because the sources and configurations of those effects remain external to and uncontrolled by the suspect. Thus, the degree of control the suspect has over his guilt is greater than the degree of control the suspect has over his shame.

Chinese collectivism, which emphasizes sources of value *external* to the suspect such as the extended family ties and guanxi ties, is concomitant with an accurate description of Chinese culture as a shame culture. American individualism, which emphasizes sources of value *internal* to the suspect, is compatible with an accurate description of America as a guilt culture.

Where emphasis is placed upon the maintenance of social relations to retain the social goodwill and to strengthen the requirement of others to respond successfully to one's potential requests of support and assistance, then the telling of "white lies" and the ability to nimbly sidestep the need to utter the blatant truth without regard to the social or personal consequences is advisable and prudent. If this assumption is taught and shown in one's family, clan, and circle of friends in a high-context culture, such as that of the Chinese and the Vietnamese, then the degree of anxiety and the explicit behavioral signs associated with "bending the truth" will be less than with those individuals where this assumption is absent. Furthermore, in the American low-context culture, where the values of accurately telling the truth often override the nuances of social harmony, the theoretical absence of deception remains an important value. Furthermore, the violation of that American value of nondeception will generate behavioral signs of deception more often than in members of a high-context culture. Empirical tests in one research project have shown that Chinese-Canadians do in fact indicate less anxiety when not telling the truth and are less concerned about it than are non-Chinese Canadians.[32]

Furthermore, as a generalization, when the Chinese attempt deception (lie) during interrogation, they lie more often by omission than by direct commission. Lying is a conscious decision to deceive by deliberately not telling the truth in response to an interrogator's question or by avoiding the mention of a relevant but sensitive topic. A deceptive answer to protect and/or honor obligations to others is more probable and harder to control and camouflage in a shame culture than in a guilt culture. Thus the conclusion here is that if a suspect is Chinese or Sinocized, the probability that he will violate his family, guanxi, or hui obligations is more strongly *thwarted* by the ever-present potential of shame than would be true for an American in the same situation who is equally haunted by the potential of guilt. Thus, the ability of a trained interrogator to detect behavioral indications of deception may be reduced by these cultural factors. (The author is engaged in a study of these cultural factors and their effects, *if any*, on the efficacy of the John. E. Reid method of interviewing and interrogation.)

Pragmatic Contextualism (Fang Bian, STC 2455 0189)

Another deep-level cultural difference is the often-admired business nimbleness, social flexibility, and political pragmatism of many Asians. This may be partly attributed to an underlying Asian cultural "habit of the mind", fang bian. Fang bian is a model of processing information and reconciling perceived incompatibilities and their resulting tensions. This influential hermeneutic is the 1800-year-old Buddhist concept of "Skill-in-Means". The religious foundations of Buddhist contextualism (fang bian) are discussed in Chapter 19.)

Most Asian Mahāyāna Buddhists will have noted the term in the second chapter of the *Lotus Sūtra* (Sanskrit original: *Saddharmapuṇḍarīka*, "The

Lotus of the Good Teachings", Bai lian jao yi, STC 4101 5571 2403).[33] The idea of fang bian may be described in a simplified manner as the adjustment of one's message to one's audience. That is, one should adjust or modify one's message, actions, and/or demeanor to accommodate the forms, means, stratagems, and methods appropriate to the cultural anticipations, contrary pressures, communicative capacities, and social contexts of the target audience. This, in turn, gives rise to the second corollary that there are legitimate alternative, but apparently incompatible, ways of saying or doing what is normatively appropriate or "true" for a specific context. And fang bian is a fundamental component of the deep grammars buried in the Chinese mindset for guiding and justifying behaviors, attitudes, and ways of communicating to accomplish these goals. This collection of ideas is referred to by the author as Chinese "pragmatic contextualism".

Buddhism pragmatic contextualism means that all ideas, ideals, good acts, and evil acts are and should be subject to judgments according to pragmatic possibilities within the shifting, ever-changing *context* of the partially unpredictable human actions and the unknown future. (Obviously, this is a compatible corollary of Chinese high-context culture.) Also, in daily life within a culture where political and social stability have not been reliable, one is constantly pressured to maintain external relationships and obligations while one is molded and restricted by time, place, history, strong personalities, the need to circumvent the letter or the spirit of the law, conflicting talents, luck, and one's karmic fate. Moreover, there is the ever-pressing need to accommodate the externally defined obligations and conflicting collectivist pressures of "face", other's "face", one's family, various guanxi and hui obligations, and the humanly indifferent, cosmic power-plays of outrageous fortune.

These collectivist and contextualist pressures, coupled with the deep cultural strategy of fang bian, give rise to the generalized cultural model that there are legitimate alternative, but apparently incompatible, ways of saying or doing what is normatively appropriate or "true" within a specific context. Thus, for some Chinese, an analysis of a "known truth" is not the accurate correspondence between a statement and a fixed unchanging reality as in many mainstream Anglo-European philosophical traditions. Rather, a "known truth" for the Chinese philosophical traditions, is an appropriate but flexible relationship between a sentence and the holistic context of the (karmic) social framework of its utterance. The idea that one's experienced context includes the continued maintenance of all one's obligations, a juggling of all the analogically determined possibilities one has, is coupled with the awareness that things are always changing.

Thus, pragmatic contextualism also includes the realization that one has to nimbly dance along one's path in life, a path that one partially invents as one goes along, creating paths of action which, it is hoped, allow one to meet the obligations one has inherited by being born into an extended family and a plethora of specialized mutually supportive societies and views of human life. From this multifaceted, ever-shifting model of accommodation to life's changing features, many Chinese have inherited a history of seeing the world silently shaped by this Buddhist cultural habit: fang bian.

Roughly speaking, similar things happened in the course of the Anglo-European tradition as well. The internalization of Buddhist pragmatic contextualism in China since 200 A.D. was analogous to the slow spreading of the Judaic-Christian-Greek philosophical ideas throughout the developing Anglo-European traditions. Two "Western" examples are "Word" ("logos") as "In the Beginning was the Word … ", which meant essence, rationality, Christ, and "soul" (pneumena); allegedly unique personal "self". To most Americans, the two ideas that all things have some sort of "essence" which defines them and that there is within us a "soul/personal eternal self" are two deeply buried cultural "habits of mind". To most of us, it is obvious and "just plain common sense". Likewise, a major Chinese Buddhist, deeply buried cultural "habit of mind" for solving problems and resolving incompatibilities is fang bian — another obvious common sense strategy. Just as the soul was based on Near Eastern and Greek philosophical ideas, Chinese contextualism (fang bian) was (and is) based on the Indian idea of karma ("moral causation" and rebirth; see Chapter 19) as imported by Buddhism.

For example, when the obvious incompatibilities between various Buddhist ideas surfaced in the Chinese translations of Indian Sanskrit texts, the Chinese "explained away" these "theological" incompatibles and contradictions by saying that they were merely fang bian — provisional accommodations for people with different Karmic abilities. Ideas and practices which were said to be merely fang bian — contextually appropriate or "true" — were only apparently contradictory. If one had a deeper understanding, these various ideas and practices could be seen to be accommodations to specific and limited human contexts. Since people and situations differed, not every idea or practice was "true" in every human context. Thus, fang bian ideas used to justify diverse social-religious practices were said to be benevolent strategies developed to fit the religious and practical needs of different people whose situations, abilities, and capacities for understanding and religious practice were uneven and varied. Therefore, since human knowledge and human self-discipline were finite, vague, and limited by one's karmic capacity to understand and act in accordance with that understanding, different "truths" and different ploys, varied ways of saying or doing what is appropriate or "true" within the specific context of each individual, develop. Also, pragmatic contextualism is strongly associated with "face", guanxi; and, for many criminals, the varied forms of illegal associations (hui) such as Triads are reconciled with one's family life and public status as an "accomendation" to the real world of obligations and/versus illegal opportunities to make money. In short, "truth" always has to be "fine tuned" to one's context, particular experience, situation, specific obligations, and pragmatic choices.

Thus, all other things being equal (which never occurs in police work), a traditional Chinese suspect being interrogated about an alleged burglary will probably feel a somewhat wider range of external shame culture pressures through "face", guanxi, and hui connections than will an American of comparable intelligence, education, and analogous social background. In addition, independent of whether he knows anything of Buddhism at all, the Chinese suspect will also probably sift and weigh his choices using the model of fang bian (contextualism) and guanxi. For the suspect, the greater pressures to minimize the straightforward correspondence between his actions and the law prohibiting his actions and to maximize the opportunities to meet his external obligation, fang bian serves as self-serving rationalization. Cross-culturally, this contrasts with our reliance on legalistic, quasi-deductive chains of proof and evidence within an adversarial style so characteristic of Anglo-Europeans legal discussions of ethics and law.

Where there are good connections (guanxi), careful maintenance of "face" (as the success of overseas Chinese investments in the PRC has illustrated) and the general absence of experience in processing international law controversies, many in the PRC hold that this historical absence of the Anglo-European legalistic style can be overcome with guanxi and its cultural foundations. Thus, guanxi becomes a temporary (?) surrogate for the Anglo-European emphasis upon formal legal systems. As Lee Kuan Yew, former Prime Minister of Singapore, once said:

> There is [now] a momentary glow of fraternity [between the overseas Chinese and the PRC]. It is at this stage, when China has not established clarity and transparency of law, that the [overseas] Chinese Diaspora can play a critical role. They have proved that if you develop guanxi (connections), you can make up for the lack of the rule of law.[34]

Thus, the Chinese emphasis upon guanxi and the implicit model of weighing and considering alternative courses of action focus on relationships between known associates who possess mutual obligations and opportunities and between whom the relationships are "worked out" and negotiated without sole reliance upon the letter of the law — business, international, or civil. However, it is worth repeating that this guanxi-driven, cultural model of "making up for the lack of the rule of law" is done without the degree of reliance on legalistic, quasi-deductive chains of proof and evidence within an adversarial style so characteristic of American's legal discussions of ethics and law which is so often missing from the Chinese methods of resolving major disputes in ethics and law and in their justification of their decision. Perhaps this is one (but only one) of the major reasons the PRC has so few attorneys. In short, guanxi and fang bian epistemic models act as surrogates or functional substitutes for the legalistic appeals to universal ethical principles and/or the application of Anglo-European and Anglo-Saxon traditions of egalitarian law and quasideductive chains of proof and self-discovery. Thus, the appeal to legalistic principles to which we habitually make has been traditionally superceded by the twin cultural habits of fang bian and guanxi.

In the interrogation of Chinese, it is probable that many of the same general cultural models and expectations hold. By contrast with Americans, the Chinese person's subjective decision to attempt deception is not implicitly restrained by the common epistemic models, "habits of mind" such as a Western legalistic emphasis on "the letter of the law" or deductive models of evidence.

To illustrate the contrast, the American position would hold that one ought to turn to the "common sense" idea that an ethical course of action can and/or should be proved by a binary analysis of a chain of ethical values ultimately founded upon two types of ethical principles. First, there are appeals to ethical absolutes (called "deontological ethics") such as in the Golden Rule — "Treat each person as an end in and of him/herself, never as a means" — or simple imperatives to "love one another".

Second, there is an appeal to one form of a group of "consequentialist ethics" where the decision of what is good (ethical) is made on the basis of whether the consequences of an action are good (ethical). In both types of appeals, the ethical questions are justifiable within a chain of deductive links that stretch back to basic principles. If everyone agrees with the basic principles (often they don't!), the ethical questions are thus decidable and can be used as guidelines for action. Thus, this chain of justification would lead one to a conclusion supported by a connected chain of deductively drawn conclusions — a semi-axiomatic, deductive model of proof. While the Chinese have and can think about ethical questions this way, this model of thinking and processing information is often absent in traditional and everyday Chinese mindsets.

On the other hand, what is more often present in the everyday Chinese mindset is the Chinese awareness of mutual guanxi/hui obligations, the comparatively reduced importance of the individual values over collectivist group values. The idea of individual values is coupled with a habitual emphasis on a pragmatic awareness of the long-range shame context rather than on guilt-induced individualism. This emphasis upon the collective fang bien aspects is coupled with the occasional absence of the correspondence with socially neutral law and universal principles of ethics so characteristic of American ideas of rights, entitlements and fairness.

These differences would certainly force the Chinese suspect to feel greater pressure from external cultural and social models, roles, and obligations than Americans. Therefore, as with all suspects, deception is more probable when the pressures and consequences are great. However, between Chinese and Americans some of the evidence for determining the probability of attempting deception may be based on different reasons and more externalized reasons and from different cultural sources.

Face (Mian-Zi, STC 7340 1311)

In most police situations where Asian culture may be a factor, it is best to allow a suspect to keep "face" to some degree. "Face" can be thought of as roughly similar to the American idea that we all exhibit to others a socially approved image of oneself which we strive to maintain in order to receive social approval, social identity, and self-respect and to remain safely predictable among one's friends and fellow workers ("Yeah, he's a steady guy … one of us."). Thus, respect shown and respect given is *very* important and should be maintained on both sides between police and the Asian community. In addition to revenge, gossip, paybacks, and money, the threat of the loss of "face" and bringing shame on the Asian family are good types of leverage for the recruitment of informers.

Most Asians, particularly the Chinese, Japanese, and Vietnamese, put great emphasis upon maintaining recognizable personal characteristics which constitute one's dignity, integrity, status, and self-respect. In any social situation, one has a built-in self-interest in maintaining one's own "face"; and with Chinese "face", one has a built-in-interest in preserving everyone else's "face". This mutual maintenance of "face" preserves the fabric of social coherence and stability. Thus, tact, understatement, polite courtesy, and an occasional "white lie" to save "face" all contribute to the kind of interpersonal social stability that has been so diligently practiced in Asia for thousands of years. American informality and our half-hearted egalitarianism confuses the boundaries of these images of "face". Also, the habitual style of descriptions about one's self among Chinese tends to be much less positive than with Americans. If asked, we Americans experience little discomfort in speaking of our personal accomplishments; if by contrast, Chinese tend to be much more self-effacing and appear to many others to have a less positive sense of "face" and less appreciation of their own self worth. Not so. They may — and do — attribute more of what happens to them as being external to their control, but Chinese have as realistic an assessment of their own self worth as we do — sometimes inflated and sometimes under- or overinflated.

In part, what seems at contrast between Chinese and Americans is not that Americans are more "positive" than Asians, for that means only that we have redefined the word "positive" to mean what we think we ought to and habitually do. Rather, one contrasting factor is the degree to which one thinks one has some control over one's life and how probable it seems that one will be confronted by a predictable, stable world-environment in which one can expect that one's efforts will meet with success. Twenty-five hundred years of Chinese historical records suggest that, as warranted by the historical evidence, the Chinese have generated a far less optimistic view of the individual's potential for realizing personal goals in life than Americans have generated from our 300 years of history. In fact, American optimism is often considered a cultural anomaly among other members of our Anglo-European heritage, which does not mean that we are wrong or naive; it simply means that Americans assume that possibility of attaining personally derived goals to be more probable than do many in other cultures.

Furthermore, this non-optimistic view attributed to the Chinese is neither pessimistic nor implausible — especially for the population of a highly ranked, authoritarian society with few opportunities for formal education and little chance for social mobility. In that social situation, restricted goals, modesty, the maintenance of everyone's "face" and mutual obligations of one's guanxi, the avoidance of confrontation, and deference to authority are "common sense"; they are prudent and straightforward means and for the betterment of one's family and supportive of harmony and stability within one's country.

A cautionary note is also in order. There are many variations in the degrees to which all these factors may be manifested in the behavior of *different* Chinese subcultures. Just as individuals differ regarding many of the traits described here, groups of Chinese from Hong Kong, Taiwan, Singapore, and the PRC may well differ greatly on many of these cultural dimensions as well. Also, non-Chinese such as the Pakistanis or the Indians may be more family oriented and socially conservative than some Chinese. Thus, these human ways of coping with the world are not the sole property of any one cultural group.

However, if an Asian person has little experience with American lifestyles, this blurring of the limits of social roles and the confusing North American ways of talking about aspects of oneself, coupled with the inherited suspicion of official authority, may make him/her very uncomfortable and unwilling to communicate with police. So, you should not be overly impressed by their apparent modesty; do not treat them as "just another guy" and slap them on the back. And last, do not touch them even though you consider it a friendly gesture. Do not smile and laugh too much. You will lose "face" — and you need to keep it.

Guanxi (STC 7070 0190)

"Guanxi" means networking, having and using connections. Networking, or "guanxi", is a model of how Chinese society actually works. That it is the real model of how things get done among Chinese people is an open secret in contemporary China (PRC) and in almost all Chinese and American-Chinese communities. A quick word about the spelling is in order. The two Chinese characters are transliterated as "guanxi" within the Pinyin system and "kuan-hsi" in the Wade-Giles system. These transliteration systems — not "translation" — are standardized systems within which the sounds of Chinese are described with prescribed matching letters from the Roman alphabet (the English language alphabet). Wade-Giles is an older transliteration system which is quickly being superseded by the Pinyin transliteration system adopted by the PRC and most international scholars. The legacy of virulent anti-Communism of Taiwan lingers on in the refusal of Taiwanese to use Pinyin transliteration because it is used by the PRC Maoist-Leninists.

Cordell Hart offers an initial explanation of guanxi/kuan-hsi in his excellent *Dealing with the Chinese:*[26]

> Compared to Americans, Chinese make a sharp distinction between their behavior towards strangers and towards acquaintances. Put simply, Chinese distrust strangers and trust associates to a greater degree and for other reasons than do Americans. Chinese dislike doing business with strangers, much preferring to conduct their affairs within a network of persons with whom they have established "kuan hsi" [a network of special pragmatic semi-personal relationships], an understanding of mutual support and relative rank.
>
> The purpose of "kuan hsi" is not friendship, but the exchange of goods and services. Americans, in particular, make this mistake and are shocked to find that their Chinese "friend" has no real affection for them; or the American, because of his cultural training not to rely on others, will make few demands on his Chinese "friend", thus leading to an impossible situation where the Chinese is denied an opportunity to fulfill his perceived obligations to the American.

However, there is a dark side to guanxi:

> Guanxi also can be a euphemism for bribery — or, to put a positive face on it, incentive payments to trusted contacts in local governments, all in the name of expediency. The line between culturally correct and seemingly corrupt often is impossible to draw. But these methods are ideally suited to doing business in developing China, where the legal system is primitive and peevish bureaucrats are easily bought. Smart business deals are not cemented by paper contracts that cannot be enforced, the theory goes, but by informal relationships of trust and mutual obligation. Many overseas

> Chinese entrepreneurs have considerable experience in this gray ethical area, having for years conducted business across an unstable jigsaw puzzle of Third World legal systems and political regimes.[35]

Thus, the ancient question remains: Where should one draw the line between bribery, grateful gifts, and legitimate exercise of influence? The answer seems to be that it depends on to whom you are talking, from where you are asking, and whether you are asking it in a high- or low-context culture!

High-Context Asian Cultures vs. Police Low-Context Culture

Some Asians live in quite crowded cities, and even villagers live out their lives with few secrets and without most Western notions of privacy. Certainly, Chinese cities are among the biggest in the world. However, as in India and most of South, Southeast, and East Asia, roughly 80% of the people live in the countryside. (Obvious exceptions are Singapore, Japan, and Hong Kong.) In China, this means the farmers, the peasantry — the "Old One Hundred Names". Even with China's recent and amazing economic growth, the vast majority of Chinese and Asians live in rural areas, many in relatively primitive towns and villages. For most, there is almost no economic base for mobility, no alternative path for the kind of social movement we take for granted. Simply missing from most of the Asian social landscape — and certainly in the People's Republic of China — is the kind of mobility we expect and find in the more industrialized countries of the world. There are a few exceptions, however; the socially mobile Chinese immigrants — legal and of illegal PRC immigrants — will be of urban backgrounds.

Rural Asians and most urban Asians live in a relatively conformist, homogenous local culture — in a village/small town setting where everybody knows everybody and everybody's business. Another phrase to describe such a setting where everybody knows the rules of the game is "high-context culture".

Chinese and Vietnamese cultures are very high-context cultures; Canadian and U.S. cultures are very low-context cultures. Thus, high/low-context cultures are not a function of whether you live in a crowded city or village. A high-context culture is one in which — for cultural comfort — most of the needed information is already known to the senders and receivers and relatively little explicit additional information is required or expected in most everyday situations. A low-context culture is just the opposite; most of the needed information is not felt to be already known to the senders and receivers and a relatively greater amount of information is required and expected to be made explicit.

Most North American police live and work in a low-context culture, quite the opposite of the Asians, especially Chinese and Vietnamese.

For example, Germans, Swiss, Scandinavians, and Americans (much less so the French and Spanish) are low-context cultures and demand that things be spelled out carefully. That is, they like detailed contracts and clear legal agreements about what will happen if X occurs or if Y occurs, and, most importantly, who pays the bills. By contrast, the Japanese, Arabs, Chinese, and many Mediterranean peoples:[36]

> … have extensive information networks among family, friends, colleagues and clients … [and live their lives] … in close personal relationships … do not require, nor do they expect, much in-depth, background information [for cultural comfort].

It is not that high-context cultures ignore contracts and contingencies; it is that they have different expectations about both how much information should be known by everyone, how much "obviously" needs to be supplied, and how they expect to handle and resolve such contingencies about what is known.

In summary, to function comfortably in their respective societies, North Americans demand more explicit information than do Chinese and most Asians. There are at least three major aspects to the problems generated for law enforcement by the different demands of highs vs. low-context cultures.

First, the subcultures of North American law are derived from English common law which were highly influenced by Roman law and Greek philosophy, all of which are very low-context, formal, *theoretically articulate* subcultures. Thus, our legal system demands a very high level of explicit information about actual or alleged crimes; causally relevant, verifiable evidence; and a demonstrable, uncontaminated chain of evidence. This means that Asian crime investigators must perform some of their work in high-context, but unfamiliar, cultures (Asian) and succeed within a low-context culture. That is, they must interact in the streets, in interviews with victims, and in interrogating suspects, to gain information in circumstances where Asian *expectations* about sufficient information to establish grounds for arrest and/or bail, incarceration, and convictions may be quite different. Finally, the evidential and procedural products of police investigations must meet the demands of our low-context North American social and legal cultures which may seem excessive or unimportant to some Asians or Asian-Americans.

Therefore, it is the gap and the resultant tensions between the contextual and attitudinal expectations of these two cultures that generate some of the stress and the intercultural problems associated with combating North American crime within Asian-American communities or international crime committed by ethnic Asian people. However, to become aware of the cultural context of such tensions allows one to understand attitudes and behaviors which may seem baffling or irrational at first contact. Also, it allows one to choose appropriate actions in light of increasingly accurate knowledge of the cultural similarities and differences — and get the job done.

The second set of problems generated by the different demands of high- vs. low-context cultures is that both North Americans and Asians are culturally hampered because we and they do not know each other's ways of doing things in some crucial situations. That is, we and they lack knowledge and the culturally approved skills about the explicit ways in which the other does things (shaking hands, forms of address, touching) and the implicit ways in which the other does things (personal space, eye contact, punctuality). More important, we lack the unconscious level of cultural knowledge and social and linguistic skills that enable an experienced officer to make a clear accurate judgment about the status of a person who may be involved in a crime in progress, or during the interrogation of a suspect, or during the interview of a crucial witness.

The third set of problems generated by the different demands of high- vs. low-context cultures is that most foreign-born Asians are culturally hampered by their lack of understanding of our cultural ways of doing things in some crucial situations, e.g., traffic stops, hospital care, arrest, bail, testifying, the responsibilities of a witness. That is, we and they lack knowledge and the culturally approved skills about how to *participate* in a culturally sanctioned way of doing things common to each culture.

If you think such "culturally implicit ways of doing things" are trivial or do not play a part in the actual lives of "real" people, try spitting into a clean glass and then drinking it! That is a "cultural-bound implicit way of doing things" — indeed!

Formal Manners and "Paybacks" Are Important

Among most traditional Asians, formality and courtesy in personal style is important and one's manners *do* count. The external appearance of one's behavior is important even when one participates in group activities which one may personally dislike. Therefore, unless you are working undercover, do not try to "be yourself" in the usual laid-back American style. While you do not have to be stiff, be quietly considerate, particularly of the senior persons, the guest of honor, or the elderly. Never omit the small courtesies and considerate signs of respect and welcome.

For at least 2300 years, the Chinese have been influenced by the Confucian ideas of polite formality, proprieties, and overt considerations (li, STC 3810); these ideas were also carried into Japan, Korea, and most of Southeast Asia through Chinese models of education and government. Theravada Buddhism and Chinese Mahāyāna Buddhism also supported these qualities. This quiet insistence on politeness, humbleness, public nonaggressiveness and humility are seen as human-to-human channels through which we can, and should, express in a well structured way the very best of our human-heartedness (ren, STC 0088) and our concern that we and our extended family be humbly "civilized" and considerate.

These ideas are also easily compatible with a rather rigid awareness of differences in social class and educational and ethnic backgrounds. In short, everybody is *not* equal! The popular American notion of equality because "we are all human beings" is just not present. Neither is the idea of "fair play" between social classes, two almost untranslatable words. Furthermore, this does not mean that there are no Chinese bastards and that they are all humble, etc. Wait until you have to negotiate or try to drive a bargain with them!

However, it does mean that if you wish to gain their trust and their willingness to communicate and cooperate with you, that you should never become overbearing in your attempts to be friendly. Likewise, you should be careful not to appear boastful, loud, and aggressive. Nor should you ever indicate a demeaning attitude towards anything Asian or over-emphasize how proud you are that you are an American-born citizen, or give the impression that you feel culturally superior in any way. Last, if you have lunch with an Asian, do not go "Dutch Treat"; it just is not done, but make sure that either you pay the first time or that you politely insist that you will pay for the second meal together. Always keep the score even over time; likewise for gifts and small favors. In part, that is how face and guanxi networking work in a high-context culture.

Business Contracts, Time, and Negotiations

Many traditional Asians often view negotiated contracts as mutual agreements which are not to be interpreted by referring only to the "letter of the law". That is, the details of business relations are not to be considered absolutely final. Rather, contracts are viewed "quite naturally" as outlines of mutual understanding to be revised and modified for the long-range mutual benefit of both parties in light of short-term business fluctuations and in light of life's ever-changing circumstances.

General negotiations may be enhanced by anticipating and emphasizing the following points (where possible):

- Expect to take a longer time with Asian groups than with non-Asian groups.
- Use guanxi relations and established relationships of interpersonal trust; they will.
- Keep cool and dampen the emotional and rhetorical levels of verbal and non-verbal communication.
- At the early stages of negotiation, send in respected but second-level negotiators to get a feel for the overall position of the Asian negotiators.
- Focus your appeals on the advantages for the group, not necessarily for particular individuals.
- Understand that the negotiators may not have the final authority to make the final decisions without consulting other group members or even authorities not obviously among the negotiating team.
- Understand that many of the negotiator's decisions may be made and conveyed to you only after the greater group has had a chance to discuss among themselves your positions and consult everyone to reach a consensus.
- Understand that their ability to agree to reduce their demands or expectations can only be agreed to in such a way that it preserves the public appearance of group harmony and consensus.
- Give them as many short breaks as they seem to want in order for them to conduct their in-group discussions and reach a sufficient degree of internal agreement to be able to display public consensus.

Another XC dimension of negotiation among culturally diverse business groups are the expected timeframes regarding investment returns and business relations. As reflected in Chinese-American business negotiations as compared with American-Japanese business negotiations, national business cultures differ in how long Asian and non-Asian business groups expect to wait before they begin to receive profits. For example, Lebanese tend to be in and out of business dealings within a year (if possible); Americans, 3 to 5 years, Europeans, 6 to 10 years, and the Japanese, 8 to 16 years. These ideas reflect their cultural expectations about how long is long enough to reap profits or the results of the negotiations.

Also, these varying expectations about timeframes may influence how Asians view the length of time that must pass before they will conclude that you are trustworthy and of good character. In general, unless there is evidence to the contrary, Americans tend to be quicker to establish trust than most Asians; American business tends to rely more on business documentation and formal education than on "ol' boy" networks (guanxi) of mutually known friends and extended family connections that are so important to most Asians. Guanxi is absolutely essential to doing business. This suggests that police must learn to establish trust, "face", and connections over a longer period of time than they or their administrative superiors would anticipate. This constitutes no small problem if the departmental assumptions are that *all "good" officers are functionally interchangeable* and that *all crimes should be handled in roughly the same way.* Some skillful police instinctively establish "face", trust, and good guanxi, and some learn that it is important and learn to do it — unfortunately, others do not — and therein lies the refutation of the two assumptions in the previous sentence.

> Knowing the Chinese art of using guanxi — personal connections — is essential for succeeding at business on the mainland, because government officials interpret rules as they see fit. Companies that do not understand guanxi frequently find themselves unable to get enough electric power, supplies or transportation for their products. The frustrations and peculiarities of the guanxi system are one of the chief factors inhibiting investment by Japanese and U.S. firms; in many cases, they find themselves forced to team up with overseas Chinese partners to cope.[37]

In general, Asians, as most others, take each situation as it presents itself and adjust their actions according to the specific characteristics of a particular set of people, specific political pressures, and business-related local circumstances. However, in reference to most people and to many Americans whose culture varies considerably from that of most Asians, almost all Asians prefer to examine, closely and slowly, key people within corporations and always prefer the possibility of long-term business relationships. There may be a gradually established sense of mutual trust; a knowledge of each other's traits, strengths, and weaknesses; and a sense of mutually beneficial dependence that is not tied to legalistic nit-picking (the letter-of-the-law) and the verbal nimbleness of lawyers.

Thus, with regard to legal, business, and long-term relationships, be prepared for the long haul and the slow building of a network of "friends" who are mutually well known and who have worked together for some time, thus establishing guanxi-like networking relationships. Establishing these relationships is not always easy and usually takes longer than most Americans would expect.

Suggested Readings: Asian Crime and Cross-Cultural Studies

In compiling this reading list, I assumed readers may have access to federal, state, and municipal police-generated Asian crime publications, but are unfamiliar with the XC aspects of Asian organized crime. Also, many standard academic Asian studies materials may seem abstract and seldom focused on Asian criminal activity. Thus, what seems appropriate here is a reasonably brief reading list relevant to understanding some cultural aspects of Asian and Asian-American criminals and the large majority of law-abiding Asian-Americans. In compiling this list of readings, I remembered the statement of a self-described street cop: "To understand the crime, you have to understand the culture." The following are general, introductory readings about crossing cultures and crime; more focused readings will be found at end of Chapters 17 and 18.

A good initial source of nuts-and-bolts information about Asian crime is the *IAACI News*, the bi-monthly newsletter of the International Association of Asian Crime Investigators (membership: $35/year). It offers "wanted" photographs, case surveys, background articles, and intelligence updates by AC specialists. In addition, regional and annual conferences are sponsored in North America; contact IAACI. Also, the California Asian Crime Investigators Association newsletters and regional conferences are equally good sources.

Note: "NCJ" = National Institute of Justice Accession Number.

Senate Hearings on Asian Organized Crime, U.S. Senate Committee on Governmental Affairs, Permanent Subcommittee on Investigations, October 3, November 5 and 6, 1991, Washington, D.C.

Organized Crime of Asian Origin: Record of Hearing III, October 23–25, 1984, New York, U.S. President's Commission on Organized Crime (NCJ: 108891, 1984).

Constraints on the Effective Prosecution of Asian Organized Crime in America, John Dombrink and John Huey-Long Song, prepared for the U.S. Department of Justice Multinational Conference on Asian Organized Crime, San Francisco, September, 1991. Contact Professor John Dombrink, Program in Social Ecology, University of California, Irvine; Irvine CA, 92717.

Asian Americans: Emerging Minorities, Harry H.L. Kitano and Roger Daniels, Prentice-Hall, Englewood Cliffs, NJ, 1988 (paperback, ISBN 0-13-049164-0). This brief overview describes Asian-American minorities, their histories, patterns of arrival, and present status in the U.S. Also, there is a general bibliography.

The Harvard Encyclopedia of American Ethnic Groups, A. Orlov and O. Handlin, Eds., Greenwood Press, Westport, CN, 1986 (ISBN: 0-674-37512-2). A standard reference work on ethnic immigration, social, and historical characteristics and patterns of dispersal throughout the U.S.

Intercultural Press, Inc., publishes good books on ethnic groups and/or their cross-cultural interaction(s) with Americans, here and abroad. Many are short and sharply focused for quick reading. Address: P.O. Box 768, Yarmouth, ME 04096. Phone: (207) 846-5168.

Interesting Readings About Cross-Cultural Practices and Cultural Groups

Arranged in ascending levels of difficulty. Check references at the back of each book for other readings.

Gestures: The "Do's and Don'ts" of Body Language Around the World, Roger E. Axtell, John Wiley and Sons, New York, 1991 (ISBN: 0-471-53672-5). Simple, basic, and mildly interesting but with little explanation.

Two very interesting, popular zoological-anthropology books by Desmond Morris are *ManWatching,* Abrams Publishing, New York, 1977 (ISBN: 0-81-91-3100); and *The Naked Ape,* Dell Publishing, New York, 1980, (ISBN: 0-440-36266-0). In 1995, Morris hosted his own excellent television series, first shown on PBS.

Brit-Think, Ameri-Think: a Transatlantic Survival Guide, Jane Walmsley, Penguin Books, New York, 1987 (ISBN: 14 00.9367 2). This is a quick, humorous, and pointedly accurate survey of "two nations divided by a common language." It contrasts our most familiar American and British "mindsets" and illustrates that these two cultures are often assumed to be more compatible than they are in practice.

For a more substantial, but very readable book about cross-cultural perspectives, try *Understanding Cultural Differences: Germans, French and Americans,* Edward T. Hall and Mildred Reed Hall, Intercultural Press, Yarmouth, ME, 1990 (ISBN: 0-933662-84-X). Building on his previous work, this is a fascinating, easily readable account of how these three cultures differ in actions, organizations, anticipations, and wide range of attitudes. Also, try Edward Hall's classic *The Hidden Dimension,* Anchor Books, Doubleday, New York, 1990 (ISBN: 0-385-08476-5).

Australians and North Americans, George W. Renwick, Interact 2, Intercultural Press, Yarmouth, ME, 1980 (ISBN: 0-933662-16-5). This is a 60-page, accurate survey of another book focused on "two nations divided by a common language." It examines Australian and American "mindsets". In spite of that fact that I have never met an Australian cop (or citizen) I did not like, the interactions between two cultures that seem so obviously compatible may be less smooth more often than one would think.

A newer version of an old classic is *American Cultural Patterns: A Cross-Cultural Perspective,* Edward C. Stewart and Milton J. Bennett, Intercultural Press, Yarmouth, ME, 1991 (ISBN: 1-877864-01-3). This is a marvelous book that allows us to see ourselves from new perspectives much in the same way we look at "foreign" cultures. Its only limitation is that it does not go deep enough. Highly recommended.

Local Knowledge: Further Essays in Interpretative Anthropology, Clifford Geertz, Basic Books, Harper-Collins, 1983, NY (ISBN: 0-465-04162-0). Try Chapter 8, "Fact and Law in Comparative Perspective", pp. 167–234. Geertz is one of the most imaginative, well-traveled, fundamental, comparative thinkers in one of the most interesting, but methodologically insecure academic disciplines in the Anglo-European intellectual tradition — anthropology.

Asian Values and the United States: How Much Conflict?, David I. Hitchcock, Center for Strategic and International Studies, Washington, D.C., 1994 (ISBN: 0-892060-311-4). An excellent, sweeping overview of Asian and contrasting values and attitudes towards the U.S. written by an experienced Asian specialist who recently retired from the State Department.

Ways of Thinking of Eastern Peoples: India, China, Tibet, Japan, H. Nakamura, East-West Center Press, Honolulu, 1964 (Library of Congress card: 64-63438). A comparative, philosophical study of great originality, insightful (if abstract) XC analysis, and technical sophistication by one of Japan's most respected scholars. More difficult than Geertz (above), this a is a great source of fundamental but very complex XC ideas. Moreover, it is not a book for the "impatient" reader, the quick reader without a good Asian studies background, or even a slow reader with a good dictionary. Certainly, it is not a book for one who thinks "everything is really just a matter of simple common sense". Complex, rare, and stimulating!

Thinking Through Cultures: Expeditions in Cultural Psychology, Richard A. Shweder, Harvard University Press, Cambridge, MA, 1991 (ISBN: 0-674-88416-7). Scholarly and oriented within the field of anthropology, ethnopsychology, and philosophy. Provides excellent and exciting intellectual journeys, such as Chapter 3 "Does the Concept of the Person Vary Cross-Culturally?" and Chapter 7 "Rethinking Culture and Personality Theory". Heuristically fascinating, fun, and formidable when universalized for Chinese guanxi, li, and fa vs. Anglo-European egalitarianism, geometric models, and formalistic legal systems, none of which are explicitly mentioned but which "shout for attention" by the careful, comparative reader. A great heuristic source for cross-cultural studies.

Ethnic Profile: The Chinese

14

關係

"Homage to Guan Di": Traditional deity of war, justice, righteousness, and, thus, law enforcement.

Introduction to the Scope of Chinese Crime

Chinese Organized Crime

To help the reader gain an overview of this aspect of Chinese and Chinese-American organized crime, the following summary of Chinese organized crime has been taken from the publication of the U.S. Senate Hearings on Asian Organized Crime, organized by the Permanent Subcommittee on Investigations:[38,39]

> For a variety of reasons, Chinese criminal groups now warrant separate and more detailed attention. First, there has been a substantial increase in Asian-based organized crime activity in the United States during the past decade. Traditional organized criminal activities within the Chinese community, such as illegal gambling and prostitution, have expanded to include money laundering, business extortion, alien smuggling, computer chip theft, and narcotics trafficking, among other crimes.
>
> Indeed, ethnic Chinese groups, the infamous Triads, have substantially taken over the rapidly expanding heroin importation market in the U.S. Moreover, repeated warnings have been heard about the possible migration of secret criminal triad organizations from their base in Hong Kong prior to the assumption of control by the People's Republic of China in 1997.
>
> While Triad organized crime resembles the La Cosa Nostra in some interesting ways, the Triads are far older and apparently range farther throughout the world than the LCN. The well organized heroin-intensive Triads are suspected to supply over seventy percent of the heroin used

domestically (U.S.A.). Triads are secret Chinese societies some centuries old which often link up with domestic Chinese Tongs. Tongs are legitimate societies created by Chinese to offer mutual assistance which live up to their admirable public aims. While it is not the function of Tongs, they sometimes provide the link between the street gangs and the Triads. Clearly, some Tongs and street gangs are engaged in a variety of illegal activities here and via connections based in Thailand, Hong Kong, Taiwan and through Europe, West Africa and South America. After the LCN, Chinese organized crime is thought to be the most important concern of the FBI.

A DEA estimate[40] is that:

> ... 68% of the heroin available in the United States ... is distributed through a combination of ethnic Chinese brokers from Mandalay, Chiang Mai, Bangkok, Hong Kong, Taiwan, Kunming, Kuala Lumpur, Singapore, New York, Seattle, Vancouver, or Toronto. While the United States is probably the largest overall drug-consuming nation, there are other important emerging markets, including China with an estimated 350,000 heroin addicts, Pakistan with an estimated 1.2 million to 2 million addicts, Taiwan with an estimated 2,500 to 3,000,000 addicts, and even Hong Kong with an estimated 30,000 to 40,000 addicts. Considering the well-established cocaine and heroin markets in Western Europe, along with the emerging markets in Eastern Europe and the former Soviet Union, and the significant "ice" consummation in Japan, Korea and the Philippines, it is easy to imagine a worldwide illicit drug trade of $100 billion.

Another example follows. The "Big Circle Boys" (BCB) (Dai Huen Jai, STC 1129 2120 1367) are headquartered in Toronto and Vancouver, Canada.[41] They have become heavily and skillfully engaged in the fraudulent production of very high quality counterfeit credit cards, Canadian provincial medical treatment cards, counterfeit U.S. $100 bills, and other counterfeit documents throughout North America. The Big Circle Boys (BCB) received their name "Big Circle" because most of the early BCB members were ex-Red Guards in the 1960s and were later confined in re-education camps located in secure compounds that encircled the southeastern city of Guangzhou (formerly Canton). Apparently, they were not initially connected with Triads in Guangzhou (see Appendix A for George Harkin's country-by-country list of Triads). Filtering throughout Canada as a result of the country's relatively permissive immigration laws, they immediately secured social services and financial support. Soon after beginning criminal operations, pickpocketing, and other small crimes in 1987, the BCB progressed to the more lucrative and complex forms of crime such as credit card fraud and alien smuggling. Since crossing the U.S.-Canadian border appears quite simple for them, they have now established themselves in the the U.S. as well. Also, contrary to most Asian crime directed to the victimization of other Asians, the BCB have directly and indirectly begun to prey on non-Asians as well.

Although it appeared initially that there was no formal connection with any of the traditional Triads or Tongs, newly formed alliances among Triads, some newly minted southern Chinese "entrepreneurs", and North American criminal groups (perhaps a few PRC government officials?) may prove otherwise. After many clever maneuvers in the U.S. And Canada, they have secured the machinery not only to duplicate stolen credit cards, but also to manufacture new "real" credit cards. Concentrating on the more lucrative gold cards which have minimum credit limits of $10,000, they have achieved a turn-around time of 2 to 3 days to duplicate a gold card; this includes spanning Canada, the U.S., and Hong Kong! In addition to counterfeit credit cards, they have been developing clone cellular phones. For assistance and training, contact the U.S. Secret Service, Visa and MasterCard companies, Cellular Telecommunications Industry Association (CTIA, (202) 785-0081), and the International Association of Credit Card investigators (IACCI, (415) 981-5300). Also, relevant publication for dealing with the BCB, is the 100-page *Cantonese-English Dictionary of Cantonese Gang Slang,* edited by Mr. Fritz Chang, FBI, Boston, may be secured by authorized personnel by phoning (617) 742-5533.

These criminal activities generate major increases in fraud-related expenses of credit-card and cellular-phone companies here and abroad. And while Japan has tremendous credit card problems, overall counterfeit credit cards are down in Asia. For example, credit card losses of one major company were estimated to be:

	1992 (millions)	1993 (millions)	1994 (billions)
Asia and Pacific	$13	$16	—
United States	16	37	—
Worldwide	43	70	$1.2

Alien Smuggling

Since the 1980s, particularly since the massacre at Tiananmen Square in Beijing in 1989, the rate of Chinese alien smuggling has increased to record proportions. One estimate suggests that the influx of aliens is reaching 2500 to 3000 per month into the rapidly expanding Chinese communities in the New York area, predominately Queens and Brooklyn.[42] Most of the aliens are funneled through the southeast Chinese province of Fujian, centered in Changle county and around the city of Fuzhou, the capital of Fujian Province.[43]

> The transformation of the Chinese economy in the Special Economic Zones from agrarian to industrial, virtually overnight, is producing another commodity for export, the one that is showing up on our shores at the rate of 100,000 per year, surplus people.... These displaced people make up the floating population estimated to be more than 100 million, nationwide. It is from a comparatively small portion of the Fukienese floating population that the more than 600,000 Fukienese have been drawn and transported to the U.S. with funds raised by close and distant members of the Fukienese overseas Chinese community in the U.S. In the U.S. even with the minimal job skills they possess, they are able to find employment within the ever expanding Fukienese population.[44]

These global smuggling activities are generally influenced, if not totally controlled by, the long-standing kinship and linguistic ties between the Taiwanese and the Fukienese.[45] Both groups speak subdialects of Min (Fukienese) derived from Fujian province in southeastern China; "Northern" Min is spoken in the northeast Fujian and in the capital of Fuzhou; "Southern" Min is spoken widely in the southern Fujian province, a large part of Taiwan, and parts of Guangdong province (Canton area). Furthermore, of the 100,000 Chinese admitted to Canada every year,[46] it is predicted that about 60% will eventually find their way into the U.S. Other countries are not immune to alien smuggling. In 1992, 68,000 foreign nationals were forcibly deported from Japan because of illegal entry; between July 1992 and November 1993, Malaysia held in immigrant centers over 64,000 illegal immigrants, mostly Indonesians, Thais, Myanmar (Burmese), and residents of Bangladesh (formerly east Pakistan of the Northeastern Indian subcontinent).[47]

Recent intelligence overviews suggests that a recent drop in smuggled aliens (20,000 in 1994) is not due to efforts on the part of the governments in North American or PRC but rather to the fact that in some villages in Fujian province, about 80% of the population has entered the U.S. by illegal means. Consequently, recruitment efforts have now been extended to the city of Wenzhou, Zhejiang province, where " ... they speak a subdialect of Wu, not widely available through Chinese interpreters in the U.S. Like the Fukienese migrants, the Wenzhounese irregular migrants have only a rudimentary understanding of Mandarin [the most widely known and used Chinese dialect] or none at all." Alien smuggling into Japan, Europe, Canada, and the U.S. generates an estimated $3.2 billion per year.[48]

However, the big money is with those targeted for North America. It is estimated that each alien pays the smugglers (called "snakeheads") about $20,000 to $50,000. A 10% downpayment is required. Although this downpayment is relatively small by Western standards, it represents a very large financial burden for most PRC Chinese. However, in the eyes of Chinese who have little knowledge of North American cultures, the goal seems very desirable. For example, an annual income of $10,000 gained by working in the kitchen of a North American Chinatown restaurant appears to many PRC Chinese who are ignorant of the cost of living in North America, to be far a larger income than they could ever hope to earn at home in the PRC.[49]

Their appalling ignorance about the economics of living in the U.S. is illustrated in Beijing's best selling novel of 1991, *Beijinger in New York*, which was made into a 20-episode television series on China's CCTV network and viewed by an audience estimated at over 900 million people. The sadly inaccurate rumors of great wealth to be earned quickly and easily in the U.S. are voiced by one of the characters, Xiao Zhen: "I hear one can earn hundreds of dollars a month abroad simply by washing dishes."[50] Such inaccuracies cannot help but tempt some young Chinese to strive for the means to leave Fujian with the hope of a prosperous future life in North America.

To help ensure the collection of fees, each alien must supply to the "snakeheads" not only family guarantors in PRC but a mentor or relative in the U.S. or Canada. On the arrival of the alien in the U.S., the family members and/or mentors are contacted and the balance is to be paid or the alien will be forced into a position as an indentured slave.[51] Many unable to pay these fees are forced to work 20 hours a day, 7 days per week, for years at extremely low wages. The smuggled aliens often are beaten to hasten family responses, and women are forced into prostitution. Other fates which await a smuggled alien who owes money include being forced to become a smuggler, a smuggler's enforcer, or a drug courier.

Another way smuggled aliens may be forced to pay off their passage is by "smurfing", where the individual either helps directly to disperse and deposit — to "launder" — large amounts of money obtained in criminal enterprises. He sets up bank savings or checking accounts in his name, then turns over the bank documents, including signature card, to the criminals for their use.[52]

In the previous 3 years, the " ... INS [Immigration and Naturalization Service] has managed to deport only 190 of the tens of thousands of undocumented Chinese immigrants."[53] Even those who " ... were arrested in the act of immigrating illegally ... cannot simply be sent back home. First, they must go before an immigration judge for an 'exclusion hearing', ... [which] could take four to six months. At that point, all are likely to request political asylum, requiring further hearings."[53] Delays are likely in that process, for "... the INS has a backlog of 260,000 asylum cases."[53]

Furthermore, while the possibilities for economic gain lure many illegal immigrants, it seems likely that the immigration policies of the U.S. may increase the flow of illegal Chinese immigrants. The recent decision of a federal judge to grant a Chinese illegal immigrant asylum was made because:

> ... China's population control strategy is political persecution, a violation of a basic human right ... Most of the Chinese refugees seeking asylum are married men in their thirties who have one child ... the refugees, their wives or both are facing mandatory sterilization in most cases ... [54]

Obviously, because of all these cultural and economic factors and the return of the British Crown Colony of Hong Kong to the PRC, there will be more groups engaged in criminal activities. Therefore, the need for trained and informed Asian crime investigators can only increase.

On Introducing and Summarizing Chinese Cultures

To understand the problem of trying to summarize this huge, ancient, oddly powerful civilization, think about the following facts and descriptions.

- Of every five people in the world, one (20%) is of Chinese descent!
- China is the world's most populous country, with a population of over 1,177,000,000!
- Since the demise of the former Soviet Union, China is the third largest country in the world after Russia and Canada and is slightly larger in area than the U.S.
- As is the case for the U.S., Russia, and Canada, China's land mass is very large, stretching some 3500 miles from north to south and, in places, approximately 3200 miles from east to west.
- China is *old*; excavations have yielded evidence of early Chinese civilization 4000 years old and evidence of early rice cultivation 7000 years ago.
- Within China, over 80,000,000 people are categorized ethnically as being non-Chinese (non-Han), who include over 56 recognized minority populations, all of whom have (in theory) the same political rights as citizens in the Han Chinese population.
- In addition to the Han and non-Han Chinese, there are the Overseas Chinese (Hua Qiao) who number about 55,000,000 and who contribute much to the overall economic strength of their ancestral homeland, providing ready-made linkages and networks (guanxi) for business — legal and illegal.

In some Asian countries, the small populations of overseas Chinese control an amazing percentage of the economy: in Thailand, the overseas Chinese comprise only 10% of the population (8 million) but have 60% control over the economy; in Malaysia, 35% and 60%; in the Philippines, 2% and 60%; in Vietnam, 5% and 60%; in Indonesia, 3% and 85%. In countries where

Chinese have been the dominant group for much longer, the percentages are higher: in Singapore, 75% and 95%; in Taiwan, 100% and 100%. The percentages for Hong Kong are slightly different; Chinese represent 96% of the population and 90% of the economy.[55] Chinese newspapers and Chinatowns abound all over the world; for example, Lima, Peru, has three Cantonese-language papers and there are Chinese newspapers in Sydney and Melbourne, Australia. Calgary, Alberta, Canada has 42,000 Chinese[56] who have built a very beautiful (and expensive) Chinese Cultural Center.

One seasoned observer of China and the Chinese described their many-sided characteristics as follows:

> They are the most paradoxical of nations. Masters of agriculture, they have to import grain. Possessed of the most refined musical tradition, they write the worst modern music in the world. Their ancient political theorists rivaled the Greeks and made possible a stable society which survived invasion, famine, and civil war for more than two millennia, yet their modern political theory is crude and derivative — little more than a set of rationales for what they find it expedient to do. With a per capita national income less than many countries generally accounted poor, they have launched earth satellites and have developed nuclear weapons and ICBMs. Child-loving to a fault, they have made it virtually a crime for a couple to have more than one child. Skeptical of religion, they turned a man into a god for ten years and then discarded his memory without regret. Always mindful of personal comfort and good, they can endure hardships beyond the breaking point of most other people. They are admirable, infuriating, humorous, priggish, modest, overweening, mendacious, loyal, mercenary, ethereal, sadistic, and tender. They are quite unlike anybody else. They are the Chinese.[57]

Thus, the problem of introducing the scope of Chinese civilization and the various Chinese subcultures to North Americans is not simple. For example, just as the physical scope of China is quite large compared with Vietnam or Japan, the historical Chinese tradition is large, old, varied, complex, and scattered. Some comparative generalizations have been offered in the preceding chapter. In this chapter we will try to encompass the varied body of cultures we call "the Chinese". We will focus on comparative descriptions of some of the differences between main*line* (but not necessarily main*land*) Chinese culture and American culture. Specifically, we will focus on that one quarter of the world's population that consists of people who are (1) citizens of mainland China, the People's Republic of China (PRC); (2) of Chinese descent and live in largely Chinese nations such as Taiwan, Singapore, or Hong Kong; or (3) among the very large numbers of overseas Chinese (Hua Qiao) who remain very important to family sites and provinces and to the economy of PRC.[58]

By way of contrast, India, a quite different but equally impressive civilization, maintained few reliable historical records, but the Chinese were a very historically oriented civilization and maintained good internal historical records since very ancient times. For the most part, China's energies and attention have been directed inward, not out towards the rest of the world. However, until the rise of what we now call "science", the European industrial revolution some 500 years ago, and the pervasiveness of applied science (technology) in this century, the sophistication of Chinese technology was probably superior to that of the rest of the world, but remains virtually unknown to the Anglo-European world.

All major civilizations of this planet, including the ancient Chinese, developed sophisticated social practices and political theories to guide and justify their beliefs, attitudes, and actions. In short, they gradually developed cultural frameworks — theoretical models of themselves, PAEFs, — to make sense of the world (see Chapters 11 and 12.) The Chinese models emphasized harmony, balance, and a context-restricted, authoritarian set of social and political standards for behavior and expectations about the world. Above all, they valued, and still value, *social stability.* They developed a largely non-theistic naturalistic view of the world in which there was a sense of what some might call the "divine" but without the concept of interpersonal relationships between individual humans and "heaven" (T'ien). However, the idea of heaven (Tien) did not include human characteristics, nor was heaven responsible for the creation of the world. Thus, it did not play an anthropomorphic[59] role in the creation and maintenance of the universe, as found in the Judaic-Christian-Islamic ideas of a single agent-creator god.

Furthermore, the Chinese did not assume, as we contemporary North Americans have assumed, an egalitarian view of humanity, social equality, or self-evident legalistic appeals, nor universal rights to personal freedom and the pursuit of happiness. Nor was there a strong emphasis on individualism and historical progress. In the Chinese tradition, rather than an emphasis on the desires of the individual, there was an emphasis upon the welfare of the family as the root institution of a multileveled society, coupled with a rather pragmatic ("do whatever works") view of human struggles to survive in a morally neutral universe. The Chinese tradition exhibits a cool, sensitive, but "in your face" realism about life's hard and unpredictable struggles.

Also, Chinese society continues to be strongly structured by social class divisions where appeals to individual rights were very seldom recognized nor successfully defended against the central government. Suspects taken into custody are seldom found innocent, for the police usually only round up suspects for which there is considerable evidence; thus their 'stats" regarding convictions are comparatively high. It is most important to emphasize that the stability of the social order and obligations of the individual to the larger family/clan unit have been strong Chinese values for thousands of years, as they are today. In short, as in most of the world, life was tough and unpredictable and the primary goal was the survival of the family/clan into the future. Other values were subordinated to those of one's family and one's guanxi.

With this general model of society, the Chinese maintained for almost 3000 years a relative stability and very high (and very elitist) culture built upon hundreds of thousands of human lives full of misery, infrequent joys, nastiness, brutishness, and pain. Thus, in spite of all the shortcomings of the Chinese, Indians, Greeks, or French, it is obvious that the Western models of society are not necessary conditions for high culture and for orderly, stable civilizations.

Furthermore, while there were (and are) many different spoken dialects of Chinese that could not be mutually understood, the Chinese were administratively and culturally united by the same written language and also by the general similarities in the education of the elite social classes from which China drew its administrators for thousands of years. This constitutes no small advantage to any civilization, as can be seen in the contrasting example of Africa. The latter remains a geographical unit, but because it lacked a unifying written language and, thus, a unified culture, it does not exhibit the cultural continuity we find in Chinese history. Thus, while we may not agree with everything the Chinese have done during the centuries, we cannot doubt that they have maintained an admirable, relatively stable civilization.

Moreover, until the last century, China had never encountered a country or a culture that could contest its cultural status as the complete "center of the world" or "middle kingdom" (Zhong gou). Thus, given the deceit, imperialism, and exploitation of China by North Americans and Europeans during the last two centuries, the Chinese understandably remain extremely sensitive about any projected sense of cultural inferiority or attempts on our part to criticize Chinese institutions and practices. For example, in cross-cultural negotiations with Anglo-Europeans, they often appeal to this point to gain an advantage.[60] As noted before, it is appropriate and helpful for us to be sensitive to our own assumptions about China; it is also helpful to us to be sensitive to Chinese views of themselves.

However, because China has entered the multicultured twentieth-century arena of international communication and criticism, they must respond to a wide range of criticisms of them and cultural contrasts within the global arena. They have learned that multifacetted, multicultural analysis remains a rough game. Overall, the Chinese do quite well in anyone's comparisons of world cultures throughout recorded history. If one looks throughout the timespans of several distinct European cultures (the Hellenic, Roman, Renaissance, and rise of the West European empires in and out of the Northern and Southern Americas) one can see the hills and valleys of both deep catastrophic change and the most admirable features of civilization. However, while we should be sensitive to Chinese history, exercise careful rhetoric, and maintain civil discourse with them, this does not mean that we necessarily should agree with their recommendations, their claims, or their points of view.

Ultimately, the differences in both cultures make a difference for law enforcement. Therefore, some knowledge of these cultural factors will reduce the difficulty, complexity, and stress for most law enforcement personnel in their communications with the Chinese-American communities and as they identify and apprehend Chinese and Chinese-American criminals.

Potential Chinese Global Economic Power

As is well known, North America has a greater trade balance with the Pacific Rim than with Europe, 31% vs. 24% in 1994. What many North Americans may have not realized is that it is likely that the huge sleeping giant, China, is fully awake and is about to develop the "Greater Chinese Economic Zone".[61] Furthermore, it is possible that this Chinese economic giant could be taller than the Japanese economy. Or, as some economists expect, the Chinese economy may "double in size before the year 2010. More feverish optimists suggest that within a few decades after the turn of the century, it may be the world's largest economy"[62] or its GNP (gross national product) may (but only "may") surpass the U.S. around the year 2010. But this rapid expansion is only possible rather than certain, because the giant, given its own internal history, might shoot itself in the foot once again by allowing something similar to the cultural revolution of the 1970s to occur. This would, of course, bring economic development and all international confidence in its stability to a halt.

Thus, while China remains a relatively poor country, its potential economic power is enormous. However, its troubles are also substantial as it continues to wrestle with rampant and rabid decentralization, international reactions to its destabilizing weapons and nuclear sales to third world countries, rising internal crime, frequent official corruption, drug transportation in the southwest from the Golden Triangle, public executions for drug sales and use, growing inflation, worker discontent, and rapidly rising expectations about consumerism among its populace. Equally important are political developments that will occur during the period of Deng Xiaoping's successor(s).

To help the reader appreciate the range of the other Sinosized countries, some information about the major players in the potential/actual "greater Chinese economic zones(s)", namely Taiwan, Hong Kong, and Singapore, is introduced. It is taken from *The World Factbook, 1993* (a publication prepared by the Central Intelligence Agency, Washington, D.C. 20505; Phone: (202) 783-3238). The purpose of this description is to give the reader a very brief idea of the relative geographical size, population, growth, rates of birth and death, life expectancy, and percentage of literacy in these other Chinese/Sinosized countries in comparison with the PRC. Thus, all percentages will refer to comparisons with the PRC.

Country	Population (in millions)	Compared to PRC (percent)	Size (kilometers)	Compared to PRC (percent)	Population Growth (percent)	Births/ Deaths (per 1000)	Life Expectancy (years)	Literacy (percent)
PRC	1177.5		9,600,000		1.1	18.3/7.3	68	73
Taiwan	21.0	1.8	36,000	0.380	1.00	15.9/5.5	75	86
Hong Kong	5.6	0.47	1040	0.013	–0.06	12.3/5.7	80	77
Singapore	2.8	0.24	633	0.007	1.2	17.1/5.2	76	88

However, the brief information given here should not lead the reader to assume that all Chinese or those of Chinese descent share all the same values, work habits, or social customs. There are significant differences between peoples from the PRC and peoples from tiny Hong Kong, Singapore, and Taiwan, but these details are generally beyond the boundaries of this book. However, as mainland China is both the historical source of Chinese culture and remains the homeland and a partial model for many Chinese today, the PRC continues to be the legitimate focus from which to generalize about the various Chinese subcultures around the world which are themselves derivative from those of the homeland — a homeland in all the senses of the word.

Potentially, a combination of natural resources and the huge labor pool of the PRC combined with financial resources and expertise and the commercial sophistication and international nimbleness of overseas Chinese, may converge to generate an economic force — a "greater Chinese economic zone" — which could rival or even surpass the economic power of cash-rich Japan. Chinese extended "overseas" families are large and pervasive in Asia. For example, in Malaysia the total population is about 15 million, of which 5 million are Chinese. In Thailand, similar figures are 56 and 8 million; Indonesia 183 and 6 million; Australia, 18 and 1 million; and Canada, 12 and 2 million. The approximate numbers in the U.S. are 250 and 2 million.[63] Furthermore, at this date, China has the fastest growing economy in the world. Its combined production of goods and services grew 12.8% in 1992, doubling its growth of 1991.[64] Its gross national product is worth about $2.6

trillion, and it manages to send about $7 million in foreign aid to southeast Asia.

> The market forces have unleashed economic and social changes that have transformed China from top to bottom, affecting everything from sex to stock markets. Driven by ruthless opportunism and the get-it-while-you-can mentality, Chinese are radically changing the way they work, eat, invest, consume and even the way they talk to each other…
>
> China today is no longer the Maoist monolith of the 1970s; myriad contradictions are pulling the country in all directions. Peasants on the outskirts of Beijing can watch Phil Donahue courtesy of their satellite dishes. While free-wheeling call-in radio shows give advice about sex, the torture of prisoners is more widespread now than a decade ago, according to Amnesty International.[65]

In addition, North American police are certainly feeling the effects of the illegal importation of Chinese firearms into the U.S.[66]

> Since a 1987 decision by the State Department allowed Chinese arms imports, Beijing's army has emerged as one of the largest suppliers of small arms on the American market, [ATF spokesman John C.] Killorin said. In 1993, the Chinese supplied 30% of all guns shipped to the U.S. and 54% of the rifles.

In his fascinating book, *Tribes: How Race, Religion, and Identity Determine Success in the New Global Economy,* Joel Kotkin devotes a chapter to the new configuration of transnational Chinese businessmen called "spacemen" (tai kung fai jen):[67,68]

> As residents and citizens of various countries … the Chinese spacemen learn far more than the rotating Japanese salarimen about their countries of residence and naturally adopt a more cooperative, flexible approach in dealing with partners. U.S.-based research and development operations — critical to all but a few Taiwanese technology companies — are run by American-educated executives, sometimes family members, fluent in English and with long experience living in the U.S. Japanese firms, on the other hand, are largely outposts manned by rotating executives whose only true standards are those of the home islands and whose foreign minions are largely consigned to irrelevance.

To grasp the potential economic importance of the combined PRC and overseas Chinese transnational financial groups, Kotkin offers several relevants facts, some of which are taken from a Washington Post article:[72]

- Taken together, the three leading centers of Chinese capitalism — Taiwan, Hong Kong and Singapore — boast [financial] reserves two and one-half times those of the Japanese; Seagrave notes that Singapore may control liquid assets of as much as $2 trillion
- The economic growth and saving rate of the PRC and the overseas Chinese are roughly twice that of Japan; Taiwans' foreign exchange reserves surpassed Japan's to become the world's largest.
- The combined investment of Hong Kong, Singapore and Taiwan in such key countries of Malaysia, Thailand and Indonesia have begun to surpass those of Japan.
- The Chinese invest eight out of every ten dollars entering China and are the largest investors in Vietnam.
- Beyond Outer Mongolia, the oil-rich Tarim Basin nearly the size of Texas may hold nearly as much oil as Saudia Arabia [and have] … three times the U.S. proven oil reserves and nearly twice the remaining U.S. proven natural gas reserves.[69]
- Once flattened by Maoist excess, China's graduate enrollment rose five-fold between 1980 and 1986 … [and] now China graduates more scientists and engineers than Germany and France combined.
- Nationwide, students of Chinese descent claim one-third of all U.S. doctorates in science and engineering awarded to foreigners.
- Although some … will return home, two out every three of the estimated 80,000 Chinese students and scholars have opted to stay [in the U.S.].[70]
- Well-educated Asian immigrants have established themselves at the top of the scientific and medical professions in the U.S., outdistancing native-born African-Americans and Hispanics both in achievement and earnings … [71]

However, the less encouraging side of the worldwide activities of Chinese organized crime was noted by Willard H. Meyers. His comments follow:[72]

- Drug production, smuggling and distribution of methamphetamine and heroin: earnings in excess of $200 billion per year.
- Alien smuggling principally to the U.S.: earnings in excess of $3.2 billion per year.
- Weapons smuggling and distribution from Russian and Chinese military stores throughout Southeast Asia, North and South America: earnings estimated to be in excess of $3 billion per year.

As these close Chinese social ties constitute *de facto* economic confederations that span many different political systems, the guanxi "networking" relationships are found to be crucial in maintaining the webs of international business arrangements. These webs of trust and personal vetting by Chinese people are linked and crosslinked by shared dialects, the ability to read written Chinese, and the long-standing cultural ties of dialect, regional and village lineages, and other relationships based on the (extended) family and surrogate family associations and their obligations.

> The Chinese are a closely knit community, wherever you find them; over the first forty years, they have established ties with each other. Sometimes it seems like everyone's related. I know someone in Taiwan, and he knows someone else in Hong Kong, and you link them together and you have this network, and you find this opportunity. That's how it works.[73]

While all cultures have guanxi networks to some extent, this is a particularly important cultural trait regarding the Chinese, for it shapes and explains how their amazingly sophisticated global networks of trading — legal and illegal — can function while U.S. and Canadian law enforcement organizations are still looking at Chinese organizations as if they were organized in an Anglo-European chain-of-command model as found in the Mafia and the LCN. (See Chapter 15 for a discussion of these differences.)

A Geographical Sketch of China

In the last decade, since the PRC became more receptive to cooperative economic development and increased its worldwide trading relationships, existing ties with the 58 million overseas Chinese have been strongly reinforced by business and travel. For example, the gross national product of the PRC has been 10 to 13% and continues to increase. It is now among the ten biggest exporting countries, and its consumption of energy is only surpassed by the U.S.[74] It is important to remember that China is the third largest country in the world after the former Soviet Union and Canada. It spans 3,692,244 square miles or about 9,326,410 kilometers in land mass, and is slightly bigger than the U.S. It consists of 22 provinces in which, except for the overloaded rail services, communication is relatively poor and technologically primitive.

To the north, China is joined with Inner Mongolia, Mongolia, the easternmost reaches of the former Soviet Union (now referred to as "Russia"), and other members of the new Commonwealth. To the northeast, China is bordered by Manchuria, the Yellow Sea, Korea, and Japan. Taiwan lies to the southeast, directly across from China's Fukien province from which much of the alien smuggling originates. Further to the Southeast lies Hong Kong, which reverts back to the PRC in 1997, causing many of the "big money men" to move their operations to Singapore, Canada, and the U.S. Tracing China's long southern border from east to west, China touches Vietnam, part of Laos, considerable miles along Myanmar (formerly "Burma"), and India; with brutal political turmoil China absorbed Tibet which borders little Bhutan, Nepal, and India. Xinjiang Uygur stretches upward to the northwest.

In their widely used university textbook, Professors Reischauer and Fairbank characterized the central geographical features of China:[75]

> China is … a less united area than either India or the traditional zone of Western civilization. It lacks the easy communications made possible by the Mediterranean or by the geographical unity of the plains of other regions. The North China Plain, the largest stretch of level terrain in the whole area, is very much smaller than the plain that extends across North India, to say nothing of the still greater North European Plain or the American Middle West.
>
> China is broken up into a sort of checkerboard by two intersecting sets of parallel mountain chains. One … from southwest China northeastward through Shansi and Western Manchuria. A parallel range extends from Canton northward … [to] the Shantung Peninsula and again in the mountains along the Korean and Manchurian border. Intersecting these two southwest-to-northeast ranges, three parallel mountain chains … protrude from west to east toward the Pacific.… This cross-hatching of mountain ranges has created a number of distinct geographical regions. It has inevitably given rise to problems of economic and political unity and has determined military strategy.

The climate of most of China is temperate. However, the extreme southern areas are subtropical, while the north can be a " … battleground between cold, dry continental air and warm, humid oceanic air which brings it most of its rainfall."[76] Although much of the land in the southeast has been exhausted and leached out by centuries of desperate farming, it is still possible to secure two crops per year; the North, by contrast, has a short growing season, sparse and chancy rainfall, and is beset by the constant threat of either floods or drought.[77]

It is amazing that about 22% of the world's population depends upon the food raised in an area about the size of the combined states of New York, California, and Texas:[78]

> The great bulk of China's population lives in east and south China, the highest concentrations being along the Yangtze River and the eastern seaboard. This good arable land comprises only about 12% of China's territory.[79]
>
> China's most populous cities are found here, the largest urban areas include Beijing (population 9 million, and rising fast) and the nearby metropolis of Tianjin (8 million) in the north, Shanghai (12 million) in east-central China, and Guangzou (5 million) in the south. Inland and to the west along the Yangtze River lie the industrial city of Wuhan (4 million) and Chongqing (7 million), the largest city in the most populous province, Sichuan.[80]

In some newly prosperous areas, particularly in the southeast, the enormous rise in new industries and the expansion of towns has generated a severe pollution problem in the rivers, water, and air. The government acknowledges the problem and is making efforts to assist in this aspect of China's contemporary "industrial revolution". However, with the lack of environmental legislation and experience in pollution control, coupled with a high level of bureaucratic corruption, these pollution problems are not likely to lessen in the near future.

Cultural Sketches

The Family: The Model of Chinese Society

For most Asians, and certainly for the Chinese, the (extended) family comes before the State, the Church/Temple, the individual, one's profession, and one's friends. Not only do brothers and sisters count, as with us, but respect for grandparents counts heavily — usually first. All the aunts, uncles, and cousins count as part of the tight, dependable source of power, protection, status, money, safety, connections, education, and help. The large extended family living together or very close is common. If family members live at great distances, all are part of the extended family for several generations; they all are bound together as family and family dialect, the basic social foundations for the Chinese mindset and the basic model for all other Chinese organizations and institutions. As a China specialist put it," ... blood ties are [usually] stronger than marital bonds. It is not unusual for Chinese to feel a greater sense of obligation to their parents, children and brothers and sisters than to their spouses."[81] Laws permitting a parent to sue a child for lack of support already exist in China and Taiwan, and the National Assembly of the government of Singapore has recently approved such a bill.

These ranked social relations based on birth are rooted in the oldest surviving Chinese texts of ancient history and organized philosophy. They were expressed most clearly in the teachings of the ancient philosopher we call "Confucius" (Kong fu zi). His ideas shaped the Chinese world view and echoed throughout Chinese society for 2500 years (see Chapter 19). Confucius claimed to be no more than a humble but diligent student of the ancient classics; he was never considered divine in the Judeo-Christian sense. He taught that the five desirable relations to be encouraged in human-to-human relationships were: (1) kind benevolence in the ruler and loyalty among those ruled, (2) respect and honor for the elders and respectful deference in the younger toward the elders, (3) the father's kindly but stern wisdom coupled with filial piety and obedience in the children, (4) gentility in the eldest brother and respectful humility in the younger brothers, and (5) righteous behavior in the husband and obedience and proper deference in his wife. Note that these relationships are not relations between equals; these are relationships between persons not of equal worth, equal opportunities, nor equal moral rights. In fact, there were no "rights" as we know them; obligations are not the same as legal or moral rights.

Therefore, ethics and morality have a different basis and history in China than in the Anglo-European traditions. This is not to say that more Chinese exhibited these ethical goals of human behavior more often, or less often, than did Anglo-Europeans. Furthermore, differences in ethical systems does not necessarily mean better or worse. For example, contrary to the ideas of most North Americans, Confucius and later Confucians would never have asserted that all men were of equal worth nor that they should all have equal political/social rights — whether legal rights or moral rights. In fact, the abstract concept of context-neutral legal or moral *rights* is an Anglo-European invention and does not exist as a socially neutral foundation for law and morality in the Chinese traditions. Furthermore, unequal social ranks have unequal social privileges and responsibilities; for example, those who have had the opportunity to educate themselves and to study the classics have greater ethical responsibilities than those who have not. However, as with some of the ancient Greek philosophers, one strong Confucian emphasis was on the roots of ethical development, namely, knowing and developing yourself as a self-conscious moral agent. In other words, "conduct yourself so that you become someone worth knowing."

Ideally, within the five relationships there is a chain of levels of learning and status, and when each is known in the proper sequence, all lead (supposedly) to morality, peace, and ethical self-knowledge. Propriety (li) leads to (proper) knowledge which leads to proper social action. This relationship was thought to be the behavioral channel through which the humane but natural biological urges and social needs of humans could be shaped and given harmonious behavioral expression as the best of human-heartedness (ren). Because of this, manners, style, and knowledgeable social skills are viewed as ethical reflections of the very human person behind the face and are not viewed as artificial, "put-ons", or unnatural pretentions. In short, human manners count. The learned development of one's natural good-heartedness is compatible with the recognition of the dark side of human behavior as well as the deliberate development of the best in human behavior by means of an all-pervasive moral sense of human-to-human social manners and self-cultivated, ethical self-knowledge. Thus, mutual respect for oneself and others, explicit knowledge of how things ought to be done, and a Chinese version of the "Golden Rule" lead one to know how to maintain and improve the five relationships.

Therefore, if one does not just blindly follow the social customs of the family but wishes to analyze the basis of one's own ethical conduct, the general Confucian tradition suggests that one should start with "things at hand" — oneself. Hence, one should start with one's own character by learning what is correct, developing the self-discipline to act accordingly, and knowing *from within* what it is to be an ethical person. This inner character building will radiate like the ripple from a stone thrown in a pond. Knowing what one should do and having the discipline to do it will bring about harmony and prosperity within one's mutually supported family/clan. This, in turn, will bring about stability and good relationships between families, villages, townships, and states. This, in turn, will bring about a benevolent, human-hearted (ren) and balanced (zhong yong) state administration in accordance with the natural way (tao/dao) of nature.

Customarily, it is the eldest son who will remain with the parents and represent the family during the holidays and when commemorating the ancestors at the grave sites. At the death of the parents (usually the father), the eldest son will become the proud head of the family. Of course, sometimes the eldest son is not as able as, say, the third-born son. In that case, responsibilities and adjustments would be made within the family with a view to maintaining "face" for all concerned. However, the eldest son is the customary focus of support of the parents and the potential head of the family.

However, while all family/clan members are "family" and are helped before any outsider, social obligations, help, and even "love" are graded virtues; the strength of the appropriate family response is a function of where in the family or how close to the core of the family is the recipient. Family responses to social/family obligations are negotiated and justified on the basis of specific (not general) obligations.

For example, the statement, "He's my father's cousin and should have access to our blood donation of the rare type Z," is a recommendation justified on a specific, non-universal set of values. By contrast, the statement, "He's a human being and he is entitled to have access to our blood donation of the rare type Z," is a recommendation justified on a nonspecific, universal set of values. (Public voluntary blood donations are largely unknown, even in urban China.) Thus, from our Anglo-European point of view, the sources of our social virtues and obligations are, at least in theory, *universally applicable* — not so with the Chinese. Even the third son of one's wife's second cousin remains "family" and will usually be considered before any outsider.

This applies to informants, for unless the individual informant is a member of, say, a Triad, the family is the most important group to which a Chinese informant belongs. To all family members — and to members of his parents' village or region — the informant has many more obligations (including not losing "face") than most Americans have to their relatives. Consequently, and to his/her benefit, most Chinese can expect and will usually receive social, physical, and financial assistance far beyond the expectations of most North Americans. Even third cousins count for help and revenge. This contrasts with our narrower emphasis upon the nuclear family, parents, children, and, sometimes, the grandparents.

By contrast, it is urban and suburban North Americans who have "little" families that, for many mobile people, consist only of Mom, Dad, and the 2.3 kids. The grandparents count, of course, but even they are subordinated to the needs and benefits of the immediate American family. After the family/clan, others to whom the Chinese have strong ties, affiliations, and obligations are those members of name associations, dialect associations, secret societies (economic brotherhoods, hui, kongsi), professional societies, trade guilds, one's childhood friends, and those of upper school and higher schooling. They are all sources of very strong affiliation and loyalty. Even college alumni are usually closer to their former schools than most North Americans. This scale of loyalty leads, of course, to guanxi "networking" and maintaining face.[82] (See Chapter 15.)

Thus, the togetherness of the family model extends to many, many other aspects of Chinese life. One example of this sense of "us vs. them" can be seen in the predicable Chinese neighborhood response of respectful suspicion toward government personnel gathering personal information about a neighbor to approve the neighbor's security clearances. Such personal information gathering, by contrast, is commonly conducted relatively easily in the U.S.

Other accurate generalizations about the Chinese are:

- Being thrifty, saving money, and not spending any more of the resource available to all members of the family than is necessary
- Typically, expending time to save money (Americans will spend money to save time)
- Acquiring education and new skills
- Working very hard, being strategically diligent and cooperatively persevering over the (very) extended long run, and not settling for short-term or quick-turnaround goals or rewards
- An absence of equality between members of the family; some count more than others — men over women, elders over the young, the socially superior over the socially inferior
- Founded on mutual obligations where the superior owes the inferior respect, protection, assistance, and tact and the inferior owes the superior respect, loyalty, and obedience
- Patience (keeping one's anger suppressed) and moderation in all things (not flaunting one's wealth)
- Subordination of emotion and feelings to duty, obligations, and the eventual achievement of long-range goals

Finally, trust and cooperation in Chinese and Chinese-American crime and in business (sometimes intertwined in practice) is often gained through guanxi, an ever widening web of familial relations, old friends, the opinions of friends and trusted acquaintances, and the face-to-face (mian zi) relationships generated and maintained by personal contact rather than legally binding "paper trails" and contracts.

A Chinese Sociological Summary of the Chinese

The following section is an academic summary of Chinese cultural traits and/or socialization from the research of Chinese sociologists based in Hong Kong and Taiwan as summarized in the excellent book, *The Psychology of the Chinese People:*[83,84] (*Italicized* words draw your attention to connections [guanxi] within the book.)

> A distillate of the literature reviewed may be summarized in the following propositions. At the present state of our knowledge, they represent permissible generalizations which have received relatively strong and consistent empirical support or on which there is overall agreement among observers.
>
> 1. Chinese parents tend to be highly lenient or even indulgent in their attitudes toward the infant and young child, in sharp contrast to the strict discipline they impose on older children. Many observers believe that the change in parental attitudes occurs when the child reaches the age of "reason" or "understanding", at around 4 to 6 years.
> 2. Traditionally, great emphasis was placed on *obedience*, proper conduct, moral training, and the acceptance of *social obligations*, in contrast to the *lack of emphasis* placed on independence, assertiveness, and creativity.
> 3. Chinese parents tend to be highly concerned with *impulse control.* The child's exploratory, adventurous, or risky activities tend to be discouraged. Compared with other areas of behavior, sex training and the control of aggression tend to be severe; in particular, expressions of physical aggression are suppressed. Chinese children tend to be physically nonaggressive; in particular, aggression directed toward authority figures is rarely expressed.
> 4. Traditionally, the father has been perceived to be a harsher disciplinarian than the mother, and is the parent of whom the child is more afraid. Father-child affectional distance is greater than that between the mother and the child. However, contemporary mothers appear to be assuming a more important role as disciplinarians.
> 5. Variation rather than uniformity has been observed among Chinese parents in the control and disciplinary techniques they use. Important factors underlying variations in the use of these techniques are parental education, social class, geographical location (urban or rural), the sex

and age of the child and same-sex vs. opposite-sex parent-child relationships. It appears that punitive and power-assertive techniques are receiving less emphasis.

6. In comparison with Caucasian infants, Chinese infants tend to be less vocal, less active, less likely to smile, and more apprehensive in social and separation situations — that is, disposed toward *inhibition.*
7. Educational programs in mainland China place a stronger emphasis on achievement motivation than educational programs in Republican China in the past, or in present-day Taiwan. Efforts are directed towards training children to become active, self-reliant, competent, intellectually critical, and achievement oriented.
8. Achievement motivation is more firmly rooted in the *collectivist* than in the *individualistic orientation.* Cooperative efforts by members of a group toward achieving collective goals are emphasized more than individual competitiveness.
9. Most results conform to the expectation that *positive parental attitudes* are conducive to desirable effects (higher achievement motivation, superior cognitive development and academic performance, and better personal and social adjustment) and that negative parental attitudes have the opposite effects in Chinese children.

A number of studies, however, suggest that boys and girls may be influenced differently by patterns of parenting (for example, the relationships with the father vs. the mother, and the quality of these relationships). These differing patterns are far from simple and the evidence in support of them is far from unequivocal.

Tongs, Triads, and Asian Gangs as "Families"

While a detailed description of Triad, Tongs, and Chinese gangs may be gained elsewhere,[85] the relevant factor here is that Tongs are quite different than Triads and that it is misleading to lump them together. However, Triad and Tong members and Chinese gangs do share at least one characteristic. They may function as surrogate families for different Chinese groups and may exhibit many of the same qualities of obligations, loyalty, and support as found in the all-important extended Chinese family/clan. (See Appendix B for a country-by-country list of Triads prepared by George Harkin, an outstanding federal official who is very knowledgeable about Asia and Asian crime, is fluent in several Asian languages and who has lived in Asia over several years.)

Tongs are Chinese-American self-help associations organized toward the end of the last century by Chinese working in the railroads, agriculture, service businesses, laundries, etc., of the U.S. Today, as before, Tongs serve the Chinese communities, usually headed by leaders who are respected and

Figure 13 Views of the same Tong alley: (left) from *Harper's Weekly,* Feb. 13, 1886 and (right) today. (Courtesy of Sgt. Tom Perdue, San Francisco P.D.)

able to wield influence. However, some Tong leaders were already influenced by or were members of Triads. On occasion, Tongs have demonstrated fewer legitimate functions — such as their relations with, but not control over, Chinese-American gangs in the cases of the On Leong and the Hip Sing of New York.[86] Thus, it is important to distinguish between the quite legitimate purposes for which a Tong was started and the multitude of other good or bad uses to which it may be put today.

In the words of Cordell Hart:[87]

> Some Tongs are crooked to be sure, many of the larger ones employ criminal youth gangs to police certain Tong activities, but Tongs are not inherently criminal associations, as are Triads. In the Chinese language, a Tong is simply an association, while a Triad is clearly understood to be a secret society with illegal aims. A parallel of inaccuracy would be to say that U.S. labor unions are criminal associations, given their infiltration and subversion by the Mafia.

Thus, Triads are illegal, secret Chinese societies begun in the 17th century for patriotic but antigovernment reasons.[88] Soon, through their powerful cultural connections and their sense of mutual obligations between Chinese people linked by dialect, regional lineage, and family, Triads became the avenues to make contacts to develop many illegal activities in China and for their development among the overseas Chinese. While some Triads direct criminal activities, *a major function of the Triads is to furnish a range of vetted contacts with whom individuals may establish short- or long-term criminal relations.* Thus, if members of two separate Triads are seen talking to each other, it does not always follow that both Triads are engaged in developing new criminal activities. By contrast, one would expect a quite different set of results if one came upon two "made" members of two Mafia families talking together. In this case, a plausible conclusion would be that the two organizations would be involved, that exclusive loyalties would be maintained within in apparent negotiations between individual Mafia members; however, this assumption should not be drawn regarding Chinese Triads. As noted in Chapter 15, the Mafia exhibits a chain-of-command model in which personal allegiances are usually exclusive within the Mafia family; the Triads exhibit a more fluid, relational model where personal allegiances for short-term criminal "business" are not always exclusive nor do they involve the whole Triad structure.

While there is great fluidity and flexibility among shifting relationships between members of the Triads, there is a vertical command structure which guarantees the vetting and mainframe of Triad personnel and its profitability. For example, some internal ranks are (1) Red Pole, a fighter-martial arts Triad official; (2) White Paper Fan, an advisor official; (3) Grass Sandal, a messenger official; and (4) an ordinary member, designated by special hand-signs and by numbers.[89a]

In this century, Triads have become increasingly involved in criminal acts such as smuggling narcotics (especially China White heroin), extortion, money laundering, and prostitution. Today, particularly among the Fujianese-Taiwan connections, alien smuggling to the U.S. has reached tremendous proportions. Since the early 1800s, the most active Chinese Triads in the U.S. are the Sun Yee On, Wo Hop To, 14K, and the United Bamboo. Furthermore, the enormous swell of Fujianese-Taiwan illegal immigrants into North American cities is gradually supplanting the older, settled, Cantonese Chinese-Americans, and Chinese-Canadians.

In his testimony at U.S. Senate hearings, Willard H. Meyers succinctly defined the self-image and innerconnections between Triads and the larger overseas Chinese communities scattered throughout the world:[89]

> We may and should define transnational ethnic Chinese criminal activity as a global trade in prohibited commodities and services conducted by and among suppliers, refiners, exporters, shippers (transporters), importers and distributors who are members of culturally recognized affinity groups, who are strategically located far from point of supply to point of distribution.

> This definition not only corresponds with the empirical data, but mirrors very precisely how those engaged in the trade define themselves — as persons engaged in business not crime ... Chinese transnational criminal activity is carried out as a form of entrepreneurial activity by and among persons who are linked by language (dialect group) and lineage (ancestral birth place), who may or may not be a member or affiliate of an organization recognized by law enforcement.

Publicly, the Triad societies have been mythologized as protectors of the poor and the underdog. Historically, and especially for some Chinese-American Tongs, this Robin Hood image often has been accurate, for they have functioned as surrogate families to help Chinese people when there was no one else to help them. However, while this holds for the most part today and almost all Tongs engage in many legal and admirable activities, some Tongs have been found to be engaged in some illegal activities as well, most often gambling. It would appear that the intentions of the Tong chairman seem to determine the Tong's activities. And while the Tongs may use Asian youth gangs as muscle to protect their local gambling activities, they do not always have direct paramilitary control over the Chinese youth gangs.

Figure 14 Gang members in front of Tong building. (Photo courtesy of Sgt. Tom Perdue, San Francisco P.D.)

Furthermore, the ritualized recruitment for the secret Triad societies is supported by the image of the Triad as an extended family beyond the biological family. The Triad guanxi relations, reinforced by initiation rituals; Tong, village, and regional lineage connections; and family name associations serve to strengthen the Triad member's recruitment, commitment, and illegal activities. However, this image of a "guanxi" family and its extended networks among the overseas Chinese is not only felt to be "true" by many Triad members, but helps to explain their strong commitment to follow orders in spite of the very dangerous and violent life of many low- and middle-ranking Triad and youth gang members.

One of the few options Triad members working the streets have to escape their Triad activities is to marry and start a family, to marry out of the Triad and seek other work. This does not mean that the member is free from Triad opportunities, connections, and obligations; clearly, he is still a member with a member's obligations. However, this option may provide police with a wedge of opportunity to pressure a gang informer by helping him get a better job, one farther away from the street. Another wedge of opportunity is to threaten to bring shame on the informer's family, resulting in his loss of "face" and (thus) his place in the guanxi network. While many good cops know this, many do not. Therefore, if, and only if, one knows something of these social aspects of Chinese culture faced by a potential Chinese informant, can these possible pressures be brought to bear on him to ensure cooperation.

Marriage, Sexuality, and Divorce

Throughout most of China's history, arranged marriages were the norm. Traditionally, parents would decide one's marriage partner through negotiations between family elders. They would be little concerned with whether the bride and groom would be personally compatible. Thus, PRC Chinese custom in particular, has not had a long social tradition of causal dating where young men and women get to know a wide variety of people and choose a marriage partner from among them. In varying ways, arranged marriages are still a partial norm, but without the prospect of the bride and groom being totally ignorant of each other before the actual marriage ceremony. In other words, there are still arranged marriages but the arrangements have been modified and loosened over the years, particularly since 1949, the beginning of the PRC. In general, the degree of traditionalism exhibited by the family indicates the degree to which one could expect traditional marriage arrangements to be followed.

Today, as across most of the world, it is often assumed that any two young people who are consistently seen together have already decided to marry. Particularly in the PRC, the couple's families, friends, the neighborhood, and the work units will expect that a wedding will occur in the near future and they will express strong disapproval if they fail to marry. While this is less true in Singapore, Hong Kong, and urban Taiwan, these procedures differ by social class but remain the basis for significant cultural clashes about *face* between families, gangs, and individuals.

In ancient times, (and sometimes today), the marriage broker was almost as important as the potential marriage partners. She was almost always an older woman who knew a range of appropriate families in the town or province. She would act as a "go-between", a negotiator who suggested and selected candidates, conveyed messages and inquiries between families, and protected all parties from premature contact and the possibility of losing "face" if personal, social, or political incompatibilities or other difficulties arose. After extensive negotiations, and at the arrival of the groom at the bride's house, the groom is usually admitted only after he offers a red envelope (hong bao) containing money in some multiple of 99 or 999. Those numbers symbolize a long, happy marriage.

Today in the PRC, couples usually meet at work or at dances arranged by their work units or the neighborhood; other alternatives are marriage bureaus which try to mix and match interested singles and the activities of matchmaking friends. Thus, potential couples get a chance to meet and know one another to a greater extent that was possible before. Also, with a minimum of loss of "face" for both the individual and the family, they can quietly reject a potential mate if one finds the other objectionable.[90]

One interesting contrast made by Godwin Chu identifies the *practical* rather than the romantic aspects of a possible spouse. This practical approach is emphasized more among Chinese than among Americans. These aspects include: " ... the prospective spouse's income, ability to provide housing, unwillingness to have parents living with them after marriage ... Romantic considerations like intense feelings, physical attractiveness, a sense of spiritual partnership were relatively less important."[91]

In the Chinese tradition, sexual relations are obviously pursued, enjoyed, abused, and exploited within the usual wide range of human sexual activities. However, from the equally biased North American point of view, there is an apparent and real sense of sexual prudishness in *public* Chinese relationships which is reflected in public media. In Singapore, this is maintained with particular tenacity.[92] In general, the Chinese mindset about sexuality and sexual activities is not rooted in a sin-based, anti-physical body religious worldview, as in Protestant Calvinism and Jansian Roman Catholic interpretations of Christianity; neither are Chinese views of sexuality based on dualistic rational-mind vs. emotional anti-bodily urges. Rather, the general Chinese view is that sex is a natural, compelling human urge, easily capable of obsession and abuse and, thus, in need of balance and moderation. However, since sexuality is a taboo subject in Chinese society, little research about actual sexual practices has ever been published.

Furthermore, during the first half of this century, particularly in the 1920s and 1930s, the trends of modernization and nationalism in Republican China opened the door to many of the "progressive modern" attitudes about sexuality now regarded as quite faulty. Among these ideas were the need to preserve the finite amount of male sperm to maintain health and the enormous emphasis on "scientific medicine" and eugenics; there were strong prohibitions against masturbation, homosexuality, and menopause for reasons which stand discredited today.[93] Also, in China there has been no psychotherapeutic tradition of treating sexual disorders, nor traditions of public talk therapy from to gather information necessary to generalize about Chinese attitudes and values about sexuality. In general, there is simply little information about particular Chinese aspects of sexuality other than those biological facts found among all of us which are then inferred and filtered through the multifaceted lens of Chinese culture. Historically, Chinese ideas about sexuality, pleasure, and our physical bodies reflect a wide range of cultural ideas.

While all known cultures are amazingly complex, within the highly sophisticated tradition of Chinese culture there remains a tension between the non-Cartesian desires of the demanding body-as-physical-person (shen) and the calculating self-as-heart-affections-mind (xin).[94] To some degree, this tension can be kept in check by means of self-chosen pragmatic strategies within the realm of Chinese social possibilities — *what can be gotten away with*. As in most societies to some degree, these strategies are chosen to gratify the relentless human striving for sex, power, fame, security, and gourmet food in a medically safe, physically satisfying, and socially acceptable way while maintaining family and guanxi obligation and opportunities.[95]

During most of Chinese history prior to this century, the predominate attitude about sex was that sexual activities were to be restricted and channeled within the family-oriented Confucian view of society. The goals of such social channeling were to support family and social stability, produce legitimate well-raised children, and gratify the constant and understandably pleasure-filled natural human urges of heterosexual sexual relations. Of course, prostitution played its usual socially regulated and exploitative role throughout most of Chinese history, although strong exceptions to that role exist today in the PRC and somewhat less so in Singapore.

As a part of the PRC's program to limit population growth, the government encourages marriages at a later stage in life, 26 to 29 years old for men and 24 to 26 years old for women. In the countryside, the average ages at marriage are somewhat younger. In the other Chinese populated countries such as Singapore, Malaysia, and Taiwan, to the extent that they have adopted less traditional ways, marriage is still heavily influenced by the tradition of arranged marriages. Thus, families still play a central role in the ultimate decision of a man and a woman to marry and begin their own lineage of children within the larger family/clan.

Divorce is legal in the PRC and in all other countries where the Chinese have large majority or minority populations. Divorce is avoided if possible and a wide range of family, friends, co-workers and neighborhood people will attempt to help with reconciliation. However, while there remains some stigma attached to divorce, especially for divorced women, the cruel almost trivial "sufficient reasons" for a husband to divorce his wife have been greatly reduced. These included being talkative, inability to bear a son or being disrespectful to her parents-in-law![96]

Children

All people love their children, but the Chinese, whether in the PRC or in any one of the numerous countries to which the overseas Chinese have migrated and usually prospered, are particularly strong in their emphasis and focus upon their children and their future. Moreover, differences in child-rearing practices drive home the importance and visibility of cultural differences. While parents living outside of the PRC are not restricted as to the number of children they can have, those within the PRC must conform to the " … family-planning policies begun in 1979 that limits each couple to one child … [Thus] spoiled only-children have become so common that Chinese have dubbed them "the little emperors".[97]

By tradition, a child is considered 1-year-old at birth. A second year is usually added at the Chinese lunar New Year.[98] Thus, it is possible that a baby girl born three weeks before the holiday would be considered two years old at six weeks! (Obviously, Chinese-Americans reckon these relationships in both North American ways and the traditional Chinese ways.)

An important milestone in the child's early life is the "first month" celebration, especially for the first-born boy or girl; later children will be celebrated in somewhat similar fashion but usually without the fanfare focused on the first-born. For first-borns, relatives and friends are invited to a fine dinner which includes the traditional red-stained shells of hardboiled eggs. Sometimes, instead of a celebration, red eggs and sweets are sent to the homes of relatives and friends.

In some very traditional overseas Chinese communities and in the PRC, a good child is said to be "guai", a well-behaved and obedient child.[99] In the PRC, a warm, caring, strict emphasis is placed upon group values which are taught from a very early age, including obedience, de-sexualization, nonaggression, and achievement-oriented behavior. Discipline to discourage or punish nonconformity includes isolation from the group and shaming the child in front of others. Many children are restricted from doing what they want to do when they want to do it by being swaddled from birth through the child's very early years, perhaps for as many as three or four years. A

Chinese physician's justification for swaddling was " … to recreate the physical security and warmth of the womb".[100] Critics who are partial to different visions of what humans should be have held that Chinese rearing practices inhibit some learning patterns and tend to produce docile, nonindividualistic children and passive, docile adults:

> Thumbsucking, pacifiers, security blankets and cuddly stuffed animals are not allowed. Toilet training starts within months of birth. Crawling, the main way infants learn new skills, is discouraged. Left-handedness is a no-no.[101] There is much less opportunity to explore by moving around, and this restricts your world view and your sense of being able to act independently.[102]

However, these practices are viewed as means toward the general Chinese ideal that children should be obedient and respectful towards their parents, relatives, teachers, and other elders: "For Conformity, Children Are Bound by Custom".[103]

Chinese societies, for the most part, exhibit low levels of aggressive behavior:[104]

> Low homicide rates, an aversion to violent sports, and an absence of public brawling are just some of the consequences of the vigilant response by parents, teachers, and other caretakers to any hostility or willfulness in their charges.

It is almost always appropriate to bring a gift for the children when a gift for a Chinese acquaintance (or informant) would be awkward. Gifts for the child could be clothing, rings, toys, talcum powder, etc. The joyous colors for gifts are red, pink, and yellow. Also, always give things in even numbers. Flowers are NOT appropriate, for they suggest sickness in the mother.

Also, avoid any representation of a stork. For example, in the subculture of the Hokkien province, the stork resembles the heron, and there, the heron is a well known symbol for the death of a woman. This is indicated in the funeral procession by the presence of a heron image on the hearse.

While it is a safe rule that one should never touch a child on the head among traditional families, interest in children and family is reassuring and may be an avenue through which to develop communication and mutual trust in the Chinese-American community. For example, bring your own children into the Chinese community on a day off and let a genuine shared interest in Chinese ways be observed in you and in your children. For those Chinese who recognize you, your role as a responsible father and the head of a family will not be lost on them; it might (but only might) help your attempts to develop better community relations.

Death and Funerals

Today, in most North American cities of moderate size, there are one or two funeral homes — usually owned and administered by non-Chinese who receive most of the funeral business of the Chinese community.[105] Just as you should get to know the motel mangers near the interstate exits in your community with whom to communicate about nomadic gangs, you should get to know these funeral directors so that they will recognize you if you attend to observe who shows up at a funeral. They may also be able to identify suspects or visitors who pay their respects at odd hours or in groups — identities that would be relevant to you and the department's intelligence database.

Chinese-American funeral services in North America are an amazing combination of traditional funeral practices from the homeland province, villages, and clans, as well as adaptations of local customs from within the Chinese-American communities. To many non-Chinese, the funeral and the procession to the gravesite may seem noisy, strange, and inappropriate because of the blowing of horns, the wailing of mourners, and the beating of gongs. However, the critic ought to remember that one's grief and pain at the death of a child or a parent hurts just as much for Chinese and any Asian-Americans as it does for any other North Americans. Furthermore, one's inability to fully express one's grief is as much of a problem in the Chinese language as it is in English.

Traditionally, in China in most cities and among some of the well-to-do in the countryside, the bodies of the deceased are cremated. Otherwise, as in the PRC, traditional burials mounds are found throughout the countryside. Unless the deceased was very wealthy, he/she is usually buried (or cremated) within one week; if wealthy, he may not be buried until 29 to 49 days after death.

In both traditional and modern funerals, there remains the cultural assumption that the proper performance of the rituals and practices associated with the dead will guarantee happiness for the deceased and good luck for the future and living family members. Thus, every appropriate effort is made to ensure the wellbeing and comfort of the deceased.

Funeral Behavior

The following are some suggestions of appropriate behavior for visitors expressing their sympathy and/or attending a Chinese funeral. Visitors who come to pay their respects to the mourning family are usually expected to arrive in the evening after 7:00 p.m. Appropriate dress should be dark colored or white (the color of death); avoid bright colors. The coffin is usually behind a screen at the foot of which the Asian visitor should bow three times. There is often a small opening to allow the *hun* aspect of the soul escape to be judged in the underworld. Family members usually kneel at the coffin; visitors do not. If (for whatever reason) you kneel, the family mourner should burn the long joss sticks for you.[106] Then, after withdrawing slightly, you may offer quiet sympathetic comments about the deceased.

At the funeral, either Buddhist or Daoist monks or priests usually chant prayers and sacred texts for the welfare of the deceased. Paper replicas of prized material things — cars, televisions, houses, furniture, jewelry — are ritually offered and then burnt as gifts sent toward heaven (tien) to accompany and comfort the deceased. The gravesite is to be selected by a geomancer, a practitioner of *Feng Shui* (see below) who will determine a favorable location for the grave. The grave will face south and be protected by high ground. Ideally, the grave is to be enclosed/protected by a horseshoe-shaped wall at the front of which is placed the gravestone (tombstone). A small table holds joss sticks and/or offerings of fruit.

Some other details related to funerals and death are[107]

- White is the color of death and mourning, and it is the color of the paper flower funeral wreaths exhibited in the funeral procession as it progresses towards the grave site.
- Gifts of odd amounts of money ($30, $70) in an odd number of bills (three $10 bills) are common and should be distributed in white or brown envelopes, if one is a close friend, or in red envelopes, if one is a respectful visitor.[108]
- Since handkerchiefs are sometimes given to mourners at a funeral and suggest sadness, mourning, or the potential breakup of a friendship, they are inappropriate gifts.
- White, blue, and black are colors associated with funerals and thus are inappropriate colors for gifts or other items.
- "Clock" (zhong, STC 6945) in Mandarin Chinese sounds the same (homophonous) as "end", that is, death, and is to be avoided.
- Odd numbers and separate, single things suggest separation, loneliness and death. Always give gifts in pairs or multiples of an even number.
- Flowers may be sent to the site of the funeral.

Education

For at least 4000 years, in one form or another, Chinese civilization has honored and encouraged education and the acquisition of the beneficial skills and humanizing knowledge of a good education. That tradition continues today as North American college admissions officers sort through an astounding number of high-quality applicants who are of Chinese and other

Asian ethnic backgrounds. The universities and schools in the PRC, Taiwan, Singapore reflect this emphasis upon respect for the written word, history, scholarship, memorization, and tremendous self-discipline. Much less emphasis is placed upon the skills, knowledge, and school experiences cherished by American education such as: flexibility in what is taught, questioning of authority, verbal dexterity and argumentation, creativity, problem-solving skills, athletic ability, personal fulfillment, and social skills. A child is not taught "to agree to disagree" in Chinese general education; one is taught to be able to repeat back to the teacher what the teacher considers worth knowing for a child at a certain stage in his/her education. As is obvious, the forms of teaching, the institutional organization, and the degrees of political and academic freedom reflect the particular culture and political ideologies of specific counties.

Although many organizational forms of Chinese education, classical and modern, have been focused on rather rigorous rote memorization and a conservative curriculum, it has produced the type of personnel with the technical knowledge and skills the Chinese tradition deemed most valuable. The Chinese Confucian emphasis on education as the means for a deep understanding of one's social and private moral relationships was to build the foundations for social harmony and public and private morality. This view of the social and moral utility of education has pervaded the cultures of Taiwan, Japan, Korea, Vietnam, Singapore, and other parts of Asia.

Therefore, Chinese respect for the *moral utility* of education rather than the occupational utility cannot be stressed too strongly. In addition to its subtle humanistic and aesthetic examination of the themes of social harmony, stability, and the pragmatic politics, Chinese education was also accompanied by the stultifying effects of rigidity and rote memorization developed to an amazing degree. In balance, traditional Chinese educational and cultural developments were achieved by an admirable people living in a dangerous world riddled with poverty, sickness, famine, floods, human greed, and treachery. Given these factors, traditional Chinese teachers have much of which they can be, and are, deservedly proud of.

Physical and Mental Illness

Within the Chinese tradition, there is a very long complex tradition of medicine to cure physical illness. However, there is no tradition in China which addresses, identifies, or cures mental illness, per se. That is, there is no tradition of a systematic description and treatment of mental illness by means of such familiar activities as psychotherapy and psychiatry; these ideas are simply absent. Overall, the tradition of Chinese medicine is quite different from the germ-based, science and art of healing common to 20th century Anglo-European medicine. Of course, neither tradition is without its variations. For example, there are very significant cultural differences in the emphasis and implementation of Western medicine among France, Great Britain, Germany, and the U.S.[109] Similar variations exist in the Chinese traditions, as well. Although a few examples of Chinese medicine are known in the West and are sometimes compatible with Anglo-European medicine (such as acupuncture and acupressure), Chinese medicine is based upon quite different assumptions, relationships, and patterns of treatment. A very simplified description follows.

In general, the Chinese distinguish between drugs used in traditional Chinese medicine and the multitude of herbs (about 45,000) used in Chinese folk medicine. Before the introduction and partial synthesis of Anglo-European germ- and virus-based medicine, the standard source on disease was the *Encyclopedia of Plants and Roots* (Ben-cao gang-mu) compiled about four hundred years ago, in which the qualities and medical uses of plants and herbs are described.

> More than two thousand years ago, attempts were made to provide Chinese medicine with a theoretical basis, by correlating it with the system of the five elements, or 'states of being' (wu xing). Illness occurred when the balance of forces in the body was not in equilibrium with the environment. Correct uses of the adequate medicine could restore lost harmony, and the patient got better. To take a simple example: a cold could be cured by taking a medicine that contained warmth. Due balance between warmth and cold, between dryness and moistness, is of universal significance over the whole corpus of Chinese medicine.[110]

Today, many herbs in use are not recognized as "official" drugs in traditional Chinese medicine, and some of the herbs (which seems quite exotic to us) are used by traditional "herb doctors". Today, in small stores in Chinatown, one finds bear galls, deer horns, various seeds, chrysanthemum petals, grubs for cleaning wounds, and other exotic Chinese pharmacopoeia.[111]

There are significant variations in Chinese medicine including differences in organizational principles, different assumptions about the body, and systematic systems and vocabularies. An example of these differences can be illustrated by examining the general principle of "qi" (this is pronounced "chee" and is also transliterated in the Wade-Giles system as "Chi", (STC 3051).[112] Qi is held to be a central energy force which is found not only in humans but in everything in Nature:[113]

> Qi … follows routes through the human body called meridians, or channels. There are twelve major channels divided into three parts: (1) the limbs through which the channel flows; (2) the modality of yin and yang, which describes the type of qi/chi energy in the channel; and (3) the body organ to which the channel is linked.… in Western herbalism, most drugs are used in their crude form. In China, however, almost all drugs are processed before use. This increases their clinical effect and, allegedly, enhances the quality and safety of the medicines.

In her very readable book, *Chinatown: a Portrait of a Closed Society,* Gwen Kinkead offers an interesting description of visiting two practitioners of traditional Chinese medicine. As Ms. Ng, a former head doctor in a hospital in Guangdong Province near the city of Guangzou (formerly Canton) explained:[114]

> In our view of disease, any imbalance in the systems causes illness. Imbalance can be between yin and yang, hot and cold, excess and deficiency, or the five adverse climates and emotions … or in a person's qi — the invisible life principle animating all living things.

Western medical science, with its demonstrably effective emphasis upon empirical germ-theory and demonstrations between biochemical causes and effects, is often unreceptive to alternate medical systems that do not meet its public, empirical scientific standards of verification and falsifiability. Worse, Chinese traditional herbal medicine has severe limits, for it cannot be used to discover the pathology of a disease nor is it any substitute for surgery.[115] On the other hand, "for example, [in] post-radiation cancer therapy, they [Chinese herbal medicines] have proved useful in preventing hair loss and increasing stamina by activating the body's immune systems in ways Western researchers cannot explain."[116]

Mental illness and the occasional need for medical treatment among Asians and Asian-Americans is a field in which cross-cultural aspects rise to the surface immediately. A summary of the major problems related to what we term mental illness follows.[117]

First, as mentioned above, the interlocking components of a Chinese mindset — the themes of past orientation; the quest for social harmony and stability; social ranking and senior authority figures in the father, the educated, and the governmental bureaucrat; the potential shame of resorting to outside medical help; the difference between a fundamental emphasis on individualism vs. collectivism — all generate significant cultural differences. These, in turn, generate a significant psychological tension regarding the mental health of Asians or Asian-Americans undergoing the inherent stress of being in a bi-cultural situation:[118]

> Racism, discrimination, language barriers, immigration traumas, and financial problems often complicate the process of development for Asian Americans.... They must work out how many aspects of their original cultural heritage to maintain and how many aspects of their new cultural home to take on.

Second, because there is no tradition of "mental medicine" in China, some Chinese and some Chinese-Americans often *experience* psychological problems in the form of physical symptoms and clearly expect that the way to cure them is to receive medicine for these symptoms and advice about how to use it; often, they do not expect nor accept extended talk-therapy common with many psychotherapists, psychologists, and psychiatrists.[119]

Third, discussion in talk-therapy of one's personal intimate knowledge and feelings and of the family are strongly prohibited in most Asian cultures. A display of emotion or family discord is both very bad form and embarrassing. Thus, these cultural expectations render such discourse unexpected, distasteful, and very uncomfortable for the Asian or Asian-American patient.

Fourth, "most models of therapy emphasize independence and focus on helping the individual develop an increased sense of autonomy, while many Asian cultures place a high value on interdependence and maintenance of strong ties to one's family."[120]

Fifth, mental illness and its explicit treatment raises the possibility of bringing disgrace and loss of "face" on the whole family/clan for not handling their own problems within the group.

Sixth, this absence of any familiar knowledge about psychotherapy, even if only potential knowledge, clouds the Asian person's response. Then, in light of this response (or its absence) may often be interpreted as a resistance to getting at their problems or as an attempt to shift the responsibility for resolution to someone else, "when in fact it reflects genuine cultural differences in how emotional distress is *experienced and understood*".[121]

Seventh, in many Asian contexts of mental health, there is a "tendency to view problems in biological terms [not psychological terms] or as fully under the individual's conscious control.... Asian Americans generally believe that mental health is maintained by avoiding bad thoughts and exercising will-power ... [and who, if mentally troubled, often think of] themselves and others as weak-willed."[122]

Eighth, in the following excerpt, I have substituted the word "investigator" for "therapist" and "suspect" for "client"; I suggest that it fits quite well.

> How families work out the amount of separateness and connectedness among family members is heavily influenced by culture as well as by individual family dynamics.... but over-involvement [of suspect with family or gangs] needs to be understood and evaluated in the context of Asian, not

> American cultural norms. Investigators working with Asian-American suspects need to be aware of the natural support networks that exist within the family and Asian community as a whole.... It would not be unusual for an Asian-American suspect to expect his investigator to be involved with and available to his whole family or to include other family members in problem-solving efforts.[123]

As police know only too well, law enforcement personnel who are "real friends" will be called upon to help and advise their Asian-American friends/informants about overt or disguised "psychological" problems. Some understanding of the differences in culture newly arrived Asians all feel and confront from time to time, plus some knowledge about the common attitudes they may have about mental illness, may assist police in offering a helpful and appropriate response. Also, such knowledge will help in interrogations, interviews, using witnesses, and educating prosecutors and judges.

Values and Law (Fa) in a Naturalistic World View

We all start with the assumptions about values and laws our own world view. In inquiring about the general Chinese world view, our own assumptions will probably block our paths to an accurate understanding as often as different Chinese assumptions. Thus, we will start with descriptions of differences and contrasts. First, as outlined in more detail in Chapter 19 on Confucianism, Daoism, and Buddhism, the Chinese view of the universe is *not* the result of the assumed creative powers and intentions of either one god or several gods. Therefore, the world is not a product of "God's will"; it *is* a product of natural, not supernatural forces as in the Judeo-Christian-Islamic traditions. Although there are occasional similarities between these world views, there are no conceptual equivalents of the Anglo-European religiously-based God-created finite universe.

Second, as noted above, there is not a clear equivalent of Natural Law theory for justifying semi-absolute values and social principles which in turn, are often used to justify Anglo-European civil and criminal law. In China, criminal law (fa), ethics, and morality/propriety (li) more often have their sources in deeply rooted public custom, the balancing functions of "face", and guanxi, historically sanctioned social obligations as shown in the Confucian, Neo-Confucian, and Legalist traditions. These sources contrast strongly with Anglo-European universal, semideductive inferences from Natural Law theory, Judeo-Christian and secular basic principles, and precedent-setting cases.

However, in Chinese civilization, there are other very deeply buried basic ideas and expectations about the world that shape their expectations and views of what is moral, lawful, and "reasonable". Some examples of the foundations of morality, are the Dao (Tao, the "natural way"), a sense that balance and harmony are built into the structure of the natural and social worlds; other basic values are a learned sense of virtue, obligations, reciprocity which we should follow; a deep respect for authority, learning, public, and private propriety (li), and the carefully taught possibility of discovering one's human-heartedness, a much debated sense of goodness allegedly possessed by all humankind.

With morality and propriety (li), there was of course, penal law (fa) as well. In ancient times, li meant rituals and codes of rites and ceremonies regarding social and religious institutions; fa meant quasi-legal hearings where judgments were passed regarding punishment. As Chinese society grew from clan/family-oriented values to those of a feudal society, both li and fa were inflated and expanded until they overlapped. Later, li became a term that included all the mores, customs, and values of society and their justifications in the moral character of both the ruler and his magistrates; fa slowly became a term that included threats and the implementation of punishment to enforce denials and violations of much of li. However, the justification of neither morality (li) nor penal law (fa) ever lost its close ties — the social glue of guanxi — with ranked, unequal social obligations and interfamily values. The appeals to justify laws and morals were not to supernatural gods or mosaic tablets from on high but to the moral obligations and fears of society and the hope that Confucian education would lessen the need for law. However, with the rise of the Legalist tradition of Han Fei Tzu, as in *The Book of Lord Shang*, there arose a shift in the purpose of law from enforcing li intimidation, deterence and its fear of punishment. Here the characteristics of the law (fa) shifted from quasi-moral sanctions to the objective, clear, explicit rule of law. Thus, law (fa) became a firm replacement and substitution for religion and morality, controlled for by the ruler for his own interests, who remained the only person immune from law. Once again, the values enshrined in law came not from the heavens, a religious-based view of the universe, but from the anticipations, fears, and collective efforts of men — men of property, men of education, and family-oriented people in society who looked to quasi-secular society rather than trans-secular sources for justifications of law. Thus, just as Christianity, Anglo-Saxon common law, and secular history remain the (oversimplified) basis of why and how things work for most Americans, guanxi, "face", secular history, Confucianism, and Legalism remain basic sources of why and how things work for most traditional Chinese.

From an Anglo-European perspective, the Chinese assumed a strong "naturalistic" rather than a religious-based view of the universe. Many Anglo-Europeans tend to link morality, ethics, and their justification with religion; the Chinese based their considerable moral and ethical views not on religion (except for the Buddhists) but in the more secular emphases of Confucianism and Legalism. While the Chinese tradition is not without great periods of religious fervor, the general Chinese world view lacks an equivalent of the Judeo-Christian "ultimate purpose (teleology)" presupposed in the God-created view of the universe. While there is a popular southern Chinese view of a world creator (developed by 11th century Neo-Confucianists) — ugly old Pan-gu — this mythology played almost no part in the sophisticated life of the Chinese elite from whom the basis of ethical, political, and social theory and practice evolved. In short, the general Confucian, Legalist, and Daoist traditions are not what most Americans (or Anglo-Europeans) would recognize as fundamentally religious-oriented traditions. For example, Confucius withheld his opinions about the existence or role (if any) of religious deities. Compared with North-American single-god religious traditions, within the more naturalistic Chinese world view religious entities certainly abound. Big and little deities, gods, godlings are found everywhere and at all levels — family, house, local, earth, city, and national. However, these are not creator gods, nor are they the sources of ethics, morality, and law. Very loosely, they are divine bureaucrats who oversee their small domains and are the "contact points" for people who wish to make requests of them.

In contrast, the "ultimate teleological purpose" common to the Judaic-Christian-Islamic tradition is a theological view of the universe created by a single, causal-agent deity for which there is a simple order or structure and an implicit ultimate purpose. That is, there is an implicit purpose built into divine creation within the Judaic-Christian-Islamic traditions; most Jews, Christians, and Moslems would deny that God created the universe merely on a whim. Therefore, He did it for some purpose and built into that implicit purpose is Natural Law, partially upon which our varied traditions of civil law are based. This is not the Chinese view.

The effects of these hidden contrasts about world views run very deep. To understand some of the whys of Chinese thought and their contrasts with our North American views we shall look at these contrasts with care; they deserve scrutiny. For example, from the implicit sense of a purposeful universe, a "teleological" universe, there has evolved the Anglo-European sense that the development of personal morality is not merely personally or socially desirable, but that it is *cosmically necessary* that is, God willed it and needs it. Also stemming from that implicit sense of a purposeful universe is the American optimistic sense of progress through time, the idea that social justice involves public fairness and equality — that the social and legal rules are applicable to all, that they are universal. Think about what the following familiar sentences mean. "Things are gradually getting better." " Justice is blind." "There is a reason for whatever has happened." These are basic ideas within the Anglo-European, Judaic-Christian theories of history and they express cultural values held particularly strongly by North Americans; they are grounded in our world views of progress, cosmic purpose, and equality before the law as well as before God.

The Chinese world view was and is different. Optimism and historical progress were not major ideas in the Chinese world view. Before 1948, there was maintained in the Chinese image of themselves and their expectations, a world view which was not wedded to universal social rules and laws equally applicable to all. Values, obligations, and one's world view was never universal for the Chinese; it was almost always context-restricted to the incidents of secular history. It did not hold for "all cases and for all people", but only for those cases related to the needs and mutual obligations of one's family/clan/village/guanxi.

The next level of supreme value, held almost as strongly as that of the family, is that of being Chinese, being *Han*. For most of Chinese history, sheer survival was the desperate goal of the non-elite classes (the peasants, farmers), who constituted over 95% of the Chinese population. It is equally true, that such a survivalist outlook was shared by most of Europe until the last two or three centuries. However, the vast majority of Chinese never experienced even the possibilities of the relative affluence hoped for and experienced by many European and the North American immigrants and postimmigrants of the last 300 years. Of course, the degree of literacy was much lower as was the available means for acquiring education and systematic public knowledge.

Another contrast is the universal sense of Anglo-American "fair play". This constitutes an example of a largely untranslatable "common sense" value for which there are few equivalents in traditional Asian cultures. The American and British sense of "fair play" is that set of ideas and assumptions about how we and the world should be aligned, with an underlying principle of cosmic justice and universal benevolence built into the structure of creation. In short, this simply does not translate without tortuous paraphrasing into Chinese, or into Japanese or Korean. This does not mean that Asian cultures lack the idea of fairness or equity; they are fair and loyal, honor their obligations to others, and are certainly honest people, about as often as we are. However, the Chinese world view lacks the North American/European expectation of a theologically driven sense of "historical progress" (Meliorism, that things get better through time) and the constant quest for and expectation of the ultimate betterment of social justice and equality within society.

A general Chinese view of fate (ming, STC 0730) means "destiny", a partial sense of "predestination", and "that's the way things are". Fate was what can and might happen if one did not take steps such as prayer or formal sacrifice to thwart the approaching situation. It was not the fate decreed by God or by Buddhist karma. Thus, good intentions and acting at the right time could allow one to escape a careful prediction of future disaster. Good timing and clever precautions might well thwart an unwanted event and these are quite human, secular qualities.

Thus, the Chinese take (perhaps) a more realistic view of human differences and acknowledge the "obvious and natural" inequalities of birth, social position, intelligence, talents and luck. Although the Chinese may desire these values and sometimes pass public laws to encourage them, and insofar as they retain some remnants of their Marxist-Maoist view of history, the traditional Chinese historical world view did not lead them to expect that their historical experiences would exhibit historical progress, "fair play", social equality, or equality of justice; nor did that traditional world view lead them to expect the ultimate betterment of social justice and equality within society. In contrast, most North Americans habitually expect to find these qualities being supported and valued in human history.[124]

Thus, there was never developed in China to any great extent, the sense of equal public responsibility theoretically shared by all citizens which extended beyond family, clan, and village or province. The surprise with which many PRC Chinese react to our volunteer organizations and especially our public blood donations illustrates (not proves) this nondeveloped (not undeveloped) expectation of universal public values independent of social rank. Thus, the family/clan, not the state, remains the core of Chinese society. One could say that many clever and industrious Chinese see themselves as semi-independent but very small cogs in a very large impersonal social machine, a machine riddled with all kinds of ranked and shifting relationships. The aim of successful individuals then, is to attain a position within the social machinery from which to exercise the maximum power for the benefit of themselves and those to whom they feel responsible. A contrast has been noted in most Americans who see the acquisition of wealth or power as enabling them either to "drop out" of or rise above the daily constraining structures of society.

Today, out of necessity, sheer pragmatism, attempted efficiency, poor resources, and poverty, the educated, sophisticated Chinese may wish to learn from the Western barbarians for a few decades, but in the end they feel that they really do not need us and that in the long run they can and will do it all better, more efficiently and with far more subtlety and grace. In the eyes of many Chinese, they are still the "middle kingdom", the deserved center of the world. Moreover, that quiet but enormous sense of pride in being Han, being Chinese, is a very deep source of determination, discipline, and ultimate superiority (see Chapter 15). These factors are coupled with a world view which assumed social and economic inequalities and which lacked the universal idea of inevitable religious progress within a purposefully created universe. In other words, justice was never blind in China and thus the police were neither "blind" nor politically impartial.

To bring our comparisons of values and assumptions to a close, even as the present PRC government seems to move down the path toward political change or down toward the path of another decade of social convulsions such as the Cultural Revolution of the 1970s, these habits of mind, these cultural mindsets will continue to function within the Chinese cultural software, their versions of "common sense". Finally, these remain the context-restricted habits of mind: known by *all* peoples as "our way of life, the way things are and obviously should be".

The Triad's Threat of Revenge

Compared to an informer from either the Sicilian Mafia, or, in the U.S., the La Cosa Nostra (LCN), a Chinese informer against a Traid group is usually far more convinced that the Triad (not the Tong) will hunt him down and/or will severely injure his extended family. Thus, the recruitment of Chinese-American informers is sometimes far harder because the threats of revenge and exposure, and the resulting loss of "face" and shame on family, are greater.

Moreover, many (if not most) former LCN soldiers who become government informants and are protected under the federal government's witness protection program. Some stumble and reveal their new identities by "calling home" in one form or another. Some give themselves away by trying to get some culturally important item such as Uncle Benvenuto's Palermo sausage or by contacting someone in their former Italian or Mafia guanxi. Likewise, the high-context Chinese lifestyle encourages the dangerous maintenance of a Chinese informant's all-important guanxi. Also, for Chinese and Vietnamese in North America, there are fewer places to go and smaller populations within which to assume a new identity than is true for Mafia members. Thus, it is the very understandable attempt to maintain certain cultural values and culture-bound lifestyles that often identifies Mafia and/or Asian members of the federal witness program, and thus allows them to be traced and revenge to be taken. For a Chinese or any other Asian informant, it is more difficult to disappear into another Chinese or Asian community and divorce themselves from their parents, former friends, and guanxi. Thus, Chinese-Americans are somewhat more reluctant to be turned and enter the federal witness program. Of course, because exceptions abound, this explanation is offered as an indication of general behavior, not a prediction about whether a specific individual can be turned.

Furthermore, Chinese often refuse to testify in open court because of fear, loss of "face", and the shame it brings upon their families. It is not that they lack personal bravery, but it is, in part, the complex cultural differences in their images of themselves and their larger social frameworks which make them different than most individualistic autonomous North Americans and Anglo-Europeans (see Chapter 6).

Feng Shui, (STC 7364 3055 0594 0592) and "Spirits"

Geomancy (feng shui) is a particular Chinese lore and practice reputed to be as old as the 10th century B.C. It consists of a body of knowledge and calculated recommendations to ensure that gravesites, construction sites, houses, furniture, and other positioned things are placed in harmony with the natural forces and environmental contours of the earth. These natural forces are symbolized by dragons and other semimythological beasts of the countryside.

Feng shui ("wind and water") grew out of the observations and prescientific lore of an agricultural society. As with Chinese and Buddhist astrology, it has generated an extensive, if not arcane, body of internally consistent and coherent knowledge about Chinese laws of Nature, complete with charts and symptoms of both problematic and benevolent environmental configurations and locations. It has been claimed that one justification for the location of certain Buddhist temples was that they tended to "improve geomantic influences (feng shui) and thereby avert natural disasters".[125] On the other hand, if there is a sharp angle to a roof across the street, near one's upper window, this would be bad feng shui and hence bad luck. Of course, a mistakenly chosen location can be corrected during building or planning, but a feng shui specialist — a geomancer — must be consulted and his recommendations must be followed. One of the new hotels outside of Hong Kong is distinguished by the large open circle in its middle portions. The builders thus accommodated the need for unobstructed relations between the nearby mountains, the sea, and the swimming pool.

As Retired San Francisco Police Inspector John McKenna noted: "From early colonial days the British authorities have played the game in utilizing the Fung Shui masters' services in site selection for police, fire and other public buildings." Accompanying feng shui are ideas about the characteristics of "spirits", those good and bad forces that need to be honored, placated, and thwarted. Sometimes, such spirits were thought to be ancestors who were not properly honored and supported with food and ritual or who were improperly buried according to the groundrules of feng shui. One interesting assumption held throughout most of Southeast Asia is that spirits and bad luck or good luck cannot turn corners; that they must travel in a straight line. Thus, corners are a protection against their entering a dwelling or institution:[126]

> The siting of the entrances of the Hang Seng [Hong Kong] Bank as diagonal to the road to stop money flowing out, or having to turn right or left upon entering certain buildings to block the entrance against evil spirits who cannot handle corners causes no concern for the old China hand.... very

> seldom will you find a new house design where the stairs face right out the front or the back door. Mirrors, long respected in the history of China, are used to correct adverse Fung Shui situations. The Regent Hotel and the Hong Kong Bank headquarters have open space or walls of windows at their back. This is to allow the dragon occupants of the hills free access to swimming waters.

The influence of feng shui was also felt in many parts of southeast Asia. For example, among the Hmong tribes, geomancy (feng shui), known as loojmem, constituted guidelines whereby the "deceased must be buried at a certain time, along the loojmem, or veins of the dragon, which run through the mountains … [The dragon] has connotations of natural strength and energy and is associated with underwater creatures, royalty and ancestors."[127]

Thus these ideas of feng shui have pervaded most of Asia in some form or another and certainly remain important in the different Chinese societies spread throughout the world. Hence, they remain relevant for Asian crime investigators as well. As Inspector John McKenna stated:[128]

> Any officer whose career takes him into Asian investigations should be conversant in these beliefs and understand Feng Shui and numerology. It is imperative as even today these elements play their part in Triad activities. These hoodlums are believers and followers of these principles as Fung Shui may determine "joss" (good luck or bad). Propitious dates and numbers may set the tone for the date and location of a crime, the target site or the victim and his address. Certain locations or addresses reflect good "joss" or bad. If an officer can understand these sciences, then one may be able to further the intelligence gathering for the investigation or interview. It should not be treated as a great mystery, but as an asset in furthering the determining facts of a case. It was a tool used quite effectively by British police in Shanghai and in Hong Kong as well as police forces in the Portuguese enclave of Macao.

Make no mistake, not only traditional Chinese but some internationally oriented, technically sophisticated Asian people — no matter how expensive their Rolexes and their Mercedes — may take feng shui very, very seriously. On occasion, Asian crime investigators and intelligence analysts should, too.

Food Prejudices and Uses

There are many sources that describe the amazing varieties of Chinese food, noting the virtues and special styles of Canton, Beijing, Sichuan, and Shanghai and the "lesser" types, the Mongol and Manchu. Attention here will be focused on aspects which may be relevant to an Asian crime investigator. Some culinary prejudices are worth knowing. For some southern Chinese:

- Both the idea and the smell of cheese make them feel sick to their stomachs.
- The smell of lamb is very repugnant.
- Drinking cold liquids during a traditional dinner is considered repulsive.
- Drinking cold liquids during mealtime is considered unhealthy.

According to one experienced writer about the PRC Chinese, some untraveled naive Chinese, usually peasants with access to television, have tended to view some North Americans as those "huge Americans [who] eat gigantic meals with disgusting amounts of meat and hardly any vegetables. Little wonder these white-skinned ghosts are all overweight and bloated."[129]

As noted in the "Do's and Don'ts" (see Chapter 4), the availability of Asian food is a more important piece of psychological-social leverage to most Chinese (not necessarily Chinese-Americans) than most Americans imagine. Therefore, when interrogating a Chinese suspect, order the appropriate regional food for a carryout lunch or dinner. Let him pick his favorite dish from the restaurant he prefers. This may (or may not) give you some idea of the dialects he might speak. (On the other hand, lots of Americans love tacos, moussaka, and spring rolls.) You place the order in English and do not convey any words or phrases from Chinese or his native dialect. (You do not wish to convey the hidden message that Jimmy [Chi-Mei] must have been picked up. Who else would order X with "M-sauce" to be delivered to the South Precinct station?) Ordering the suspect's favorite food gives him "face" and he will not forget it.

Five Deep Cultural Mindsets 15

關係

Because these five sets of ideas — "face", self, collectivism, guanxi, and being Chinese — play such a pivotal role in the cultural background of the Chinese and Chinese-Americans, law enforcement officers and analysts will encounter them sooner or later. Also, in light of the multi-level structure of this book, these five interrelated topics are described in greater detail and depth.

"Face" (Mianzi) and Losing "Face" (Diu Lian)

To some degree, all societies possess some fear of the loss of "face" or honor, that required public and private image of ourselves we present to others. For example, when our boss "chews us out" in front of our subordinates, we lose "face". Thus, losing "face" is not something unknown to us. The difference in the Chinese (and Asian) attitude to loss of "face" is a matter of the degree of sensitivity. In contrast with comparable Chinese cultural traits, some of the reasons for this sensitivity may be, in part, that we are less crowded in North America but have existed as a unified nation for only for three centuries — only a blink of the eye of Chinese time. These admittedly incomplete reasons may be coupled with Anglo-European philosophical and religious traditions that emphasize individualism, personal independence, autonomy, and self-reliance. While some North Americans are extremely sensitive to notions of "face", the Chinese generally tend to put more emphasis upon "face", one's social reputation, one's public image and social predictability, one's rank or place in the social structure — that is, guanxi. Thus, "face" is a mixture of our public image of ourselves, to ourselves, and to others. It supports our dignity, our self-esteem, our sense of worth in the eyes of others. "Face" expresses and reflects Chinese notions of mutual obligations to other people about whom we care and to whom we have mutual obligations by virtue of birth, village, dialect, surname, or extra-family ties, such as Triads or hui.

Also, some China-born or first generation Chinese-Americans live in much smaller, culturally restricted communities — Chinatowns, for example — than do many Americans. This tends to inhibit the kind of directness that is prized by many North Americans, especially the young from U.S., but is usually incompatible with explicit "face" and the respect due the social rank and the older members of a society. Coupled with the sensitivity about rank, "face" and guanxi are the basis for establishing trust.

Our indifference to different cultural values and our ignorance and indifference to how we appear through the cultural sunglasses of others with whom we wish to cooperate often hinders our aims.[134] While not everyone shares our cultural traits of directness and almost-instant intimacy, all of us dislike or fear "losing face", especially the Chinese. To gain sufficient experience with another person to cross cultures and establish trust, interpersonal comfortableness, mutual "face", and guanxi take more time than we usually expect. The point here is that we need to be aware of and to understand possible differences; then, if we so choose, we may change our behavior.

Figure 15 Late 19th century (1882?) portrayal of the (racist) "Crusade against the Chinese in San Francisco." (Courtesy of Sgt. Tom Perdue, San Francisco P.D.)

On the Chinese idea of losing "face" (diu lian), Cordell Hart states:[135]

> ... what we Westerners commonly think of as Chinese concern for [losing] "Face" is Chinese concern for their rank or position in the particular "kuan hsi" [guanxi]. To lose "face" is to lose position, and this does not mean simply to move down a notch in the hierarchy, it means to lose membership in the group. Whatever a Chinese may feel about losing "face", it does not alter the effect it has on his "kuan hsi" [guanxi, "network"]. A loss of "Face" may be embarrassing, but embarrassment is not a loss of "Face". [Words in brackets are the author's.]

However, the process of giving and receiving "face" can become rather complicated. In his excellent small book, *Beyond the Chinese Face: Insights from Psychology,* Michael Bond illustrates the subtleties of guanxi:[133]

> The process is fair, but in Chinese culture the *quid pro quo* is extended across greater periods of time than in other cultures and can be repaid indirectly to a third party. This is where the Chinese world of associates becomes so important. If an individual (X) needs a resource from a stranger (Y), he may be able to obtain it by "pulling on his relationship" (la guanxi) with an associate (Z), who is also associated with Y, so long as Z is indebted to X and Y is indebted to Z. This Z may then be able to repay the debt which he owes to X by allowing Y to repay the debt owed to Z indirectly by granting Z's request. Complicated!
>
> Of course the intermediary must first decide if he has sufficient 'Face' in his relationship with the more powerful person to ensure that the request is granted. After all, to ask and be refused would be acutely embarrassing, since one would clearly have miscalculated one's own 'Face value' and a man who does not know his place in Chinese society disrupts the fine balance of privilege and obligation.
>
> Given the importance of having Face and of being related to those who do, there is a plethora of relationships politics in Chinese culture. Name dropping, eagerness to associate with the rich and famous, the use of external status symbols, sensitivity to insult, lavish gift-giving, the use of titles, the sedulous avoidance of criticism, all abound, and require considerable readjustment for someone used to organizing social life by impersonal rules, frankness, and greater equality.

To amplify our understanding of the details of "face" we turn to a Chinese sociologist, Professor Yang:[134]

> Basically, ... ["face"] represents a tendency for a person to act in accordance with external expectations or social norms, rather than with internal wishes or personal integrity, so that he would be able to protect his social self and function as an integral part of the social network.

> Westerners and more modern Chinese give greater weight to their own personal standards in making the same behavioral decisions. Yang ... considers that some consequences of the traditional Chinese concern for the reaction of others are their submission to social expectations, social conformity, worry about external options, and non-offensive strategy in an attempt to achieve one or more of the purposes of reward attainment, harmony maintenance, impression management, Face protection, social acceptance, and avoidance of punishment, embarrassment, conflict, rejection, ridicule, and retaliation in a social situation.

The application of proper "face" to the social framework sometimes results in what is called "face-work":[135]

> Another strategy which is frequently used for enhancing one's influence over others in Chinese society is Face-work. Since an individual's power and status as perceived by others can guarantee an allocator's help, it is important for a Chinese to maintain his or her Face and to do Face-work in front of others in the mixed tie. He or she may deliberately arrange his or her appearance, and behave in a specific manner, in order to shape a powerful and attractive image when dealing with others. The more skilled this impression management is, the more likely the allocator will be to accept his or her request. If the allocator dares to reject his or her plea, the petitioner will lose Face and both sides may feel disaffected in the long run. Thus, the allocator is generally well advised to "do a favor" (renqing) and grant the request.

However, if law enforcement officers can utilize or manipulate the strong cultural value to save "face" — mutually — while maintaining an awareness of what other Chinese cultural possibilities may occur, the threat of the suspect's loss of "face" may provide a powerful tool with which to "massage" or pressure a potential informant.

Likewise, the relationship between "face" (mianzi) and one's position in the guanxi networking system is also important. There are only finite possibilities for any informant within any network (guanxi). It is important to realize these limits and not push the informant too hard to do something which is not culturally possible. To push him/her to violate what is culturally possible in his guanxi network requires the handler to understand the types and edges of those limits:[136]

> When the allocator is neither willing to grant the petitioner's request, nor to hurt his or her Face, the allocator may adopt the strategy of deferment and give no definite answer to the petitioner. The latter may then "forget" the request and both parties proceed as if it had never been made, but with

> a clear understanding of the limits to their relationship. Should, however, the request be pressed further, the potential for disruption to the two parties and their social network escalates seriously.

Thus, from the subtleties and dimensions of "face" we shall turn our attention to three equally important mindsets: self, collectivism, and guanxi.

Self and Its Status

For most periods of Chinese history, few worried about the nature of the self. Of course, few Chinese or Americans entertain this question today. Classical Chinese literature and philosophy — the roots of Chinese civilization — do not exhibit as much interest in the nature of the self as is found in much of the Greek-Roman-based, Anglo-European traditions. Moreover, on the basis of worldwide empirical evidence, Americans are the world's most individualistic people and the second most religious. It seems quite clear that Americans repeatedly emphasize the importance of self, of our individuality, no matter how vague the ideas may seem when examined closely.[137]

Certainly, Chinese and Vietnamese ideas of the self and its status differ considerably from the equally unexamined ideas of the self in North America. However, these differences are differences which make a difference with regard to behavior, values, community policing, interrogation, and intelligence. Furthermore, while some version of the idea of the self is found in almost all literate, theoretically articulate cultures, there is little agreement regarding what self is, its form, or its content. Obviously, to use the word "self" is not necessarily to be able to explain why it is important, in what form it exists, or exactly why it is valuable. For example, following is a contemporary legal and operative presupposition in Central African criminal trial law regarding the public examination of the self as evidence regarding whether a person is sane and thus able to stand trial. This African law explicitly:[138]

> forbids the examination and testing of defendants by forensic psychologists and psychiatrists to establish competency to stand trial under any circumstances, because the human psyche is considered a sacred and inviolable territory never to be revealed to profane investigations.

Other examples of the wide range of ideas about the self and the wider range of values about its permissible use — conceptual habits of mind — is found in the contrasting ideas of selfhood in the cultural traditions of the

Judeo-Christians (personal self/soul), Hindus (deep nonpersonal ātman), and the Buddhists (nirātman: everything is impermanent and the self neither exists nor nonexists). Equally varied are the social-cultural constructions of the persona of self from Java, Bali, and Morocco which are marvelously illustrated in Clifford Geertz's *Local Knowledge.*[139] Thus, ideas of what the self actually is and how it should be used are varied and not at all obvious. For most of Chinese thought, the self was not an effect of a god's creation, nor a uniquely valuable core of a person; nor was the self the essential feature which makes a person human or religious. Rather, the self was a product of natural forces which received its status and characteristics from within the social and cultural context of one's birth, family, education, and public social network of mutual dependence, obligations and responses to events. Very little of the personal self survived:[140]

> The Chinese considered that man's personality was a composite. When he dies, one part of it, the *hun* [the heavy animal aspect], rose up to join his ancestors in Heaven; another part, the *p'o* [the lighter aspect], lingered by the grave [near the wooden grave tablet, around 18 inches high and three inches wide with the deceased name inscribed on it] until it [the p'o] weakened, sank down in the earth to the Yellow Springs, and gradually expired; both these parts were animated by the *ch'i* or "life-breadth," which simply dispersed at death. If a man's descendants failed to nourish the hun and p'o with sacrifices, these became malevolent ghosts which wreaked havoc upon all who had neglected them. This is the reason for Chinese "ancestor worship" and, to a large extent, for the shape of Chinese society.

(See Chapter 19, "On Chinese and Vietnamese Ancestor Worship".)

Thus, what was important and essential about oneself was a product, an effect, a relational spin-off of the physical, social and family environment within which one was born and lives and to which one owes obligations and loyalty and from which one receives support and identity. Of course, within the Chinese social network, we find as many individual characteristics and traits as we find anywhere else in the world. However, oneself was neither seen as an essential essence nor unique personal inwardly-oriented core; nor was the self theologically related to the actions of a creator deity as in the Judeo-Christian tradition. It is also important to note that the cultural emphasis on social relations external to the individual's inner experiences does not mean that the Chinese or other Asians do not differ from one another. Rather, the general point is that their personal idiosyncratic individual characteristics are not held to be as important in and of themselves as their external social relations and their accompanying obligations, duties and collectivist expectations.

Collectivism: Individualism vs. Chinese Group Orientation

The style of individualism we North Americans emphasize to our children and in our schools is not an integral part of Chinese culture. Some significant XC differences can be found in what we expect out of life — what we expect it will bring us. A major difference between us and the Chinese is that American expectations are primarily focused on the individual and his/her individual expectations as an individual, not as a member of an extended family or of an all-important collective, guanxi group. Thus, our expectations are expressed in our attitudes about adversity and constitute an important part of our culture.

We North Americans are activists; we do things. Not only do we expect to feel fairly happy and remain generally optimistic, but we expect to do something about it if we are not happy or optimistic. We do not expect that human misfortune, depression, loneliness, or the loss of loved ones are the norm. Just as we view peace as the norm and war as a violation of it, so we view happiness (or at least its pursuit) as the norm — and that we should do things to ensure that we get it. Rationally, we know that bad things happen to everybody sooner or later. However, somehow we feel that we can and should remedy the situation and improve it, as if human misfortune was a disease and we have the unopened medicine bag. Indeed, we expect to experience and think we should experience more happiness than sadness, more successes than failures. Furthermore, some of us appear to others in our talking, acting, and planning as if we are immortal, although we would all readily admit the contrary. Thus, as seen by other cultures, our attitude about unhappiness seems to go against the grain of life's natural course.

We note, of course, that these differences about XC expectations are differences of degree, not differences in kind. For example, it is clear that all groups subordinate individual preferences to group preferences to some extent:[141]

> The Chinese have a strong anti-Good-Samaritan tradition; there has long been in China a superstitious belief that to aid a stranger in trouble may bring bad luck. Thus in both Hong Kong and the mainland, it is not uncommon for the victim of an accident to lie helpless in the roadway, or drown in a lake, before someone finally fetches the police or an ambulance. There is an intense reluctance to get involved in inauspicious situations or over-step the limits of one's strict obligations to one's segment of society.

In a famous study of the cross-cultural dimensions of over 50 cultures, Prof. G. Hofstede concludes that Americans are the most individualistic national group in the world.[142] His characterization of individualism and its corollary, power distance follows:[143,144]

> Individualism stands for a preference, for a loosely knit social framework in society wherein individuals are supposed to take care of themselves and their immediate families only. Its opposite, Collectivism, stands for a preference for a tightly knit social framework in which individuals can expect their relatives, clan, or other in-group to look after them in exchange for unquestioning loyalty (the word "Collectivism" is not used here to describe any particular political system). The fundamental issue addressed by this distinction is the degree of interdependence a society maintains among individuals. It relates to people's self-concept: "I" or "we".
>
> Power distance is the extent to which the members of a society accept that power in institutions and organizations is distributed unequally. This affects the behavior of the less powerful as well as of the more powerful members of society. People in large power distance societies accept a hierarchical order in which everybody has a place which needs no further justification. People in small power distance societies strive for power equalization and demand justification for power inequalities. The fundamental issue addressed by this dimension is how a society handles inequalities among people when they occur. This has obvious consequences for the way people build their institutions and organizations.

In Foreign Service Institute orientation materials for U.S. Department of State Foreign Service Officers and their families, the nonadversarial legal system and the collectivist emphasis of PRC society is noted. Here, everyone shares in the blame — even if, by our standards, one party was "not to blame":[145]

> Traditionally, the institutions possessing legal authority have viewed their role as one of achieving social harmony and consequently sought when making judgments to offer an equitable and harmonious resolution of the conflict, rather than to assign one party exclusive guilt. In general, it is assumed that in any dispute all of the disputing parties are at fault to some degree, and hence none should be awarded a judgment totally at the expense of any other.

Guanxi (Networking): A Key to Chinese Society

This is an amplification of the introduction to guanxi (STC 7070 0190) in Chapter 13, the sense of benefit-driven networking or "having connections"; also American "guanxi" is introduced and compared. In short, Chinese society, there and here, operates through guanxi. Many a North American businessman has learned this the hard way. After many attempts to work directly through "public" and explicit government offices, many have chosen to employ Chinese who have good guanxi. Only a handful of foreigners have good guanxi in China; they usually lack sufficient understanding of how small- and medium-sized Chinese businesses work through guanxi. S. Gordon Redding, author of *The Spirit of Chinese Capitalism* and a business professor at the University of Hong Kong, stated:[146,147]

> A recent study commissioned by the Hong Kong government suggests that local businesses investing in China typically spend 3% to 5% of operating expenses on "gifts and guanxi." … Other sources say that the guanxi margin is closer to 10% and recently had caused consternation as it rises as high as 20%.… The fuss over the questionable payments in business transactions betrays a deep-seated misunderstanding of alternative moral values. Chinese entrepreneurs build guanxi payments into their cost structure [just as Westerners anticipate burdensome legal fees]. To me, it's preferable to paying lawyers, and the lawyer is the functional equivalent to this kind of middleman [guanxi].… Within a circle where the trust is implicit, they keep their word. If you're an insider, you can trust. If you're an outsider, they'll screw you blind.
>
> To establish such trust, it helps not only to know the relevant language(s), but to possess other connections. As noted above, the connections of dialects, family and clan associations are of primary value, thus rendering the infiltration of such groups extremely difficult. Clannishness among the guanxi capitalists might be attributed to the fact that many, indeed, do business through their clans. But geographic links are considered even more important. A preponderance of Taiwanese investment in China, for example, is believed to be routed surreptitiously through Hong Kong banks to Fujian Province, just across the Taiwan Strait, to which the vast majority of Taiwan's 21 million people trace their [kinship] roots.

To illustrate guanxi in the larger context of Chinese mindset, we shall turn to a pedagogical ploy, an illustrative source more comfortable for those law enforcement personnel whose internal, culturally loaded model of reliable knowledge points towards sociology — the underlying cultural model of reliable knowledge presupposed by most university educated North American police. This discussion of guanxi is taken from the works of a Chinese sociologist in *The Psychology of Chinese People*:[148]

> Guanxi, which is a term used to denote particularistic ties in China, is a key concept for understanding Chinese behavior in social, … political, … and organizational … contexts. Having evolved from an agricultural society where the major social resources were controlled by a few powerful figures, traditional Chinese developed a complicated cultural system focused on li (courteous ritual), which encourages an individual to maintain hierarchical

> order and harmonious interpersonal relationships in a relatively stable and permanent social fabric. The Chinese cultural norm of li demands that an individual interact with people across different guanxi in accordance with various standards of social exchange. Thus the manipulation of interpersonal relationships has long been a strategy for attaining desirable social resources in Chinese society.

To explain how Chinese interact with one another through the guanxi "back door" rather than the "front door" of appealing to formal power relations or legal entitlements, K.K. Hwang[149] developed a conceptual framework for Chinese power games to integrate such indigenous Chinese concepts as guanxi (relationship), renqing (favor), mianzi ("face"), and bao (reciprocation):[150]

> The most popular strategy for strengthening ganqing and guanxi in China is to increase the social interaction between two parties deliberately, by visiting, the giving of gifts … and inviting the other person to banquets on such occasions as weddings, funerals, or birthday parties, and festivals in one's home village … Even if an individual is barely acquainted with a resource allocator, he or she may "pull" or "work" the connections (la guanxi or gao guanxi) by asking an intermediary of high social status to introduce the petitioner to the allocator and to solicit a favor from the allocator on his or her behalf. Once the strategy of utilizing guanxi has been successful, people generally say that a "back door" has been opened.

In the following description, a Harvard Professor of Education illustrated his awareness of the functional differences between Chinese and American ethics. The quotation contrasts the Chinese guanxi model of selected ethical relationships and guanxi obligations with the American, Anglo-European emphasis on appeals to universalizable normative-moral rules and principles independent of personal-social contextual connection which are uniformly applicable to all in all circumstances:

> From an early age, Chinese children are introduced to certain role models … and to certain attitudes about communism, China, their family, their peers; and these are drummed into them regularly. So far as I can tell, Chinese citizens do not as a rule make much of an effort to test these precepts and models against the evidence of their own senses, but simply accept them as a part of what it means (or what is considered to mean) to be a good and educated Chinese. My hosts seemed genuinely surprised when I suggested that these moral standards are being violated right and left by such common practices as guanxi, or helping out one's friends via the back door, instead of making a decision based on its merits.[152]

Contrasts Between American and Chinese Guanxi

Americans have guanxi, too, but their expectations of organized crime networks are usually based on what North American police have seen in the Mafia, LCN, or Russian Mafiya. First, Chinese, North Americans, and many others have some form of guanxi networks. For example, Cordell Hart has noted that North Americans use and support family relations, ancestral ties, old school ties, fraternity and GDI connections, teammates, social and business obligations, duties and debts owed, continuing business deals, co-workers, "back-door" power, etc.[151]

Second, Chinese guanxi has additional components for initial contacts that offer greater breadth, depth, and options regarding potential sources of criminal guanxi relationships than most Americans would anticipate regarding Chinese organized criminal activities. For example, among the 55 million overseas ethnic Chinese (many of whom are speakers of the Fukienese-Taiwanese Min dialect group) and among citizens of the PRC, the Republic of China, Singapore, and Hong Kong, most honor and use guanxi ties and sources to a greater extent than Americans by using major guanxi ties of birthplace, village, same-surname associations, and especially dialect, in addition to economic brotherhoods (hui), refugee-camp connections, and other regional ties.

Third, in North America, analysis of the Mafia and the LCN organizational structure occurred before Asian organized crime was "discovered". As a result, the LCN structural model became the primary model for analyzing the organizational structures of all organized crime, Asian and non-Asian. The general LCN model is a typical Anglo-European organizational model, comprised of absolute, vertical, hierarchical relationships. During a member's lifetime, exclusive allegiance is required to those in authority above and below each level by means of absolute chain-of-command relationships located within exclusive, geographically defined turfdoms.

Fourth, Chinese Triads and gangs do exhibit a hierarchical structure; by contrast, the middle and upper echelons of Chinese and Sinosized crime largely exhibit a set of guanxi relationships but not a rigid LCN model of absolute hierarchical structures.

Fifth, as a result of our unfamiliarity with Chinese culture, the LCN model has often been wrongly projected into the analyses of the middle and upper levels of Chinese organized criminal enterprises and has led some analysts to search for LCN hierarchical relationships within Chinese heroin and alien smuggling groups where they are frequently absent. Since the LCN model is often an inappropriate model for analysis of Chinese organized criminal enterprises and guanxi is a more appropriate model, the guanxi model of criminal organization should be integrated into analysis of Chinese and other Asian organized criminal enterprises.

Comparisons of American and Chinese Guanxi

Compared with American expectations of organized crime networks, Chinese criminal guanxi networks are wider, bigger, deeper, quicker, and more anonymous and are composed of semivertical, optional links that are not well known. Guanxi relations radiate farther, reflect more sources of assistance and obligations, reflect more types and degrees of nonlegalistic, nonentitlement connections, reflect a stronger sense of obligation to more people, and offer more flexible and less turf-governed options for new criminal enterprises and cheaper criminal "start-up costs. Guanxi blurs and conflates the identification of corruption and bribery and the distinctions between crime and sharp business practice and decreases the role and impact of universal formal systems of law.

Compared to American expectations, Chinese criminal guanxi networking is:

1. Wider, because it extends to a wider range of sources, relatives (seventh cousins), schoolmates, business acquaintances, family friends and their relatives, and people with the same family name who speak the same dialect and are from the same village, county, or locale, even when such relationships are scattered throughout the world, as in the Fukienese-Taiwanese snakehead connections.
2. Bigger, because it embraces seventh generations of relationships between each member of the additional sources noted above.
3. Deeper, because it embraces assistance and obligations to the seventh generations of relationships between people, at each level of which many know only one other member of the guanxi chain.
4. Quicker, because criminal entrepreneurs can make contact through person-to-person guanxi relations within pre-established ethnic/cultural linkages where such vetting is relatively rapid.
5. Composed of nonvertical, optional links, not chains of command of absolute allegiance as in the LCN.
6. More anonymous, because there is usually no obligation to reveal the vertical connections and/or identities of those in the guanxi chain.
7. Not well known, because North American police, usually unfamiliar with the operational structure of Chinese society and criminal organizations, assume that most nongang Chinese criminal activities are directed through a chain of command of hierarchical organizational structure, rather than the typical Chinese modus operandi, guanxi.
8. Able to radiate farther, because it potentially embraces members of the most populous country in the world and the pool of 55 million overseas Chinese, many of whom speak or can speak the Fukienese-Taiwanese Min dialect. While many have lived out of China for many

generations and have never visited China, they will maintain, honor, and utilize guanxi relationships.

9. A reflection of more sources of assistance and obligations and more types and degrees of nonlegalistic, nonentitlement connections of obligations, because it embraces more sources than most Americans would choose, cultivate, maintain, or embrace by virtue of mainline American culture.
10. A reflection of a series of person-to-person obligations and situational ethics as defined by social context and not by legally defined social entitlements, because it embraces more sources than most Americans would choose, cultivate, maintain, or embrace by virtue of mainline American culture.
11. A reflection of a stronger sense of obligation to more people, because while Americans exhibit the most individualistic traits among the world's population, the Chinese exhibit the most collectivist traits, and the sense of obligations to others decreases among individualist cultures and increases among collectivist cultures.
12. Able to offer more flexible criminal options and is less turf-governed in setting up new criminal enterprises, because Chinese criminal entrepreneurs need not secure formal permission as often to set up new "business" in someone else's territory because the guanxi relationships of criminal power are far less frequently defined in terms of geography and turfdom in Asian criminal enterprises than in the LCN.
13. Able to offer cheaper criminal startup costs, because there is no need to bring in new, nonlocal personnel and the local personnel are more likely to have helpful local connections to plan locally appropriate criminal tactics. However, long-term costs of maintaining such guanxi-driven criminal groups may constitute an additional expense..
14. Able to blur identification of corruption and bribery, because there are many mutually observed favors and debts within cultures throughout the world in which there is a sufficient variety of types of public vs. private morality such that what one group views as corruption and bribery may be viewed by others as deserved tokens of gratitude and rewards for requested mutual assistance between guanxi-linked friends.
15. Able to blur the distinctions between crime and sharp business practice, because Chinese often claim to be more tolerant, flexible, and realistic. Some tend to view what we consider as crime to be merely an accommodation to good business entrepreneurship, the simple attempt to supply publicly desired goods and services between trusted guanxi "friends" even if these goods and services are abstractly deemed illegal.

16. Able to decrease the role and impact of universal formal systems of law, because of the cultural preference for the primary organizational model of guanxi relationships rather than law. The result is a pragmatic diminution of strict legal interpretations of crime as a consequence of the ever-balancing mutual interplay of guanxi, "face" (mianzi), deeply rooted public custom, and ranked social obligations. This results in the diminution of the explicit Anglo-European model of common egalitarian law, in spite of the public facade of legalism the PRC Chinese offer as a public surrogate for the legalistic, universalistic emphasis so commonly expected of — but fiercely resisted by — the Chinese when engaged in international or cross-cultural negotiations with North Americans.

Pride in the Ultimate Superiority of Being Chinese

Within the long scope of Chinese history, there have been many attempts to throw off the ties of oppressive authority and rigidly structured bureaucracies and to temper internal fits of political self-mutilation (as in the "Cultural Revolution"). However, for all these instances of turmoil, there remains another all-pervasive mindset component, the enormous pride in simply being Chinese, being *Han*. Although this is not unique to the Chinese, the traditional Chinese sense of its long history and its well demonstrated determination to endure, survive, and work for the future of the extended family have generated a very strong sense of quiet pride of ethnic superiority — sometimes approaching the Greek sense of *hubris*, excessive pride. While a Chinatown restaurant owner may be poor, overworked, and extorted by other Chinese and while a few of his waiters may sleep in 8-hour shifts in "hot beds", he and they still remain Chinese (Han) and for that they consider themselves ultimately superior among nations as they believe history has shown and will show once again.

An institutionalized concept of ethnic pride is common to many people. The U.S. has reveled in its sense of "Manifest Destiny", the New World's mandate from Heaven to lead the way into this century and the next. The American sense of itself as a moral and a deserved moralistic leader is illustrated quite clearly in the controversies over human rights in China and their one-child-policy. These controversies arose in debates about America's decision to retain China's trading status as a "most favored nation" which avoids high tariffs on imports to the U.S. Also, American special interest in China was exhibited in the internal political controversies of who lost China to the Communists in the 1950s. Projections of a special American interest in China arose once again at the opening of China to increased trade and international investment in the 1960s and 1970s. This was accompanied by the underlying American hope that exposure to our democracatic ways would bring them around to be "just like us". These naive hopes were dashed in the public American consciousness with the televised brutality in Tiananmen Square.

However, this sense of the inherent superiority of being Chinese is a particularly acute sensibility for those traditional Chinese who are broadly educated and aware of the many lifestyles and values in other cultures throughout the world. This sense of inherent superiority is also a formidable problem for those educated Chinese who remain acutely aware of the shabby humiliating treatment of China during the last two centuries at the hands of the Europeans, Americans, and certainly the Japanese. With no small accumulation of evidence, they feel that the light of recent history reflects and confirms that they, as a distinct people, are more determined than most others, can and have endured more, are more disciplined, work harder, and possess a sheer superiority in inherent cleverness, realistic tactics for good living, superior strategies for survival, and a winning, subtle, flexible intelligence, second to none.

Many internationally astute Chinese are all too conscious of their economic, political, and industrial shortcomings; lack of technical resources; and the absence of an educated work force. Furthermore, especially for the young Chinese, the superior sense of "being at the center of civilization" (Zhongguo) has been severely challenged by several internal Chinese experiences, such as the "in your face" contrasts between China's low levels of technology, PRC's low standard of living, excessive corruption and the indulgence of Western luxuries by PRC officials and their wholesale greedy love of Mercedes Benz sedans and Western luxury hotels built in most large Chinese cities from which Chinese were excluded. From individual reports of students studying in North America, most of whom wish to remain here, the foregoing Chinese qualities of life contrast strongly with the obvious higher standard of living in North America and Europe. The indifference of the non-Chinese world to China's self-proclaimed superior morality is highlighted in two illustrative facts: between 1985 and 1995, China's per capita GNP had fallen from 108th in the world to 126th, plus, as one of my Chinese PRC students once said about the U.S., "Wow! The goddamn phones work everywhere and at any time!"

In spite of these experiences, many (if not most) traditional Chinese also feel deeply in their hearts that they are, in the long run, inherently superior and that the setbacks and subordinate positions China has been forced to hold during the last few centuries are temporary setbacks within the long view of history. Thus, from the traditional perspective, they also know that their natural qualities of superiority will eventually return them to the positions of respect and authoritative preeminence that they assume they rightfully deserve. For many, if not most Chinese, they have always been, and have always deserved to be, the “Middle Kingdom”, the center of the world. For the rest of us, we shall wait with respect, skepticism, and occasional admiration, but we shall wait to see what happens.

Is the Reading of Chinese Ethnic Strategists Relevant for Police? 16

關係

Within all major civilizations, there are always a few reflective individuals whose hard-nosed, pragmatic views of war and politics focus on military strategy, domestic and political intelligence, and the problems of enforcing the law of the land. Worldwide examples are Machiavelli's 16th century Italian *The Prince*;[152] in India, during the time of the great epic, the *Mahābhārata* and Kautilya's *Arthaśāstra;*[153] and in ancient China, Sun Tzu's *The Art of War* ("Skills of the Soldier").[154] At Asian organized crime conferences, usually in the bar in the late afternoon, some naturally curious, energetic officer who has been reading about Asian cultures may bring up the famous Chinese book on strategy and warfare, *The Art of War*, wondering whether it is worth reading to understand "the Chinese mindset". Perhaps someone else has seen the new translation and commentary on other ancient Chinese strategists, *The Seven Military Classics of Ancient China.*[155] Another officer may have read a translation of the famous *Thirty-Six Stratagems*[156] and wonder if they bear upon the way Asian organized crime is conducted. Since the influence of these works has been and remains substantial in China, Japan, and Korea, their content and relevance deserve our attention. However, at the other end of the scale are found more exotic claims about Chinese strategic thought, which deserve at least a debunking warning.

At the outset, reading Sun Tzu's *The Art of War* would seem relevant, because reading any basic thought about Chinese military and law enforcement culture would seem potentially helpful. However, an important question remains: Would reading *The Art of War* be helpful to police whose professional goals are to identify, assess, thwart crime, and arrest criminals? To that question, I answer that they *could* be but they usually are *not.*

The following quotations and commentaries illustrate that the thrust of Sun Tzu's *The Art of War.*

> [It was] … the first known attempt to formulate a rational basis for the planning and conduct of military operations.… He believed that the skillful strategist should be able to subdue the enemy's army without engaging it, to take his cities without laying siege to them, and to overthrow his State without bloodying swords.

Written about the 4th century B.C., Sun Tzu's book is a collection of compact one-liners (aphorisms) and terse paragraphs which describe and recommend strategies for the military leader — usually there were no separate police — who is carrying out the internal and external policies of the state by threatening war or waging war. It summarizes internal military policies and the many uses of strategic, tactical, and political intelligence — including culture.

> He considered the moral, intellectual and circumstantial elements of war to be more important than the physical … He did not conceive of war in terms of slaughter and destruction; to take all intact, or as nearly intact as possible, was the proper objective of strategy … based on sound information of the enemy.

On general strategy, Sun Tzu's thesis is typically Chinese and may be paraphrased as follows. Be indirect. The best policy and the height of military skill is not to ruin the enemy, nor is it maximizing killing or winning all your battles. The best indirect approach and the highest standard of military skill is to subdue without fighting by thwarting the enemy's plans. The next best strategy is to disrupt his alliances and next to attack his armies. The worst approach and the worst policy is to directly attack cities. Thus, Sun Tzu's implicit strategy is to approach your enemy indirectly, from an oblique, unexpected angle. Obviously, this indirectness could be justified by appealing to lower expenditures in military and civilian lives and physical, financial, and natural resources. In the following two tactical examples, Sun Tzu illustrates this indirect strategy regarding intelligence — the first, systematic and carefully assessed; the second, ruthless and clever:

> Now there are five sorts of secret agents to be employed. These are native, inside, doubled, expendable and living.

The commentary of Chang Yu describes an expendable agent:[157]

> ... Chief of Staff Ts'ao once pardoned a condemned man whom he then disguised as a monk, and caused to swallow a ball of wax and enter [the land of the enemy] Tangut. When the false monk arrived, he was imprisoned. The monk told his captors about the wax ball and soon discharged it in a stool. When the ball was opened, the Tanguts read a letter transmitted by Chief of Staff Ts'ao to their [own] Director of Strategic Planning. The ... [Tangut's were] ... enraged, put his [Tangut] minister to death, and executed the spy monk.... But expendable agents are not confined to only one use. Sometimes I send agents to the enemy to make a covenant of peace and then I attack.

In a terse fashion, the *Thirty-Six Stratagems* are divided into six general positions, stratagems, and tactics for commanding superiority, confrontation, attack, confused situations, gaining ground, and desperate straits. For example, Gao Yuan notes Sun Tzu's aphorism, "He who knows the art of the direct and the indirect approach will be victorious. Such is the art of maneuvering." Then, to make the connection between them, Gao Yuan translates Stratagem 2 as, "Besiege the kingdom of Wei to save the kingdom of Zhao," and offers the following explanation:[158]

> The stratagem of besieging Wei to save Zhao plays on the yin-yang relationship between directness and indirectness, concentration and division, and solidity and void. It may mean concentrating one's forces to strike at the enemy's weakest point, taking advantage of an opponent's shortcomings, solving a problem by focusing on an aspect that seems tangential but is actually key, or deflecting a problem onto something or somebody else.

Are these stratagems relevant to Asian crime investigators? First, to assume that they are presupposes that Sun Tzu has been assimilated by criminals so deeply that *The Art of War* has become an almost unconscious guide to their behavior. The indirect approach is typically Chinese; the tactics that exemplify that strategy require analysis. However, while this strategy of indirect approach might be explicit for a few specialized elite among the sparsely educated classes and perhaps a few extremely intelligent criminals, the majority of Chinese criminals are seldom members of such an elite group. Second, others have argued that these tactics (and thus) strategies are learned by criminals in the many Chinese games such as Wei Chi, which somewhat resembles Anglo-European chess. Once again, this may be true for a few, but, even as an informal tradition in folk games, these strategies would be deeply assimilated by relatively few. Few criminals would have the ability to analyze the situations in such a way as to appropriately recognize how to apply the tactics. Most American and Chinese criminals are not too bright and are certainly not the type of persons predisposed to the explicit use of such abstract models of conflict strategy as a blueprint for their criminal behavior. Rather than using such a blueprint, Cordell Hart has affirmed this last point by noting that many ruthless, highly successful tacticians and strategists have an innate sense of operations and are successful without the benefits of education, training, or reading in such matters. He mentioned Dr. Bergan Evans's comments on Machiavelli's book *The Prince*:[159]

> I don't suppose really that anybody ever learned anything practical from Machiavelli's writings. Power politicians, dictators, warlords, duces, fuhrers, and their like do not have to learn from books to be cunning and treacherous and ruthless. Machiavelli's book has survived not solely as a manual of how to do it, I'm sorry to say, probably, but as a description of how it is done.

If the foregoing is true, then there is even less merit in reading the writings of Sun Tzu and company without an accompanying historical and cultural grounding, a necessary background for being able to see and justify the alleged *connections* between Sun Tzu et al., and the tactical crime problems of today. To connect means to know both sides; without a background about Asia, it is difficult to see and articulate the alleged connections between Sun Tzu and the nuts and bolts of Asian crime investigations. Thus, Sun Tzu is clearly relevant but making use of *The Art of War* as a way of understanding Chinese thought and behavior and then applying it to modern police problems is complex and far more difficult than it first appears.

We now turn to the more controversial end of the scale of readings about Chinese "strategy" of possible relevance to police. There is a contemporary compilation of claims about Chinese strategy (allegedly) within the Sun Tzu tradition which also incorporates the *Thirty-Six Stratagems*. This book, claiming to offer deep insights into the contrasting ways of Chinese of thinking, is entitled *The Chinese Mind Game: The Best Kept Trade Secret of the East*, by Chin-Ning Chu.[160] This series of exotic gems is claimed to be "A Guide to Penetrating the Forbidden City of the Asian Inner Business Culture". For example, some of the subdivisions of the chapter entitled "The Inner Chinese" are Creative Interpretation of the Law, North-South Prejudices, Peace-Loving, Endurance, Slippery and Tricky, Lack of Innovation, Mooching, Lack of Involvement, Jealousy, Strategy Oriented, Judgmental, Love of Gossip, and Wife-Fearing.[161] It is not to say that these brief descriptions are not without any insights which might be helpful to police. Rather, it is to say that these characteristics are true of a good many people beside the Chinese and are thus neither the essence of any Asian inner business culture nor a hitherto hidden trade secret. In my opinion, most of these 13 characteristics are true of the Vietnamese and the Cambodians; at least 11 of these 13 would be equally applicable to the Arabs and Japanese, 10 of 13 to the French, and at least 7 or 8, or perhaps all, to the North Americans of the U.S.

While all these aphoristic gems are moderately interesting, one wonders who, how many, and what kind of readers will be able to recognize the connections between these alleged insights into Chinese behavior and North American police problems. Also, one wonders who, how many, and what kind of readers will be able to recognize the slippery relationships between most officers' understandable absence of a knowledge of Asia and their lack of a comparative framework in which to carefully compare cultures of Asia, Canada, and the U.S. Moreover, one wonders who, how many, and what kind of readers will know how to apply these relatively abstract stratagems appropriately (even with their illustrative stories) to the tactical practicalities of the everyday, nuts-and-bolts police work of Asian investigators.

Furthermore, one wonders who, how many, and what kind of readers will be able to convince their administrative superiors to act in accordance with their knowledge about Chinese strategies. In light of these implicit criticisms, wholesale swallowing of this "best kept trade secret of the East" encourages an unrealistic sense of cross-cultural competency, inaccuracy in police intelligence, skewed planning, and, worse, reinforcement of ignorant views of admirable Asian people. Furthermore, analyzing Sun Tzu's implicit strategy yields the following three-part admonition: (1) approach Asian criminal activities indirectly, (2) be aware that Asian criminals will most likely approach you indirectly, and (3) be aware that direct steamroller approaches may easily dissipate connections with possible informants (cop guanxi) and the Asian community. Thus, this statement of strategy offers very little tactical information for the good cop on the street.

Therefore, these gems of Chinese exotica, these "penetrations of the Forbidden City of the Asian inner business culture", omit the alleged connections to contemporary Asian crime problems. Moreover, this omission leaves to the reader all the hard work of determining what the actual connections are and how he/she ought to apply these cross-cultural insights. Furthermore, in this author's opinion, there is generated an analogy between the "penetrations of the Forbidden City of the Asian inner business culture" and a portion of the Uniform Code of Military Justice (about which the author was instructed when in Navy bootcamp), wherein are used the words "penetration, however slight". The analog so generated strongly suggests an appropriate use of a familiar vulgar verb to describe what is being done to you when you buy any book of Asian exotica which states that it is "the best kept trade secret of the East".

Thus, the lack of instruction about how to apply these insights renders these readings inefficient and inappropriate ways to convey cross-cultural information to Asian crime investigators. Even worse is that, since the difficult task of applying cross-cultural skills and knowledge is ignored in the book, the burden of application is shifted to the inquiring reader who is seeking such information by reading such books in the first place. Furthermore, an experienced former CIA intelligence officer suggested that it is also a major mistake to think that we should strive to become so familiar with and so insightful into Chinese culture as to "out Chinese the Chinese"; that is, to try ...[162]

> ... to behave totally as a Chinese in dealing with them. Many an Occidental, even those with great and learned command of the Chinese spoken and written language ... met with disaster because, among other reasons, they thought they could deal with the Chinese as Chinese. Not so. The other [recommendation is that] we should allow for the fact that Asians generally prepare for us better than we prepare for them. [Moreover,] if we do not act in the Western ways they allow for, they are most befuddled — and both sides lose.

Therefore, reading a simple translation of such books as Sun Tzu's *The Art of War* is barely helpful at best. As general background reading, such books are interesting; however, as sourcebooks or "cookbooks" for the straightforward application of cross-cultural skills and knowledge to Asian crime problems, they are neither effective or efficient, nor do they deliver what they seem to promise. In short, learning to cross back and forth between cultures remains complex, interesting, and full of surprises. As with most things worth knowing, cross-cultural knowledge is generated, not by exotic "penetrations", but by sustained, straightforward, analytical *hard work.*

Chinese Language, Names, and Holidays 17

關係

The Chinese Language

Just as English is a late-born descendant in the large family of Indo-European languages (French, German, Spanish, Latin, Greek, Sanskrit, Old Persian, etc.), modern Chinese comes from a family of languages called Sinitic or Sino-Tibetan. Geographically, Sino-Tibetan group languages cover China, Vietnam, Tibet, Thailand, Laos, and most of Burma.[163] Since 1949, the standard Chinese dialect has been Mandarin (putong-hua, "ordinary people's language"), the dialect around the northern capital of Beijing. It should be noted that some (spoken) Chinese dialects are as mutually incomprehensible as Swedish is to German or as Spanish is to Italian; some are as different as English is to Finnish.[164]

As was noted in discussing the two Chinese characters of the term "guanxi", they were transliterated as "guanxi" within the Pinyin system or as "kuan-hsi" in the Wade-Giles system. These transliteration systems, as opposed to translation systems, are standardized systems within which Chinese sounds are described with prescribed matching letters from the Roman alphabet (the English language alphabet). Wade-Giles is an older transliteration system which is quickly being superseded by the Pinyin transliteration system adopted by the PRC and many international scholars. However, Pinyin is still officially rejected by Taiwan because of their lingering anti-communistic policies.

Many of the early Chinese who became contract labors to lay railroad track throughout western Canada and the U.S.[165] were born in a very small area of southeastern China, Guangdong Province. They spoke a dialect of what we call "Cantonese" which is the subdialect common to the city Guangzhou, formerly known as "Canton". Cantonese, in turn, is a subdialect of the dialects grouped under the name "Yue", the dialect(s) of many early Chinese immigrants to North America.

The impression of most North Americans and Europeans at their first view of written Chinese is bewilderment — no letters, a series of squiggles written up and down and from right to left. Worse, the squiggles have no relation to the sounds; therefore, there is nothing recognizable at all! Understandably, North Americans conclude that they could not possibly learn anything about the written Chinese language which appears so foreign and so different from English. Unfortunately, this conclusion is usually extended to the spoken language as well. However, this conclusion is unfortunate because spoken Chinese is easier than it appears. The word order of spoken Chinese, at least at the beginning levels, more closely resembles standard English than does German or Latin; for example, subject + verb + object. Also, Chinese has no inflections, no endings (no "-ed", "-ing", "-es" or affixes "anti-", "a-", "super-"). Furthermore, this unfortunate conclusion discourages many law enforcement people from learning how to use a few helpful words and simple courtesy sentences that would assist them not only in straightforward communication ("Where did he go?"), but also in understanding, assisting, and developing better police-community relations with Chinese-Americans.

While it is clear that written Chinese is strange and difficult to most Anglo-Europeans, the conclusion to stay at arm's length away from the spoken language is not warranted. In short, more can be done with even written Chinese than its formidable appearance would suggest. Also, the negative conclusion discourages many law enforcement personnel from learning a few helpful techniques about using a dictionary and benefiting from learning how to use the Standard Telegraphic Code (STC) or Chinese Commercial Code (Chapter 20). Some benefits do occur at different levels of complexity and knowledge, and there is no reason not to use STC to some degree to determine the exact name of a Chinese or Chinese-American or Chinese-Canadian person. However, the exact name of an ethnic Chinese person is in *Chinese characters*, not in some semi-arbitrary combination of American perceptions of Chinese sounds loosely symbolized in English letters. Furthermore, to use STC to determine and identify a specific Chinese name to some beneficial degree, you do not have to be able to read or speak Chinese.

Appendix B offers a large supplement on Asian languages, dialects, and names, prepared by Robert Hearn, an outstanding federal intelligence analyst who has lived in Asia over many years and is fluent in several Asian languages. The FBI's excellent publication, *A Guide To Chinese Names and Language*,[166] outlines the formation of Chinese characters, the major dialects that are not mutually understandable, and the tone systems such as the four tones of the Mandarin dialect. Also explained are the two major systems of transliteration, Wade-Giles and Pinyin. There is a description of Chinese name order (surname first, personal names second) and a proper sequence of decoding and conveying Chinese names in STC. Also, other reference materials especially prepared for police are listed at the end of the chapter.

Chinese Names

Uses of the most common Chinese names are discussed and illustrated with Chinese characters and their STC equivalents in Chapter 20. A survey of the major Chinese dialects and other aspects of Chinese names can be found in Appendix B.

As we look at Tommy (T-chang) Wang's Chinese name, we should realize that of the traditional 200 Chinese family names, the family name being written first rather than last, only about 45 to 90 Chinese family names are in fairly common use. Therefore, given the population of ethnic Chinese in PRC, Singapore, Taiwan, Hong Kong, Amsterdam, Los Angeles, and Houston, there are many, many Chinese named Wang. Also, there are villages whose inhabitants all have the same family names. (Imagine the guanxi connections there!) Furthermore, Wang might well be an Anglicized version of several possibilities such as Wong, Won, and Wan, just as Tommy is a somewhat anglicized version of T-chang. Cordell Hart offered the example of a Cantonese by the name of Au Hoy who might take the name John Auhoy. Many others merely pick a common Western surname such as John or Sam, as do many African students.

Two well known differences between English and Chinese are that Chinese write the family name (xing) first and then the personal name (ming). Very often, the family name consists of one syllable and the personal name of two syllables. The renown Sinologist Dr. Wolfram Eberhard summarizes what is usually not popularly known about Chinese names:[167]

> When a child is born it first receives a pet-name such as "little lion" or "little fatty". A little later, it gets its personal name, its *ming*. ... The *ming* is chosen according to certain rules which are often set out in verse form. All the children or at least all the sons belonging to the same generation, get the same character as [the] first ... character of the *ming* [personal name]. ... Millions of Chinese have identical family names and two persons with the same family *may* be related. It is here that the code poem plays a part. For example, suppose that a visitor shows up who has the same family name and who also knows the code poem in which his *ming* appears. From this the host and visitor can at once establish whether or not they belong to the same generation of one family. This in turn, will affect the manner in which the visitor is received, and the way in which he is addressed. Thus, it is almost impossible for an impostor to pass himself off as a relative.

> At the age of ten, or shortly thereafter, the child is given a second name. This is a monosyllable or disyllable which is chosen by the father as particularly suited to the child in question with an eye to its future success and happiness. This second name — the *zi* — is therefore symbolic. It is used by friends and strangers alike. Adults may add further names to those they already possess. Within the family, brothers and sisters are referred to in terms of relationships only: "older brother number two", "younger sister number three", where "older" and "younger" are with relation to the age of the speaker. Again, within the family, such forms of address as "old two", "maternal aunt two" and so on may be used.

Many, Chinese, both U.S.- and China-born, often allude to their birthplace as part of their name illustrating their very strong attachment to their ancestral home or province. Also, nicknames and honorifics (old, elder brother, etc.) are widely used. People of about the same age call each other old (lao) or little (xiao) followed by either their full name or their surname. Only family members use their personal name; others using it would be considered pushy and/or trying to be inappropriately intimate. The younger address the older by their surnames plus Uncle (shushu or bobo), Aunt (ayi), Grandpa (yeye), or Grandmother (nainai); personal or first names are never used.[168] Even these simple differences in Chinese names may complicate law enforcement efforts to identify, process, and retrieve ID information in NCIC and from other databases; this supports the need for greater knowledge and use of STC.

Chinese Holidays and Festivals

Since there will be special visits of distant relatives and friends and increased telephone activities during holidays, surveillance and telephone teams should take advantage of the holidays and special family activities. Since suspects who have gone underground may surface for family visits, watch the parents', grandparents', and eldest sons' homes. Analysis of holiday telephone calls would generate a definitive matrix of the suspect's guanxi and business contacts. Not only are the Asian holidays an opportunity to seek suspects, but they are instructive for officers concerned with community policing. Holidays offer opportunities to learn about the people of the Asian-American communities and for them to get to know you — and the food is terrific!

Most of the holidays are placed within the Chinese lunar calendar which is based on the changes of the moon. If you are using the standard Western solar calendar, the exact date of these lunar holidays may shift from year to year. The PRC, Singapore, and Hong Kong have adopted the Western Gregorian calendar for public holidays, and dual calendars are common. In North

America, check with a friendly Chinese merchant for a traditional almanac (tong shu) within which there will be represented both calendar systems.[169] Some of the major holidays are briefly described below. Many local ones will be of equal importance within your Asian community. Ask about them.

Chinese Lunar New Year's Day
(Yuan Dan, Yuan Tan, STC 0337 2481)

Now officially refered to as the Spring Festival (Chunjie), this holiday occurs in late January or early February, usually the first day of the first moon, the 15th day of the new lunar month. These days of festival may last from 3 days to 2 weeks. They are family holidays when all debts to friends and businessmen are to be paid, grudges reconciled, and honor restored; visits of respect and affection to elders, other family, and friends should occur; inexpensive prints of the kitchen god, peaches, fish, and well-fed, plump children are displayed to symbolize prosperity; messages written on red paper expressing confidence, good luck, and prosperity are hung in doorways of businesses; children are given "lucky money" in small red envelopes. Wearing black is considered unlucky during the holiday.

Special foods are prepared before the holiday because no knives or sharp objects can be used during the beginning of the New Year to prevent good luck from being cut off. For Southerners, the favorite foods are sweetened glutinous rice pudding (nian gaom); for Northerners, steamed wheat bread (man tou) and small dumplings filled with chopped meat, peanuts, dates, and chestnuts. Among the wealthy, gold coins were added; the finder of such a coin was (supposedly) never to be without money.

Employees usually get about 4 days off starting on New Year's Eve and lasting through the third day. They — and informants on a regular retainer — should also receive a month's salary (the "13th" month) if they have worked at their jobs for a year or more, two weeks salary if less than one year. Red envelopes of "lucky money" are left under the plate for the servant of a good friend to whose house you have often been invited. It is thought best if the bills in the red envelopes are new crisp bills and the amounts are even, $6, $8, $10. Some Chinese will not venture out of their homes on the third day, for fights are likely to occur and "devils" roam the streets and countryside. Some refrain from washing their hair during the holidays to prevent "washing away good luck".

During the holiday period there are lantern and lion dances and, of course, the famous Dragon dances. At any Dragon dance/parade, it is sometimes claimed that the presence of a black Dragon constitutes a challenge to other gangs in the vicinity. Also, during the parade watch for gang members flitting about the stores to collect "protection" money or pick up money for mooncakes sold to merchants at very inflated prices.

Honoring the Graves of the Ancestors: The Pure Brightness Festival (Qing Ming Jie, STC 3237 2494 4636)

This family holiday is coordinated with the solar calendar and, in some overseas Chinese communities, often with Easter. It usually occurs about April 4th, 5th, or 6th. This is a time in which members of the family gather to honor, remember, and commemorate the ancestors of family/clan. (They do not literally worship the ancestors; see Chapter 19) Sometimes in a picnic-like spirit and sometimes soberly, one should fast. One is forbidden to light fires. The extended family gathers at the gravesites which they sweep and neaten. In their home, at the location of the family lineage tablets on which there are inscribed the names and dates of birth and death of their forbearers, family members honor former members of the extended family. In the local temples, paper money is burned for the dead. The sober side of the festival is lightened by the ancient tradition of kite-flying. Offerings of food for the dead are followed by family feasts and friendly visits between families and friends, thus offering advantages for law enforcement intelligence.

Feast of the Hungry Ghosts (Gui Jie, STC 7607 4636)

This occurs in July or August on the 15th day of the 7th moon. The purpose of this ancient Buddhist observance is to placate the souls of wandering hungry ghosts (Sanskrit: pretas; Chinese: e-kuei), uncared-for spirits, so that they do not turn against the living. Some mark this period from the first to the last day of the 7th month when the gates of Hell are open and the wandering spirits of the dead are honored by burning joss sticks and offerings of food. Thus, to ensure salvation and comfort for the wandering spirits, these activities culminate in a ritual ghost-feeding on the 15th day during which paper clothes, spirit money, incense, and food are offered in the appropriate temples and outdoor altars. Also referred to as the Festival for Burning Clothes (Shao Yi Jie), this process is a way to honor and help one's ancestors, as is the burning of paper money at the Temple.

Mooncake Festival (Zhong Qiu Jie, STC 0022 4428 4636)

The 15th day of the 8th lunar month is a special full-moon day and night celebration. Relics of a former harvest celebration, the mooncakes are prepared 2 weeks before the evening of the festival day, when they are eaten by moonlight.

> Today, mooncakes are made with various fillings. Some have lotus-seed paste, others red-bean paste and some even contain meat and egg yolk filling. Lanterns, made with bamboo frames and translucent colored paper, are delightful gifts for young children who carry them in the moonlight during the festival.[170]

Also on this day, gang members extort merchants by intimidating them and forcing them to buy mooncakes at highly inflated prices. Sometimes around this holiday period, gang members can be seen carrying mooncakes into businesses for what they claim are "legitimate" sales.

The Kitchen God (Zao Wang, STC 3501 3769)

Sometimes thought to be the inventor of fire, this old household ritual occurs on the 23rd day of the 12th lunar month; the kitchen god's birthday was said to be the 3rd day of the 8th lunar month. On the back wall where the family cooks, the kitchen god is often represented as a young man with a writing tablet on which he records notes for his report on the family's activities to the heavens. Among the poorer families, the kitchen god is sometimes represented by a patch of red paper on which the god's name and title are written, accompanied by an apology for not offering more for him.[171]

Suggested Readings

An excellent bibliography may be found in *East Asia: The Great Tradition*, by Edwin O. Reischauer and John K. Fairbank, Houghton-Mifflin Company, Boston, 1960, pp. 679-686. The Association for Asian Studies generates a bibliographical issue (roughly) each year which categorizes scholarly research publications. However, there are few (if any) articles on Asian based crime in North America since it is clear that the relationships between Asian culture and Asian crime are clearly hybrid specialties. Other bibliographies may be found in the publications listed below, within the endnotes and list of references.

Asian Names and Language References

To assist in understanding and deciphering Asian languages and the recording and tracing of Asian names, some relevant references designed for law enforcement are listed below.

A Guide to Chinese Names and Language, U.S. Department of Justice, Federal Bureau of Investigation, Washington, D.C., September, 1991.

Standard Telegraphic Codes, Financial Crimes Enforcement Network (FinCEN), U.S. Department of the Treasury, Washington, D.C., 1991.

Three Way: Chinese Commercial/Telegraphic Code Book, Royal Hong Kong Police Force, Hong Kong, June, 1989.

Vietnamese and Thai Names — Law Enforcement Considerations, prepared by Peter F. Vandivier, Financial Crimes Enforcement Network (FinCEN), U.S. Department of the Treasury, Washington, D.C., 1992.

Distinguishing Between Vietnamese and Chinese Names, Financial Crimes Enforcement Network (FinCEN), U.S. Department of the Treasury, Washington, D.C., 1991.

Thai Names: Reference Aid, Office of Intelligence, Drug Enforcement Administration, U.S. Department of Justice, Washington, D.C., February, 1992.

Standard Telegraphic Code, television interview with M. Cordell Hart (Senior Analyst) and Paul N. DerGarabedian (Analyst, FinCEN), produced by the Law Enforcement Television Network (LETN); #153-0087, Crime Scene: "Asian Gangs"; LETN, 1303 Marsh Lane, Carrollton, TX, 75006-5430, Phone: (800) 942-2786.

Japanese Names: A Comprehensive Index by Characters and Readings, P.G. O'Neill, Weatherhill, New York, 1989 (ISBN:0-8348-0225-2). While this reference would not be directly relevant for Chinese names in a database, etc. it might be useful as a secondary reference to check a name that you cannot find; the names at issue are actually Japanese names in kanji (Chinese characters as used in Japanese) that are mistaken for Chinese names.

Chinese Crime and Chinese Culture

Hearings on Asian Organized Crime, U.S. Senate, Committee on Governmental Affairs, Permanent Subcommittee on Investigations, Washington, D.C., October 3, November 5 and 6, 1991.

Chinese Subculture and Criminality: Non-Traditional Crime Groups in America, Kolin Chin, Greenwood Press, Westport, CN, 1990 (ISBN: 0-313-27262-X). Excellent study of Chinese gangs in New York and the background of Chinese Traids; contains an extensive bibliography.

Triads: The Growing Global Threat from the Chinese Criminal Societies, M. Booth, St. Martin's Press, New York, 1991 (ISBN: 0-312-05524-2). Contains excerpts from *Triad Societies in Hong Kong* (below), which is out of print.

Law Without Lawyers: a Comparative View of Law in China and the United States, V. H. Li, Westview Press, Boulder, CO, 1978 (ISBN: 0-89158-161-8). Two cultural views on law and order.

Policing in China, Chapter 12, Comparative Perspectives, in Policing America, Kenneth J. Peak, Regents/Prentice Hall, Englewood Cliffs, NJ, 1993, pp. 387-393.

"The Police in China", Richard Ward, in *Justice Quarterly,* Vol. 2, 111-115, 1985.

Sons of the Yellow Emperor: History of the Chinese Diaspora, Lynn Pan, Little Publishing, 1990 (ISBN: 0-316-69010-4). A short overview of the Triads and Chinese-American Tongs within a very readable book on Chinese and Chinese-American history, customs, and culture.

Warlords of Crime: Chinese Secret Societies, the New Mafia, Gerard L. Posner, Penguin Books, New York, 1990 (ISBN: 0-14-012340-9). An interesting, very readable overview of the heroin trade beginning in the Golden Triangle and ending in Europe and the U.S. I am told on excellent authority that the statements attributed to a federal analyst in Hong Kong were severely misquoted, garbled, and, in some cases, never uttered.

Triad Societies in Hong Kong, 3rd printing, W.P. Morgan, Hong Kong Government Printing Office, Hong Kong, 1989. A comprehensive, excellent survey, with many photographs. It is out of print, but copies were sometimes available at IAACI conferences.

Chinatown: A Portrait of a Closed Society, Gwen Kinkead, Harper-Collins Publishers, New York, 1992 (ISBN: 0-06-016776-9). A very readable overview of recent Chinese history in our cities, their successes, troubles, adjustments, and crime.

Chinatown No More: The Taiwanese in New York, Hsiang-Shui Chen, Cornell University Press, Ithaca, NY, 1992 (paperback). Reviewed: *IAACI News,* International Association of Asian Crime Investigators, September, 1992.

Fires of the Dragon: Politics, Murder and the Kuomintang, David Kaplan, Atheneum, NY, 1992. Reviewed: *IAACI News,* International Association of Asian Crime Investigators, September, 1992: "Based on the life and the 1984 assassination of Chinese-American journalist Henry Liu, killed by the United Bamboo Gang who were hired by Taiwan's Military Intelligence Bureau." An excellent work on Chinese-Taiwan intelligence operations in the U.S. written by a trusted, careful investigative journalist who was the co-author of the respected book on Japanese organized crime, *Yakuza: The Explosive Account of Japan's Criminal Underworld,* with Alec Dubro, Addison-Wesley Publishing, Menlo Park, CA, 1986 (ISBN: 0-201-11151-9).

The Soong Dynasty, Sterling Seagrave, Harper and Row, New York, 1989 (ISBN: 0-06-091318-5). A history of a very prominent Chinese family/clan and the interplay of politics and Triads in this century.

Year of the Dragon, Robert Daley, Simon and Schuster, New York, 1981. This is fiction which was also made into an inaccurate but interesting movie about crime and the clash of cultures in U.S. Chinatowns and the Golden Triangle. Uneven, but worth the video rental.

Encountering the Chinese: A Guide for Americans, W. Hu and C.L. Grove, Intercultural Press, 1991 (ISBN: 0-933662-95-5). A good introduction to Chinese manners and assumptions, e.g., "face", friendship, negotiation, and other cultural relations.

Chinese (formerly *Dealing with Chinese*), M. Cordell Hart, Financial Crimes Enforcement Network (FinCEN), U.S. Department of the Treasury, Washington, D.C., 1991. Other contributors are Christopher Ballou, William Donnett, David Collier, George Harkin, and James Schnell. This is an excellent 20-page introduction to aspects of Chinese culture written and edited by a former senior intelligence analyst who is a speaker of fluent Mandarin, now a mid-level manager, FinCEN, U.S. Department of the Treasury.

Americans and Chinese, Francis L.K. Hsu, Natural History Press, Doubleday, Garden City, NJ, 1972 (paperback). Many comparative insights are made explicit.

The Chinese Mind Game: The Best Kept Trade Secret of the East, Chin-Ning Chu, AMC Publishing, P.O. Box 1420, Beaverton, OR, 97075, 1988 (Phone: (503) 644-2438, ISBN: 0-929638-19-0). An AOC specialist who lacks Chinese claims that this interesting book reveals a fundamental Chinese mindset. That there is great room for doubt, I noted in Chapter 16.

Chinese Religion: An Introduction, L.G. Thompson, Dickenson Publishing, Belmont, CA, 1969 (Library of Congress Number: 69-17301). An outstanding small survey of Chinese religious culture.

Mooncakes and Hungry Ghosts: Festivals of China, C. Stepanchuk and C. Wong, China Books and Periodicals, San Francisco, CA, 1991 (ISBN: 0-8351-7481-9).

Chinese New Year: Fact and Folklore, William Chao-Chung, Ars Ceramica, Ann Arbor, MI, 1991 (ISBN: 0-89344-037-x). Four hundred pages of details and illustrations of the food habits, social customs, tales, and festivals associated with the Chinese New Year.

Traditional Chinese Festivals, Marie-Luise Latsch, Graham Brash (Pte) Ltd., 227 Rangoon Road, Singapore, 0821, (ISBN: 9971-947-80-3.) (No date noted.)

A Dictionary of Chinese Symbols: Hidden Symbols in Chinese Life and Thought, Wolfram Eberhard, Routlege and Kegan Paul, New York, 1986 (ISBN: 0-415-00228-1). A very readable, fascinating collection of Chinese symbols, myths, common ideas, and lore about numbers, holidays, directions, colors, and practices. A good source of background materials.

The Seven Military Classics of Ancient China: Including the Art of War, translation and commentary by Ralph D. Sawyer, with Mei-chun Sawyer, Westview Press, Boulder, CO, 1993 (ISBN: 0-8133-1228-0).

The Art of War, Sun Tzu (translated and with an introduction by Samuel B. Griffith, foreword by B.H. Liddel Hart), Oxford University Press, New York, 1963.

Chinese-English Bilingual Glossary of Traditions Medicine, (no author listed), Science Press, Elmhurst, NY, a subsidiary of the Science Press, Beijing (PRC), 788 pages, 1993, (ISBN 7-03-033528-3/R-181. This publisher offers a wide range of scientific dictionaries and bilingual paterials on modern and traditional Chinese science as well as some culturally relevant topics.

Weapons in Ancient China, Yong Hong editor. Science Press New York, Elmhurst, NY, 1992, ISBN: 1-880132-03-6. Telephone: (718) 476-0238.

The Psychology of the Chinese People, edited by M.H. Bond, Oxford University Press, Oxford, 1987. Very academic in style but excellent in content. A 1991 "layman's version" by Michael H. Bond is *Beyond the Chinese Face: Insights from Psychology,* Oxford University Press (ISBN: 0-19-585116-1), paperback. It is a clear excellent source largely free from excessive academic machinery and the social scientist's jargon.

The Parting of the Way: Lao Tzu and the Taoist Movement, Holmes Welch Beacon Press, Boston, 1960. A classic study of Taoism.

Three Ways of Thought in Ancient China, Arthur Waley, Doubleday and Company, Garden City, N.Y., 1956. A super-classic by one of the smoothest, most revered translators in this century.

A History of the World's Religions, David S. Noss and John B. Noss, Macmillian Publishing, New York, 1990. Good, solid, clear university textbook.

Culture Shock!: China, Kevin Sinclair with Iris Wong Po-yee, Graphic Arts Center Publishing Company, Portland, Oregon, 1990 (ISBN: 1-55868-060-8). One of the best "what-to-read-before-you-go to-China" books.

East Asia: The Great Tradition, Reischauer, Edwin O., and Fairbank, John K., Houghton Mifflin Company, Boston, 1960. A deservedly famous (and comprehensive) university textbook written by two (deservedly) famous and respected scholars in Asian Studies.

Bulls in the China Shop and Other Sino-American Business Encounters, Randall E. Stross, University of Hawaii Press, Honolulu, 1990 (ISBN: 0-8248-1509-2). A delightful and very informative post-1970 history of American and PRC perceptions and interactions while trying to continue to do business and understand and predict the other.

Family, Field, and Ancestors: Constancy and Change in China's Social and Economic History, 1550-1949, by Lloyd E. Eastman, Oxford University Press, Oxford and New York, 1988 (ISBN: 0-19-505270-6). An excellent, readable jewel of facts about Chinese economic history, commerce, agriculture, rising social classes, religion and manufacturing. In Chapter 10, "The Yin Side of Society: Secret Societies, Bandits, and Feuds", there is a three and one-half page description of the hui, "secret brotherhoods" of which the Triads are one example. This is accompanied by a description of similar folk sects and protective societies, that, together, gives one an expanded understanding of how the Triads fit into and are an ancient part of the whole of Chinese society. For example, it supplements Ko-lin Chen's *Chinese Subculture and Criminality: Non-Traditional Crime Groups in America* (No. 10) and Lynn Pan's *Sons of the Yellow Emperor: History of the Chinese Diaspora* (No. 15).

Gifts, Favors and Banquets: The Art of Social Relationships in China, Mayfair Mei-hui Yang, Cornell University Press, Ithaca, NY, 1994 (ISBN: 0-8014-9592-X). This excellent new book is an academic study but very readable analysis of guanxi relationships within the context of contemporary PRC.

When China Ruled the Seas: The Treasure Fleet of the Dragon Throne, 1405-33, Louise Levathes, Simon and Schuster, New York, 1994 (ISBN: 0-671-70158-4).

The East Asian Region: Confucian Heritage and Its Modern Adaptation, Gilbert Rozman, Ed., Princeton University Press, NJ, 1993 (ISBN: 0-691-02485-5). A superb series of essays on Confucianism and its pervasive influences throughout east Asia.

Race and Culture: a World View, Thomas Sowell, Basic Books, New York, 1994 (0-465-06796-4). A fascinating book with pages of empirically grounded information about the factual and normative aspects of culture, ethnicity, and "race" containing very controversial implications for public policy in the U.S. and Canada.

Tribes: How Race, Religion, and Identity Determine Success in the New Global Economy, Joel Kotkin, Random House, New York, 1992 (ISBN: 0-679-41282-4). See Chapter 6, The Spacemen Have Landed, pp. 165-200. Well worth reading because of the many insights regarding different quasi-transnational ethnic groups in international businesses and the cultural aspects of their actual or potential success.

China and the American Dream: a Moral Inquiry, Richard Madsen, University of California Press, Berkeley, CA, 1995 (ISBN: 0-520-08613-9). This is an excellent socio-cultural analysis of the American and Chinese mindsets regarding the origins, developments, and our reactions to the Tiananmen Square Massacre of June 4, 1989. On that date, the Chinese Army confronted students and workers who were protesting official corruption and encouraging "science and democracy" but who clearly threatened the cherished Chinese need for social stability. The book adroitly describes how Chinese and Americans interpreted the event, each from within its own perspectives, and how each found different themes of disillusionment because of the cultural assumptions and projections of the other which each brought to the event. I have woven in strands from this excellent book into the mindset section of Chapter 12.

China White, Peter Maas, Simon and Schuster, New York, 1994 (ISBN: 0-671-69417-0). An entertaining novel about aspects of Chinese organized crime and law enforcement efforts against them in fictional form. A good story by an author who has talked with many of the right Asian crime investigators. It is an effortless way to gain some begining knowledge about Chinese and AC but no substitute for reading *Chinese Subculture and Criminality: Non-Traditional Crime Groups in America, Sons of the Yellow Emperor: History of the Chinese Diaspora,* and *Chinatown: A Portrain of a Closed Society* (above).

Outrageous Chinese: a Guide to Chinese Street Language, James J. Wang, China Books and Periodicals, San Francisco, CA, 1994 (ISBN: 0-8351-25327). A helpful, short compilation of idioms, slang, "taboo words", obscenities, parts of the body, and easy "slips of the tongue" in Chinese and in English. Easy and fun to read.

China Town Gangs, Extortion, Enterprise, and Ethnicity, Ko-lin Chen, Oxford University Press, 1996 (ISBN: 0-19-510238-X). This excellent new book on Chinese gangs in New York came out just as this book was going to press. Thus, material from it has not been included but is very highly recommended.

Ethnic Profile: The Vietnamese

18

關係

An Introduction to the Scope of Vietnamese Crime

To assist the reader in gaining an overview of Vietnamese and Vietnamese-American organized crime, the following excerpt is taken from the hearings on Asian Organized Crime held by the Permanent Senate Subcommittee on Investigations, of which Vietnamese crime was a part. The Subcommittee's subsequent report summarized Vietnamese crime as follows:

> In the United States, a few Vietnamese operate within the context of Chinese organized crime, but the largest Vietnamese crime problem is that of extremely, vicious street gangs. These gangs typically do not have the tight organizational structure of Chinese or Japanese organized crime groups, and have a much younger membership than other Asian criminal groups. Also, unlike the Chinese and Japanese groups, Vietnamese gangs do not have a centuries-old tradition of organized crime in their homeland. Vietnamese street gangs include both Vietnamese and Chinese-Vietnamese (or Viet-Ching), who are most likely to forge functional relationships with Chinese organized crime groups.
>
> The Vietnamese gangs sometimes serve as extortionists or enforcers for Chinese-American syndicates; their use of violence is common and frequently brutal. Some Vietnamese gangs also specialize in violent home-invasion robberies, often of other Vietnamese-Americans. These gangs are highly mobile and prey on Vietnamese in various parts of the U.S.
>
> The Born To Kill gang, headquartered in New York City, exemplifies the Vietnamese street gang. The Born To Kill was allegedly formed in 1988 by 35-year-old David Thai, who split off from the Flying Dragons. Many of the members of the Born To Kill are in their teens and early twenties. Born To Kill members engage in a variety of criminal activities in New York City,

> including extortion and armed robbery, and frequently travel to such places as upstate New York and Connecticut, and even as far as Georgia to commit armed robberies and crimes of violence against other Asians and Asian businesses. We have seen significant Vietnamese gang activity in New York City, New Orleans, Houston, Miami, Arlington, Virginia, San Francisco, and San Jose.[173]

As stated above, Vietnamese organized crime focuses on large currency transfers, auto theft for transfer to Vietnam, and high-tech theft such as computer chips. Many of the Vietnamese leaders in computer theft are ethnic Chinese (Viet-Ching).[174] Vietnamese have also been used as muscle for Hong Kong-based Triad members and auto insurance fraud scams in this country.[175] Other violence-prone crimes of Vietnamese criminals include gambling, arson, murder, prostitution, weapons and explosives violations, drugs, and extortion. Vietnamese have been involved in the smuggling of prescription medications impossible to obtain in Vietnam such as ampicillin, streptomycin, and tetramycin. Smuggling routes include South America and France. Tax evasion or the under-reporting of income is not uncommon; very few individuals paid taxes in Vietnam and that expectation has been transferred here.

However, the most widely publicized Vietnamese crimes are the home-invasion robberies where Vietnamese or Chinese are the abused but often silent victims. These vicious home-invasion criminals are known for their brutality, careful planning, and extreme mobility. (See *Born To Kill*, by T. J. English.) The victims are usually other Vietnamese, many of whom are suspicious of banks and keep large amounts of cash in their homes. Some of the gangs remain together but some are pick-up gangs and disperse at the conclusion of a job. On occasion, Cambodians, Laotians, and Amerasians are included. Excellent sources describe the specific techniques or typical methods of these particular Vietnamese criminals, such as William Cassidy's *Nomadic Vietnamese Armed Robbery*,[176] Jack Willoughby's *Vietnamese Traveling Criminals*, Philip Hannum and Al Lotz's *Nightmare*, and the Bureau of Alcohol, Tobacco, and Firearms' *Vietnamese Traveling Criminals*. In the 18-page BATF pamphlet, it is noted that the favorite weapons of gangs are Uzis, Mac-10s, AK-47s, M-16s, sawed-off shotguns, small caliber pistols, and knives.[177]

Some gang members are on the road almost all of the time; some have no permanent home and shift from motel to motel. After extensive phone connections or planning meetings (e.g., Carthage Marian Days), they may pop in and out of a city or town where neither their faces nor their fingerprints are known and make quick connections at another gang banger's room or motel. There, usually treating each previously unknown member as family, they carefully plan (and sometimes rehearse) a home-invasion robbery. Included in their deliberations are such issues as the number and placement of phones in the victim/s house; the use of torture; backup plans if something goes wrong; acquiring "cold" backup cars; coordination and uses of walkie-talkies between lookouts and getaway cars. Then they often execute the plan with precision and ruthless violence, change cars before driving onto the interstate, and are out of the county or state within minutes. It is often claimed by experienced investigators that they are neither intimidated by law enforcement nor afraid of shooting police. Thus, police should take every precaution in traffic stops and when questioning gang members.

A Geographical and Historical Sketch

Vietnam is located on the coast of the Southeast Asian peninsula surrounded by the China Sea on the East, Laos and Cambodia on its west. Relatively narrow, it is about the size of California, or slightly larger than New Mexico — 329,560 km in total land area. It stretches in a north-south direction and consists of three types of terrain: fertile village farmland and river delta in the south, mountains and highlands west of the central coast, and mountains and cooler plains in the north.

To the north, China looks down upon Vietnam which it conquered in the second century B.C. and retained as a colony until the 10th century A.D. Before the French invasions of the last century, Vietnamese education was modeled on the Chinese system of studying Chinese classical texts such as those of Confucius and Mencius. Furthermore, Vietnamese Buddhism has been heavily influenced in form and content by Chinese Mahāyāna Buddhism. However, in spite of the strong influences of almost two centuries of French colonialization, China remains the major cultural influence in Vietnam.[178]

During the early part of the last century, the French conquered Vietnam and revamped the educational system on the French model. This permanently changed the way the Vietnamese looked at themselves. As with many former colonies, the Vietnamese had to fight internal ideological battles to determine their own national identity. Various Vietnamese have tried to determine with whom their identities lay — with the classical Chinese heritage or with the modern but foreign ideas introduced by the French. Furthermore, the introduction of the foreign ideas of Marxists and Communists, made the problems of a national identity even more complex.[179] It might be well to remember that the U.S. has never had to fight an ideological battle of such a magnitude to determine who and what we are. Thus, it is easy for Americans to overlook how important most Vietnamese and Vietnamese-Americans consider questions about their cultural identities and the tensions built into questions of assimilation and ethnic pride in North America. Such controversies can also make a Vietnamese person cautious in developing immediate trust in others.

Today, Vietnam has a population of about 72 million people, of whom about 20% live in urban areas; 80%, mostly farmers, live in the countryside. It remains one of the poorer nations on the globe. Although most inhabitants of Vietnam are ethnic Vietnamese, about 7 million ethnic minorities also live in Vietnam, the majority of whom are ethnic Chinese (Viet-Ching). The latter identify themselves ethnically rather than politically, as Chinese with Vietnamese citizenship. They usually live in the south, speak Cantonese, read and write both Chinese and Vietnamese, and are commercial vendors engaged in small manufacturing. In 1978–1979, the numbers of Chinese-Vietnamese were substantially reduced through official "stimulation" to leave the country. Also, there are a few other indigenous minority groups in Vietnam such as the mountain-dwelling Montagnards and Hmong (Meo, Miao). Those that did not flee because of their involvement with the CIA during the Vietnam War generally continue to live independently of Vietnamese culture in the mountainous highlands.[180]

In North America, Southeast Asian refugees are clustered in California (223,000), Texas (51,000), and Washington (29,000); approximately 18,000 to 21,000 are in the states of Pennsylvania, Illinois, Minnesota, Virginia, New York, and Oregon. The Vietnamese population in the U.S. today is about 750,000. During the decade of 1982 to 1992, the Vietnamese population of the U.S. increased by 135%.

There were two initial waves of Vietnamese immigration.[181] The first wave was at the fall of Saigon in April, 1975 during which many of those 132,000 Vietnamese leaving had close connections with the American presence in Vietnam. In general, the first wave of immigrants on or before 1975 were middle- or upper-class, military or civil service personnel. They tended to be better educated, as 48% had over 4 years of college; they were more fluent in English, usually came from urban areas, and were considered to be friends of America to whom we had a moral obligation.

Two years later, the second wave of about 127,000 began as a result of the Vietnamese government's decision to expel the ethnic non-Vietnamese such as the Homg (Meo), Cham, Montagnards,[182] and Khmers, who were linked to the Cambodians. However, other Vietnamese, often referred to as the "boat people", continued to flee Vietnam and eventually arrived in North America. These people were less educated and unfamiliar with North American cultures. They tended to be rural farmers and fishermen trying to escape the chaos caused by the war. Many of these people were without adequate documentation and encountered severe difficulties as they found their way to the U.S. through several other countries.[183] After the second wave, there has been a smaller but steady stream of immigrants coming here by means of their connections to family and friends, legal and illegal. By 1993, those fleeing Vietnam has dwindled to relatively few.

Two particular groups among those of the second wave are those children and teenagers who entered with little documentation and without parents or family through the Unaccompanied Minors Program and as a result of the abuse of Amerasians by Vietnamese trying to get into this country. Amerasians are children born in the early 1970s of (usually) American military personnel fathers and Vietnamese mothers. The unaccompanied minors have been placed in North American foster homes after existing in Asia under severe and sometimes dangerous, survive-at-all-cost conditions in refugee/resettlement camps. Their lack of documentation and their absence of commonly learned social survival techniques do not make their transition into North American society a smooth one.

Amerasians constitute a small but growing problem in two special respects. As Shirley Y. Chin noted, "In Vietnam, they are considered half-breeds, pariahs to be shunned by the 'normal' Vietnamese community".[184] Thus, they were considered the "lowest of the low", particularly the children of Afro-Americans. With the establishment of the resettlement program, the Amerasian Homecoming Act of 1987, this method of getting to the U.S. has been " … permeated by fraud at every level. The scam starts with the purchase of the Amerasians, includes bribery of Vietnamese officials and culminates with fake families receiving U.S. resettlement benefits in the U.S."[185]

Furthermore, U.S. officials and voluntary agency officials estimate that perhaps one half of the 50,000 Vietnamese who have been brought into the U.S. at a cost of about $6000 per person were brought in on the basis of fraudulent documents and claims. After arriving in this country, many of the Amerasians have been abandoned by the Vietnamese families who purchased them in Vietnam for amounts ranging from $800 to $2000. The fraudulent actions and the human consequences of the importation of such people do not bode well for American law enforcement, for most of the Ameriasians possess exactly those characteristics that make them potential gang members.

While most of the older and second generation Vietnamese in North America have tended to cluster together and exhibit what some have called "a passive resistance to change and assimilation", their children are walking the path of most immigrant children and becoming more and more "Americanized".[186] However, some Vietnamese who arrive too late to assimilate the English language and North American culture have become a crime problem. Lt. Jack Willoughby, New Orleans P.D., noted the traumatic influence of the of the refugee camps in Thailand, Malaysia, or Hong Kong:[187]

> Gangs formed in camps, for self protection and survival, continue when the members are transported to the U.S. Not all gang members from the camps come to America; some are so vile they will never be allowed to leave the camps. It is thus so, that when many refugees from Vietnam reach our shores they have undergone trials worse than any in any American prison. They have seen the worst that life can deliver, and because of their experiences of the past years expect and look forward to nothing.
>
> Survival is all. This is part of the culture of many newly arrived, young Vietnamese and the only survival some of them see is as a member of a gang. These psychic burdens of the new refugee, including Post-Traumatic Stress Disorder, must be recognized and dealt with by an investigator working in an Asian community. Any failure to understand the violent background of these refugees will be a failure affecting all criminal investigations involving these subjects. You may be assured that in a criminal trial, a good defense attorney will have figures and facts at his finger tips, making an ignorant, testifying officer look like a jerk and milking sympathy from the jury, as cheerfully as a hippie milks a goat.

Furthermore, while many North Americans have tended to view Asians as a whole as a "model minority", the economic and social realities are less admirable and far more painful. They include:[188]

> A poverty rate for Asians in Los Angeles, San Francisco, and New York that is nearly twice as high as that of whites. For every Asian household with an annual income of $75,000 or more, there is another making less than $10,000 a year. A growing reliance on welfare. In fact, Southeast Asians — Vietnamese, Cambodians, Laotians — have the highest welfare dependency rate of any racial group. Southeast Asians comprise only about 13 percent of Asian Americans but account for up to 87 percent of all Asian Americans on welfare. An explosion of entrepreneurship that focuses on low-margin, low-profit businesses. One-third of self-employed Asians are in the highly competitive retail sector, most commonly operating restaurants. Asian American entrepreneurs accounted for 2.6% of all firms in 1987, but only 1.7% of all receipts.

Cultural Sketches

The following section consists of sketches of some important aspects of traditional Vietnamese culture with an emphasis on cultural contrasts.[189] While these descriptions constitute reasonably accurate cultural guidelines (not rules), individual Vietnamese are as varied in their personal actions, choices, and lifestyles as anyone else.

People

Traditional Vietnamese greetings are first directed toward the elders and/or the head of the family. Except for more "internationalized" Vietnamese, men do not shake hands with the opposite sex and often not with each other. Usually they show greetings and respect (as in India, Srị Lānka, etc.) by placing their two hands together, palms pressed together before the chest coupled with a slight bow of the head. However, in the U.S. one sees an occasional greeting between men where there is only a slight bow; but, to show special respect, a mutual two-handed shake of the hands is used. Respect is often shown by using an appropriate or polite title in addressing a senior or person of the same social level as one's self. Manners count!

Offers of dinner, snacks, tea, or other refreshments should be repeated at least two times, for it is impolite to accept at the first (or among the very traditional, even the second) offering. Calling ahead before visiting, rather than dropping in (just "popping in") is seldom observed. If guests arrive at dinner time, they are invited to share whatever is in the house to eat.

Between friends, men may hold another man's hand, as do women; however, public touching between men and women is severely criticized. Kissing is never done in public, except with babies and only by parents or close relatives. Friendly slaps on the back are usually considered insulting. It is not unexpected that two or three members of the same sex would be regularly sleeping in the same bed; naps ("siestas") are common. Because they consider the human head the place of the essential "spirit" of the person, a person's head should never be touched, even in a friendly pat on a child's head. Expressions of thanks are not used as often as in North America, not between friends, not to those of lower social rank, not to people who are merely implementing their professional or work responsibilities, e.g., a salesperson or secretary.

The traditional social levels ("caste system") are: (1) scholar, (2) farmer/fisherman, (3) laborer, and (4) businessman.

Humility and indirectness are highly valued. Thus, they tend not to speak of themselves, their families, or their accomplishments. Often, Vietnamese have to be asked to respond to inquiries about their families to which most Americans would deliberately volunteer information to try to establish mutual feelings of friendliness. Also, "small talk" about trivial personal things or giving or receiving praise is sometimes awkward for them. When speaking, some consider it polite to cover one's mouth with one's hand or a napkin, etc.

The older a person is, the less inclined he may be to request information or assistance. Since he is older, he is expected to know more; to ask may be to lose "face". Moreover, the assumption is often held that a stranger would have no interest in giving them accurate assistance and that it is better to check and re-check with family and respected friends to secure help. Among friends or acquaintances, someone may suggest that he needs help, but in a very indirect manner. For example, someone might suggest that his situation would be improved with a loan or some assistance. However, these needs will be described in such a way as to allow both to keep "Face" and to allow the listener the choice as to whether he will or can loan money or help.

Punctuality is not a social value. American punctuality (within 3 to 5 minutes) is not observed. Vietnamese are much more "laid back" about time; showing up an hour late for an appointment should not be considered a deliberate insult nor would it be considered particularly rude by traditional Vietnamese (see "Deep Mindsets;" this chapter).

Given the openness of traditional Vietnamese country homes, American homes, to some Vietnamese, seem strangely closed up and stuffy.

In general, Vietnamese standards of physical attractiveness are:

- Fair complexion
- Tallness
- Modesty
- Soft, well-spoken voice
- Naturally red lips
- Straight posture
- Bright eyes
- Straight nose
- White teeth
- Slimness
- Straight legs (a sign of good health and bountiful parents).

Other facts about the Vietnamese include:

- The average height of Vietnamese is about 5'4"; weight, 110 lb. As has been observed with recent Japanese and Chinese immigrants to the U.S., the size and weight (and certain forms of cancer and other illnesses) of Vietnamese generally increase with Western diets.
- American cultural styles of dating are rejected and such social pairing off is viewed as either evidence that a couple is very close to being married or that she is a bad, immoral woman.
- Whereas direct and sustained eye contact and staring straight into a person's eyes as one talks to him/her usually shows honesty and frankness among Americans, in traditional Vietnamese society these behaviors would be impolite and disrespectful, especially to superiors and/or elders.

- With Americans, a smile means pleasure, happiness, and sometimes agreement; with Vietnamese, a smile could mean anything from happiness to sadness, agreement to disagreement, or polite indifference to interest. Laughing loudly or speaking in a loud rough voice is thought rude, especially for women.
- To lose one's temper in public is very bad manners, and one loses a great amount of "face". Stay cool.
- Traditional working hours are from 8:00 a.m. to 12:00 a.m and from 2:00 p.m. to about 5:00 p.m. Retail shops often stay open in the evenings. The work week is 5½ days (Saturday morning).

Contrasts of American and traditional Vietnamese cultures regarding clothing include:

- Pajamas are acceptable in public.
- Women seldom wear socks and the older women often wear the national/regional ethnic clothes.
- Men may often wear Western clothes.
- Shoes are removed before entering a house.
- Some aspects of common American summer clothing are considered much too revealing for traditional Vietnamese mothers; other Vietnamese, however, do not find this an issue.
- Some Vietnamese businessmen find American business attire too heavy and formal for their traditional tastes.

Chopsticks, spoons, and a bowl are used without napkins; however, people are expected to wash their faces after every meal. Traditionally, two equally large meals are consumed. Vietnamese usually eat lunch and dinner in equally large portions each day; the choice portions of food — rice is the staple — are served to the parents and elders first from the large central serving bowl. In general, the younger or social inferiors do not begin to eat until their elders or social superiors begin to eat. Appreciation for food is sometimes expressed by deliberate "slurping" sounds while eating, especially with soup — they are not silent eaters. Publicly, women are expected to eat small portions (like a cat); men, large portions (like a tiger).

The "OK" and "thumbs up" gestures are acceptable; as in most all of Asia, the "thumbs up" gesture means good, great, super, number one! However, a Vietnamese-American made the following interesting cross-cultural point: "The OK sign is universal language which is fine to use [with the Vietnamese]. However, for unknown reasons many Americans make a face when they make this gesture. Refugees may become confused. They see the OK sign with what they interpret as a negative facial expression. The two cancel each other out and they are back to zero."[190]

Human Nature and World View

As in much of the Confucian and Neo-Confucian traditions, the Vietnamese view of human nature has been that it is basically good or at least capable of being improved by proper education and humane activities. However, human nature can easily be corrupted and/or thwarted by social and economic circumstances. As with many others, Vietnamese will be reluctant to settle for short-term progress and short-term friends. A Vietnamese is interested in adjusting and maintaining a reasonable, workable, pragmatic harmony in his/her life. The Chinese were the first realists and pragmatists, and the Vietnamese learned the lessons of Chinese pragmatism and the quest for social harmoney and stability from them centuries ago.

In general, the Vietnamese view of the world was that there is:[191]

- Order, regularity, reasonableness and pattern to the cyclical physical universe (Vietnamese: ly; Chinese: li, STC 3810)[192] and that what was observed in nature — hierarchy and ranked relationships — provided a balanced model for human relationships, humans being only one complementary aspect of the natural universe. Thus, not only are humans to help to maintain this balance by acting in proper ways which reflect this natural order, but also humans are a natural part of this order, not something created by something outside of the natural order.
- Filial piety, a natural (ly) order of obligations and duties found in the Vietnamese (and Chinese) sense of the ranked, specialized, and unequal bonds, birth-based obligations and ethical oportunities, (Vietnamese: hieu; Chinese: xiao, STC 1321) between younger members of a family towards their elders, much as in the five relationships of Confucius.
- Moral debt (Vietnamese: *on*) to one's parents for being raised by them which cannot be discharged except by raising one's own children in the proper (ly, hieu) ways.
- "A righteous path" (nghia) is described by Neil L. Jamieson:[193]

> These role-based behvioral ideals, with *hieu* [filial piety] and *de* [brother to brother obligations] at the core and combined with the concept of *on* [moral debt to one's parents] instilled in Vietnamese a rigid code of conduct and strong sense of duty.... the primancy of social obligations was summarized by the value of *nghai*, perhaps best translated as "righteousness". Nghai

> implies duty, justice, and obligation. It inculcates the willness to do what one must do to fulfill one's social obligations, to repay *on*, to meet the demands of *hieu* and *de*. *Nghai* demands calm rationality within the structure of *ly*, the nature of things, and that one live scrupulously by an unbending set of rules, regardless of circumstances, regardless of personal preferences, regardless of the apparent consequences.

Thus, the behavioral guidelines are internal and village oriented. As one educated Vietnamese put it, "Because of centuries of domination by the Chinese and the French and years under the Communists and/or the Americans, the Vietnamese tend to be wary and cautious of unknown persons or authority." This should never be taken as an indication that Vietnamese are liars, as Americans use the term. Rather, Vietnamese tend to find it more difficult to immediately tell the truth in a direct way without learning more about the possibilities built into the social and political situation and/or the real agendas of unknown people involved. The quest for survival breeds caution and skill in weaving one's responses to fit the situation; this, in turn, constitutes another exported version of the old Buddhist idea of social contextualism and pragmatic behavioral expediency: Sanskrit upāya, Chinese fang bian, Japanese hōben (see Chapter 13).

Also, because of centuries of domination by the Chinese and the French and then the years under the Communists and/or the Americans, Vietnamese have a somewhat more difficult time finding a deeply trusted, intimate friend than do most more trusting North Americans who are less cautious of unknown persons or authority. As always, it is a matter of the degree of difference between Vietnamese and Americans, as both share some of both the same qualities of trust and suspicion.

Family

The central focus of the Vietnamese (and the Chinese) is the family; ideally, it is a large extended family including aunts and uncles living together in busy, hardworking harmony. This major influence can be seen in the Chinese Confucian social ideals of social harmony, defined and ranked mutual dependence, family goals, and mutual assistance. This interrelated focus on the family and the regional home village of the family is well expressed in the following excerpt from a cultural profile of the Vietnamese prepared by the Australian Customs Service.[194,195] Note the echoes of Chinese culture.

> The Vietnamese are also strongly attached to their land and native village because it is the home of their ancestor's tombs. There is great respect for ancestors' spirits and achievements, and due to these strong emotional

> attachments, Vietnamese do not usually wish to leave their villages or home towns.... for the Vietnamese, age is wisdom and deserves high esteem. As a consequence, elderly people are accorded the highest standing in society and in the family. Any insult to the ancestors of a Vietnamese or to a respected older person is taken very seriously.... Family loyalty plays a very important role in the conduct of its members. Each person is aware of his position in relation to every other family member and this is reflected in the way they behave and are addressed. Family identity can be a tremendous source of pride or dishonor, and family loyalty engenders a strong sense of duty and responsibility. Each child is taught to carry out these two obligations in order to pay off the debt of birth and rearing by their parents.

The extended family/clan consists of not only the parents and children, but also uncles and aunts, nephews and nieces, and numerous cousins. Furthermore, honorary family status is sometimes extended to members of the home village. The parents and grandparents are expected to live within the extended family complex of married children until they die. Compared to most Americans, traditional Vietnamese are not socially or physically mobile. That is, they do not change social classes nor do they travel much.

The father is the leader of the household and will not hesitate to physically discipline his sons, although he does not possess an absolute right over the lives of other members of the household as in traditional China. However, the father remains the absolute leader in family decisions. (By contrast, this is somewhat less so with the Khmer and Lao families.) Before marriage, a woman is to be subordinate to her father, and after marriage, subordinate to her husband; when she is widowed, she is to be subordinate to her sons, certainly to the all-important eldest son. These are public expectations about social roles, although some women and/or widows have become very powerful leaders within and without the family and are anything but subordinate. However, the overriding goal (again, as with the Chinese) is the long range continuance of the family, and this requires sons. Thus, a lack of sons is both a family disaster and a sad example of life's uncertainty.

In the urban and suburban areas of Hanoi (north), Hue (central) and Ho Chi Minh City (south; the former Saigon), these are areas which reflect shared religious preferences or shared economic or occupational interests. However, even there, the village mentality (see below) is carried with them. The needs and desires of the family take precedence over the needs and desires of the individual and, similarly, of the elders over the young. Roughly, all other things being equal, being over 45 years of age generally entitles one to receive the appropriate respect for a senior or a respected elderly person. The husband focuses on the world outside the family. While the wife focuses within the family, she wields considerable power and influence through family actions. Praise or blame are held to reflect on the whole family, not just on the individual who acts:[196]

> A violation of social and moral codes can seriously damage or destroy a person's acceptance in the community. A behavioral deviation by a Vietnamese will hurt not only him but also his family. Pregnancy in an unmarried girl, divorce, living together or a socially unmatched marriage, for example, can lead to family dishonor, and may result in the family disowning the family member or forcing them to move to a distant place where their identity is unknown. On the other hand, the successful completion of a difficult or competitive examination can boost family pride and prestige tremendously.

All things equal, men are considered superior to women, a husband to his wife, a brother to his sister. In this country, second and third wives are prohibited even though older such relations may have been quietly incorporated into the family. Of course, this does not always work out in practice, for some women have wielded great power in and out of the home. However, because of decades of war and the increasing influences of Western lifestyles and feminist ideas, these general cultural traits remain in force more for those Vietnamese who live in the countryside than those who live in or near the city.

In North America, the Vietnamese husband's position as head of the family is occasionally diminished if his wife must work to maintain more than a minimum level of care for their children. In light of the stress of adjusting to a new culture, the maintenance of traditional social roles and the avoidance of losing "face" remains important and sometimes quite difficult in a strange land. Abuse of wives and children by the male head of the household was more widely tolerated in Vietnam than in North America. Because Vietnamese wives and children are not usually near their relatives, the stress of living in a different culture increases the frequency of battered wives and children who are without the companionship and help of their extended family. Most women are reluctant to report such abuse, and many calls to police come from a neighbor or relative.

Marriage

Custom holds that both parents should approve the match of their children. Men marry between 20 and 30, women between 18 and 25. Until a marriage is agreed upon, a woman may not accept gifts from a man, for doing so is a polite symbol of encouragement or acceptance of him. The marriage celebration is usually held in either or both households, not in a temple — the temple is home of the gods. The new wife becomes part of her husband's family and although she may legally retain her own maiden name, many take their husband's name. Second and third wives are allowed, but the first wife is senior in almost all things. Divorce, uncommon but not unknown, brings intense social and family pressures if it is openly contemplated. An unmarried daughter of marriageable age is often thought to be a very worrisome burden indeed for the family. As Neil Jamieson put it, "So a family had to groom girls for export, so to speak, and to bind boys emotionally to the family in which they would remain for the rest of their life."[197]

Based on very strong cultural traditions, the bride must be a sexual virgin at marriage. Sex education, formal or informal, is almost always absent. Rape is very *under-reported*, for rape renders the young woman unmarriageable and "used goods", in the eyes of traditional Vietnamese. Thus, date rape usually is not reported, and some Vietnamese young men have taken advantage of this, knowing that raping their dates will never be told to families or reported to the police. Spousal rape is traditionally considered brutal and blameworthy, but the concept of "raping one's wife" is almost never considered as bad as the rape of an unmarried woman. Some of these ideas may simply need to be explained to those first or second-generation Vietnamese who may be unfamiliar with North American laws and customs or legal alternatives. In general, the woman has few alternatives in a bad marriage and is usually blamed for any troubles in the marriage: "Leaving the marriage would also probably mean that she loses the children, as they belong to the husband's family. Remarriage is uncommon, and widows are also expected to remain single, although this changing."[198]

Children

Outside the cities, childbirth is traditionally supervised by a midwife assisted by married women of the family within the family home; husbands, men, boys, and girls are excluded. Sons are preferred over daughters. As with the Chinese, a newborn infant is deemed 1 year old at birth. Children are closely supervised. The eldest son is (in theory) the most powerful of the male children. Boys are strictly disciplined and often closely supervised and kept relatively apart from their sisters. Young girls have strict household duties to learn in preparation for future marriage, and education for them has often been considered a waste of time and resources — except at higher levels of traditional Vietnamese society. Children are expected to exhibit filial piety toward their parents, grandparents, elders in the community, and elder brothers and sisters. They are to use good manners, give great respect to their elders, and generally remain passive and shy when meeting people outside their family. While children are the extremely important responsibilities of the parents and are the constant focus of the family, it is also generally true that children have no operative legal rights which would or could bring them in opposition to any customary or "socially reasonable" decisions of their parents.

Death

Most Vietnamese wish to die at home among their family, not in a hospital. Cremation, if requested, is not uncommon. As with the Chinese, white is the color of death and of mourning. (Gifts are given in red envelopes, not white ones.) Traditionally, the family should wear white clothes for two weeks after the death in the family and a white head band for several months. For family members, the appropriate periods of mourning are:

> When the husband dies the wife should wait three years;
> If the wife dies, the husband should wait one year;
> If one of the parents dies, the children should wait three years to marry or re-marry;
> If brothers or sisters die, they should wait one year to marry.

Using the lunar calendar (as many Asians do), a special ceremony to assist and honor the dead will occur one week after the funeral and be repeated for 7 weeks. After 49 days (7 days times 7), the ceremony honoring the deceased will be repeated each year at a nearby temple/pagoda or at home. (A pagoda is the Chinese Buddhist architectural form of an ancient Indian Buddhist structure for housing sacred relics; Sanskrit: stupa, caitya; Chinese: xie, STC 1044.)

Education

Education has been considered of utmost value and teachers are regarded as the highest level of society because of their moral character as well as their knowledge. Hence, in traditional Vietnamese eyes, education, as opposed to technical skills, is thought most important and presumes high cultural and moral discipline. Showing respect for an educated person, a teacher, or an elder is done by a modest bow of the head. Giving respect and precedence to an elder or highly educated person is taken very seriously. Skilled professions are distinguished from educated persons and the former are not honored in the same ways as are educated persons, nor is the social status of a (merely) skilled professional person very high.

Today, Vietnamese education is highly centralized and rigid from kindergarten through grade 12 and among the 91 multipurpose colleges and two universities. Literacy is officially claimed at just under 80%. However, nationwide economic problems have reduced the quality and availability of education and the 9 years of compulsory education are not always achieved. Additional emphasis has been placed on vocational and managerial training in the lower grades which is often shunned by those who aspire to high status "white-collar" positions. The numbering of the grades is now parallel to the American pre-university grade system. At the end of the 12th grade the student takes a national examination to try to secure the Tu Tai, the equivalent of the French Baccalaureate. Values placed on class rankings are not similar to the American system of A, B, C, D, E; however, the American 5-point scale may be illustrated by comparing it against a 20-point scale with the qualification that grades or class marks 17 through 20 are almost never awarded; the grades of exceptional students, usually an A grade, are usually about 15 or 16.[199]

Vietnamese Religions

The Anglo-European assumption that one should have an exclusive allegiance to the "practice and belief in" one, and only one, religious sect is not shared in much of Asia (see Chapter 19). While most Vietnamese are Buddhists, there are influences from China in the centuries-old traditions of the Confucian and Neo-Confucian social and political traditions. Other influences are found in the Vietnamese Buddhist religious schools, particularly Thien (Chinese: Ch'an; Japanese: Zen; derived from the Sanskrit word for trance or meditation: dhyana). A more devotional tradition is Amidaism in which the devotees practice the recitation of "Amita", the name of the Bodhisattva Amida, the Bodhisattva of the Western Paradise to which one may wish to be reborn (Sanskrit: Amitābha; Chinese: A-mi-t'o; Japanese: Amida, the Bodhisattva of the Pure Land, Jōdo and Jōdo Shinshū). The repetition of the sacred name of "Amita" (often simply called "Buddha") and another female Bodhisattva Quan-The-Am (Sanskrit: Avalokiteśvara; Chinese: Kuan-yin; Japanese: Kwannon) are common forms of religious devotion among Vietnamese Buddhists. The chanting of the sacred Buddhist name often takes place at a Buddhist shrine where there are also contained intertwined observances to the Earth god and the animal gods of the old Vietnamese religion.[200]

Most villages have a pagoda, a Buddhist relic shrine, but as with most south and southeast Asian Hinduism and Buddhism, there is no "congregation" which "belongs" at the temple. While there are exceptions, Buddhist monks are usually uneducated and have little influence in the villages; they are there to preserve the traditions, recite the Buddhist texts, and see to the temple grounds, relics, and statuary. The most popular groups found at many pagodas are women praying for male children or old women engaged in pious devotions. Often there is an annual Buddhist ceremony on the Buddha's birthday followed by a banquet.

There are two smaller but important Vietnamese religious groups, the Hoa Hao and the Cao Dai. Hoa Hao is a hybrid messianic Buddhist sect founded in 1939 which dispenses with the venerable positions of the monks (priests or bhiksu) and allows no temples. This allegedly prevents religious "professionals" from coming between the people and the supreme "God", probably the Buddhist Bodhisattva Maitreya and the Luminous King or Prince Moonlight (yueguang tonzi). Cao Dai is an odd (to us) combination of Confucianism, Daoism, Buddhism, Christianity, and popular versions of Anglo-European romanticism. Begun in the 1920s, with close to 2 million devotees today, Cao Dai reveres, and attempts to contact in seances led by Vietnamese mediums, prominent Anglo-European and Asian leaders and literary figures such as the Chinese Sun Yat-Sen, Britain's Winston Churchill, and France's Joan of Arc.

As in China, the three religions commonly known as "The Three Teachings" are usually honored equally; they are (1) Confucian ethical and social ideals, (2) Mahāyāna Buddhist paths of salvation and rebirth, and (3) Daoist (also spelled "Taoist") teachings of harmony, balance, and subtle simplicity in all things including traditional medicine, martial arts, and cooking. A person may burn incense at local village altars to ensure good crops and fertility, honor (not literally worship) the family ancestors with Confucian rites. Often, Buddhist monks are honored and invited to funerals, festivals, and special occasions. A common attitude is "After all, religion is good so why should not we honor all forms of it?".

Animist Religion

In the countryside, most Vietnamese practice some form of animism which holds that there are hidden local spirits in agricultural places and in inanimate objects. Examples are the gods of the Earth, animals, and the spirits of the river and special local sacred trees or groves. Coupled with local animistic cults, most country people practice some type of village-level devotional Buddhism which is sometimes mixed with local country godlings important at festivals and annual holidays. In suburban and urban areas around the large cities of Hanoi, Hue, and Ho Chi Minh City (former Saigon) there are sizable numbers of French Catholic Christians and larger numbers of more sophisticated sects of Mahāyāna Buddhism. The distinctions among all these semi-religious Vietnamese themes have become blended and blurred, just as Lady Luck, Santa Claus, Mother Nature, Satan, and Elvis are blurred in popular American TV culture. In contrast with the monotheist (one god) religious traditions of Judaism, Christianity, and Islam, there are, in both China and most of Asia, no fundamental creation myths or theologies of a single god creating the universe out of chaos or out of nothing to attain some implicit purpose, in the way most Anglo-Europeans believe. For many traditional Vietnamese, the universe is held to be infinite in time and size, and the earth is (more or less) square; this folk belief is often symbolized in the round and square rice cakes prepared for the Tet (New Year) holidays.

Reincarnation

Belief in reincarnation or continual rebirth (Sanskrit: karman or the Anglicized karma; Pali: kamma; Chinese: ye; STC 2814) is extremely widespread due to the influences of Buddhism and Hinduism.[201] As Greek and Latin were the classical languages of the Anglo-European traditions, Sanskrit was and is the sacred classical language of almost all classical Hinduism and almost all of Indian Buddhism; the derivative classical language of Theravāda Buddhism is Pali. The belief in karman, usually called karma in English, contrasts with the Judeo-Christian-Islamic belief in a single, agent-creator god. There is no theological/philosophical idea in the Judeo-Christian traditions equal to or analogous with karma. On the other hand, few if any Buddhist or Hindu deities are inclusive, all-powerful creator Gods in the way in which Christians, Jews, and Muslims usually think of God/Allah as the one and only causal agent of the creation of the universe.

Asian belief in karma is coupled with the presence of many, many great gods, little gods, and semi-divine godlings each of whom manifests countless types of religious ritual and ceremonial machinery and are present in an enormous range of religious practices. Karma is a belief about moral causation furthered by intentional actions, physical or mental. Karma is a Hindu idea, originating in India and first found in the books of the *Vedas* called the *Upanishads.* This occurred around the time of the historical Buddha, about the fifth and sixth centuries B.C. The ideas of karma and rebirth spread to China and Vietnam about the second century A.D. with other Chinese influences of Confucianism and Taoism.

The doctrine of karma presupposes that (almost all of) the circumstances of this life are causally determined by the accumulated effects of intentional moral and immoral actions in both this life and in many past lives. Also, depending on one's present and past actions, one can be — and has been — reborn as other human beings, animals, insects, or ghosts (preta) or angelic messengers (apsura) in or out of numerous Hells and Heavens.[202] Good intentions bring about good effects and vice versa — bad intentions cause bad results. Right knowledge (vidhyā) and the diminution of ignorance

(avidyā) are the double-sided keys to right understanding and, thus, to right intentions, right actions, and right morality. Karma then, constitutes a very deep idea, a conceptual axiom which explains and justifies the way the world is and the way it "works" — from the Buddhist perspective (naya).

Fate and Fatalism

The idea of karma is often and mistakenly equated with fate or fatalism. The generalization is often heard that the Vietnamese will struggle very hard to improve their lot in life but that at a certain point — if they have done all they possible can — they will cease struggling and accept their "fate" peacefully. Aside from the trivial point that many non-Vietnamese also do that, there is a difference in the point at which many Vietnamese will give up, as opposed to the point at which mainline Americans give up. Americans are oriented toward the future and habitually hope that the future will be better. We, and some Japanese, emphasize that struggling is admirable and we admire those who never give up, even when taken to ridiculous lengths.

Another internal perspective of some Vietnamese is that because of the constant armed struggles since the World War of 1939 to 1945, they feel that they are a "people wronged by fate". As noted by T.J. English, this is expressed in the Vietnamese term "oan" ("wronged") and in the 200-year-old epic poem about the tragic life of a Vietnamese woman, *The Tale of Kieu.*[203] The fate (or karma) of some Vietnamese has been to suffer in and out of the homeland and, for some, to be scattered throughout the world. T. J. English describes a former gang member's feelings: "Whether they see themselves as victims or survivors, all Vietnamese refugees have been severed from the land of their ancestors. Like Kieu, they have been compelled to serve false masters, to do things they otherwise might not have done were it not for the cruel demands of fate."[204]

From Asian cultural traditions we find contrasting attitudes rooted in Theravāda Buddhism, various forms of Mahāyāna Buddhism, in which one's bad fortune is seen to be an effect of bad karma, and karmic effects are known to be inevitable. Also rooted in Chinese culture is the quiet emphasis of Taoism, the twin Confucian virtues of submission to one's social superiors and accepting the consequences of one's chances in life by responding appropriately within one's social station. In short, Asians may sometimes publicly accept the inevitable, but their energy and work ethic refute the sweeping claim that they are fatalistic. On the other hand, if Americans and many other Anglo-Europeans were not so imbued with public optimism, the constant rejection of theodicy, and the idea of progress in human history, Asian contrasts would not seem as great as our generalizations and rhetoric would lead us to believe.

Behavior with Police

In Vietnam, corruption and bribery have been common, and police have been considered as representing political authorities, not the people. Penalties have been severe and swift. Procedures common in the American system of justice with energetic public defenders are unknown. Most traditional Vietnamese settle disputes by themselves, within the family, clan, or village without reference to or interference from the national legal system.

Several special cross-cultural features are noteworthy for North American police. In North America, during a traffic stop, some Vietnamese may not always pull over immediately. Furthermore, after stopping, they may leave their autos and walk back to the officer as a gesture of respect rather than sit in their cars and wait for the officer to approach them. This difference makes some officers nervous and they may draw their weapons as a result. Also, remember that direct eye contact (looking someone straight in the eye) is considered rude, especially to an elder or a person in authority. Thus, their avoidance of your gaze may not be a sign of deception or guilt.

A few relevant but scattered points are worth noting once again. Their identification cards/papers and official documents are not kept in the usual places for fear of theft. Their names and addresses may be incorrect, out-of-date, or misinterpreted because of misunderstandings and/or frequent moving. In the experiences of many Southeast Asians, only the most serious criminals were handcuffed. Furthermore, the kneeling position or on-the-ground position was thought to be a forerunner of death; that is, kneeling was followed by execution. Hence, their extreme nervousness may (or may not) be due to such cross-cultural factors. In interviewing nonfluent Vietnamese speakers of English, do not mix Chinese-Vietnamese (Viet-Ching) with other Vietnamese. When interviewing non-gang bangers, speak politely and in a moderate tone of voice; use short sentences and simple words. Since they are operating in a second (and difficult) language, don't use long words or lots of American slang ("bottom line", "hit the deck", "screw up", etc.).

And don't ask, "Do you understand?" As noted, it is polite in much of Asian culture to avoid negative replies; they will usually nod or say yes. Also, avoid negative questions, as these are cross-culturally confusing. For example, regarding the question, "Do you not like egg rolls?", the appropriate answer for most Southeast Asians who do like egg rolls, would be "no" ("I do like egg rolls."). Rather, ask the Vietnamese to repeat what he thinks you said so that you will have a chance to evaluate his English and be able to correct and explain your messages to him. Remember that they are more likely to tell you things if you have some understanding of their cultural background and can concentrate on making them think you are a friend. Getting bangers drunk, making some sort of trade, or offering them a (legal) advantage are some tactics used; however, in all contacts, be calm, cool, and patient.

Two Deeper Cultural Mindsets: Village Mentality and Time

What is a deep cultural mindset? For example, Americans find the passage of time precious and expensive: "Time is money!". We also tend to be oriented toward the future rather than the past or present. Thus, the ideas of a better future, of boundless opportunities, the open possibilities of individual recognition and personal change — the American frontier spirit — are part of the buried ideas that make up our American mindset. Some sources of important Vietnamese mindsets are a result of their surroundings, the farming village, the central role of the extended family, and the ideas of Confucianism, Chinese Mahāyāna Buddhism, and animistic local religion. Viewing the world from the standpoint of the farming village is deeply influential in Vietnamese culture, even when they have lived in urban and suburban areas for some time.[205] To describe this particular idea, I have adopted the term "village mentality" from William L. Cassidy's excellent book, *Nomadic Vietnamese Armed Robbery: The Fundamentals of Nomadic Vietnamese Residential Armed Robbery Investigation.*[206]

Vietnamese Village Mentality

Law enforcement personnel often wonder at the brutal way some Vietnamese home burglars abuse and torture other Vietnamese. Quite simply, because we don't understand the Vietnamese mindset, many ask what kind of an idea of humanity and of human compassion — or the lack of it — can they have? How can they be so brutal toward their countrymen who have shared many of the same hardships of their parents or themselves?

A set of ideas that remains unconscious in most Vietnamese but that make sense of these questions is the concept of Vietnamese village mentality. It is as deeply held a mindset about human relations for many Vietnamese, just as the American (unconsciously held) ideas of individual freedom and the constant potential for greatness in the future. To understand how this largely buried notion about human relations is relevant to Vietnamese home invasions, we need to examine the idea of Vietnamese village mentality and several related assumptions. Unfortunately, they are connected in ways we might not easily notice. An oversimplified analysis of village mentality follows in six points. These are guidelines for attempting understanding; they are not an all-encompassing explanation of Vietnamese behavior.

1. Most Vietnamese have lived in the countryside in small villages. Even for those relatively few who live in the few cities, the village mentality is part of their way of viewing the world; their deep mindset is a village mindset about whether one has social obligations to certain classes of people. More importantly, one is not just a "Vietnamese". Rather, one

belongs to a particular (extended) family lineage in a specific village, in a specific delta or highland, near specific mountains or a river, in the north or south. It is of that specific place and of that specific group that one is a member. And it is from that family and that village that one gets one's identity, one's sense of self. More important, it is to the village members that one owes loyalty; one has obligations of mutual protection and help only to members of one's family lineage, then one's village.

2. One's village has finite resources; there are clear limits to the amount of land, crops, durable goods, and money available. Since the resources are limited, the totality of the members of the village possess all there is to possess.
3. Any increase in anyone's wealth means that somebody else is going to lose some of what they have, and that someone else's increase in wealth will hurt some fellow villagers. Although violated in daily practice, the gist of the connection is that hurting one's fellow villagers is wrong; to be wrong is to be immoral.
4. One need not have any feelings of guilt or compassion toward those who are immoral; they deserve what they get.
5. If one's robbery victims are wealthy then they could only have gotten their wealth by being immoral, and the immoral do not deserve the concern one should have for one's family or fellow villagers. Thus, accumulating money and property is antisocial and a mark of selfishness because it is obtained at the expense of many others.
6. One need not worry about the degree of pain, violence, or pleading of one's victims if they are immorally selfish, for such wealthy (and thus immoral) people do not deserve the compassion that one extends to one's fellow villagers. Therefore, one ought to and can be as vicious as one needs be to get (and redistribute) wealth as quickly and easily as possible.

Of course, no one ever quite thinks through these things in this systematic explicit fashion and for most Vietnamese gangbangers, this would be a blatant rationalization of greed. To many traditional farmers this would just seem to be the way things are and the way one does things. However, these ideas of finite wealth and maintaining the status quo are what makes some people judge material success, not as a desirable reward for one's own efforts, but as the mark of wrong, immoral actions. Furthermore, in spite of the influence of Buddhism which emphasizes the spirit of compassion (Sanskrit: Karuṇā) and empathy (Sanskrit: muditā ; sympathetic joy), this narrow village mindset partly helps to explain why many Vietnamese nomadic gangs are so vicious to other Vietnamese and Asians. Obviously, the social rootlessness of the generations of war victims, the raw needs of survival, and the overthrow of the Confucian styled repression of anger breed callousness and brutality.[207] Also, some of these Viet bangers were never integrated into groups who practiced ethical values.

However, things are never quite so simple. One must also balance this reasonable and plausible explanation about village mentality against the hard fact that hundreds of thousands of Vietnamese left hamlet and home to band together to challenge and defeat the huge, technologically sophisticated armies of the U.S. Furthermore, hundreds of thousands have come to North America, Europe, and the rest of the world and have blended and prospered as hardworking, decent, family-oriented citizens who contribute to the cultural and economic wealth of the U.S. and Canada. Thus, as with any identifiable cultural group, there are significant exceptions to any true generalization. This is particularly true if social, economic, historical, philosophical, and political circumstances merge in a way sufficient to move cultures in different directions, as was done during the decades of Vietnamese conflict with the French and then the Americans, and as was done in the U.S. in late 1941 and in Europe in 1939.

Time

Time is something about which we assume that there can be no misunderstanding; after all, we all agree that "time is money and time is time." As with many basic ideas, this does not hold in all cultures — certainly not with many Asian cultures. Between most Vietnamese and mainline North Americans, neither punctuality nor appointments are as important to Vietnamese as to North Americans. They seem more relaxed, laid back, and easygoing. Our tolerance for being late is much lower than theirs.

One of the best summaries of Vietnamese concepts of time — which sometimes is said to stretch like a rubberband — is in the late Paul James Rutledge's *The Vietnamese Experience in America*:[208,209]

> For the Vietnamese, time encompasses the past, the present and the future and has an element of permanence. Time is perceived as having an integrity of its own and it cannot be hurried, rushed or changed by human beings. Consequently, the Vietnamese workers are not "clock-conscious" or "time-oriented" as are many Westerners. The attitude towards time is more relaxed than American attitudes and as long as one works hard the completion of the task is not important. The process is important; the fulfillment of the goal may require another lifetime.
>
> Since … [we Americans] … place great emphasis on time, perceptual differences have sometimes resulted in cultural clashes. To Americans, "time is money", "time is fleeting", and "life is short". Underlying this … is the belief that one has only one lifetime, that it is necessary to quicken one's

> pace to accomplish as much as possible in that brief life span. Vietnamese refugees share with Americans a strong achievement orientation, but many do not believe that accomplishments are limited to a single lifetime [because of karmic rebirth]. This … [indeed is] … a different way of looking at time."

As all immigrants have learned to adjust to the oddities of their new homeland under the pressure of economics and society, the Vietnamese have also learned to adjust to the time-conscious American style. However, the adjustment of the Vietnamese (Chinese and other Southeast Asians) goes on, particularly with the new immigrants and the increasing possibilities of renewed diplomatic relations with the nation of the yellow dragon, the home country.

Names, Language, and Scripts

In contrast to the use of Chinese characters and Japanese kanji and Korean hongul, the Vietnamese use a Roman (our) alphabet but with special tonal and diacritical marks. This was devised in the 17th century by Roman Catholic Jesuit missionaries and replaced Chinese and other indigenous scripts.[210]

There are six tones in Vietnamese as compared with four tones in Mandarin Chinese. These six tones and their corresponding diacritical marks refer to the inflections and pitch of the pronunciation of a name or a word; the tones and diacritical marks make as great a difference in the meaning as does the spelling of the words. The tone/diacritical marks should be carefully copied where possible. For example, "Ngáy" (acute accent over the "a") means "snore"; "Ngay" means "straight"; "Ngày" (grave accent over the "a") means "day." Thus, it is necessary to preserve these diacritical marks as much as is possible. However, it is still possible to record Vietnamese names without diacritical marks with much less difficulty than with Chinese or Japanese names where every aspect of the character is necessary in identification.

The family name (or surname), as with the Chinese, is usually written first followed by the given name which usually consists of two syllables. Vietnamese often use first (personal) names as middle names, particularly with women. Usually, there will be no repetition of the same personal names within the core family. Married Vietnamese women legally maintain their own name but usually will use their husband's names and "Mrs." In social situations. For example:[211]

Husband's name	Nguyễn Văn Hai
Wife's maiden name	Lê Thị Ba
Wife's married name	Lý Thị Ba
Wife's formal name	Mrs. Nguyễn Văn Hai

Quite often, "Vietnamese middle names are "Văn" for males and "Thị" for females. "Văn" means literature, supposedly a male should be learned or at least literate; and "Thị" signifies female (or market), but middle names can be other than Văn and Thị."[212]

The following material is taken from an excellent Australian Customs Service profile about the Vietnamese people.[213]

- Male given names are:

DÂN	HẢI	HÙNG	PHƯỚC	THANH
ĐÔNG	HIỂN	LONG	SƠN	TRUNG
DŨNG	HOA	MÌNH	TÀI	TÙNG

These names normally mean something strong, tough, or hard. However, some given names can be used by both sexes, e.g., DŨNG (good endeavor) or PHƯỚC (happiness).

- Female given names usually mean flowers, beautiful birds, or some similar form of flattery:

ANH	HỤÊ	MỸ	SƯỞNG	TUYỀN
CÚC	LAN	NGA	THANH	TUYẾT
ĐAO	LÀNH	NGỌC	THU	
HÀ	LÌÊN	NU	THỦY	
HOA	LÌNH	PHONG	TRANG	
HỒNG	MAÌ	PHÚC	TRÚC	

At marriage, Vietnamese women do not change their family names to that of their husbands on marriage. If NGUYỄN CAO QUANG marries HOÀNG THỊ THANH, then both Mrs. THANH and Mrs. QUANG are acceptable titles, but never Mrs. NGUYỄN. Mr. And Mrs. QUANG is the formal way of referring to the couple.

- The children are given the father's family name. Names may also indicate the child's rank of birth, such as ANH HAI (elder son) or CHI BA (second daughter).
- Titles are used in conjunction with the given name and not the family name:

Mr.	ÔNG
Mrs.	BÀ
Miss	CÔ

- THƯA is a polite form of address used before a personal pronoun when addressing someone superior to oneself in family or social rank:

CHA, MẸ	Father
BA, MÁ	Mother

- THÍCH preceding the family name indicates the bearer is a follower of the Buddha. Buddhist monks take a religious name.

The 12 most common Vietnamese family (last) names are:

NGUYỄN ("WIN")	NGÔ
TRẦN	PHẠM
PHAN	LÊ (LAY)
LÝ (LEE)	HUỲNH
VÕ	ĐINH
TRƯỞNG	TRỊNH

Other relevant information about names may be found in the Bureau of Alcohol, Tobacco, and Firearms' *Vietnamese Traveling Criminals: An Identification Manual* and the two FinCEN publications, *Distinguishing Between Vietnamese and Chinese Surnames* and *Vietnamese and Thai Names: Law Enforcement Considerations.* (See "Suggested Readings" at the end of this chapter.)

Some Vietnamese who are ethnic Chinese are referred to as Viet-Ching. They may obscure this fact if they consider it to their advantage, especially to an arresting officer who knows nothing of Asian names or of STC.[214] After determining their possible Chinese Viet-Ching status, ask for the Chinese characters of their name. If they are older Viet-Ching, they will certainly know their name in Chinese characters and probably their STC numbers as well. Then, secure the services of someone who can use the Standard Telegraphic Code reference book and find the STC numbers for each Chinese character. Use those STC numbers in every communication about the suspect. Underline or capitalize the family name; do not refer to it as the "last name"; always refer to it as the "family name".

Holidays and Calendars

Tết (New Year's Day) and Vu Lan

The most important Vietnamese holiday of the year is Tết or Tết Niên, the celebration of the new year. More important than Christmas, Tết is the first day of the Chinese lunar calendar, usually between January 19th and February 20th, somewhat similar to the Chinese-American (Chinese) New Year celebrations. In Vietnam, Tết continues to be a time for the gathering of the whole family, honoring the family lineage, and performing the proper rites for ancestors. It is like our Christmas, Easter, and Thanksgiving all rolled into one holiday. Tết is the time for paying all debts, forgiving grudges and settling disputes. It is often celebrated with culturally familiar traditional theater, dancing, dragon dances, fireworks, and contemporary songs and dances — all with lots of flowers. Traditionally, the first person outside the family to enter the house at Tết will bring good or bad luck. Thus, a respected "good-luck" person will often be invited to guarantee a prosperous year. In Vietnam, Tết was the high point of all the cultural, familial and religious ceremonies; to be Vietnamese was to fully celebrate Tết. Today, for most Vietnamese-American refugees, Tết has become *the* occasion to re-assert their identity as Vietnamese and to celebrate their dual Asian heritage and American citizenship.

Tết is both a good and bad time for police. In Vietnamese communities, a lot of money is there to be earned, gambled, received, and given out around Tết . Holiday gambling abounds, and gang activities, home invasions, and store robberies are more frequent. Surveillance teams (and wire taps) are more likely to find something of interest than at any other single time of the year.

The second major holiday is Vu Lan, the festival of the Wandering Souls, usually held in mid-July. It is analogous to the Chinese Feast of the Hungry Ghosts and the Japanese Bon Festival, all of which are based on Buddhist history, festivals, and theology. It has some parallels with the Anglo-European Halloween or All Souls' Day. However, the general religious purpose of this ancient Buddhist observance throughout Buddhist Asia is to placate the souls of wandering hungry ghosts or uncared-for spirits (Sanskrit: pretas; Chinese: e-kuei) so that they do not turn against the living.

Other Holidays

Other holidays are Trăng Trōn, festival of the full moon; Lễ Phật Đãn (April), celebration of the Buddha's birthday; and Trung Thu, the "woman in the moon", the festival of the harvest moon in which the face in the moon is supposedly that of Hằng Nga, a wife who would not listen to her husband. After being banished by him, her face looks out to us in sorrow and regret — a folk myth doubtless favored by men. Because of two centuries of French Catholic influence and the conversion of many Vietnamese to Christianity, some Vietnamese and most Vietnamese-Americans also celebrate Easter, Halloween, and Christmas. Vietnamese also celebrate what might be called "Death Days" when families and friends of a deceased member gather at a festive dinner and tell stories to recall many of the admirable aspects of the dead person. In Vietnam, secular holidays are May Day, Liberation Day, Hồ Chí Minh's birthday, and National Day.

Marian Days: Carthage, Missouri

There is one special annual celebration not found in Vietnam, but which is celebrated by Vietnamese and other Southeast Asians in the very middle of North America: Carthage, Missouri! Marian Days is a 5-day religious celebration, usually held in August and celebrated at the excellent facilities of the Roman Catholic Seminary of the Fathers of the congregation of the Mother Co-Redemptrix, a Vietnamese religious order. Much like a large family reunion, over 40,000 Vietnamese and other Southeast Asians from Canada and the U.S. congregate in motor homes, RVs, campers, cars, tents, motels, and hotels for a series of Masses and religious celebrations. There are over a dozen Vietnamese temporary restaurants, well-organized social services coordinated by both the and the Catholic Order, and smooth, professional police protection to generate a happy, safe, celebration for these Asian-Americans.[215]

Figure 16 Entrance to the Catholic Church, the center of the Marian Days religious and festive observances in Carthage, Missouri. This event is patrolled regularly by officers of the Carthage Police Department, area law enforcement officers, and an invited group of federal and municipal Asian crime investigators. (Courtesy of the Carthage Police Department.)

However, a small number of Vietnamese gang members and "wannabees" also gather to have fun, watch the girls, eat good food, quietly intimidate others, and exchange information about planned home invasions and other robberies. For the last few years, the careful policing by the excellent Carthage Police Department and surrounding law enforcement personnel have been

Figure 17 Southeast Asians attending the Marian Days festivities. (Courtesy of the Carthage Police Department.)

supplemented by a team of Asian crime specialists from around the country who roam the crowded grounds, talk to Asian-Americans, photograph gang bangers, gather intelligence, and run license plate numbers through various law enforcement data bases. For the last few years, several felons and at least one alleged murderer have been apprehended each year. Marian Days, then, remains a holiday especially relevant to law enforcement personnel interested in Asian crime and Asian culture. It is well worth a trip for exposure to the customs of Southeast Asian-American people and for the potential apprehension of some vicious gang members.

Suggested Readings

Hannum, Philip with Al Lotz, Eds., *Nightmare: Vietnamese Home Invasion Robberies (and Jewelry Store Robberies), Selected Interstate Cases: 1987-1992*, occasional paper of the International Association of Asian Crime Investigators, Falls Church, VA, 1992. Contact Phil Hannum at (703) 241-4911.

Willoughby, Jack, *Vietnamese Criminal Activity with an Emphasis on Traveling Criminals*, occasional paper of the International Association of Asian Crime Investigators, Falls Church, VA, 1991. Contact Lt. Jack Willoughby at (504) 244-4600.

Vietnamese Traveling Criminals: An Identification Manual, Bureau of Alcohol, Tobacco and Firearms, Tactical Intelligence Branch, U.S. Department of the Treasury, 1994, 18 pages. For copies for official use only contact Asian Intelligence Analyst, 650 Massachusetts Avenue, NW, Room 7150, Washington, D.C. 20226; (202) 927-7900; fax: (202) 927-8001.

Martin, Michael L., Ed., *Asian Gang Activity*, Fourth ed., Asian Service Unit, Gang Suppression Unit, Garden Grove Police Department, 1994. pp. 23-50. (Confidential: for law enforcement personnel only.)

Cassidy, William L., *Nomadic Vietnamese Armed Robbery*, occasional paper of the International Association of Asian Crime Investigators, Falls Church, VA, July 4, 1991.

Cassidy, William L., *Recognition Guide to Vietnamese Banknotes in Current Circulation*, occasional paper of the International Association of Asian Crime Investigators, Falls Church, VA, July 4, 1991.

Distinguishing Between Vietnamese and Chinese Names, Financial Crimes Enforcement Network (FinCEN), 2070 Chainbridge Road, VA, 22182. Contact Cordell Hart at (703) 905-3662.

Phillips, P.C., Jones, C.H., Emmett, G.W., Curran, K., *A Profile of Vietnamese Gang Activity in Victoria [Australia] '82-'86*, Victoria, Australia, 1986. (A police publication for police usage only.)

Vietnamese Crime and Culture

Badey, James R., *Dragons and Tigers*, Palmer Enterprises, P.O.Box 1714, Loomis, CA, 1988. (One of the first books on Vietnamese Asian crime for cops written by an effective, culturally attentive experienced, police officer.)

Vietnamese Criminal Activity in the U.S.: a National Perspective, Organized Crime/Drug Branch, Criminal Investigative Division, Federal Bureau of Investigation, U.S. Dept. Of Justice, Washington, D.C., 1993.

English, T.J., *Born to Kill: America's Most Notorious Vietnamese Gang and the Changing Face of Organized Crime,* Morrow Publishing, New York, 1995 (ISBN:0-688-12238-8). An accurate, detailed, and very readable book on Vietnamese gangs and their social environment and rough cultural backgrounds. The book is arranged through the story of a Viet gang member who became an informant. Reviewed by David Chanoff, "How the Gangsters Got Rapped," Book World, *Washington Post,* January 30, 1995, p. D2.

FitzGerald, Frances, *Fire in the Lake: The Vietnamese and the Americans in Vietnam,* Vintage Books, New York, 1972.

Toai, Doan Van, and Chanoff, David, *The Vietnamese Gulag,* Simon and Schuster, New York, 1986.

Woodside, Alexander Barton, *Vietnam and the Chinese Model: a Comparative Study of Vietnamese and Chinese Government in the First Half of the Nineteenth Century,* monograph of the Council on East Asian Studies, Harvard University, Harvard University Press, Cambridge, MA, 1988 (ISBN: 0-674-93721-x). A scholarly, comparative study of the historical Sino-Vietnamese and southeast Asian roots of modern Vietnam.

Butler, Robert Olen, *The Deuce,* Henry Holt, New York, 1989. The hard life of a teenage Amerasian in New York.

Rutledge, Paul James, *The Vietnamese Experience in America,* Indiana University Press, Bloomington, IN, 1992 (ISBN: 0-253-20711-8). An excellent, sympathetic description of the sequences and characteristics of the Vietnamese refugee immigrations and settlements into the U.S.

Karnow, Stanley, *Vietnam: A History,* Viking Press, New York, 1983.

Jamison, Neil L., *Understanding Vietnam,* University of California Press, Berkeley, CA, 1993 (ISBN: 0-520-20157-4). This very fine book contains the best short overview of the Vietnamese world view the author has found.

Butler, Robert Olen, *A Good Scent from a Strange Mountain,* Penguin Books, New York, 1992 (ISBN: 0-14-01.7664-0). This 1993 Pulitzer Prize winner has composed a beautiful set of short stories all of which are written from the standpoint of Vietnamese men and women, young and old. Terrific but gentle insights into the character and problems of Vietnamese spanning two cultures.

Huong, Duong Thu, *Paradise of the Blind,* William Morrow, New York, 1993.

Pike, Douglas, Ed., *Indochina Chronology,* Institute of East Asian Studies (Quarterly), University of California at Berkeley, CA 94720.

19 Asian Buddhism and Chinese Confucianism

關係

A Brief Comparative Introduction

Attempts to bridge the immense gap between the fundamentals of culturally scattered religious traditions (Buddhism, Confucianism, Christianity, Anamism) and the effects of that tradition that are found in the everyday lives of people are difficult and necessarily oversimplified. However, to lay a foundation for further understanding and for informed inferences between what is read and what is observed in street behavior, these overviews of Confucianism and Buddhism, plus the comparisons of mindsets in Chapter 12, may help the reader to gain a more inclusive view of some of the religious and cultural roots of Asian cultures, particularly Chinese.

All cultures have deeply buried ideas which influence the way people of that culture *see* the world and *shape* their expectations of the way things "must" be. These influences include the complex but different ways people process information; other influences are history, law, place of birth, native language, and religion. Of course, other accidents of one's experience also influence one's personal profile within a culture. Examples are one's parents, stature, race, handicaps, intelligence, talents, and just plain luck.

In any culture, certain things are held in common, and one of those commonalties is the object of this chapter, namely, religion. However, religion is shaped by culture as much as it helps to shape culture. For examples of how religion is shaped by culture, look at the contrasts between Zulu Christianity vs. Mexican Christianity vs. Vermont Christianity vs. Indonesian Christianity. While these are all culture-specific examples of "styles" of Christianity, the degree of variation by culture is about the same for other religions such as Buddhism. Confucianism and Taoism (Daoism) are native to China, and as with Buddhism, they have greatly influenced aspects of Japanese and Korean cultures.

Cross-Cultural Religious Mindsets: Deep and Surface

First, for a minute, try to suspend your Western Judaic-Christian (JC) ideas about religion, God, gods, or reincarnation. Second, unless you wish to enter into some extremely complex arguments about the justification of types of proofs across cultures, it is easier to just assume that the Buddhist religious ideas and Confucian social ideals are not necessarily better, just different.[216] Third, if we are America-born Americans we are all at least "cultural Christians" in the way some Jews differentiate between religious Jews and cultural Jews. Because we live in North America, we are at least minimal cultural JCMs even if we *are* Jews, Christians, or Muslims; we remain semi-*cultural* JCMs to some degree, if we are Hindus, Buddhists, Jains, agnostics, atheists, evangelical snake handlers, or indifferent to religion.

North American culture is obviously strongly influenced by the ideas held in common in the Judaic-Christian-Islamic traditions (JCI) and its mixture of Greek philosophy, Roman law, Arab cultures, West European ideas and cultural styles, and Anglo-Saxon common law and applied technologies.[217] Some of these ideas are buried in the deep levels of our JCI mindsets; others linger at the surface. For two quick examples of surface mindsets, we North Americans of Canada and the U.S. expect to see progress in human history and we emphasize our individuality and our self-earned accomplishments. Thus, the ideas of a better future, of boundless opportunities, the Frontier Spirit, the open possibilities of individually-driven and personal change are surface-level components of our 300-year-old U.S.-Canadian history that makes up a general North American mindset.

In any culture, religious mindsets are among the deepest and most fundamental. Deep mindsets consist of a interlocking set of beliefs, assumptions and attitudes. In the Judeo-Christian-Islamic traditions, it is assumed that there is only a single agent deity who created a finite universe for an assumed purpose imperfectly (at best) known to us; Christians hold that people have only a single enduring personal identity (a personal soul) which did not exist prior to this life but which does exist in this life. After death, the soul is maintained throughout a single everlasting life, the state of which may be either earned or awarded peace and joy or deserved torment and punishment. This single personal identity is maintained throughout this life and the next life — one identity in two (and only two) states of existence. An extremely important assumption is that the development of the person as a self-conscious moral agent is an apparent prerequisite for the attainment of the presupposed purpose underlying God's creation and mature moral choices. These examples of surface and deep mindsets grow out the intermixing of

Anglo-European cultures and the influences of and the reaction to 2500 years of Western religious and secular experience.

To those Western traditions we will now contrast 2500 to 3000 years of Asian religious, historical, and ethnic influences. Analogous to the JCI tradition, a somewhat similar mixture of history, ideas, and religions occurred in the development of Asian mindsets. Thus, keeping in mind our JCI orientation, we will take a look at some strong Asian religious influences and their effects, namely Confucianism, Daoism, Buddhism, and the deeply pervasive communities of East and Southeast Asian gods and spirits:[218]

> In fact, ... Chinese of all economic classes and social rank were, over the centuries, deeply concerned about mystical forces and the supernatural. Spirits and gods were thought to be everywhere — usually unseen, but nevertheless real. The largest and most ornate buildings in every town and village were customarily temples; along the roadways and even beside paths and in the fields, untold numbers of small shrines house effigies of various deities; virtually every home contained at least one altar and place of sacrifice. Spirit gates stood just inside the entrances to family compounds to prevent entry of evil spirits. And in any town or village, regardless of the day of the year, a visitor could see incense and spirit-money burned, food sacrificed, and fire-crackers exploded — evidence of an active belief in denizens of a supernatural world. The sense that supernatural beings were omnipresent was expressed by the small boy who, before relieving himself alongside a dark street, warned the spirits lurking in the dark: "I am going to urinate. Please stand aside."[218]

Thus, the Chinese world of religious gods, godlings and spirits was a varied one indeed.

> The spiritual world, as conceived by believers in the popular religion, reflected the social landscape of human existence. It was inhabited by bureaucrats and ordinary citizens, police and soldiers, beggars and ruffians. Some were good; some, bad. Although all these supernatural beings possessed powers transcending those of mere mortals, they were also endowed with human characteristics. They felt emotions — such as pride, jealousy, anger, and pleasure. And they had needs — for food, money, and housing. Because of their ability to intervene in the lives of the living, it was important for the human condition to win the favor and to forestall the malevolence of the supernatural beings.[219]

It is important to note five contrasts with Anglo-European versions of the Judeo-Christian traditions. First, as in most of Asia, temples and other sacred buildings are the homes of the gods and sacred spirits, not institutions or assembly halls for the social and communal religious benefit of believers, as are Anglo-European churches. Thus, temples are places where believers might visit to contact, worship, or beseech the deities for favors or guidance. Second, priests and monks are there to support the locale of the deities, not primarily to offer religious guidance for the believer. For example, although some Theravada Buddhist monks are wise counselors, their primary goal is to lead the religious life and retain and maintain the Theravada traditions and monastic practices, not to counsel lay believers.

Third, many Chinese temples, especially Daoist ones, may house religious figures from other religious paths, exhibiting Buddhist Bodhisattvas, a local earth God, Guan Di, and Confucian wise men. Others remain more strictly defined and narrower in scope. Fourth, in China, "popular religion tended to be diffused; its theology and ritual had no existence separate from the major social institutions, such as family, lineage, merchant guild, and village. The popular religion lacked … the independent organizational strength of, say, Christianity or Islam."[220] Fifth,[221]

> One thing the popular religion did *not* supply, as do institutional religions in the West, was a *distinct and independent* set of moral values. From an early time, Confucianism had been the dominant source of China's ethical precepts, and the moral priesthood — those who were primarily responsible for interpreting the rules of morality and passing judgment on right and wrong actions — consisted of the Confucian scholars and officials. The Taoist and Buddhist clergy who served the popular religion were generally so poorly educated and of such suspect morality that they lacked the social and moral stature necessary to perform that role.

On Chinese and Vietnamese Ancestor Worship

Americans celebrate the birthdays of those in the family who are still alive, and, of course, Chinese and Vietnamese celebrate birthdays, too (especially for children). However, Chinese and Vietnamese also celebrate the deathdays of their deceased family — the (so-called) worship of the ancestors (ji zu, STC 4385 4371). It is the occasion in the Spring (Mua Xuan, the Spring festival similar to the Chinese festival) when (if possible) the graves are swept and cleaned. Within the home, with the family gathered around the family ancestor tablets, or at the family gravesites, offerings of food and flowers are made to honor the dead. The elder male(s) gather the family to celebrate and commemorate the continuity and wellbeing of the family lineage.

A partial analogy would be a military veteran's group of former shipmates who honor with a toast those shipmates who died in battle and those shipmates who have since died. Then they tell stories and recount experiences which continue to reinforce and strengthen the bonds of the living regarding their shared military experiences. Analogously, ancestors are honored, celebrated, recalled and (metaphorically) embraced within the Confucian extended family/clan; they are not literally worshipped. Gods and godlings are worshipped; dead people may be feared, and honors must be performed for the benefit and placation of both the dead and the living, but people are not worshipped as the Christian Yahweh or the Buddhist Amitābha are worshipped. However, when Anglo-Europeans observe unfamiliar Chinese and Vietnamese devotion and reverential rituals performed to honor the memory and the semi-divine status of the dead elders, they may confuse what appears to be religious worship with what is actually a religious manner of celebrating, placating, bonding, and nurturing one's extended family — dead or alive.

Chinese Confucianism

What Is Confucianism?

This major contribution of the Chinese to various Asian civilizations is usually described as a religion. In some aspects, the Confucian temple and its rites do have religious qualities as the West understands aspects of religion, but it would be inaccurate to deem Confucianism a religion in the same sense that most Americans would refer to Christianity or Islam. Moreover, few Chinese would call themselves a Confucian, in the sense in which a North American might call himself a Baptist or a Catholic or a Reform Jew. For example, some American Jews call themselves a cultural Jew rather than a religious Jew. That distinction might be helpful here since a Chinese (Han) person would seldom (if ever) deny his/her Chineseness" whether he/she lives in Singapore, Kowloon, Beijing, Soho, or Mott St. in New York. Furthermore, for him to be Chinese is to be a *cultural* Chinese, and that is tantamount to him calling himself a Confucian — a Confucian in spirit if not always in conscious practice.

Confucius (Kong Fu Zi, "Master Koong", Kong fu zi, STC 1313 1133 1311) was a highly educated, traveling teacher of social and ethical philosophy; about himself, he said that he was merely a student of the ancient classics. He was neither a religious prophet nor a self-conscious innovator. In fact, he remained an agnostic regarding supernatural religious claims.[222] He lived from about 551 to 479 B.C. and founded one of the three major intellectual, ethical, social, and political traditions that influenced all of East Asia and Southeast Asia — the others being Chinese forms of Mahāyāna Buddhism — and to a lesser extent, Daoism, Dao, The Natural Way. Also, in much of Chinese history, Chinese Daoists and the Buddhists (after 200 A.D.) acted in accordance with or in opposition to the developing Confucian traditions.

Moreover, it was the Confucian model of society which strongly influenced Vietnamese, Japanese, and Korean societies and other Sinocized countries. For example, the Vietnamese developed their social structure using the Confucian values of propriety (li), harmony, order, mutual respect (shu STC 2611), and inner-family benevolence or filial piety (xiao, STC 1321).[223] The Chinese, Vietnamese, Japanese and Koreans embraced the Confucian ideal of the morally guided development of the humble but ethical "superior man" (jun-zi, STC 0689 1311) from within the potential humanness found in each person (ren) could and should be developed.

Confucian Social Relations

Confucius taught that the five desirable (and ancient) values to be nurtured in all human relationships were:

1. Kind benevolence in the ruler and loyalty among those ruled
2. Respect and honor for the elders and respectful deference in the younger toward the older
3. The father's kindly but stern wisdom coupled with filial piety and obedience in the children
4. Gentility in the eldest brother and respectful humility in the younger brothers
5. Righteous behavior in the husband, and obedience and proper deference in his wife.

This was the source of the view that the extended family should be the basic model for almost all Chinese in the Confucian theory of social assumptions about relationships.

There is a chain of levels of learning; when each is known in the proper sequence, all may lead to morality, peace and ethical self-knowledge. Propriety (li) leads to proper knowledge which leads to proper social action. Correct social action was thought to be the behavioral channel through which the humane but natural urges and social needs of humans could be shaped and given balanced, harmonious expression. Thus, manners, style, and knowledgeable skills count. Mutual respect for yourself and others, explicit knowledge of how things ought to be, and a version of the "Golden Rule" leads one to know how to maintain and improve the five relationships (noted above).

Confucius and later Confucians did not claim that all men were of equal worth nor that they should all have equal political/social rights. Furthermore, unequal ranks have unequal privileges, but those, for example, who have had the opportunity to study the classics have greater ethical responsibilities than those who have not. However, as with some of the ancient Greek philosophers, one Confucian emphasis was on the roots of ethical development, knowing and developing yourself: "Conduct yourself so that you become someone worth knowing." In thinking about ethical conduct, one should start with things at hand — oneself. Thus, one should start with examining one's own character — knowing what is correct and developing the self-discipline to act accordingly. This inner character building, in turn, will bring about harmony and prosperity in a mutually supported family/clan. Family stability will bring about social stability and good relationships between families, villages, townships, and states. This, in turn, will bring about a benevolent, human-hearted (jen), balanced state administration in accordance with the natural way (Dao) of nature.

Two Views of the Worth of Individuality

In another contrast with Confucianism, Hinduism, and Buddhism, there is a JCI assumption of one and only one permanent identity. The JCI tradition lacks assumptions affirming reincarnation or multiple earthly lives. In the JCI tradition there are no existences before one's present life, nor are there an almost infinite series of lifetimes after this present life. In short, those of us of the Anglo-European traditions know that this does not mean that we necessarily agree with others of different views; but, to *know* of our differences may enable us to understand others and, thus, to have some basis on which to judge how we ought to act towards others who do not share many of our deep, hidden assumptions about human life and its values.

To understand the contrast between the Chinese Confucian view of the individual and the general American version of the Anglo-European, JC view, we need to look at the development of moral values by focusing on the underlying ideas of individualistic obligations and self-directed values vs. Chinese, Confucian inner-group obligations and collectivist social values. The Confucian path from individual self-development towards an ethical society was not designed to achieve the goals or freedoms for the individual, but rather to achieve the goals of the group; the individual was merely the starting point. Whatever ethical attention is focused on the individual as emphasized in the Confucian tradition is not for the reasons most North Americans would expect. Americans prize "individuality", personal uniqueness, and personal freedom. That, in turn, is rooted in our JC theological ideas of an individual, unique soul with one (and only one) personality. It is this personality that generates an unique destiny justified by personal choices and personal values made over a single lifetime. By contrast, the Confucians focused on the social group and its ranked obligations to others.

Within the Confucian tradition, the family, the extended family-as-clan, is the ultimate source of value; with established guanxi relationships, the family dictates the boundaries of human trust and obligation. Whatever attention is focused on the individual is emphasized to support his/her contributions towards the goals of the family/clan (or the surrogate gang family) and the private network of obligations or connections (guanxi). While there exist tremendously diverse traits in the personal characteristics of specific Confucian oriented peoples, the American concept of the ultimate worth of the individual person and less so of the group is based on different ideas and different values:[224]

> Lacking a concept of [Christian] original sin [and a tradition of dualism as in a creator God vs. Satan], Confucian philosophy professes optimism about the perfectibility of man, whether human nature is seen as basically good or bad. It takes a positive outlook on the family's and the teacher's ability to guide an individual into seeking to serve the family's interest. The individual is not sacrificing but fulfilling himself by learning to cooperate. Parents teach children, largely through positive reinforcement, to find gratification through long-term undertakings in which great effort must be invested. They learn to feel moral through self-control.

Both Confucian and North American cultures recognize the merits and demerits of specific traits of individual people, but that is not the central issue here. What is crucial is what Americans and Chinese think about the *importance* of that individuality and how individuality should be treated within their respective societies. Americans think the unique value of the individual and the freedom to pursue individual goals built into the "furniture" of the universe; the Chinese think the furniture is quite different. Of course, Chinese notice individual traits, but think that individuality is only occasionally relevant and that personal goals are, and should be, subordinate to the goals of the family-group. For the American, his/her unique worth is as an individual human being who also has a family and lives within a variety of social associations, which calms the excesses of rampant individualism. The Confucian concept of the unique worth of the individual is as an individual member of a human clan and his/her worth is *externally* defined. The worth of the individual is defined as an interwoven member of a larger social network for which his/her character and expectations are based on a prior functional social definition of himself/herself. This social context of one's personal life is shaped by the larger social values of the network of human relations with whom the individual has culturally legitimate, externally defined relationships. However, one should remember that persons in both the JC, American, Anglo-European and Chinese cultural traditions are as unconscious of these underlying assumptions as you and I are unconscious of the style of type fonts of the letters you are now reading.

Formality, Etiquette, and Manners as Moral Training

Because of this highly structured, externally oriented social background, many traditional Asians tend to be much more formal than many North Americans. They place a much higher value on manners, etiquette, and decorum than the more informal, apparently egalitarian Americans.[225] Most of the perceived need of many Asians for such formality is historically rooted in the Confucian models of ranked, formal relations in society. Once again, we note that the development of moral and social values is not rooted in religion or universal declarations of independence or self-evident truths; rather, Chinese moral and social models are rooted in the self-discipline and social discipline outlined in the five Confucian relationships. Also, we note that these relationships are not relations between equals; these are relationships between persons neither of equal worth nor with equal opportunities nor equal moral rights.

These Confucian ideas have echoed for centuries in Vietnam. Two related examples are those of the Vietnamese word for politeness — le phep — literally means "rules of propriety", and the Vietnamese personal pronoun toi (I) also means "servant" or "subordinate". They echo today, in Fairfax, VA, and in Orange County, CA.

Echoes of Confucianism Today

The merits and demerits of the Confucian traditions echo in the following summary, a summary which reflects many Chinese and non-Chinese attitudes about this venerable tradition:[226]

> The importance ascribed by Confucianism to the need for human beings to model themselves on the virtues of a long-lost golden age held back social progress and the use of scientific thought to create industry and wealth. Through its insistence on stable family and social relationships and an overwhelming, even exaggerated, respect for the elderly, [Confucianism] stifled the spirit of enterprise and adventure in young men and subjugated women to an extent thought shocking even in the far-from-emancipated Europe of the day. It discouraged speculative thought and looked down on manual labor and mechanical inventions. In the first half of the twentieth century, there was every reason for it to be regarded as the biggest single obstacle to progress in China.
>
> Nonetheless, Confucianism had its good points: care of the aged, mutual help in stable family units, admiration for uprightness and loyalty even unto death, a plain and moderate life-style, rejection of wild superstitions and barbaric practices masquerading as religion, and respect for principle. Confucianism saw the prosperity of the peasants and the justness of official acts as the key indicators of the strength and weakness of a dynasty

> and in theory, at least, despised mercantile self-enrichment. It revered music and the arts and exercised a civilizing influence wherever it was spread.

Law enforcement personnel will observe the continuance of several central Confucian ideals which remain in force today, namely, hard work, social cohesion, and family or group loyalty. Today, it can be found in the tight cohesion of Asian street gangs, in the emotionless unloading of frozen fish, each of which had somehow — completely unknown to anyone who was questioned — swallowed a neat packet of white powder. Strange fish. Thus, the Confucian ideals of stability, balance, harmony, and loyalty to the family/clan echo in the dogged determination and discipline of Asian family syndicates, family-like businesses, the loyal guanxi networks of clan and village and language groups, family name societies, and other Chinese-American guilds of mutual help (Tongs) and the Companies. All these are rooted in and shaped by the family-oriented discipline of the Confucian tradition.

To some non-Asians, Confucianism sounds like a rigid, stuffy way to smother individual ambition; without doubt, it certainly does smother (at times) those American buzz words of "imagination," "creativity" and "informality". However, for 2500 years, not only has the Confucian perspective worked fairly well, but it still shapes the emphasis upon family responsibilities and benefits found in Asian societies today. Also, the legacy of Confucianism echoes within Vietnamese and Korean gangs (their surrogate families) and within the Chinese Triads and the Japanese Boryokudan (Yakuza) organized crime societies. The formalities and loyalty between ranks, the initiation ceremonies, the emphasis on and attraction to the symbolism of numbers and history, the intense sense of belonging, and the restrictions of dialect, ethnic background, and narrowly focused outlook are supported and encouraged by the echoes of Chinese Confucianism:[227]

> Observers have rightly contrasted the Western ideal of impersonality, individual calculation of self-interest, and management by [legal, formal] contract to the [Far] Eastern ideals of [family-oriented] human emotional bonds, regard for group harmony, and management by status or by consensus. The gap is narrowing, but will likely remain for a long time.

Taoism (Daoism): The Internal Chinese Counterbalance

It would be as great an oversimplification to reduce Chinese religious traditions to three simplistic strands — Confucianism, Buddhism, and Taoism (Daoism) — as it would be to reduce the Anglo-European traditions to Judaism, Christianity, and Islam. In North America, we are too close and know too much about the latter religions and how they differ internally and from country to country to accept such an oversimplified picture. With Chinese religious traditions, we are too far away and know too little. Furthermore, what we do think we know is often the skewed result of projecting our own expectations on Asian traditions. However, with a few exceptions and Vietnamese developments, we shall focus on the second of the three major religious traditions of China: The Daoist/Taoist traditions.

In many popular sources concerning China, one reads about the "third strand" of Chinese religion (Taoism), Confucianism and Buddhism being the first two strands. Therefore, and with a warning that things are always more complicated than they seem, a sketch of Taoism (Daoism) is included here to give some sense of proportion regarding its many roles in the long traditions we call Chinese civilization. While Taoism is the traditional spelling, the pronunciation of the word "Tao" is closer to "Dao", thus, we use the latter, more widely adopted Pinyin spelling.[228] Over time, the greatest influence was the philosophical, rather than the religious side of Daoism. However, compared with the Anglo-European religious traditions, the Chinese religious traditions lack that sense of an exclusive allegiance to one and only one God. Thus, one can assert the accurate generalization about China that Daoism functioned more as a balance to Confucianism than as a rival; of course, at different times, Daoism did engage in intra-court fighting for political power against both the Confucians and the Buddhists, and, later, the Neo-Confucianists.

One obvious problem about describing Daoism is that:[229]

> … the word "Tao" (The Way) is used by every school of Chinese thought or religion, and because the English word "Taoism" is used to refer to both Taoist philosophy (Tao-chia) and Taoism religion (Tao-chiao). Besides, there has always been a certain shroud of secrecy surrounding Taoism, which as a philosophy of recluses and for recluses, prefers anonymity, chooses to articulate its teachings in riddles, and, as an esoteric region, discloses many of its secrets [only] to the initiated.

However, while religious Daoism and moralistic Confucianism may seem to be clear opposites in style and content,[230]

> In [religious] Taoism, we can find those formally religious features that are lacking in Confucianism, including the clearly enunciated belief in a hierarchy of gods and the saving power, the acceptance of man's sinful condition (ch'eng-fu), and the attempt to bridge the gap between the human and the divine through ritual practices of prayer and penance. Yet the Taoist religion has been at times an uneasy ally of Confucianism, particularly when the

> two joined forces against Buddhist competition. Confucian rationalism is basically incompatible with Taoist fantasy and what may be called superstition. But Confucian rationalism is also a weakness, in a system which does not provide for consolation in distress, while Taoism offers a different option as personal religion.

On the other hand, philosophical Daoism reflected the elite Chinese literary background of the scholar-gentleman-administrator, their love of the poetic, and their ideas of the natural way things occur in what we call "Nature". Some points of literary-philosophical Daoism are that

- The Dao flows in all of nature, in the natural flow of all things, including ourselves.
- Simplicity, quietude, spontaneity, and naturalness in human affairs are best.
- The theory of wu-wei (non-action, not doing) means noninterference with nature as it/she flows along in the most humble but powerful fashion, taking the lowest, most humble position rather than the highest.
- As with water, the Dao overcomes the strongest substances with quiet persistence and without the false sophistication of rigid, rule-governed education and modern complexities.
- Simple virtues will give rise to sincerity, love, compassion, humility and kindness when government and individuals do not interfere with the simple naturalness common to people in their "natural" state:[231]
- The nature of water is that if nothing is mixed with it, it remains clear; if nothing ruffles it, it remains smooth. If it is obstructed so that it does not flow, then, too, it loses its clearness. In these ways, it is a symbol of the heavenly powers that are in man.[232]

The interplay between Daoism and Confucianism, the two currents of mainline Chinese thought were often expressed in the yin-yang symbol where each curving side of the circle balanced the other and in each was something of the other contrasting side. The thoughts of the individual were often summarized in the ancient saying, "A Confucian while in office; a Daoist while out of office."

> Chinese thought has manifested a certain rhythm: a moment of activity, its yang side, in Confucian moral and social philosophy — usually dominant during the periods of political unity and social order — and in a moment of passivity, its contemplative, yin side, in Taoist "naturalism" and quietism.[233]

Finally, the Daoist traditions have, without doubt, influenced the general Chinese outlook on life. If warranted, and this may sound strange to the reader, the investigator should use these ideas to influence an Asian suspect. As one experienced intelligence operative has suggested, "Law enforcement officers consider Taoist concern for inexorable and predetermined waves of history and events as a way of convincing Chinese (and other Asians) to do or not to do something the officer has in mind. Certainly, U.S. intelligence officers working abroad have used this appeal to definite effect."[234]

However, while Daoist thought influenced Chinese traditions, the law enforcement professional will seldom encounter the direct influence of these aspects of Daoism, even with an occasional visit to a Daoist temple. Furthermore, were this to happen — and be recognized — it would probably be best for the officer/agent to seek the help of a professional Sinologist who specializes in Daoism within a discipline relevant to the law enforcement problem at issue:[235] A rare bird, indeed!

Buddhism

What Is Buddhism?

Buddhism (Baudhadharma) was founded in northeast India around the fifth century B.C. by the prince of a small kingdom, Siddhārtha Gotama (563–483 B.C.). As a mature young man, he chose to become a wandering religious seeker (śramaṇa: striver). After leaving his royal family and becoming a (socially) nonperson, and a religious ascetic and after many years of searching and meditative self-analysis (bhāvanā), he became enlightened (bodhi, wu, STC 1889) and thus achieved Nirvāṇa (Nibbana in Pali). At enlightenment, he became "The Buddha", the Enlightened One (Fo He; STC 0154 0735). After a long life of teaching, he attained final Nirvāṇa (parinirvāṇa) and died, a beloved saintly teacher and the founder of one of the world's great religious traditions.

During the approximately 1500 years after his death, the Buddhist tradition became the largest missionary religion to spread through all of Asia. Buddhism migrated to China by 150 A.D., to Southeast Asia by the end of second century A.D., to Korea by the fourth century, to Japan around the sixth century, and established itself strongly in Tibet by the eleventh century. Today, there remain two general types of Buddhism, Theravāda ("Teachings of the Elders"), and a large, varied collection of Buddhist sects grouped under the term Mahāyāna ("The Great Path"). Theravāda Buddhism is quite old, but it is not the original Buddhism of the Buddha, as some naive believers would assert.

Many of the Mahāyāna groups are non-Indian-based Buddhist sects, which developed hundreds of years after Buddhism had died out in India (by the twelfth century A.D.). Because Buddhism had taken root in other parts of Asia, it survived, adapted, prospered, developed, and merged into cultures quite different from its Indian origins. For example, Vietnam has had strong Chinese Mahāyāna Buddhist and Chinese Confucian influences. Today, the major Mahāyāna Buddhist countries are Tibet, Japan, Korea, areas of the PRC, and all portions of Asia heavily influenced by the Chinese such as Vietnam, Korea, Japan, Hong Kong, and Singapore. It remains a minority religion among the ethnic Chinese Malaysians.

Major Mahāyāna Sects in both China and Japan are T'ien-T'ai (Japanese: Tendai) which focuses upon the Lotus Sūtra (Saddharmapuṇḍarīka); Chen-yen (Japanese: Shingon), a form of Tantric Buddhism primarily worshipping the Bodhisattva (see below) Vairocana; and Ch'an (Japanese: Zen) Buddhism. Sects particular to Japan are Nichiren Buddhism, founded by Nichiren (1222–1282), which focuses on the Lotus Sūtra ; Pure Land (Jōdo), founded by Honen (1133–1212, which focuses on reciting the name of the Bodhisattva Amida (Sanskrit: Amitābha); and True Pure Land (Jōdo Shinshū) created by Shinran (1173–1263).

Taking quite a different form than Mahāyāna Buddhism, Theravāda Buddhism is found in Sri Lanka, Thailand, Myanmar (Burma), Cambodia (Kampuchea), and Laos. In theory and often in practice, a Theravāda Buddhist layman is to observe five basic precepts to abstain from (1) taking life, (2) taking what is not offered or given freely, (3) misusing sex, (4) false speech and deception, and (5) using intoxicants which confuse one's mind. In the various sects of Mahāyāna Buddhism, similar rules survive but there remains great variation in the implementation of the first and third precepts. While there are many sects of both types of Buddhism and of Hinduism and Judaic-Christianity that exhibit similar ethical practices, there are also many underlying aspects of these religions that are very different. And these differences account for some of the different practices and everyday outlooks many Asian Buddhists share.

The following is a description of what level of understanding most people *actually have* about their religious preferences; it is not a comment of whether they *ought* to have more understanding about their religious preferences. The factual truth about most people who would affirm some kind of allegiance to a specific religion is that: (1) they are usually ignorant of its more complex historical doctrines, (2) their participation is usually done without much examination of the central religious tenents, and (3) they are largely indifferent about responding to the foregoing points. As with most Christians, most Buddhists go to the temple, perform the usual rites, and make requests to the Buddha or Bodhisattvas in a largely unconscious manner. If one asks them about the difference in meanings and status between the various Bodhisattvas, the famous Zen sand gardens of Japan, and the Emptiness of Emptiness (ŚūnyaŚūnyatā, SuSu; STC 5711), one will acquire about as much understanding as if you asked a Roman Catholic, Methodist, or Baptist about the empirical falsifiability of the transubstantiation of the Blood of Christ into the sacramental bread used in the Christian Mass, or the importance of the ancient Greek philosophical background of "logos" ("In the beginning was the *Word* ..."). Consequently, the following is a thumbnail sketch of the underlying ideas of the historical origins of Indian Buddhism, about which most Buddhists know very little.

Nine Basic Ideas of Indian and East Asian Buddhism

The following is a simplified sketch of the background of some of the differences between the Judeo-Christian tradition and the Buddhist tradition which focuses on eight underlying ideas. They are neither simple nor familiar — nor are they superficial or easily explained in these few pages.

Karma

What was the Buddha thinking deeply about when and by which he became the Enlightened One? The answer is karma, moral causation. The term "karman" (or its Anglicized form, "karma"), constitutes the single most important concept in Buddhism. Karma also offers the greatest contrast with the JC tradition because Christianity lacks any idea remotely similar to karma. Similiarly, Buddhism lacks any concept of Christian aseity — the idea that God is not causally created but caused everything else. Karma is a theory about causation; it is a theory about the breadth, depth, and causal implications of thoughts, behavior, and their social and psychological effects throughout many, many lifetimes in many, many forms. The word "karma" refers to both the causal process and also to the general term for the total sum of the process, just as the word "load" can refer to both the process "to load" (verb) and the sum total of what was loaded — the "load" (noun). Therefore, in its different historical interpretations, karma is *the* central, most important assumption in Hinduism, Buddhism, and Jainism.

Karma refers to the process that causes effects in the past, present, and future; it also refers to the whole accumulated effects of intentional "willed" action associated with a given person or animal. The primary assumption of karma is that for every intentional (willed) mental or physical action, there is an automatically generated effect; this effect may occur in our experience immediately after the act, soon after, in the near or distant future, or in the next life/lives. However, no intentional action ever escapes generating an effect. Thus, at each level of karmic development while one is a person, one has the possibility of understanding the Buddhist analysis of the world. This understanding would allow one the option of changing one's behavior and intentions and turning toward a variety of ethical paths (marga) stretched over many lifetimes — towards Nirvāṇa or at least a better rebirth.

The Mutual Interpenetration and Interdependence of All Things

The idea of karmic causation refers to a closed causal network of interlocking causes, conditions, and effects (pratītya saṃutpāda). This means that everything in the world, including the human sense of a personal self, is a causal effect, a changing product of interdependent causal forces; furthermore, the self does not ultimately continue to exist (nirātman) since it is the product of constantly changing causes and effects. Thus, there is nothing which is not caused — no creator god and no viewpoint which is not part of the interdependent system; there is no standpoint independent of causation, no independent fulcrum outside the world system of causation (saṃsāra). This means that ourselves, and everything else, are not a collection of different isolated discrete elements, but that the movies in our heads, our changing experiences, are a slowly shifting, mingling of conditions and causes without an independent owner of these thoughts and experiences. This interdependence of all things is reflected in the Chinese Buddhist schools of Hua-yen and T'ien-t'ai. In Hua-yen, this intermingling of causes and conditions is compared to one's views of things if one were standing within a closed globe made of mirrors wherein each mirror reflects the image of all other mirrors.

This deeply buried idea of the interlocking, mutual interpenetration and mutual support of all things is built on this Buddhist philosophical "grammar" and is reflected in the analogy of guanxi connections in which Chinese opportunistic criminal groups briefly congregate to achieve a goal and then dissolve into other shifting temporary alliances — often without a fixed hierarchical chain of command. This Chinese Buddhist model contrasts with the deeply buried Anglo-European idea of fixed chains of causes which form a hierarchy like a pyramid with the one person who causes things to happen at the top over extended stretches of time as in the LCN model. (See Chapter 15 on guanxi; also note that there are counter-examples to all these broad generalizations.)

Furthermore, the original Indian Buddhist mindset assumed that:

1. Causation (cause and effect) in the universe is infinite and uncreated.
2. There is no implicit end or purpose built into the universe the way most JC believers would expect.
3. Although Bluddhists do not deny the everyday experience of one's personality, they assert neither any form of individual permanent personality nor eternal soul within the living person.

4. There is no god or gods who administer the invariable law of karma.
5. There is no permanent individual self (or soul) except as a mistaken belief, a wrongly constructed map of experience.
6. One's willed mental and/or physical actions in this life, plus the latent accumulated karma of one's past lives, generate one's future lives in either human or nonhuman forms.
7. Good karma generates good effects (or good merit) in one's experience, and good karma compensates for bad karma.
8. With accurate (Buddhist) knowledge of the way things really are and with the deliberate generation of good intentions, one has always the possibility of improving what happens in this life and in one's many future lives.

Thus, by acting and thinking in virtuous ways, one always has the possibility of improving both one's future experiences and the type of future rebirth which one's karma automatically generates at one's death. This obviously offers a strong contrast with the Christian ideas of a single enduring personal identity which is maintained during two (and only two) states of existence, this life and the afterlife where the final choice of one's destiny is God's, not man's.

Change

In other words, insofar as karmic causation and the dual consistency of language and behavior create the illusion of personal permanence, there is only causally driven *process* of change, albeit change at different rates of speed. Trees, men, mountains, elephants, rabbits and rivers continually change but at different rates of speed, but all change is ultimately driven by the interplay of karmic cause and effects. Roughly speaking, to actually know the way things really are (yathā bhūtam), is to come close to knowing the content (but not the process) of enlightenment ("Bodhi") as did the Buddha. The name given to the non-physical "status" of the Buddha's enlightenment was " Nirvāṇa ".

Nirvāṇa (nie pan; STC 0154 2857)

The word " Nirvāṇa " consists of two parts: "nis" and the root "va". Before the consonant "v", the "s" in "nis" becomes "r" as in "nir". The fundamental metaphorical meaning of the root "va" is the cessation of the flame of an oil lamp when all the oil which fuels its flame has been burned up. The metaphor of burning up the fuel is analogous to the cessation of karmic causation through good actions and good thoughts over many lifetimes. Religious salvation consists of *really knowing* this, digesting it thoroughly in all its hidden implications, and *acting in accordance* with that full understanding over many, many lifetimes. However, different people have different karmic capacities to know and to behave and thus Buddhism has provided — as do most religions — multiple paths (marga) for people with different needs, different apparent personalities, and different capacities. People also conceive of Nirvāṇa in accordance with their own personal, historical personalities — otherwise known as their own karmic configurations. Thus Bart Simpson and Archie Bunker may conceive of Nirvāṇa as a heaven, a marvelous place to go after they die. On the other hand, higher upon the scale of karmic capacity to know, practice, and discipline one's self, knowledgeable and sophisticated Buddhists have expressed these differences in levels of capacities to understand Buddhist Nirvāṇa as, "There is no one who goes, no place to go, and no process of going."

Afterlives

Thus, the quest to achieve ultimate religious salvation, Nirvāṇa, as understood at the lower levels of Buddhist practice, is as an afterlife within a heaven and as an almost infinite series of different lifetimes. These different lifetimes consist of a limited existence within many different sentient (knowing) forms of life — destinies (gati). These afterlives can be in the form of people; animals; Crocodile Dundee; insects; birds; Bart Simpson; big-breasted, topless, angelic messengers who flit between the various mythological gods (apsara); Al Bundy; ghost-like things that "go bump in the night"; or even beings in various Hells (Naraka) and/or various Heavens (Amitābha's Western paradise). The underlying point is that the Buddhist framework of time is a very, very long one and is implicitly much longer than the "one lifetime in two places" framework of popular Anglo-European Christian time.

Bodhisattvas (Pu Sa; STC 5476 5646)

Some 2000 years ago, the Mahāyāna tradition brought forth the religious ideal of the compassionate Bodhisattva, the Enlightened (bodhi) Being (sattva). (This deity is not observed in Theravāda Buddhism.) The general model is that of a Buddhist who practices all virtues in all life-forms and destinies throughout an almost infinite series of lifetimes and earns through karmic rebirths a status where he/she can attain Nirvāṇa. However, it is at that highest point of Buddhist salvation that the individual honors the Bodhisattva and vows to forgo Nirvāṇa until all sentient beings in all life-forms also attain Nirvāṇa. Thus, such religious supreme beings remain involved with lesser worldlings, and with their great store of resources they help others achieve Buddhahood and/or Bodhisattvahood. Bodhisattvas represent a Mahāyāna ideal of emotional and theistic expression, they are compassionate means or instruments (Sanskrit: upāya ; Chinese: fang bian; Japanese: hōben ; Tibetan: thabs) to assist all sentient beings toward ultimate salvation. A very popular example is Guanyin (STC 6034 7299) often known as the Chinese Goddess of Mercy. Guanyin was female in China and the rest of Asia, but in earlier Indian Sanskrit texts, Guanyin was known as the masculine Avalokitesvara, as in the *Diamond Sutra* (Vajracchedikā - Prajñāpāramitā-Sūtra). Guanyin is known as Kwanon in Japanese, the historical source of the name of the internationally known business firm Canon.

Four Basic Illusions

By using the word "illusion", one does not mean to infer a visual illusion but rather an idea learned in each culture which fogs one's attempts to "know things as they really are" (yathā bhūtam). The Buddhist tradition recognized a range of interconnected, conceptual, and emotionally loaded mistakes, bogus ideas of how the world and ourselves really are, which generate mistaken expectations in people's thoughts, behavior, and everyday anticipations.

Following are the types of misleading and inaccurate conceptual mistakes we would recognize if we heard someone ask:

- Where does my headache go when my headache goes away?
- What does the "it" refer to in the sentence: "It is raining."?

Many knowledgeable Buddhists would hold that such types of confused, conceptual mistakes (as in the preceding two fallacious questions) lie at the root of most human assumptions about who we are, where we are going, and what we ought to do. At a deeper level of Buddhist thought, the Buddha remains the model of understanding and practice. He, having understood causation and its clinging relationship with the ideas of desire, held that there were four basic illusions, emotionally loaded conceptual mistakes (as are the two analogous examples above). These *illusions* are that:

1. The thoughts and sensations which somehow belong to the entity that we call our personal self are *ultimately real* and that they refer to something permanent.
2. It is possible to *permanently* belong to and own anything or anybody.
3. Everything is not a fluxing staccato product of the everchanging totality of causes and effects.
4. Anything is truely permanent and that anyone is free from, or outside the scope of, the instantaneous, interlocking, world-inclusive-bundles of causes and effect (karman).

The Buddhist tradition holds that since the Buddha no longer viewed the world in relation to these (mistaken) ideas, he no longer acted with a built-in desire to grasp and cling to the effects of his actions. Thus, the Buddha no longer generated any good or bad karmic causes; without karmic causation, there is no more birth, no more re-birth, and neither any illusion of anyone, nor of anyone going anywhere.

Fate

Often, the echoes of karma and the popular interpretations of re-birth are also mistakenly equated with fatalism and a lack of ambition for the future. This conclusion is, of course, false and cross-culturally confused. Obviously, there are times when apparently undeserved grief and suffering enter people's lives. By means of their sharp-eyed realism, some Asians expect to receive an "unfair" mixture of the good and the bad; they do not expect social progress or cosmic justice in this life. Then, when they conclude that there is little to be done except persevere and get on with what is possibly good in this life, their cultural style and their theological framework appears coldly resigned and fatalistic to an Anglo-European. Dead wrong! Also, the perceived fatalism of Asians seldom hampers their ability to do business. There is nothing quite as ambitious as a Hong Kong Buddhist businessman who sees the beginning of a deal and smells a profit. Also, one must add that there is no one who will work quite as hard to bring it off.

Evil and Death

One hears the echoes of Buddhist thought in the ways in which many (but not all) Asians reconcile themselves to the human inevitabilities of sorrow, grief, death, blameless suffering, and all the other evils of humankind. Some Christians blame it on God, or assume that God knows what He is doing and our misery is part of the price inherent in His creation and our moral inferiority.

However, since in Buddhism, there is not a single all-powerful god who created the universe on which to initially put the blame for apparent undeserved evil-as-punishment. Since there is not assumed any necessary progress or implicit betterment built into human history, the reactions of many Asians to these inevitabilities of human life are significantly different from those of Judeo-Christian Anglo-Europeans. In other words, there is for Buddhists a human problem of evil, for all the mean terrible things that can happen to humans have happened to them — as with everyone else in the world. They grieve at death much as we do; they are as devastated as we are by the death or the rape of children. However, for Buddhists, there is a difference in how they see the responsibility and context of the event. For Buddhists, there is no problem of theodicy — the Christian defense of a good God in the light of the experience of human evil.

Thus, individual Buddhists, especially Theravāda Buddhists, bear the ultimate responsibility for bringing evil upon themselves, not God nor the Buddha nor the Mahāyāna Bodhisattva. Evil, as noted above, is one's own karmic fate. One is faced with the instantaneous ever-pressing need to accommodate to one's circumstances and to get on with one's life, especially the future of one's family. Some Asians would call that realism, not fatalism.

In a nutshell, the preceding section describes the underlying philosophical ideas and meanings of some important aspects of Buddhism. As you can see, Buddhism and Buddhists are admirable, sophisticated people, and no matter how different their conclusions may be, they offer a compassionate, religious mindset about human life. However, it is also clear that Buddhism is a long, long way from the fundamental assumptions and underlying frameworks of the Jewish-Christian-Islamic traditions!

Buddhist Contextual Pragmatism and Truth

As noted earlier regarding mindsets and interrogation (Chapter 9), the often-admired business and political pragmatism of many Asians may be attributed indirectly to the Buddhist concept of "skill-in-means" which has echoed in so many Buddhist countries for many centuries. The idea of "skill-in-means" may be described in an oversimplified manner as the adjustment of one's message into forms, means, stratagems, and methods appropriate to the karmic, social, personal, religious, and economic capacities and cultural contexts of the target audience. Since we have dealt with some nonreligious implications of this idea, some of the religious implications of this pragmatic contextualism follow.

Obscure as this may seem, "skill-in-means" is standard Mahāyāna Buddhist doctrine expressed in alternative words. Once again, I refer to the Buddhist technical term " upāya " and its many uses throughout Asia (Sanskrit: upāya , Chinese: fang bian, Japanese: hōben , Tibetan: thabs). The term " upāya " can be paraphrased as "skilled in alternative contextually appropriate means to help others towards Nirvāṇa ." This means that the deity, the Bodhisattva — he, as the Indian Avalokiteśvara, or she, as the Chinese Guayin-Kuanyin and Japanese Kwannon — has many "skillful means". In the Mahāyāna Buddhist context, this is taken to mean that gods, Bodhisattva, or divine agencies use benevolent strategies, ploys, devices, and/or religious deceptions that change throughout many different lifetimes. The Bodhisattva has the insight to choose means appropriate to the troubled contexts (duḥkha) and the karmic capacities of the particular individuals to understand and act properly. With the Bodhisattva's help, a Mahāyānist Buddhist may find and properly practice a path appropriate to his/her karmic capacity from among the many religious and ethical paths toward Buddhist salvation, Nirvāṇa. Therefore, by the Bodhisattva's use of these context-restricted strategies to develop these upāyas/fang bian/ hōben tactics appropriately for the person, the person is helped to achieve salvation in a form appropriate to his/her type of karmically-bound understanding and behavior. Examples of three different types of portraying such salvation, are Nirvāṇa, paramārthasatya (the highest level of insight/truth), and rebirth in Amitābha's Western paradise.

This deep cultural view contrasts with the (here oversimplified) Anglo-European, Judeo-Christian-Islamic habit regarding truth, a "God's-eye" view of truth. This holds that whether or not persons know the truth of a matter, they should try to express an approximation of the single, unchanging, accurate correspondence between what *is the case* (which is what God can see) and what is said to be the case by humans. This expression would be between what actually exists but is known only to God and what is said to be the truth of the matter by humans. Therefore, what can be known and expressed as a true expression is context-restricted to humans; but truth, as an invariable, absolute, nonconditional true expression of what actually is, is known only to God from His "God's-eye" view of truth. This latter point was found in the view of one elderly Muslim merchant whose reason for not cheating his customers was expressed in the Qur'an (Koran): "Lo! He over all things is watching."[236] This is a "God's-eye" view of truth. Chinese Buddhist contexualism was religious in its origins but it is a view of "truth" which is neither God's nor the Bodhisattva's. It is a human view based on analogical reasoning grounded in the Buddhist system of karma and Asian societies and remains systemically incompatible with the Judeo-Christian-Islamic traditions.

Some implications of pragmatic contextualism, this deeply buried, habitual way of thinking, feeling and seeing the world, are that ideas should not be judged by comparing them against some form of absolute truths or universal, law-like principles, the "God's-eye" view of truth. Rather, all ideas, ideals, goods, and evils should be subject to judgments driven by the pressures of *specific circumstances* according to *specific everyday contexts.* Led by this deep cultural habit of processing information and making contextual judgments, what is implicitly discounted and rendered to be of secondary importance is the application of absolute truths or values to social situations without regard to the social and personal conditions of the moment. What is of primary importance in thinking about truth-telling and deception is the Buddhist habit of mind of judging things contextually. Thus, truth is context restricted. This habit of mind is a fang bian-driven process which is experienced as the obvious, common-sense need to judge things in relation to time, place, history, dominant personalities, and in light of the long-term social *effects* of one's decisions on those to whom one has strong obligations and with whom one is socially intimate. In practice, the acculturated Buddhist conceptual habit of upāya /fang bian silently supports the ocassional circumvention of the letter of the law, not telling the truth and whole truth regardless of the consequences, by using one's talents, luck, and loyalty to honor and support one's social guanxi mentors.

The culturally-driven analogy is between: (1) judging one's karmic fate, one's appropriate but limited ethical capacities circumscribed by the karmic possibilities and limitations of one's rebirth (gati), the special context of one's destiny in this life; and (2) a general Anglo-European appeal to Judeo-Christian universal, absolute, timeless, unchanging principles inherent in creation and/or by appeal to Natural Law.

Thus, for the unreflective Buddhist, one decides one's actions and one's public posture and maximizes one's own future and one's family's future by appeal to the context-restricted, ever-pressing need to accommodate and dance to life's karmic circumstances and to embrace whatever measures will likely ensure the best future of one's extended guanxi family under changing circumstances. Since the introduction of Buddhism in about 150 A.D., this Buddhist idea of fang bian, contextual pragmatism, was used to reconcile Buddhist history and doctrine and thus has been deeply assimilated into Chinese culture. Furthermore, in my eyes, this assimilation now represents a basic, second-order model of processing information, just as a "God's-eye" view of truth now represents a basic second-order model of processing information in the Anglo-European, Judeo-Christian-Islamic cultures — or, "Different karmic strokes for different karmic folks!".

Thus, in generalizing about contextual pragmatism, the influence of the Buddhist Chinese fang bian mindset can be seen in the encouragement of mutually dependent strategies between people:

1. To promote harmony, duty, obligations of family, and maintenance of "face" and guanxi obligations, which involves rejecting rhetorical honesty, prohibitions against white lies, and telling the truth regardless of the circumstances without regard to the effects of loss of "face" and public shame.
2. To recognize that the truth or falsehood of socially relevant ideas should not always be considered mutually exclusive, either/or alternatives (strong disjunctions), but may be considered as endpoints on a line (continuum) where each point embodies a possibly appropriate response to maintain the desired interpersonal balances within the fluxing social context.
3. To recognize that truth depends on the changing context of human environments and needs, and as both change, the formulations of what is true are to be modified to meet changing human needs and social contexts.

4. To recognize that one should temper what one tells as true by judging and weighing the consequences to the broader context of one's family, "face", guanxi, and the maintenance of social harmony.

The merging of these mindsets, these historical and cultural habits of mind shape a person's choices, even though they are usually inconsistently and unconsciously used by individuals. Cultural factors such as fang bian may influence a Chinese person's choices whether to attempt deception, just as a Jew, Christian, or Muslim's reluctance to cheat or lie is influenced by the historical belief that an all-powerful, all-knowing, all-benevolent God is watching to see whether you cheat or lie. Likewise, with Chinese fang bian, because of the acculturated layers of these cultural traits with which ideas and values are processed and judged, the influence of contextualism has grown during the centuries of Chinese history. Finally, fang bian strongly promotes those clan and guanxi values and collectivist ends, which are perceived so often in accordance with general Chinese mindsets.[237]

Today, Buddhism remains one of the largest religious traditions and it has spread throughout the world. Within the ranks of Buddhists is a huge and bewildering variety of ethnic groups who are associated with many different Buddhist doctrines and practices. Preliterate Theravāda Buddhist Cambodians stand in great contrast to sophisticated Thai Theravāda and Mahāyāna Buddhist businessmen in all of Asia. Thus, Buddhism remains part of the cultural landscapes of Thailand, Śrī Lanka, PRC, Japan, ROC, Korea, and the many locations where the overseas Chinese Buddhists have immigrated and prospered. Also, the echoes of many developments of Buddhist thought and practice appear as unnoticed patterns within the daily lives of many Asians. One hears Buddhist (and Confucian) echoes in the gentleness, compassion, and discipline associated with the Chinese, Vietnamese, Korean, and Japanese ideals of adulthood, parenthood, family responsibility, and public and private morals.

IV

Recording, Preserving, Training, and Planning

20 Standard Telegraphic Code (STC)

關係

What Is STC?

中文電碼手冊

Standard Telegraphic Code (STC), also known as Chinese Telegraphic Code (CTC), was established in the 19th century to identify and accurately identify specific characters and convey the meaning of Chinese words and names without using Chinese to do so. STC has been used to assist in the identification of Japanese names as well. By extension, it can be applied to Korean names.

Appendix B reproduces a publication prepared by Robert M. Hearn describing the major Chinese dialects, relevant terms, and Thai and STC equivalents. It has been published in the *IAACI News*, a publication of the International Association of Asian Crime Investigators. It is reproduced here with the permission of Mr. Hearn.

Our basic problem (and it is *not* a problem to the Chinese) is that Chinese and Japanese do not use an alphabet as we do. They use written characters or ideographs, not separate letters in combinations. When we spell out the sounds of Chinese pronunciation in the English alphabet, this is known as *transliteration*. On the other hand, *translation* is the process of using English words to describe and convey the meanings of words or phrases from Asian languages or from various Asian dialects within the English language.

The way a Chinese word or character is pronounced — the way it sounds — has *no* relation to the way it is written. However, the sound of the Chinese ideograph or character is dependent on the Chinese dialect spoken. In other words, the way a Chinese character is written tells us absolutely nothing about how it is properly pronounced. Furthermore, upon hearing the sound of a Chinese character, different people will use quite different English letters to try to recreate the Chinese pronunciation. For example, take the word or character for the common Chinese name "Wang" (STC number 3769) which means "king". This has been transliterated in many different ways, such as Wang or Wong.

Therefore, STC provides the means to switch from their nonalphabetic language to a way to represent Chinese sounds and identify Chinese characters (ideographs) in our alphabetic language. We use STC numbers to make those switches with accuracy and relative ease. This switch is accomplished by matching a specific Chinese/Japanese character or ideograph with a number within the STC code. The use of STC numbers is justified by the fact that they can be more easily transmitted by most telecommunication systems than the nonalphabetic Chinese/Japanese characters.

Why Should STC Be Used? A Hong Kong Example

Quoting Tony Lee, a senior superintendent in the Hong Kong intelligence division, Gerald Posner described the acute need for STC:[238,239]

> For instance, in the U.S. the most important piece of information you can have on a criminal is a fingerprint. If we were looking for an American criminal in Hong Kong, we would get a fingerprint from the U.S. and match it to the person here. Well, for us, there is something as important as a fingerprint. It is the Chinese characters of someone's name. Since there is no standardized way of translating Chinese characters into English, the names in different files look totally different. The Chinese character that represents the name pronounced "Ing" is spelled by different people in different ways, including "Eng", most commonly "Ng", but I've also seen it as "Ong", as "Eing", and even "Enq"."
>
> So when a U.S. law-enforcement agency is seeking information [from the Royal Hong Kong Police] on a Chinese criminal or Triad member, they must give us the person's Chinese name in Chinese characters. Even though we ask for this all the time, we always get requests in English and usually with the person's adopted American name. There's no way for us to find the information. We get requests, then we tell them you must give us the Chinese characters, and then we do not hear from them for six months until we get another request in English. It is crazy. In America they cannot even ask us for the right name of a file on someone, much less work with us in catching the guys.

This is why we need to expand the use of STC! As the incidence of Asian-based crime increases, whether it be based in either the Chinese Triads or the Japanese Yakuza or others, it is clear that it is necessary to have at least one or more law enforcement professionals in every good-sized police force who are able to use the Standard Telegraphic Code to trace Chinese, Japanese, and Korean ideographs within domestic and international databases. Without this ability, one is never quite sure whether one is chasing the same person. This problem also holds for Viet-Ching (Chinese-Vietnamese) names.

Understandably, the lack of STC training for law enforcement personnel is a particular problem for small and medium-sized police departments. Although they may now have only occasional contacts with Asian crime, the present absence of widespread use of STC for tracing Asian names within domestic and foreign databases will generate serious problems for future Asian crime specialists. Thus, one of the first priorities of cross-cultural training for law enforcement personnel should be to encourage the establishment of two or three centers to instruct law enforcement personnel in the use of the STC for Chinese, Japanese, and Korean names.

Using STC, names written by means of the various Asian writing systems, such as Chinese ideographs or the related Japanese ideographs (kanji) and the Japanese phonetic writing system (kanna), can be processed for accurate tracing and easy distribution. STC can also be applied to Korean names and words, by means of special cross-reference books which illustrate the Korean Hangul equivalents for the Chinese ideographs. Thus, mutually understood numbers in a code, rather than unwieldy ideographs, may be transmitted through a range of telecommunications. For example, neither the Royal Hong Kong Police Force nor the Japanese National Police will accept inquiries about Chinese or Japanese individuals without STC identification.

Translation vs. Transliteration

If you have the Chinese character (ideograph), and if you can use a Chinese-English dictionary, you can use STC fairly easily. However, if you have only the sound of the Chinese name, without the ideogram, using STC may require some skill in the transliteration of names from within a variety of Asian language dialects into English. Another term for the transliteration process is "Romanization", or using the Latin ("Roman") alphabet as a target language for the sounds of Asian languages. Two of the most common transliteration systems for Chinese are the older Wade-Giles system used in Taiwan and Hong Kong and the Pinyin system used in the People's Republic of China. Both systems are foreign to the internal Chinese tradition, although they have been widely adopted in this century by Chinese who need to communicate with non-Chinese people.

Problems with Chinese words, transliterations, and names were described by M. Cordell Hart:[241]

> Even with identical spellings, transliterated Chinese names may well not be similar. There are far fewer distinct sounds in Mandarin Chinese than, for example, in English, but the various dialects of China all call for the incorporation of tones with sounds to form syllables of their spoken languages. And each character of the written language is pronounced in a unique sound uttered in a prescribed tone. It is this incorporation of tones which gives Chinese a quality often referred to as "sing-song". We have the same thing in English but with a major difference. In speaking English, one easily knows the difference in meaning between "O.K.?" and "O.K.!", but the root meaning of "O.K." is the same. English also has homonyms, "bear" and "bare", for example, which can only be understood in context. Chinese has a vastly greater problem with homonyms, and there are abundant opportunities for puns in speaking. In the dialects of Chinese all spoken words — whether comprising one or more characters — have essential tones that are critical to the root meaning. In Mandarin, for example, the sound transliterated as "zhong" in the Pinyin system can be spoken in three of that dialect's four tones. Indeed, searching only such common Chinese-English dictionaries as *Mathews' Chinese-English Dictionary*[240] and the *Pinyin Chinese English Dictionary*, one finds 10 characters in the former and 8 in the latter properly pronounced with the same sound of "zhong" to be said in a high-level tone, commonly called the "first tone". No characters with the sound of "zhong" are pronounced with a high-rising ("second") tone. Three characters and four characters are found in the respective dictionaries calling for "zhong" to be said in a low-dipping ("third") tone. With the sharp falling ("fourth") tone, the two dictionaries show 11 and 10 characters, respectively, as with the sound of "zhong".

In addition to the STC book, a second tool of great help to Asian crime investigators and analysts to be used as a supplement to STC is the *Sino Surnames Syllabary* prepared by Louie M. Valdivia, U.S. Customs Service. This excellent, inclusive reference offers a wide range of information about Asian surnames, nicknames, milknames, STC, and helpful tables of cross-references between Wade-Giles and Pinyin transliteration systems. Also, it lists common Chinese and Southeast Asian surnames such as Hmong, Mien, and Thai. For Thai names, there is the Romanization System (transliteration system) of the Royal Institute of Thailand. For Laotians (Lao) and other Tribal peoples of Southeast Asia, there is the transliteration system established by the Board of Geographic Names, the BGN/PCGN.

The Importance of the Word Order of Chinese Names

One well known difference is that Chinese write their family name first, their brother names (if any), then their personal name(s); we write our personal name(s) first, our middle name, and our family name/surname last. Very often, the family name has one syllable and the personal name has two syllables. Also, some Chinese, both U.S. And China-born, use their birthplace as part of their name, illustrating their strong attachment to their ancestral home or province. On occasion, Chinese will acquire an additional name if they have recovered from a severe illness or some other "close brush with death".

Common Surnames, Personal Names, and Brother Names

Among traditional Asians, there may be a second name which accompanies the personal name, the brother name, which is shared by all brothers of a particular married man and wife. Thus, if a suspect claims that another person is his brother, but if you determine that they do not share the same second or third name, it is probable that they are not biological brothers. However, of the traditional 400 to 500 Chinese family names (surnames), about 45 Chinese family names constitute about 70% of those names in common use (see Robert Hearn's materials in Appendix B).

Therefore, given the population of ethnic Chinese in PRC, Singapore, Taiwan, Hong Kong, Amsterdam, L.A. And Houston, there are many Chinese named "Wang". Furthermore, "Wang" might well be an Anglicized version of several possibilities such as "Wong," "Won", just as "Tommy" might be a somewhat anglicized version of "Ti-chang." Japanese and Vietnamese may also spell-out or transliterate Chinese names into English letters quite differently. Mr. M. Cordell Hart offered the example of a Cantonese by the name of "Au Hoy" who might take the name "John Auhoy". These issues are described with illustrative examples in the Appendices, as prepared by Mr. Robert M. Hearn. This appendix describes and illustrates the major Chinese surnames, the Chinese characters, Pinyin transliteration, tone, STC numbers and the meaning.[242]

An Example from the STC Code Book

In Figure 18, note the lower right-hand box, number 3769 illustrating the four-stroke character or ideogram and the Chinese transliteration (not translation) of the character "WANG". For this character, the representation of the Chinese sounds in our English alphabet remains the same in either the Pinyin system or in the Wade-Giles system, both of which are foreign systems to the Chinese. In Cantonese dialect, the (same) character would be written the same but would be pronounced differently; thus it would be transliterated differently. In this case, in Cantonese, the character "WANG" would be

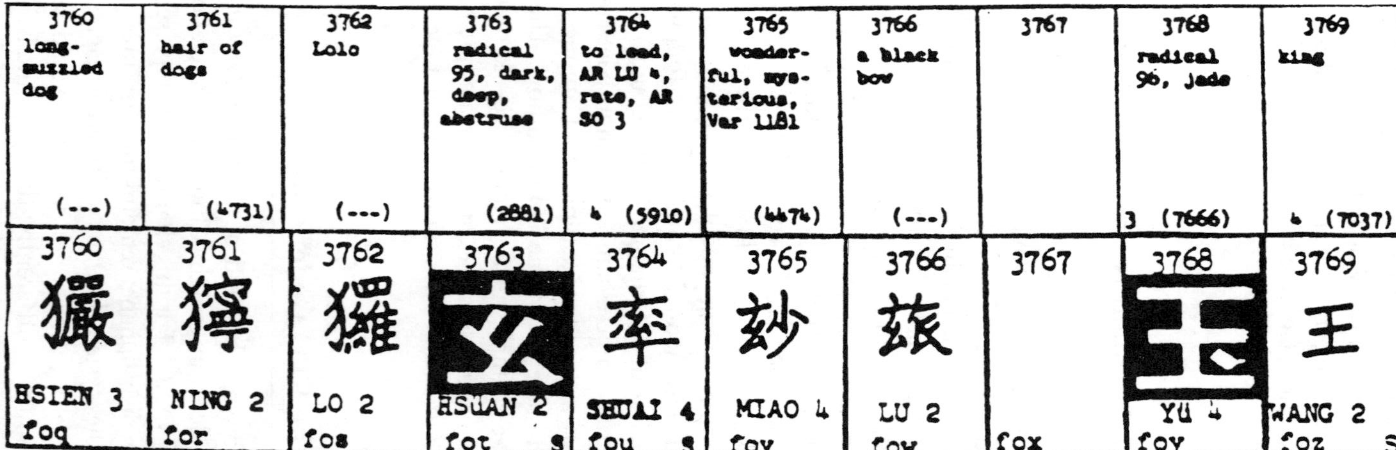

Figure 18 Example from the STC code book. Above are two rows of boxes taken from facing pages of the STC book. The bottom row shows the Chinese character and the equivalent representation of the Chinese sound in the English alphabet. The top now shows the meanings and dictionary reference to *Mathews Chinese-English Dictionary.*

pronounced and thus transliterated as "WONG". The upper right-hand box (number 3769) gives us, among other things, the meaning of the word-used-as-a-name, as analogous for example, in the English name "ARMSTRONG". Also, given in the top row is the reference number in *Mathew's Chinese-English Dictionary*, an older, standard dictionary.[243]

The Problem of Nicknames and Suffixes

There are no standards in the STC transliteration system for nicknames and AKAs which, unfortunately, play a great role in conversation about criminal activities. Rather, nicknames are usually transliterated strictly by sounds, usually the creation of the first officer/agent who tries his hand at recording the sounds of a nickname. For an example, "Old Thief Lady" has been transliterated as "Chuck Poor," "Chat Por" and "Tsat Pow." For example, it is not as if the Chinese suspect was named the equivalent of "Bubble-Gum Joe." Obviously, with an alphabetic language we could transliterate "Bubble-Gum Joe"; where "Bubble-Gum" is a standard (Chinese) word, there is a standard way of transliterating the sounds "Bubble-Gum". The problem of Chinese nicknames is different. It is as if the suspect's nickname was a southeast Dallas pronunciation of "Bubba-Wopis", where "Wopis" is not a word and for which there would be no *standard* transliteration in either Chinese or English. In many cases it is best to continue the first attempts at transliteration of the nickname so that at least the original transliteration may be retained for identification, even though there may be more accurate or alternative transliterations as more information is gathered. It remains a problem, but maintaining the first occurrence maximizes the probability of accurate identification.

Suffixes

Many Chinese and Thais use diminutive and honorific suffixes in their references to individuals. For example, "Old Wang" consists of Lau (old) plus the Chinese family name Wang (STC 3769); other common suffixes are Au and Hun, as in Tsit Chai Hung, where Hung means "dice" and his real name is Hung Tang.

Asian Police Transliterations/Romanizations

To complicate things, it is reported that the police forces of Hong Kong, People's Republic of China, Macao, and Taiwan use slightly different styles of transliteration and generally insist that these forms of names be used when requesting identification searches within their own internal records. Some Hong Kong police, for example, base their transliterations on Cantonese Chinese rather then Mandarin Chinese; PRC police offer other law enforcement officers only their own transliterations and not the actual characters or the STC numbers. M. Cordell Hart notes that…[244]

> … the Public Security Bureau of the Peoples Republic of China uses the "Five Stroke Method" (wu bi zi xing, STC = 0063/4581/1316/5887) to input names into their computer files. The Japanese National Police use a combination of "kanji" (literally "Chinese characters") and one form of "kana", a Japanese phonetic system.

Then, non-Asians and Asians must determine the original character for accurate identification — no small problem. A new Marine Smuggling Database Network has been proposed for the intelligence/investigative communities. Briefly outlined in an article by Gideon Carr, this would utilize STC and would also range across a field of some 18 variables.[245]

The Absence of Materials and Training Sources

Several senior intelligence analysts and scholars have searched for but not found a self-help book in print on STC. Thus, it seems that there are no materials to allow law enforcement personnel, unfamiliar with Asian languages, to do four interrelated things: (1) teach him/herself how to use Chinese Standard Telegraphic Code, (2) learn how to use standard Chinese-English dictionaries for STC purposes, (3) learn to understand and use the PRC Pinyin or Wade-Giles systems of transliteration, and (4) utilize dialect conversion tables to identify and distinguish Chinese names in Mandarin, Cantonese, or in other dialects. However, the *Sino Surnames Syllabary* and other materials prepared for law enforcement (listed at the end of this chapter) will greatly help those unfamiliar with Asian languages.

As mentioned earlier, in spite of the best efforts of Cordell Hart,[243] to encourage law enforcement interest in STC, there are no public-domain instructional materials written for non-Federal law enforcement personnel that provide a step-by-step instruction and a comparative overview of transliteration and dialect problems in English. Furthermore, until text scanners and more sophisticated computer software are developed, STC offers an interim advantage. However, such levels of high-tech scanners do not seem to be on the near horizons.

The FBI's clear, concise 19-page *A Guide to Chinese Names and Language*[246] remains an excellent first step, albeit incomplete. Now that the FBI may be considering the development of its own STC course, more materials may become available. Perhaps special cassettes and exercises coordinated with videotaped instructions would be useful. At this writing, the only other place federal law enforcement personnel can receive government-sponsored training in STC is at a federal language school where a federal linguist teaches an excellent 2-week course in STC and transliteration techniques about three times per year. One commercial firm teaches a 1-week course on demand.

As indicated above, both the lack of training opportunities and the differences in Chinese names complicate law enforcement efforts to identify, process, and retrieve ID information in their files or databases. However, one can easily see that the Standard Telegraphic Code represents an advantageous procedure whereby Chinese and Japanese ideographs can be more precisely identified by unique numbers in a simple code which simplifies communication and identification. It is also clear that increased uses of STC are justified because of its utility in identifying and tracing names within international and domestic police databases.

Reference Materials

A Guide to Chinese Names and Language, U.S. Department of Justice, Federal Bureau of Investigation, Washington, D.C., September, 1991.

Standard Telegraphic Code, Financial Crimes Enforcement Network (FinCEN), U.S. Department of the Treasury, Washington, D.C., 1991.

Three Way: Chinese Commercial/Telegraphic Code Book, Royal Hong Kong Police Force, Hong Kong, June, 1989.

O'Neill, P.G., *Japanese Names: a Comprehensive Index by Characters and Readings,* Weatherhill, New York, 1989 (ISBN:0-8348-0225-2).

Valdivia, Louie M., *Sino Surnames Syllabary,* U.S. Customs Services, 1993. Law enforcement officers may contact the Customs Services in San Francisco.

Posner, Gerald L., *Warlords of Crime: Chinese Secret Societies — the New Mafia,* McGraw-Hill, New York, 1988 (ISBN: 0-007-050600-0). Pages 258-259 focus on the need for STC training.

"Standard Telegraphic Code", a television interview with (Part 1) M. Cordell Hart, Senior Intelligence Analyst and Referent for Asian Organized Crime, and (Part 2) Paul N. DerGarabedian, Intelligence Analyst, both of the Financial Crime Enforcement Network, U.S. Dept. of the Treasury, produced by the Law Enforcement Television Network (LETN), Crime Scene: "Asian Gangs", #153-0087, 1303 Marsh Lane, Carrollton, Texas, 75006. (There are some inaccuracies in Part 2.)

Thai Names: Reference Aid, Office of Intelligence, Drug Enforcement Administration, U.S. Department of Justice, Washington, D.C., 1992.

Vandivier, Peter F., *Vietnamese and Thai Names — Law Enforcement Considerations,* Financial Crime Enforecement Network, U.S. Dept. of the Treasury, Washington, D.C., 1992.

Distinguishing Between Vietnamese and Chinese Names, Financial Crime Enforecement Network, U.S. Dept. of the Treasury, Wahington, D.C., 1992.

Preserving the Cross-Cultural Skills Police Already Possess

21

關係

From a national perspective, there are two unrecognized problems about Asian crime and North American police. First, many of the hard-won cross-cultural (XC) skills, tactics, and knowledge that law enforcement professionals *already possess* are being lost through transfers, promotions, illnesses, retirements, and death. Second, these cross-cultural skills and field-proven tactics are not being systematically analyzed nor cross-referenced for efficient distribution to assist Asian crime training programs.

There are exceptions. Groups of law enforcement personnel pass on or receive cross-cultural information in informal networks (police guanxi by telephone), as part of Asian language training, or from specialized groups such as the International Association of Asian Crime Investigators and the California Asian Crime Investigators Association. However, the most likely method of acquiring XC skills, tactics, and knowledge training is on-the-job-training based upon the cross-cultural experience of seasoned investigators, street cops, and special agents. Of course, these are extremely good sources of information but, unfortunately, the information is seldom distributed except at Asian crime conferences. Such information usually remains geographically fragmented and unsystematically scattered between individuals and/or teams of very effective, knowledgeable officers and special agents. Clearly, this is not an efficient way of organizing and distributing hard-won XC information. Such skills are not being compared, analyzed, or merged into larger cross-cultural descriptive systems, nor are they being merged with existing query languages, special Asian language-compatible databases, interactive training software, or video-training cassettes.

Given contemporary educational and training technology, this information *could* be gathered within retrievable training programs, organized for distribution in ways from which each law enforcement intelligence group could receive cross-cultural information and training tailored to its own needs and its own appropriate levels of complexity. That means that the analysis and distribution of cross-cultural information could be pitched at usable/pragmatic levels appropriate for hard-charging street cops, detectives, or analysts or administrative planners or specialized trainers.

Aspects of Asian culture relevant to the scholar are not relevant to the police, even though the range of XC materials requested by police is much wider and much more complex about specific Asian topics than most scholars might expect. For example, the cultural roots of Asian mindsets in religion, philosophy, social theory, law, and ideas about rebirth, fate, elite education, classical literature, formal methods of reasoning, and even some aspects of social rank and family behavior are appropriate objects of the scholar's interests. Furthermore, many of them could be relevant for law enforcement personnel in particular cases. However, for some some street cops engaged in combating Asian crime, these interesting and legitimate aspects of culture are usually thought to be far too abstract, too theoretical, and far too distant from the pragmatic needs of the police officer who must combat the deliberate illegal behavior of Asian criminals. (While this is not true of many other good cops, of course, a few will make that criticism of this book, which is why this book has been designed as a multi-leveled sourcebook.) However, these aspects of Asian culture are *requested* and relevant to analysts, administrators, and trainers.

There is a clear need for XC training materials, actual case studies, and relevant "war stories", captured on videotape, analyzed in appropriate training styles, and arranged in functional categories appropriate for different police tasks and administrative levels. This is particularly relevant when officers are learning about Asian cultural differences while at the same time attempting to communicate with and protect the great majority of hard-working, law-abiding Asian citizens who are living quietly and productively in our many Asian-American communities and who are often the victims of criminal activities.

Therefore, it is particularly unfortunate that relevant cross-cultural knowledge and skills already found within the law enforcement communities are not being systematically gathered or preserved. While training does occur for a small number, it could be done more efficiently if such training programs included: (1) extensive surveys of police-relevant XC skills and knowledge, (2) some enlightened political support, (3) some hard-nosed administrative coordination of resources, and (4) some imaginative, flexible training programs. However, these programs must be based on real police cases, coupled with videotaped interviews of experienced Asian investigators. Furthermore, these programs should be organized by those few trainers who know *why* certain nonsuperficial aspects of Asian culture are relevant, who actually know how to *teach* XC information, and who will take time to actually *listen* to cops to determine whether their programs are succeeding and why.

The Unnoticed Pressures on Asian-American Officers 22

關係

While the application of cross-cultural (XC) skills and understanding may help to understand Asian criminal organizations, reduce stress for police, and generate more support from the Asian communities, these applications are even more effective when coupled with such innovations as Asian police storefronts, more Asian-American police officers, and training in Standard Telegraphic Code. Also important is Asian language training at Foreign Service Institute competency levels between levels, 2., and higher levels, 3+, a widely used measure of linguistic performance.

Contrary to popular views, the recruitment of more Asian-American police officers is not as simple a solution as many think it may be. (It should be noted that the following remarks are to be taken as expressing support and admiration for the particularly difficult positions to which Asian-American police are sometimes assigned. Furthermore, these remarks are, in part, a result of interviewing a number of Asian-American police.) The hiring of more Asian-Americans is often thought to be a panacea, an easy solution to the many problems of Asian crime. While it is clearly a practice to be encouraged, young Asian-American police are sometimes treated badly and with gross ignorance. Most mainline law enforcement administrators know very little of the special pressures and the legitimate limitations of what can be realistically expected of first- or second-generation Asian-American police personnel.

As with other American police, Asian-American personnel are dedicated, successful law enforcement professionals. However, they are seldom specifically prepared to meet the total range of difficult cross-cultural problems that may arise. Worse, these may be problems that Asian-American police are expected to meet quite easily. This is because some Anglo-European-American and African-American police administrators may have already assumed that by virtue of the ethnic background of Asian-American officers, that they are actually prepared to meet and successfully cope with the XC aspects of Asian criminal forces. Furthermore, while they may possess clear advantages in Asian language skills and some cultural knowledge, there are also drawbacks and ethnic pressures of the types well known to Hispanic and African-American police officers. In particular, these pressures are usually found in one type of police work for which Asian-American officers are often picked, namely, undercover operations — a most dangerous and difficult task.

Historically, American law enforcement has recruited first- or second-generation ethnic Americans whose ethnic backgrounds were appropriate to infiltrate "ethnic" criminal populations. It is assumed that Asian-American police who are competent in the Asian language do have very valuable skills and knowledge relevant to some undercover operations. Their courage, too, should be admired for the risks they take in this dangerous type of police work. However, the Anglo-European, Hispanic, or African-American administrator may have assumed falsely that since an Asian-American interrogator is a street cop or that he is Asian, he will know what is really going on and know what to do. Simply stated, assigning an Asian-American officer simply does not always work, because (as many Asian-American police officers know) the administrator may be understandably ignorant of a range of crucial ethnic factors. Some of these XC factors are outlined below:

1. The wars and ethnic rivalries, e.g., Chinese vs. Vietnamese, in Asian history, accompanied by a wide variety of quite different cultural assumptions, can make Asians understandably suspicious communicators with other Asians. This familiar difficulty has been noted between first-generation Greeks and Turks, or between first-generation Protestant and Catholic Irish. However, it is a touchy point, indeed, that many times second-generation sons may lack the street smarts, the gait, the posture, the slang, the bearing, the style to attempt undercover infiltration of Asian organized crime. They make look sufficiently Asian to an understandably naive non-Asian police administrator, but they may lack the body and communicative skills and knowledge of the Asian subculture which lies beyond strict linguistic communication. Lacking these skills and knowledge, they will be discovered quite soon and their effectiveness and perhaps even their lives will be threatened. So, being a first- or second-generation Asian immigrant's son or daughter does not guarantee that one's cultural baggage is appropriate for an undercover operation. However, the culturally insensitive or the culturally ignorant administrator may not know this, and with the best of intentions, he/she may make this mistake.

2. The Asian-born or the first-generation Chinese-American and Vietnamese-American may be somewhat more susceptible than are some other ethnic groups to the tug of loyalties — the powerful ethnic guanxi — to the family homeland, to the powerful underlying sense of being Chinese, etc. Many Chinese criminals know this and will use it to reinforce ethnic ties and favors and weaken loyalties to non-Asian institutions and values. This is particularly acute when the undercover operative must maintain close relations with scumbags and other undesirables for periods of 6 or 8 months when the pressures of leading a double life and the boundaries of personal identification may become somewhat more fuzzy than normal. Very few Asian-Americans, indeed, succumb to these ethnic wiles, but it remains an additional pressure on the Asian-American undercover operative.
3. Relationships between the Asian and Asian-American communities and the Asian-American officer are often a source of social pressure for the officer. Since the social status of a policeman within the local communities is rather low, the social status of the officer is usually low and lacks the prestige of the professions to which many upward mobile Asian-American families aspire.
4. The Asian-American officer also bears the additional burdens of the history of Asian ethnic prejudice and/or problems and prejudices between speakers of different dialects (Mandarin vs. Northern Min, one the main dialects of snakehead alien smugglers from Fujian Province). For example, a second-generation Chinese-American who is a Shanghai speaker of Mandarin Chinese probably has more strikes against him when interrogating a Viet-Ching (a Vietnamese of Chinese ancestry) than does a Mandarin speaking Anglo-European "round-eye". Peasant Cantonese (Yue) accents of an interrogator do little to ease the perceived insulting interrogation of a sophisticated Hong Kong financial sharpshooter by his cultural inferior. In short, being of a similar ethnic background only solves, at best, some — certainly not all — of the an Asian-American officer's problems with Asian crime.

Furthermore, if such police personnel are expected to cope without adequate and tempered administrative knowledge of the cultural and linguistic limitations of their undercover identity or their new Asian crime positions, the Asian-American officer's admirable efforts will have been hindered; they will have been treated badly, and the likelihood of successful recruiting for other undercover work and more Asian-American police may be diminished.

23 Supplementing the Planning of Criminal Justice and In-Service Training Programs

關係

For the increasingly multicultural decades starting in 2000 A.D., skills and knowledge and training ideas and techniques from *both* the social sciences and humanities will be needed in planning cross-cultural (XC) training programs for law enforcement personnel. This supplement is required because the cultural factors of present training programs do not address the full range of cultural factors police are confronted with during Asian crime investigation. Or, to put the point in another way, it may be heuristically useful from time to time to remind ourselves that the human-to-human situations Asian organized-crime investigators confront in their everyday investigations are (at least) bicultural, not monocultural. However, almost all in-service training programs are monocultural in planning and in instruction. (Regional and the annual conference on Asian crime co-sponsored by the International Association Asian Crime Investigators, and others illustrate partial exceptions.)

In the streets, during interviews and interrogations, the bicultural mutual interplay between Asian, Asian-American, and mainline American police cultures obviously generates effects and stress on police and Asian peoples. However, these effects are seldom recognized or addressed in law enforcement training programs which focus on Caucasian, Hispanic, and African-American police. Why? One major reason is that the social science emphases within criminal justice education tend to be monocultural — usually Caucasian — and reflect a narrow point of view about crime. Thus, the bicultural mutual interplay between Asian and American police cultures is ignored, whereas it ought to be recognized and integrated into police training programs, without which they remain incomplete, and their efficiency and goals are diminished.

Furthermore, in addition to professional police training, careful *planning*, but not necessarily the implementation, of XC training programs require fivefold skills and knowledge: (1) comparative studies, (2) teaching skills, (3) background in Asian studies, (4) a solid knowledge of the cultural history of the Anglo-European traditions, ideas, and modes of processing information, and (5) law enforcement problems. Thus, short-course program planning requires solid police skills and knowledge, in addition to some background in teaching comparative studies, classroom teaching skills, Asian studies, and our Anglo-European traditions. However, less background is required in the *implementation* of XC training programs. This background is required only in the planning stages in order to:

1. Analyze the cultural assumptions and incompatibilities between cultural values;
2. Understand them in some depth;
3. Compare them regarding crime and law;
4. Select the relevant factual and normative information for the police audience;
5. Plan the pragmatic boundaries of what is to be taught;
6. Determine in what sequence it should be taught;
7. Determine in what form it is to be taught;
8. Determine on what criteria XC trainers should be selected and instructed;
9. Determine how the effectiveness of the teaching and training should be evaluated;
10. Determine who should monitor overall accountability for training effectiveness.

We note that we find backgrounds in Asian studies and a solid knowledge of the facts and the normative values of the intellectual history of the Anglo-European tradition in the humanities; we do not find them in the descriptive procedures of the proto-descriptive social sciences. And the latter is the background of most criminologists who usually lack both the cognitive skills and the backgrounds in analyzing, synthesizing, and evaluating the comparative, normative questions of incompatible values between cultures.

In short, these problems illustrate why medical ethics courses are usually taught in the humanities, not in the social sciences. Social sciences describe facts and explain and predict facts. The cross-cultural analyst, well grounded in the cognitive humanities within a global perspective, utilizes all the facts of social sciences and *adds* the systematic evaluation of the underlying cultural norms and cognitive cultural, religious, and philosophical presumptions. Then he/she draws and justifies those factual and normative conclusions to be implemented in training. For example, euthanasia, the right to refuse needed lifesaving treatment, abortion, and whether to treat severely defective newborns are not scientific questions but normative questions, just as the questions of whether rewards for guanxi friends constitute bribery is a normative XC question based on two traditions of law. An advantage of the humanities over the social sciences is that in the humanities both types of controversies (medical ethics and XC criminal issues) are subjected to systematic analysis and argumentation regarding the relevant empirical facts, factually falsifiable mindsets, and the resulting derivative, *normative* evidence from these XC mindsets. All these procedures are clearly relevant to the XC analysis of Asian organized crime. Therefore, (ideally), to plan the XC training programs, we need *both* the humanities and the social sciences. As these systematic and cognitive evaluations are regularly implemented in the humanities, we turn to the correlative prejudice often found in both the subcultures of American academia and law enforcement institutional cultures expressed in the title of the next chapter.

24

A Criminal Justice Prejudice? Cross-Cultural Studies Belong to Social Science

關係

Without a broader set of cultural perspectives and an influx of data from both the social sciences and the global humanities, North Americans, police, analysts, agents, and citizens lose in the long run. Quite simply stated, we all lose because we need all the knowledge we can get about our major Asian trading partners with whom we are learning to live more closely on our shrinking planet. If criminology and in-service training programs restrict themselves solely to social science, the world of law enforcement loses. Moreover, the pragmatic value of criminal justice research and its training products would be considerably enhanced if its paradigms were expanded and if it were to join forces with the rest of the world's various traditions of knowledge and skills which focus upon the criminal and cross-cultural (XC) aspects of Asian and Asian-American peoples. While not all relevant cultural knowledge should be integrated in training programs, it is desirable that relevant information should not be excluded from consideration because of academic or agency subcultural prejudices or narrow ethnocentrism. This is particularly so when the breadth and seriousness of acute Asian crime problems demand a revision of our assumptions about what is relevant for police who must struggle with cultural differences in language, social relations, and thought processes.

Six years ago, I noted that a similar lack of attention to cross-cultural sources and I questioned the narrow emphasis in criminology education and in-service training. Quite independently, I found that similar criticisms were also expressed in the writings about the international world of intelligence by a renowned scholar of history, Africa, and the mores and institutional cultures of the intelligence community: Dr. Ada B. Bozeman.[247]

Dr. Bozeman echoed Robert Rossow in his discussion of the training of diplomats who he likened to cross-cultural interpreters. He warned "against overdoing pure social science because it would lead to disciplinary parochialism [*it already has*!], to the conversion of methodologies into ideologies."[248] Both Bozemen and Rossow suggest that the narrow emphasis upon political science, the behavioral sciences, and economic theory should be enhanced and strengthened — but not replaced — by the additional study of relevant aspects of the humanities — "language, literature, history, religion, philosophy, and philosophical anthropology".[249]

However, North America is becoming more (not less) multicultural. Because XC differences remain unrecognized within most police training programs, the need for broadly based applied XC research and training is increasing. Moreover, the habitual model tendency to rely upon a narrow "social science" of human knowledge on which to ground police training is reinforced by another American academic and law enforcement subcultural prejudice — namely, that such XC research belongs only to social science, particularly sociology and anthropology. Whereas, if one looks closely at the range and complexity of the cross-cultural problems *actually found* in working Asian crime, one sees that XC studies that focus on the wide ranges of Asian cultures should be multidisciplinary. Moreover, this shift to include multidisciplinary and crime approaches can be pragmatically justified by an examination of the occasional inaccurate presuppositions and the underlying reasons for the frustrations of the actual nuts-and-bolts problems of street cops, detectives, and intelligence analysts who work Asian crime. To reiterate the point in the previous paragraph in a more vernacular manner, I paraphrase what one "super-cop" who has worked Asian crime for years has been saying, also for years: "If you do not know the culture, you will not know the crime — or how to get at it."

After all, North Americans are very familiar and analytically nimble with Anglo-European cultural differences — but not with Asians. However, there are as many (perhaps more) widely recognized cultural differences between a Japanese and a Vietnamese than as between a Swede and an Italian, or between an Englishman and a Greek. We simply must learn to recognize them, and as time passes, we will learn — either out of helpful XC training or out of desperate necessity! Furthermore, the need for incorporating aspects of cross-cultural "understanding" relevant to combating Asian crime has long been recognized as necessary within government, international business, international law and negotiation, international conflict resolution, comparative medicine, and comparative medical ethics.

A final suggestion to assist in explaining the narrow approaches to Asian crime training may be found in the long history of the social sciences as they have striven to emulate the "hard" sciences of physics, chemistry, biology, and the nonempirical queen of science, mathematics. This tendency, in conjunction with the law enforcement's own predilection for discrete pieces of factual data, rather than wider case-based paradigms (gestaults), has resulted in the conservative placement of undergraduate law enforcement majors within the academic departments of sociology where they imbibe a narrow, culturally provincial perspective: as Asian crime increases, this narrow perspective has now been found to be incommensurate with the wider cultural range of XC problems of Asian organized crime and Asian-American communities. Furthermore, perhaps the worst aspect of this narrow tendency toward social science is a narrow, oversimplified emphasis in most officers' college training upon what can be measured and number-crunched. This sub-cultural prejudice toward over-quantification has become the familiar paradigm of how criminal justice research *is* done today. Such a tendency, unfortunately, usually discourages XC interests and is generally held to be incompatible with "serious research". For example, a glance at hundreds of the valuable but narrow publications of the National Criminal Justice Reference Service reveals that they exemplify, and confirm this trend. Furthermore, it might be insightful for many Asian crime specialists and trainers to glance at the excessively narrow publications to guide fledgling police researchers, distributed by the Police Executive Research Forum: *Using Research: a Primer for Law Enforcement.*[250] Equally interesting would be a survey of the issues addressed by the National Institute of Justice's *Research in Brief.* All these research products exemplify four narrow, debatable aspects common to the field:

1. An absence of any humanistic-oriented research about XC methodology or questions of cultural and country-specific values
2. The clear preponderance of number-crunching articles, instances (exemplars) of an implicit paradigm of quasisocial science, and empiricism of a simple kind
3. The cultural, tunnel-vision of their research exemplars and the absence of any rigorous discussion about any cultural issues relevant to the cross-cultural problems of *any* type of crime
4. The implicit presupposition that police research is, could be, or ought to be free from implicit culturally restricted values or, worse, free from any discussion about cultural values.

This narrowness of training, education, and attitudes is incompatible with the best efforts of most police who wrestle with Asian crime. To best combat Asian crime, we need flexible, multidisiplinary approaches to Asian crime training which fit with and explain the cultural details of Asian crime and are commensurate with the depth and breadth our transnational, multicultural, shrinking world of crime.

Community Policing and Cross-Cultural Training Programs

25

關係

Now that we have traveled through most of this book and have seen many examples of cross-cultural (XC) skills and knowledge — and have raised a few controversial points as well — five comments and recommendations are offered. These five comments address law enforcement planning into the year 2000: expanding community policing in North America while multicultural problems increase.

First, we cannot over-stress the need for greater XC knowledge, skills, and mutual understanding of Asian communities as a prerequisite for effective police street-level problem-solving, administrative planning, crime analysis, preventive activities, interrogation, running informants, apprehension, trial preparation, convictions, and prison maintenance. However, improved communication and trust between the police and the various Asian communities are equally important, perhaps even crucial for the future of North American law enforcement activities. The worst possibility for the future would be that neither side, the police or the Asian community, understands the other, nor trusts the other, a possibility partially realized in some ethnic communities. Also, when making the case for training police in relevant XC skills, it is not a question of whether Asians should or must obey our laws and adjust somewhat to our varied customs. Almost all Asians do so now — and probably to a greater extent than in many mainline American communities. As with everyone else, Asians must comply only to some degree, albeit to a very high degree, to gain acceptance. Moreover, the pressures of living in North American society will continue to compel them to make adjustments in their lifestyles, just as such pressure has compelled other immigrant populations to make similar adjustments in their lifestyles. Asians, like all immigrant populations, will eventually "come along" in order to "get along".

Second, in the future, as in the present, a major hurdle for police will be to understand and act upon a realization that there remain XC differences in both the content and the processing of information for foreign-born Asians and, to varying degrees, in first- and second-generation Asians. Without this realization and appropriate training action, new and more severe XC problems will arise in everyday police work regarding the cooperation, interviewing and interrogation of Asians; the management of Asian informants; risk assessment; intelligence estimates; and operational training. Also, an absence of streetwise cross-cultural skills, knowledge, and language barriers will increase the frequency of on-the-job stress and officer burnout. Furthermore, such police officers will alienate the Asian communities; diminish potential Asian community trust; prevent the recruitment of new Asian officers, potential witnesses, and possible informers; and perpetuate bad Asian images of the police.

Third. With all the particular cultural features that make Asian crime different, the standard practice of rotating officers through Asian crime units or units which handle Asian crime in a semi-random way should be modified. Asian crime is a professional specialty and deserves administrative recognition in the same way that administrators make efforts to retain specific police expertise, language, and XC skills and knowledge.[251] Thus, additional support should be extended for the acquisition of modest language skills, attendance at Asian crime conferences, and extensive exposure within the informal but extremely effective North American guanxi networks of experienced Asian crime investigators by encouraging membership and participation in such organizations as the International Association of Asian Crime Investigators.

Fourth, while some individual police have argued, "Let them adjust to us! It is our country.", it is also the professional responsibility of law enforcement to maximize attempts to protect and to serve *everyone.* So the problem will remain with us. The XC understanding of Asians, without necessarily agreeing with any specific Asian behavior, constitutes one small avenue to support the quiet old-fashioned idealism of police to do the right thing; it is this value so often overlooked by the public and I have been surprised to encounter it so many times in the unmarkeds, in the streets, and in conversations, once their trust in me has been established.

Fifth, as planners, trainers, and administrators, we should listen to street cops, detectives and other special Asian crime investigators about how *they see* their XC problems; then and only then should we bring in a vast of array of other professional law enforcement personnel, academics, and international business personnel to generate a synthesis of knowledge and skills commensurate with the complexity and sophistication of the varieties of Asian-based crime to meet the needs of both the Asian-American *and* the non-Asian-American communities. In short, if we do not generate the perception that XC training is of real use in the streets, the worthwhile XC skills and knowledge will be neither supported nor learned — and we will all be the worse for it.

Afterword 26

關係

It has never been the author's aim to tell law enforcement people how to do the job they have been doing for years and doing it well — and usually, doing it underfunded, underfed, understaffed, underground, underloved, and underpaid! Nor has it been the author's intention to answer questions not asked by the law enforcement communities. However, it *has* been the intention of the author to suggest questions and heuristic answers which have been asked and should be asked by investigators who work Asian crime.

The professional focus of the author has been to support three goals: (1) the protection of our Asian-American communities, (2) the apprehension and conviction of Asian and Asian-American criminals in North America, and, (3) the development of cross-cultural training programs to support a more effective, nuts-and-bolts, educated network of law enforcement professionals working Asian crime. As a result of these goals, it is hoped that this sourcebook will generate greater cross-cultural understanding for readers, all of whom have different needs and different interests and capacities. This, in turn, this will result in the increased protection of our various Asian communities. Finally, it is hoped that the book will foster more Asian crime training programs, encourage professional police interest in Asian crime as a professional specialty, reduce police stress, and increase their safety and thereby facilitate the efforts of Asian crime law enforcement specialists.

Thus, to bring the book to an end, the purpose of this book has been for the author to be (once again) "a ford and a bridge",[252] to suggest possible benefits and problems in the application of cross-cultural skills and knowledge to assist our various Asian communities and those North American law enforcement personnel who strive to protect our Asian-American communities, as they are simultaneously deeply engaged in the fight against the rising tide of Asian based crime.

Appendices

Appendix A: Chinese Triads, Triad Organizations, and Triad Relationships

CHINESE TRIADS (HONG KONG) (ACTIVE)

NAME	CTC	CHINESE	AKA/OR TRANSLATION
14K Group			
14K Baai Lo	3269/4151	湃盧	-
14K Chung	1813	忠	Loyalty
14K Chung Yee Tong	1813/5030/1016	忠義堂	Hung Fat Shan,洪發山
14K Hau	1321	孝	Filial Piety
14K Kim	0494	劍	Knife
14K Lai	4409	禮	Worship
14K Lun	0243	倫	Relationship
14K Ngai	3015	毅	Resolute
14K Sai Shing Tong	6007/0524/1016 ?	西勝堂	Western Victory Lodge
14K Sai Yee Tong	6007/5030/1016	西義堂	Western Righteous Lodge
14K Sat	1395	實	Sincerity
14K Shun	0207	信	Faith
14K Tai Huen Chai	1129/0946/0098	大圈仔	14K Big Circle Gang
14K Tak	1795	德	Virtue
14K Yan	0088	仁	Patience
14K Yee	5030	義	Righteousness
14K Yee Shing Tong	5030/0524/1016	義勝堂	Righteous Victory Lodge
14K Yung	0516	勇	Bravery
Wo Group			
Wo Hop To	0735/0678/2711	和合桃	Lo Wo
Wo Hung Shing	0735/3163/0524	和洪勝	
Wo Kao Chi	0735/0046/2172	和九指	Kao Chi Lin Wan,連環
Wo Kwan Lok	0735/5028/2867	和群樂	
Wo Kwan Ying	0735/5028/5391	和群英	
Wo Lee Kwan	0735/0448/5028	和利群	
Wo Lee Wo	0735/0448/0735	和利和	
Wo On Lok	0735/1344/2867	和安樂	Shui Fong,水房
Wo Shing Wo	0735/0524/0735	和勝和	Shing Wo,勝和
Wo Shing Tong	0735/0524/1016	和勝堂	
Wo Shing Yee	0735/0524/5030	和勝義	Shing Yee,勝義
Wo Yau Wo	0735/0645/0735	和友和	
Wo Yee Tong	0735/5030/1016	和義堂	
Wo Yung Yee	0735/0516/5030	和勇義	

CHINESE TRIADS (HONG KONG) (CONT'D)

NAME	CTC	CHINESE	AKA/OR TRANSLATION
Chiu Chow Group			
Ch'iu Kwong She	3390/0342/4357	潮光社	
Chung Sun Tong	1813/0207/1016	忠信堂	
Fuk Yee Hing	4395/5030/5281	福義興	Lo Fuk,老福
Hoi Luk Fung	3189/7120/6265	海陸豐	
King Yee	2417/5030	敬義	
Sun Yee On	2450/5030/1344	新義安	Lo Sun,老新
Tai Ho Choi	1129/1170/1752	大好彩	Lucky, Si Kung
Yee Kwan	5030/5028	義群	
Big Four Group			
Chuen Chi Wo	0356/1807/0735	全志和	Lo Chuen,老全
Chuen Yat Chi	0356/0001/1807	全一志	
Luen Fei Ying	5114/7378/5391	聯飛英	
Luen Hung Ying	5114/4767/5391	聯紅英	
Luen Kung Lok	5114/0361/2867	聯公樂	Kung Lok,公樂
Luen Lok Tong	5114/2867/1016	聯樂堂	Tan Yee,單耳
Luen Shun Tong	5114/7311/1016	聯順堂	
Luen To Ying	5114/2711/5391	聯桃英	
Luen Ying She	5114/5391/4357	聯英社	Lo Luen,老聯
Tong Kwan Ying	0681/5028/5391	同群英	
Tong Lok	0681/2867	同樂	Yee Lok,義樂
Tong San Wo	0681/2450/0735	同新和	Lo Tong,老同 San Wo
Tung Kung She	2639/0361/4357	東公社	
Tung Kwan Ying	2639/5028/5391	東群英	
Tung Luen She	2639/5114/4357	東聯社	Lo Tung,老東
Tung On Tong	2639/1344/1016	東安堂	Ching Ngau
Tung On Wo	2639/1344/0735	東安和	
Tung Ying She	2639/5391/4357	東英社	
Miscellaneous Triads			
Kwong Hung	1684/7160	廣雄	
Kwong Luen Ying	1684/5114/4141	廣聯盛	Lo Kwong,老廣
Kwong Shing	1684/4141	廣盛	
Kwong Sing Tong	1684/5116/1016	廣聲堂	
Yuet Kwong	4727/1684	粤廣	
Yuet Tung	4727/2639	粤東	Sin Yan Tong,
Ching Lung Tuen	2973/7893/0957	正龍團	

CHINESE TRIADS (HONG KONG) (CONT'D)

NAME	CTC	CHINESE	AKA/OR TRANSLATION
Ching Nin She	7230/1628/4357	青年社	
Ch'ing Wah She	7230/5478/4357 ?	青華社	China Youth Society
Tai Huen Chai	1129/0946/0098	大圈仔	Big Circle Gang
Chuk Lien Pang	4554/5114/1620	竹聯幫	United Bamboo

CHINESE TRIADS AND GANGS (TAIWAN) (ACTIVE)

NAME	CTC	CHINESE	AKA/OR TRANSLATION
Ch'i Hsien Pang	0003/0103/1620	七仙幫	Seven Immortals
Ch'ing Pang	7230/1620	青幫	Green Gang
Chu Lien Pang	4554/5114/1620	竹聯幫	United Bamboo Gang
Fang Ming Chia Pang	xxxx	-	
Fei Ying Pang	7378/7751/1620	飛鷹幫	Flying Eagles Gang
Hai Lang Pang	3189/3186/1620	海浪幫	Sea Wave Gang
Ho Tsun Pang	xxxx	-	
Ho Sheng Ho	0735/0524/0735	和勝和	Wo Shing Wo
Hsi Pei Pang	6007/0554/1620	西北幫	Northwest Gang
Hsin Tien Pang	2450/1131/1620	新天幫	
Hung Men	3163/7024	洪門	Hung Family
Hung Pang	4767/1620	紅幫	Red Gang
Niu Pu Pang	xxxx	-	
Ssu Hai Pang	0934/3189/1620	四海幫	Four Seas Gang
Ssu Shih K	0577/0934/K	十四K	14K
Tien Tao Meng	1131/6670/4145	天道盟	Way of Heaven Alliance
Wen Shan Pang	2429/1472/1620	文山幫	Literary Mountain gang
Ya Tan Chiao	7700/5751/2403	鴨蛋教	I Kwan Tao (Duck Egg Sect

CHINESE TRIADS AND GANGS (CHINA)

NAME	CTC	CHINESE	AKA/OR TRANSLATION
IN CHINA			
Chen Chung Pang	7201/0022/1620	震中幫	Middle Quake Gang
Chen Lung Pang	4176/7893/1620	眞龍幫	True Dragon Gang
Chih Kung T'ang	5268/0361/1016	致公堂	
Ch'un Lung T'ang	5028/7893/1016	群龍堂	Great Dragon Gang
Hai Ch'uan Pang	3189/3123/1620	海泉幫	Ocean Spring Gang
Huang Ch'i Chiao	4106/2817/2403	皇極教	Ultimate Imperial Sect
Hung San Chiao	4767/0005/2403	紅三教	Red Three Sect
I Kwan Tao	0001/6306/6670	一貫道	Faithful Way
Kai Jih Hui	2395/2480/2585	改日會	Future Association
Mei Hua T'ang	2734/5363/1016	梅花堂	Plum Blossom Lodge
Pai Sh'ou T'ang	4101/2087/1016	白手堂	White Hand Lodge
Sha T'ou Pang	3097/2435/1620	沙斗幫	Sand Head Gang
Ta Tao Hui	1129/0430/2585	大刀會	Big Knife Association
T'ien Tao	1131/6670	天道	Heavenly way
Tou Chin T'ang	2435/1577/1016	斗巾堂	
Wo Hu Pang	5257/5706/1620	臥虎幫	Sleeping Tiger gang
IN CHINA BUT OPERATING MOSTLY OUTSIDE CHINA	(The following Big Circle names are either from common schools or Red Guard Camps)		
Ta Ch'uan Tsz	1129/0946/0098	大圈仔	Big Circle Gang
Fo Kang	0154/1481	佛岡	The Buddha Mt. Ridge
Ts'ung Hua	1783/5478	從華	From China
Ch'ing Yuan	7230/6678	青遠	Youth Far Away
T'ai P'ing	1132/1627	太平	Peace
Fo Shan	0154/1472	佛山	Buddha Mountain
San Shui	0005/3055	三水	Three Waters
Ssy Chung	0934/0022	四中	Fourth Middle (School)
IN CHINA BUT FROM OUTSIDE CHINA			
Chu Lien Pang	4554/5114/1620	竹聯幫	United Bamboo (TW)
Fuk Ch'ing	4395/7230	福青	Fukienese Youth (NY)
Ho An Ho	0735/1344/2867	和安樂	Wo On Lok (HK)
Ho Sheng Ho	0735/0524/0735	和勝和	Wo Shing Wo (HK)
Ho Sheng I	0735/0524/5030	和勝義	Wo Shing Yee (HK)
Hsin I An	2450/5030/1344	新義安	Sun Yee On (HK)
Shih Ssu K	0577/0934	十四K	14K

CHINESE TRIADS (THAILAND AND BURMA)

NAME	CTC	CHINESE	AKA/OR TRANSLATION
Ch'ing Pang Group			
Ch'ing Pang	7230/1620	青幫	Green Gang
Chien Te Tsung She	1696/1795/4920/4357	建德總社	
Hung Pang Group			
Hung Pang	3163/1620	洪幫	Hung Gang
Ch'eng She	6134/4357	誠社	
Chien Te T'ang	1696/1795/1016	建德堂	
Chih Kung T'ang	5268/0361/1016	致公堂	
Shih Ssu K (14K)	0577/0934/K	十四K	14K
Feng Kao	xxxx/2403 ?	x 教	
He Sheng Kung Szu	0735/0524/03610674	和勝公司	
Hsin I An	2450/5030/1344	新義安	Sun Yee On
I Ch'un	5030/5028	義群	Yee Kwan
Kuang Ming She	0342/2494/4357	光明社	
Kuang Ming T'ang	0342/2494/1016	光明堂	
Ling Pa	7190/0360	零八	Zero Eight, 08
Meng Tzu Wen Hua Hui	1322/1311/2429/0553/2585 ?	孟子文化會	Mencius CltClb.
Shih Pei Kao	xxxx/2403	X教	-
Ta Hung Shan	1129/3163/1472	大洪山	Big Hung Mountain
Wu He Kung	0063/0735/0361	五和公	Five Harmony Company
I Kwan Tao			
I Kwan Tao	0001/6306/6670	一貫道	
Ya Tan Chiao	7700/5751/2403	鴨蛋教	Ap Lon Kao (TW)
Lung Hua Kung	7893/5478/1362	龍華宮	China Dragon Temple
Shuang Lung Kao	7175/7893/1362	雙龍宮	Double Dragon Temple
Ch'iu Ch'ow Dialect Groups (Ethnic Gps. Not Triads)			
Hong Sun	6265/7311	澧順	Feng Shan
Kek Ia	2263/7122	揭陽	Chieh Yang
Phao Lang	2528/1380	普寧	P'u Ning
Swatow	3073/7333	汕頭	Shan Tou
Tai Pu	1129/1033	大埔	Da Bu
Theng Hai	3397/3189	澄海	Ch'eng Hai
Tia An	3390/1344	潮安	Chao An
Tia Ia	3390/7122	潮陽	Chao Yang
Yiao Pheng	7437/1627	饒平	Jao Ping

CHINESE TRIADS (MALAYSIA) (ACTIVE AND INACTIVE)

NAME	CTC	CHINESE	AKA/OR TRANSLATION
Hung Men Group	(Second Lodge Tradition)		
Ang Bin Hoay	3163/7024/2585	洪門會	Hung Men Association
Ang Bing Tong	3163/7024.1016	洪門堂	Hung Men Lodge
Ang Hor	3163/3109	洪河	Hung River
Ang Kim Leng	3163/6855/7893	洪金龍	Hung Golden Dragon
Ang Lian	3163/5114	洪聯	Hung United
Ang Min Tong	3163/3046/1016	洪民堂	Hung People's Lodge
Ang Soon Tong	3163/7311/1016	洪順堂	Hung Obedience Lodge
Cher Leng	7230/7893	青龍	Green Dragons
Chi Kung Tong	5268/0361/1016	致公堂	
Fei Lung Tong	7378/7893/1016	飛龍堂	Flying Dragon Lodge
Gee Ang Ying	5030/1344/5391	義安英	
Gee Hong San	5030/3163/1472	義洪山	Righteous Hung Mountain
Gee Hup	5030/0678	義合	Righteous Unity
Gee It Hooi	0059/0001/3189	二一海	21 Seas
Gee Ling San	0059/7190/0005	二零三	203 Gang
Gee Lung Seah	5030/7893/4357	義龍社	Righteous Dragon Society
Gee Sap	0059/2168	二拾	20 Gang
Gee Sap It	0059/2168/0001	二拾一	21 Gang
Gee Sap San	0059/2168/0005	二拾三	23 Gang
Gee Tong San	5030/0681/1472	義同山	Righteous United Mt.
Guat San Seah	2588/1472/4357	月山社	Moon Mountain Society
Hong Hong San	7685/0420/1472	鳳凰山	Phoenix Mountain
Hooi San	3189/1472	海山	Ocean Mountain
Hung Sian	3163/0103	洪仙	Hung Immortal
Hup Hor Tong	0678/0735/0681	合和同	Peaceful Harmony
It Ling It	0001/7190/0001	一零一	101 Gang
It Ling Pat	0001/7190/0360	一零八	108 Gang
It Teow Leng	0001/2742/7893	一條龍	One Dragon
Jen Yee Tong	0088/5030/1016	仁義堂	Righteous Patience Lodge
Ji Lam Cheh	5030/5663/7230	義藍青	Righteous Blue Green
Ji Tiam Ang	5030/0002/5391	義丁英	
Kow Luk Kow	0046/0362/0046	九六九	969 Gang
Kut Tow Tong	7539/7333/1016	骨頭堂	Skeleton Gang
Leng Fu Tong	7893/5706/1016	龍虎堂	Dragon Tiger Lodge

CHINESE TRIADS (MALAYSIA)(CONT'D) (ACTIVE AND INACTIVE)

NAME	CTC	CHINESE	AKA/OR TRANSLATION
Hung Men Group (Continued)			
Leng Hor	7893/0735	龍和	Dragon Union
Leng Ying Seah	7893/5391/4357	龍英社?	
Ling Pat	7190/0360	零八	08 Gang
Ling Sze	7190/0934	零四	04 Gang
Man Leng Hong	5502/7893/?	萬龍?	-
Mun Hap	5502/0678	萬合	10,000 unity
Ngo Chee San	0063/2172/1472	五指山	Five Mountains
Ngo Leng San	0063/7893/1472	五龍山	Five Dragon Mountain
Ngo Sek Kee	0063/5331/4388	五色祺	Five Color Flag
Pat Leng Foo	0360/7893/5706	八龍虎	Eight Dragon Tiger
Pat Sian	0360/0103	八仙	Eight Immortals
Pek Hor	4101/5706	白虎	White tiger
San Luk Ling	0005/0362/7190	三六零	360 Gang
San Luk Pat	0005/0362/0360	三六八	368 gang
San Pat Gee It	0005/0360/0059/0001	三八二一	3821 Gang
San Sap Gee	0005/2168/0059	三拾二	32 Gang
Sap Pat Ching Lung	0570/0360/7230/7893	十八青龍	18 Green Dragons
Sap Sim Too	0570/xxxx	十XX	
Siew Loong Choo	1420/7893/3796	小龍珠	Little Dragon Pearl
Siew Luk Kow	1420/0362/0046	小六九	Little 69
Siew Pat Hong	1420/4101/7160	小白雄	Little White Heroes
Sin Ang Bin	2450/3163/7024	新洪門	New Hung Men
Sin Gee Sap	2450/0059/2168	新二拾	New 20 gang
Sin Lian Hooi	2450/5114/3189 ?	新聯海	New United ocean
Sin Wei Seh	2450/xxxx/4357?	新X社-	
Sio Ang Bin	1420/3163/7024	小洪門	Little Hung Men
Sio Ang Eng	1420/3163/5391	小洪英	
Sio Ang Mooi	1420/3163/2734	小洪梅	Little Hung Plum
Sio Gee Sap Sze	1420/0059/2168/0934	小二拾四	Little 24
Sio Khoon Tong	1420/0981/1016	小坤堂	Little Earth Lodge
Sio Leng Hor	1420/7893/0735	小龍和	Little Dragon Harmony
Sio Ling Pat	1420/7190/0360	小零八	Little Zero 8
Sio Mooi Fa (Real?)	1420/2734/5363	小梅花	Little Plum Blossom
Sio Pek Hor	1420/4101/5706	小白虎	Little White Tiger
Sio Sam Ong	1420/0005/7160 ?	小三雄	Little Three Heroes
	1420/0005/3769 ?	小三王	Little Three Kings
Siong Foo San	7175/5706/1472	雙虎山	Double Tiger Mountain

CHINESE TRIADS (MALAYSIA)(CONT'D) (ACTIVE AND INACTIVE)

NAME	CTC	CHINESE	AKA/OR TRANSLATION
Tiong Gee Hor	1813/5030/0735	忠義和	Chung Yee Woh
Tiong Wah Tong	0022/5478/1016	中華堂	Chung Hua Tang
Tiong Yee Tong	1813/5030/1016	忠義堂	Loyal Righteous Lodge
Yee Wah Say	5030/5478/4357 ?	義華社	
Wah Kee Group	(Chow Faa Chee Thow)(Fourth Lodge Traditon)		
Kwang Tung Loh Hon	1684/2639/0577/5706	廣東十虎	Ten Kwangtung Tigers
Sap Pat Loh Hon	0577/0360/5012/3352	十八羅漢	18 Immortals
Sap Sam Fah	0577/0005/5363	十三花	13 Flowers
Sap Sam Tai Poh	0577/0005/1132/0202	十三太保	13 Princes
Siew Wah Kee	1420/5478/6068	小華記	Little Wah Kee
Sin Pin Sat Pat	xxxx	-	
Sze Kang	xxxx	-	
Sze Ko Lung	0934/0222/8914	四個X	Four Caves

CHINESE TRIADS (SINGAPORE) (ACTIVE AND INACTIVE)

A. Hokkien Faction
1. Gin Hin Group
a. 18 Subgroup
b. 24 Subgroup
c. 108 Subgroup
2. Gi Hok Group
08 Subgroup
3. Goan Seng Group
36 Subgroup
4. Ji It Group

B. Teo Chew Faction
Sar Ji

C. Cantonese Faction
1. Heng Group
2. Kwan Yi Group
3. Man Yi Group

D. Independent Faction

NAME	CTC	CHINESE	AKA/OR TRANSLATION
A. Hokkien Faction			
1. Gi Hin Group a. 18 Subgroup			
Chap San Io	0577/0005/xxxx	十三X	13 Comrades (Hokchiu)
Chap San Tai Poh	0577/0005/1132/0202	十三太保	13 Princes
Choan Gi Ho	3123/5030/0735	泉義和	Spring Righteous Harmony
Gi Ho Hup Soon Heng	5030/0735/0678/7311/5281	義和合順興	
Gi Khi Sia	5030/3051/4357	義氣社	
Gi Khun Tong	5030/2492/7825	義昆黨	Tong Min Kok同民閣
Gi Pak Hai	5030/4101/3189	義白海	Gi Hai Kan
Kun Tong	5028/1016	群堂	
Sin Ang Hap	2450/3163/0678	新洪合	New United Hung(Hokchiu)
Sin Hai Ian	2450/3189/6513	新海軒	
Sio Fei Lung	1420/7378/7893	小飛龍	Little Flying Dragon
Sio Gi Ho	1420/5030/0735	小義和	(Women's triad)
Sio Kun Tong	1420/5028/1016	小群堂	
Tiong Gi Sia	0022/5030/4357	中義社	China Righteous Society
b. 24 Subgroup			
Ang Kun	4767/6511	紅軍	Red Army
Choan Hiap Ian	3123/0588/6513	泉協軒	
Gi Ang Kun	5030/4767/6511	義紅軍	Righteous Red Army
Gi Chye Hup	5030/0375/0678	義再合	(Ch'iu Kang Hokkien)
Gi Hai Kim	5030/3189/6855	義海金	Righteous Golden Sea
Gi Hai Leng	5030/3189/7893	義海龍	Righteous Sea Dragon
Gi Hap Ian	5030/0678/6513	義合軒	
Gi Kim San	5030/6855/1472	義金山	Righteous Golden Mt.
Gi Leng Hor	5030/7893/5706	義龍虎	Righteous Dragon Tiger
Gi Leng Kiat	5030/7893/0267	義龍傑	Loyalty
Gi Leng Par	5030/7893/6283	義龍豹	R. Dragon Leopard
Gi Sam Hup	5030/0005/0678	義三合	Righteous Three Unity

CHINESE TRIADS (SINGAPORE)(CONT'D) (ACTIVE AND INACTIVE)

NAME	CTC	CHINESE	AKA/OR TRANSLATION
Gi San	5030/1472	義山	Righteous Mountain
Gi Tong Hing	5030/0681/5281	義同興	R. United Happiness
Kim Ki San	6855/1477/1472	金岐山	
Kow Luk Kow	0046/0362/0046	九六九	969 Gang
Loh Kuan	5071/0689	老君	(Chinese god)
Or Leng Tek	7815/7893/1795	黑龍德	Black Dragon Virtue
Or Pek	7815/4101	黑白	Black White
Pat Leng	0360/7893	八龍	8 Dragons
Sin Chye Hup	2450/0375/0678	新再合	
Sin Ang Kun	2450/4767/6511	新紅軍	New Red Army
Tun Hong	3545/3552	炖煌?	
c. 108 Subgroup			
Ching Leng Par	7230/7893/6283	青龍豹	Green Dragon Leopard
Gi Leng Chu	5030/7893/3796	義龍珠	Righteous Dragon Pearl
Gi Leng Huat	5030/7893/4099	義龍發	
Hai Lok Iu	3189/7120/xxxx	海陸x	
Hai Lok San	3189/7120/1472	海陸山	Sea Land Mountain
Hing Hup Yiu	5281/0678/0645	興合友	Happy United Friendship
Kim Leng Hor	6855/7893/5706	金龍虎	Golden Dragon Tiger
Leng Hor San	7893/5706/1472	龍虎山	Dragon Tiger Mountain
Ng Ling Ng	0063/7190/0063	五零五	505 Gang
Pat Ling Pat	0360/7190/0360	八零八	808 Gang
Pat Leng San	0360/7893/1472	八龍山	8 Dragon Mountain
Pek Kim Leng	4101/6855/7893	白金龍	White Golden Dragon
Por Thau Tang	2445/7333/7825	斧頭黨	Double Ax Party
San Ling San	0005/7190/0005	三零三	303 Gang
Sio Eng Hiong	1420/5391/7160	小英雄	Little Heroes
Sio Leng Hor	1420/7893/5706	小龍虎	Little Dragon Tiger
Sio Or Leng	1420/3527/7893	小烏龍	Little Black Dragon
Sio Pat Leng San	1420/0360/7893/1472	小八龍山	Little 8 Dragon Mt.
Siong Gi Thoan	7175/5030/0957	雙義團	Double Righteous Dragon
2. Gi Hok Group 08 Subgroup			
Chuan Chin Huat	3123/xxxx/4099	泉X發	

CHINESE TRIADS (SINGAPORE)(CONT'D) (ACTIVE AND INACTIVE)

NAME	CTC	CHINESE	AKA/OR TRANSLATION
Chuan Gi Ian	3123/5030/6513	泉義軒	Chuan Nghee Hean
Chuan Lok Kang	3123/3157/3068	泉洛江	(Hokkien)
Chuan Sian Ho	3123/0103/0735	泉仙和	(Hokkien)
Han Ho	3352/0735	漢和	(Chiu Kang Hokkien)
Hiap Ek Ian	0588/4135/6513	協益軒	Hiap Yak Hean
Hiap Tong Ian	0588/0681/6513	協同軒	(Chiu Kang Hokkien)
Hui Gi Ian	8409/5030/6513	惠義軒	(Hui Oan Hokkien)
Oon Luk Sia	3306/7120/4357	溫陸社	
Sin Han Ho	2450/3352/0735	新漢和	
Sin Han Kun	2450/3352/5028	新漢群	
Sin Tong Ho	2450/0681/0735	新同和	(Amoy Dialect)
Thit Ho Tong	6993/0735/1016	鐵和堂	
3. Goan Seng Group 36 Subgroup			
Chin Seng	2182/4141	振盛	
Chip Seng	7162/4141	集盛	
Gi Tiong Ho	5030/0022/0735	義中和	
Go Chap Kong Si	0063/0577/0361/0674	五十公司	The 50 Company
Luk Luk Luk	0362/0362/0362	六六六	666666
San Gee Kow	0005/0059/0046	三六九	329(Connected to HK 14K)
Sin Hai Seng	2450/3189/4141	新海盛	
Thit Leong	6993/7893	鐵龍	Iron Dragon Gang
Tiong Gi Kiam	1813/5030/0494	忠義劍	
Tong Kim Lan	0681/6855/5695	同金蘭	
Ying Choan Tan	7336/1557/7115	穎川陳	(Teng (Tan) Family)
4. Ji It Group			
Ang Jit San	3163/2480/1472	洪日山	Hung Sun Mountain
Ang Meng Tong	3163/4145/1016	洪盟堂	Hung Alliance Lodge
Ang Soon Tong	3163/7311/1016	洪順堂	
Gi Ang Eng	5030/3163/7751	義洪鷹	
Gi Chuan Hai	5030/3123/3189	義泉海	Righteous Spring Sea
Gi Hai Heng	5030/3189/6068	義海記	
Gi Hong San	5030/7685/1472	義鷗山	
Gi Lam Eng	5030/0589/5391	義南英	
Gi Lam Kok	5030/0589/7041	義南閣	
Gi Meng Tong	5030/4145/1016	義盟堂	Righteous Alliance Lodge
Gi Pak Hai	5030/0554/3189	義北海	Righteous North Sea

CHINESE TRIADS (SINGAPORE) (CONT'D) (ACTIVE AND INACTIVE)

NAME	CTC	CHINESE	AKA/OR TRANSLATION
B. Teo Chew Faction Sar Ji Group			
Kian Heng Kok	xxxx/5281/7041	X興閣	8888=32
Kun Heng Kok	xxxx/5281/7041	X興閣	
Lau Khiang Heng	5271/xxxx/5281	臻X興	
Lau Yong Heng	5071/3057/5281	老永興	Old Eternal Happiness
Sar Ji	0005/1316	三字	Three Words Gang
Sin Heng Kok	2450/5281/7041	新興閣	
Sin Yong Heng	2450/3057/5281	新永興	New Eternal Happiness
Sio Sar Ji	1420/0005/1316	小三字	Little Three Words
C. Cantonese Faction 1. Heng group	(Allied with 18)		
Heng Faat	5281/4099	興發	Heng Yau
Heng Fuk	5281/1607	興幅	
Heng Khiu	5281/0294	興僑	
Heng Tong	5281/xxxx	興X	Ng Fong Loke
Heng Wah	5281/5478	興華	China Happiness
Heng Woh	5281/0735	興和	Happy Harmony
Heng Yi	5281/5030	興義	Righteous happiness
Lo Heng Kei	5071/5281/6068	老興記	
Lok Wah	2867/5478	樂華	
2. Kwan Yi Group (Sam Fong Sai Mien, 三方四面)			
Kwan Kei	0689/6068	君記	
Kwan Luen	0689/5114	君聯	United Army
Kwan Yi	0689/5030	君義	Sam Fong
Lo Cheong	5071/7022	老長	
Lo Kwan	5071/0689	老君	Old Army
Lo Yi	5071/5030	老義	Old Righteous
San Kwan	2450/0689	新君	New Army
Tai Chap Hui	1129/7162/2585	大集會	
Yi Kwan Ying	5030/5028/5391	義群英	

CHINESE TRIADS (SINGAPORE)(CONT'D) (ACTIVE AND INACTIVE)

NAME	CTC	CHINESE	AKA/OR TRANSLATION
3. Man Yi Group			
Kwong Yi Woh	1684/5030/0735	廣義和	
Luen Wah	5114/5478	聯華	United China
Man Yi Tong	5502/5030/7825	萬義黨	Lao Chi Hor
Man Yi Woh Kei	5502/5030/0735/6068	萬義和記	
Thit Khwan	6993/5028	鐵群	
Thung Hok	0681/1331	同學	School Mates, Tai Hok
Wah Khui	5478/0294	華僑	Oversea Chinese
Woh Kei	0735/6068	和記	Cho Fah,草花
Wui Khwan	2585/5028	會群	(Si Yap Cantonese)
D. Independent Group			
Bek Poh Tang	xxxx	X	
Bun San	2429/1472	文山	(Hokkien Boatmen)
Hung Peh	4767/4101	紅白	Red White, Merah Puteh
It Teow Sin	0001/2742/1800	一條心	One Heart, Satu Hati
Li Hong Ian	7642/7685/6513	鯉鳳軒	
MGR		X	(Indian/Eurasian)
See Tong	2984/1016	死堂	Death Lodge

CHINESE TRIADS (WORLDWIDE)

COUNTRY

NAME	CTC	CHINESE	AKA/OR TRANSLATION
Australia			
Ssu Shih K	0577/0934/K	十四K	14K
Sun Yee On	2450/5030/1344	新義安	Hsin I An
Tai Huen Chai	1129/0946/0098	大圈仔	Big Circle Gang
Wah Kee	5478/6068	華記	
Wo Hop To	0735/0678/2711	和合桃	
Wo Shing Wo	0735/0524/0735	和勝和	Shing Wo, He Sheng He
Wo Yee Tong	0735/5030/1016	和義堂	He I Tang
Belgium			
Ssu Shih K	0577/0934/K	十四K	14K
Tai Huen Chai	1129/0946/0098	大圈仔	Big Circle Gang
Wo Shing Wo	0735/0524/0735	和勝和	Shing Wo
Great Britain			
Ssu Shih K	0577/0934/K	十四K	14K
Sun Yee On	2450/5030/1344	新義安	Lo Sun
Wo On Lok	0735/1344/2867	和安樂	Shui Fong
Wo Shing Wo	0735/0524/0735	和勝和	Shing Wo
The Netherlands			
Ah Kung	0068/0361	亞公	(All SR/MZ Triads)
Ling Sze	7190/0934	零四	04 Gang
Ssu Shih K	0577/0934/K	十四K	14K
Tai Huen Chai	1129/0946/0098	大圈仔	Big Circle Gang
Wo Shing Wo	0735/0524/0735	和勝和	Shing Wo
Spain			
Ah Kung	0068/0361	亞公	
Tai Huen Chai	1129/0946/0098	大圈仔	Big Circle Gang
Germany			
Ssu Shih K	0577/0934/K	十四K	14K
Tai Huen Chai	1129/0946/0098	大圈仔	Big Circle Gang
Wo Shing Wo	0735/0524/0735	和勝和	Shing Wo
Norway			
Tai Huen Chai	1129/0946/0098	大圈仔	Big Circle Gang

CHINESE TRIADS (WORLDWIDE) (CONT'D)

COUNTRY

NAME	CTC	CHINESE	AKA/OR TRANSLATION
France			
Ssu Shih K	0577/0934/K	十四K	14K
Tai Huen Chai	1129/0946/0098	大圈仔	Big Circle Gang
Wo Shing Wo	0735/0524/0735	和勝和	Shing Wo
Paraquay			
Ssu Shih K	0577/0934/K	十四K	14K
South Africa			
Cho San	2777/1472	棹山	Table Mountain (Area) (TW)
Fei Ying	7378/7751	飛鷹	Flying Eagles (TW)
San Yan (?)	xxxx	X	
Ssu Shih K	0577/0934/K	十四K	14K (HK)
Wo Shing Wo	0735/0524/0735	和勝和	Shing Wo (HK)
Canada			
(Triads)			
Chang Yee Tong	1813/5030/1016	忠義堂	
Kung Lok	0361/2867	公樂	
Ssu Shih K	0577/0934/K	十四K	14K
Sun Yee On	2450/5030/1344	新義安	Hsin I An
Tai Huen Chai	1129/0946/0098	大圈仔	Big Circle Boys (Gang)
Wo Shing Wo	0735/0524/0735	和勝和	Shing Wo
(Gangs)			
Ch'ing Lung	5478/7893	華龍	Young Dragons
Gum Wah	6855/5478 (?)	金華	Golden China (?)
Hung Che Pang (?)	4767/6508/1620 ?	紅車幫	X
Hung Ying	4767/7751	紅鷹	Red Eagles
Jung Ching	0022/7230	中青	China Youth
Kuei Ying Pang	7607/1758/1620	鬼影幫	Ghost Shadows
Lien Hua	5571/5363	蓮花	Lotus Gang
Viet Ch'ing	6390/7230	越青	Vietnamese Youth
Wah Ch'ing	5478/7230	華青	Young China
Wah Liun (?)	5478/5114 ?	華聯	X

CHINESE TRIADS (WORLDWIDE) (CONT'D)

COUNTRY

UNITED STATES (TRIADS AND GANGS)

NAME	CTC	CHINESE	AKA/OR TRANSLATION
(TRIADS)			
Kung Lok	0361/2867	公樂	HK
Chu Lien Pang	4554/5114/1620	竹聯幫	HK
Hung Men	3163/7024	洪門	TW
Chih Kung T'ang	5268/0361/1016	致公堂	TW
Chiu Lung Shan	0046/7893/1472/1016	九龍山堂	TW
Sheng Chia T'ang	0524/1367/1016	勝家堂	TW
Loong Foo Tong	7893/5706/1016	龍虎堂	Malaysia
Ssu Shih K	0577/0934/K	十四K	HK
Sun Yee On	2450/5030/1344	新義安	HK
Wo Hop To	0735/0678/2711	和合桃	HK
Wo On Lok	0735/1344/2867	和安樂	HK
Wo Shing Wo	0735/0524/0735	和勝和	HK
(GANGS)			
Chang Sha (LA)	xxxx	X	
Cheung Chi Yee(LA)	xxxx	X	
Chinatown Boys(LA)	xxxx	X	
Ch'ing Lung (NY+)	7230/7893	青龍	Green Dragons
Fei Huen Chai (LA)	7378/0946/0098	飛圈仔	Flying Circle Boys
Fei Lung Pang(NY+)	7378/7893/1620	飛龍幫	Flying Dragons
Fuk Ch'ing (NY+)	4395/7230	福青	Fukienese Youth
Heung Kong Chai(LA)	7449/3263/0098	香港仔	Hong Kong Boys
Hei Lung (LA)	7815/7893	黑龍	Black Dragons
Hop Sing Chai(SF)	0678/0524/0098 ?	合勝仔	
Joe Chai (SF)	xxxx	X	Joe Boys
Kit Chai Pang(LA)	xxxx	X	
Kuei Ying Pang(NY+)	7607/1758/1620	鬼影幫	Ghost Shadows
Oriental Boys(LA)	xxxx	X	
Pai Fu (NY+)	4101/5706	白虎	White Tigers
Pai Lung	4101/7893	白龍	White Dragons
Ping On (Bos)	1627/1344	平安	Peace Gang
Sui Sing Chai(LA)	xxxx	X	Sui Sing Boys
Tai Huen Chai	1129/0946/0098	大圈仔	Big Circle Gang
Tai Wah Ch'ing	1129/5478/7230	大華青	Big China Youth
Tai Wan Chai (LA)	0669/3494/0098	台灣仔	Taiwan Boys
Tung On (NY+)	0681/1344	同安	United Peace
Wah Ch'ing (LA+)	5478/7230	華青	China Youth

CHINESE TRIADS (WORLDWIDE) (CONT'D)

COUNTRY

UNITED STATES (TRIADS AND GANGS)

NAME	CTC	CHINESE	AKA/OR TRANSLATION
(SOME OF THE MANY NON-CHINESE ASIAN GANGS)			
Asian Boys (MD)	xxxx		(Cambodian)
Bahala Na Gang(LA)	xxxx		(Filipino)
BTK (NY+)	xxxx		(Viet)Born to Kill
Frogmen (LA)	xxxx		(Viet)
Fuk Chiu (NY)	xxxx		(Korean)
Gum Sing (NY)	6855/2502	金星	(Viet)Golden Star
Hung Pho (LA)	4767/3499	紅火	(Viet)Red Fire
King Cobra Boys(LA)	xxx		(Lao)
Korean Power (NY)	xxxx		(Korean)
Natoma Boys (LA)	xxxx		(Viet)
Sworn Sisters (DC)	xxxx		(Cambodian)
Sworn Brothers(DC)	xxxx		(Cambodian)
Tiny Rascal Gang (VA/CA)			(Cambodian)
Viet Ch'ing (NY+)	6390/7230	越青	(Viet)

Appendix B: Common Chinese Surnames and Notes on Chinese Language and Dialects

45 COMMON CHINESE SURNAMES (姓)

	CHINESE IDEOGRAM	PINYIN	(TONE)	STC/CTC	DICTIONARY DEFINITION	PRC PINYIN	WADE-GILES MANDARIN	HONGKONG CANTONESE	OTHER DIALECTS AND/OR SPELLING VARIATIONS
1.	張	zhāng	(1)	1728	open, spread, stretch	Zhang	Chang	Cheung	Tsong, Chong, Chiang, Jiang, Jang, Tia
2.	王	wáng	(2)	3769	king, monarch	Wang	Wang	Wong	Ong, Heng, Vong, Vang, Uang
3.	李	lǐ	(3)	2621	plum (a fruit)	Li	Li	Li	Lee, Ly, Leuie, Loei
4.	趙	zhào	(4)	6392	a surname	Zhao	Chao	Ch'u	Chu, Zhau, Tchao, Chiao, Jew, Jieow, Tia
5.	陳	chén	(2)	7115	to display, arrange	Chen	Ch'en	Chan	Tan, Ting, Chin, Chun, Chinn, Tin
6.	楊	yáng	(2)	2799	poplar (a kind of tree)	Yang	Yang	Yeung	Young, Yeong, Yeang, Ia, Ear, Yia, Yon, Yorn
7.	吳	wú	(2)	0702	Kingdom of Wu	Wu	Wu	Ng	Ngo, Goh, Eng, Ing, Ong, Ngow, Ung, Ngu
8.	劉	liú	(2)	0491	name of a royal clan	Liu	Liu	Lau	Lew, Liew, Low, Lou, Lao, Liou, Laow, Liw
9.	黃	huáng	(2)	7806	yellow	Huang	Huang	Wong	Wang, Ng, Wee, Oei, Ooi, Ung, Eung, Yang
10.	周	zhōu	(1)	0719	circumference, periphery	Zhou	Chou	Chau	Chow, Jiw, Tchou, Jew, Jow, Chew, Chiu

- There are an estimated 800 Chinese surnames in use throughout the world today, but only about 400 to 500 are relatively "common" surnames. Of this total, however, only 45 are truly "common" surnames, and these account for an estimated 70% of all Chinese surnames in use.
- Some surnames are more common in one province, region, or country than in another.
- The 45 common surnames listed herein were identified from international data and statistically analyzed in 1977 by Chinese researcher Li Dong Ming.
- Not all of these 45 surnames are common to all locations - - either within China or elsewhere.
- Shown above are the 10 most common Chinese surnames, listed in order of frequency of occurrence and, according to Li, account for an estimated 40% of all existing Chinese surnames.

45 COMMON CHINESE SURNAMES (姓)

	CHINESE IDEOGRAM	PINYIN	(TONE)	STC/CTC	DICTIONARY DEFINITION	PRC PINYIN	WADE-GILES MANDARIN	HONGKONG CANTONESE	OTHER DIALECTS AND/OR SPELLING VARIATIONS
11.	胡	hú	(2)	5170	ancient non-Han groups	Hu	Hu	Wu	Wo, Hoo, Woo,Foo
12.	鄭	zhèng	(4)	6774	serious, solemn	Zheng	Cheng	Cheng	Chang, Tchang, Tcheng
13.	郭	guō	(1)	6753	outer wall of a city	Guo	Kuo	Kwok	Kwoh, Gwok, Kuai, Kuei, Kuay, Guai, Ko
14.	蕭	xiāo	(1)	5618	desolate, dreary	Xiao	Hsiao	Siu	Siw, Seow, Siao, Siaow, Tok
15.	孫	sūn	(1)	1327	grandson	Sun	Sun	Sun	Soon, Soun, Sung, Seung, Swin, Tung
16.	馬	mǎ	(3)	7456	horse	Ma	Ma	Ma	Mar, Marr, Mah, Be, Beh, Bay
17.	高	gāo	(1)	7559	tall, high	Gao	Kao	Ko	Go, Gor
18.	徐	xú	(2)	1776	slowly, gently	Xu	Hsu	Tsui	Hui, Hee, Huey
19.	朱	zhū	(1)	2612	vermillion (bright red)	Zhu	Chu	Chu	Choo, Tchou, Tu, Chik, Jik
20.	林	lín	(2)	2651	forest, woods, grove	Lin	Lin	Lam	Lim, Lum, Liam, Liem

- Shown above is the second set of 10 common Chinese surnames, listed in order of frequency of occurrence. These 10 surnames, according to Li, account for an estimated 10% of all existing Chinese surnames.

45 COMMON CHINESE SURNAMES (姓)

	CHINESE IDEOGRAM	PINYIN	(TONE)	STC/CTC	DICTIONARY DEFINITION	PRC PINYIN	WADE-GILES MANDARIN	HONGKONG CANTONESE	OTHER DIALECTS AND/OR SPELLING VARIATIONS
21.	謝	xiè	(4)	6200	thank, thank you	Xie	Hsieh	Tse	Tsia
22.	何	hé	(2)	0149	what (interrogative)	He	Ho	Ho	Hoh, Haw, Hor, Hu, Heu
23.	許	xǔ	(3)	6079	praise, commend	Xu	Hsu	Hui	Hee, Huey
24.	宋	sòng	(4)	1345	Song Dynasty	Song	Sung	Sung	Soong, Soung, Tan
25.	沈	shěn	(3)	3088	a surname	Shen	Shen	Shum	Chen, Shim, Tchim, Sum, Soen, Seun, Sim
26.	羅	luó	(2)	5012	bird trap, bird net	Luo	Lo	Lo	Law, Loh, Lau, Lor, Lua
27.	韓	hán	(2)	7281	a surname; Korea	Han	Han	Hon	Harn, Hang, Horn, Ham
28.	鄧	dèng	(4)	6772	a surname	Deng	Teng	Tang	Dung, Dong, Ong, Toen, Teun, Teurn, Chang
29.	梁	liáng	(2)	2733	roof beam	Liang	Liang	Leung	Leong, Long, Lieng, Liao, Lieow, Nia
30.	叶	yè	(4)	0673	leaf, foliage	Ye	Hsieh	Hip	Yeh, Yap, Yia, Iap, Ieb, Yip

• Shown above is the third set of 10 common Chinese surnames, listed in order of frequency of occurrence. These 10 surnames, according to Li, account for an estimated 10% of all existing Chinese surnames.

45 COMMON CHINESE SURNAMES (姓)

	CHINESE IDEOGRAM	PINYIN	(TONE)	STC/CTC	DICTIONARY DEFINITION	PRC PINYIN	WADE-GILES MANDARIN	HONGKONG CANTONESE	OTHER DIALECTS AND/OR SPELLING VARIATIONS
31.	方	fāng	(1)	2455	square	Fang	Fang	Fong	Kwong, Kuang, Pang, Pung, Peung
32.	崔	cuī	(1)	1508	a surname	Cui	Ts'ui	Chui	Tsui, Tsou, Sew, Siu, Sui
33.	程	chéng	(2)	4453	rule, regulation	Cheng	Ch'eng	Ching	Tchang
34.	潘	pān	(1)	3382	a surname	Pan	P'an	Pun	Poon, Phoun, Phan, Phua, Pua, Hua
35.	曹	cáo	(2)	2580	people of same type	Cao	Ts'ao	Tso	Tsao, Cho
36.	馮	féng	(2)	7458	a surname	Feng	Feng	Fung	Fong, Foong, Pong, Poong, Pang, Fo
37.	汪	wāng	(1)	3076	collect, accumulate (liquid)	Wang	Wang	Wong	Ong, Vong, Wan
38.	蔡	cài	(4)	5591	a surname	Cai	Ts'ai	Tsoi	Tsai, Choi, Choy, Toy, Tsoi
39.	袁	yuán	(2)	5913	first, original, former	Yuan	Yuan	Yuen	Uen, Uan, Yoon
40.	盧	lú	(2)	4151	a surname	Lu	Lu	Lo	Loh, Loo, Lou, Low
41.	唐	táng	(2)	0781	Tang Dynasty	Tang	T'ang	Tong	Teng, Thang
42.	錢	qián	(2)	6929	copper, coin, cash	Qian	Ch'ien	Chin	Chien, Tsien, Tsin
43.	杜	dù	(4)	2629	birch-leaf pear	Du	Tu	To	Tou, Toh, Too, Tow, Thu, Ru, Roo
44.	彭	péng	(2)	1756	a surname	Peng	P'eng	Pang	Pong, Phoeng, Pheung, Phae, Phang, Phae
45.	陸	lù	(4)	7120	land (noun)	Lu	Lu	Luk	Look, Lok, Loo, Lek, Liw, Liu, Rok

• Shown above is the fourth set of common Chinese surnames, listed in order of frequency of occurrence. These 15 surnames, according to Li, account for an estimated 10% of all existing Chinese surnames.

NOTES ON THE CHINESE LANGUAGE & DIALECTS

CHINESE	NOTES	THAI EQUIVALENT
廣州 guǎngzhōu 1639/1558	Cantonese (Guangzhou, Guangdong, Kwangtung) A major dialect of the Yue dialect group of the Chinese language. "Canton" is the anglicized term for Guangzhao, the capital city of Guangdong Province in southeastern China. The Cantonese dialect is the standard dialect of the Pearl River delta area, and enjoys the status of a prestige or standard language, not only among Yue speakers, but even among Min and Kejia (Hakka) speakers who live in Guangdong Province. This standard dialect is also the predominant dialect in the colonies of Hong Kong and Macao, as well as in San Francisco's Chinatown.	จีนกวางตุ้ง Chin Kwangtung
潮州 cháozhōu 3390/1558	Chaozhou (Ch'ao-chou, Chiu Chau, Chiw Chow, Taechiu, Teochow, Teochew) A dialect of the southern Min dialect group of the Chinese language. Linguistically related to Fujianese and other Min dialects. The homeland of the Chaozhou speakers is in the southern port city of Shantou ("Swatow"), in Guangdong Province. Like other Min dialect groups, the Chaozhou were seafarers and fishermen. In the nineteenth century, many Chaozhou Chinese (or "Taechiu") migrated to Thailand, Vietnam, Malaysia, and other countries in Southeast Asia. Today, the Taechiu Chinese are the largest Chinese dialect group in Thailand.	จีนแต้จิ๋ว Chin Taechiu
福建 fújiàn 4395/1696	Fujianese (Fukkienese, Fukinese, Hokkien, Hokkienese) A major dialect of the northern Min dialect group of the Chinese language. Includes the Fuzhao ("Foochow") dialect of Fujian Province, spoken in the city of Fuzhao. Fujianese is also the main dialect spoken in Singapore and Malaysia. Pronounced *hok-kien* by native Fujianese speakers. The rough terrain of Fujian Province caused many Fujianese-speaking groups to remain isolated for centuries, resulting in some very distinct dialect differences. At least nine Fujianese dialects within this province are mutually unintelligible.	จีนฮกเกี้ยน Chin Hokkian
海南 hǎinán 3189/0589	Hainanese (Hailam) A dialect of the Min dialect group of the Chinese language. The periphery of the island of Hainan, like Taiwan, was populated during the 15th and 16th centuries mainly by immigrants from the southern coastal province of Fujian.	จีนไหหลำ Chin Hailam
客家 kèjiā 1356/1367	Hakka (Kejia, Khae) Major dialect group (linguistic classification) of the Chinese language. The name "Kejia" (in Cantonese, *hak-ka*) means 'guest' or 'stranger;' it was given to those Kejia Chinese who during recent times settled in areas already occupied by Yue-speaking peoples. The Kejia group includes the dialects of Taipu, Huizhao, Fengshun, Meixian, Popo and Yongding.	จีนแคะ Chin Khae

NOTES ON THE CHINESE LANGUAGE & DIALECTS

CHINESE	NOTES	THAI EQUIVALENT
果敢 gŭogăn 2654/2413	**Kokang (Guogan, Kuo-kan)** Ethnic Chinese minority group in the Shan State of Burma. The origin of the Kokang Chinese group is traced to neighboring Yunnan Province, from which the earliest groups migrated about two hundred years ago. The Kokang of Burma speak a dialect very similar to the Yunnanese dialect. Often regarded by local population as simply Yunnanese Chinese immigrants. Very little study has been done on this isolated group of Chinese emigres, particularly to determine if the dialect spoken by this group differs significantly from other Yunnanese dialects.	จีนโกก้าง Chin Kokang
國語 guóyŭ 0948/6133	**Mandarin** Refers to the main dialect spoken in Beijing as well as to a major dialect group (linguistic classification) of the Chinese language. (The latter meaning is more precisely known as "Beifang" by linguists.) About 70% of China's Han (ethnic Chinese) population speak one of the Mandarin dialects. Prior to the 1950s, few Mandarin speakers emigrated overseas, but there are now a number of Mandarin-speaking Chinese groups in many cities of Europe and North America. Mandarin dialects are spoken everywhere north of the Yangtze River except for those border regions where non-Han languages predominate. The standard language of China, called "putonghua," is based on the northern Mandarin dialect of Beijing (Peking) and, due to its prestige and wide use, exerts a strong influence on all the Chinese dialects and on the non-Han languages of China. Mandarin dialects range from Beijing Mandarin to the Yunnanese dialect in the southwestern border area with Southeast Asia. The term "Mandarin" is believed to have originated with Portuguese maritime traders using the Portuguese term *menderi*, meaning "government official."	จีนกลาง Chin Klang
閩 mĭn 7044	**Min** Not a Chinese dialect, per se, but rather a major *dialect group* (linguistic classification) of the Chinese language. The homeland of the Min dialects is Fujian Province and the northeastern corner of Guangdong Province. The majority of the inhabitants of Taiwan speak Min dialects which are closely related to that of Xiamen ("Amoy") in southern Fujian Province. The Min group includes Fukkienese, Xiamen, Fuzhou ("Foochow"), Quanzhou, Hainan, Putian, and Chaozhou (Taechiu) dialects. "Taiwanese" is a Min dialect. *Min* is also another name for Fujian Province.	

NOTES ON THE CHINESE LANGUAGE & DIALECTS

CHINESE	NOTES	THAI EQUIVALENT
名 míng 0682	name (first name, given name) Traditional Chinese names follow the surname and are generally made up of two carefully-paired Chinese characters (from a choice of about 900 characters) which have a propitious meaning. The romanized version of the name can be written as two separate elements, the first letter of each character being capitalized (as a Western first name and middle name); as two elements linked with a hyphen, the first letter of the second element not being capitalized; or it may be written in a combined form, without a hyphen. E.g., Deng Xiao Ping, Deng Xiao-ping, or Deng Xiaoping.	ชื่อ Chu
拼音 pīnyīn 2178/7299	pinyin The standard romanization system for Chinese used in the People's Republic of China. The standard pronunciation is defined as the speech sounds of the Beijing (Peking) dialect. These are represented in written form by a romanized alphabet that is taught in all the nation's schools. Pinyin has been the official spelling system of the PRC since 1958. The pinyin system is not generally known or used among Chinese outside of the PRC, unless through special training. Instead, the Wade-Giles System, or some other method, would be used.	
標准電碼 biāozhǔn diànmǎ 2871/0402/7193/4316	STC (Standard Telegraphic Code) / CTC (Chinese Telegraphic Code) 100-year-old system which identifies each of some 10,000 Chinese ideograms by individual 4-digit numbers. Originally used for transmitting telegraphic messages (in Chinese) among Chinese around the world. Although the telephone and fax machine have largely replaced the telegram and the need for such a coding system, the STC/CTC system is used for Chinese name and surname indexing purposes by some government agencies (including law enforcement agencies) in Asia, North America, and Europe.	เลขระหัสจีน lek rahat Chin
上海 shànghǎi 0006/3189	Shanghainese A major dialect of the Wu dialect group of the Chinese language. The main dialect spoken in the city of Shanghai and its environs.	
姓 xìng 1198	surname (family name, last name) Chinese surnames originated from the name of the village in which one lived or the family to which one belonged. The surname is traditionally written first, and the name (given name) follows. Hence, the term "last name" does not equate with the Chinese surname, as it does in Western cultures. (Pronounced "sae" in Taechiu dialect.) Many overseas Chinese, however, have re-ordered and modified their surname and name in order to accommodate to local practices in their country of residence (USA, Canada, Thailand, etc.) For example, the female name *Zhao Meirui* of Canton might become *Mary Chao* in Vancouver or *Maliwan Sae Chao* in Bangkok.	แซ่, ตระกูล, นามสกุล sae, trakun, nam sakun

NOTES ON THE CHINESE LANGUAGE & DIALECTS

CHINESE	NOTES	THAI EQUIVALENT
台灣 táiwān 0669/3494	**Taiwanese** A Min dialect spoken by the majority of residents of the island of Taiwan. The island was populated during the late Ming period mainly by immigrants from the southern coastal province of Fujian, situated on the mainland, about one hundred miles across the Formosa Strait. The standard "Taiwanese" dialect spoken on Taiwan today is closely related to the Xiamen ("Amoy") dialect of southern Fujian Province. Taiwanese speakers outnumber all other groups on the island, including the mainlanders who fled to Taiwan following the Nationalist (KMT) defeat by the Communists in 1950.	จีนไต้หวัน Chin Taiwan
台山 táishān 0669/1472	**Toisan (Taishan)** One of the Yue (Cantonese) dialects, spoken in the tiny, rural district of Taishan, about sixty miles southwest of Canton, in Guangdong Province. Taishan was only one of the ninety-eight districts of Guangdong (which was only one of some twenty Chinese provinces), but it had the advantage of being accessible from the sea when American sailing vessels came to recruit labor in the mid-nineteenth century. As a result, a large number of today's (Cantonese) Chinese Americans trace their ancestry to this small district.	
	Wade-Giles system of romanization A system of using the Roman (or Latin) alphabet to write Chinese words and names, devised by two lexicographers, Thomas Wade and Herbert Giles, in the early 1900s. Pronunciation was based on current Bejing (Peking) usage. Giles modified the transcription of Wade, creating what has come to be known as the Wade-Giles system of romanization. For many years this system served as the standard transcription in scholarly sinological works in English, but it is now slowly but surely yielding its place to the newer *pinyin* system.	
吳 wú 0702	**Wu** Not a Chinese dialect, per se, but rather a major *dialect group* (linguistic classification) of the Chinese language. Wu dialects are spoken in the Yangtze delta and the coastal region around Shanghai. The heart of this Wu-speaking area is Shanghai, China's largest city. Includes the Shanghainese dialect, as well as Suzhou ("Soochow"), Hangzhou ("Hangchow"), Shaoxing, Yongkang, and Wenzhou ("Wenchow").	

NOTES ON THE CHINESE LANGUAGE & DIALECTS

CHINESE	NOTES	THAI EQUIVALENT
粤 yuè 4727	**Yue** Not a Chinese dialect, per se, but rather a major *dialect group* (linguistic classification) of the Chinese language. Includes the Cantonese and Toi-san dialects. The Yue dialects are spoken over wide areas of Guangdong and Guangxi Provinces in China. The term "Cantonese," which is sometimes used interchangeably with Yue, should be reserved for the dialect of the city of Guangzhou (Canton) and not used as a general name for the Yue group as a whole. Yue dialects are spoken by a large population overseas (Thailand, Malaysia, Singapore, Indonesia, and North America). *Yue* is also another name for Guangdong Province.	
云南 yúnnán 0061/0589	**Yunnanese ("Haw")** A southwestern dialect of the Mandarin dialect group of the Chinese language. Yunnan did not become part of China until the thirteenth century, when the Mongols conquered the Tai groups living there and incorporated the area into the Chinese part of their empire. Consequently, Yunnan was settled long after the rest of South China and, as a result, the only dialect of Chinese which is spoken in Yunnan is a Mandarin dialect. Yunnanese is spoken in Yunnan Province and it also serves as the *lingua franca* among many non-Han hill tribe groups in the border areas of northeastern Burma (Kachin State, Kokang and Wa areas, and some sectors of the Shan State) and the highlands of northern Thailand and northwestern Laos. The Yunnanese dialect, as well as the Han Chinese immigrants from Yunnan Province, are called "Haw" by Tai-speakers (Shan, Thai, Lao, Lue, etc.) in Mainland Southeast Asia.	จีนยูนนาน, จีนฮ่อ Chin Yunnan,Chin Haw

Appendix C: Guanxi: An Important Concept for the Law Enforcement Officer

PREPARED BY M. CORDELL HART, SENIOR ANALYST, FINANCIAL CRIMES ENFORCEMENT NETWORK (FINCEN)

You Can Do It

For most Westerners, learning to deal effectively with Asians[a] does require some training and extra effort,[b] but there is nothing magical or mystical or particularly difficult about it. You don't have to learn to speak an Asian language or even to use chopsticks. What is important, however, is that you have an interest in people and a curiosity about how they think and act. It certainly helps if you generally like Asians. I don't know of anyone who was ever successful in working with people of a particular racial or ethnic group they disliked.[c]

Some things that you will want to learn about Asians are fairly straightforward, such as the structure of Asian names.[d] Other matters that deal with mindset and such social ways as guanxi are more involved. They are more

[a] "Orientals" and "Occidentals" may be the correct terms to use here, but my own practice is to say "Westerners" and "Asians". (Chinese often refer to Caucasian foreigners simply as "Americans".) In any case, the Asians I refer to in this paper are only those persons with East Asian cultural ways and mindset, not simply ethnic Asians.

[b] See "Overcoming Language and Cultural Barriers in Dealing With Asian Organized Crime" (U.S. Department of the Treasury, FinCEN), a paper prepared for the Multinational Asian Organized Crime Conference in Sydney, Australia, November 1994.

[c] Asians, too, have their preferences. For a discussion of Chinese perceptions of Westerners, see the pamphlet entitled "Chinese" (U.S. Department of the Treasury, FinCEN, March 1994).

[d] An extraordinarily effective training course on the listing and tracing of Asian names in databases is presented annually by the U.S. Central Intelligence Agency.

involved, but not totally new. Most differences in Asian and Western social ways only reflect slight variations on how we live and think.

What Is Guanxi?[e]

The spelling of guanxi simply provides a transliteration (by the widely-accepted Pinyin system) of 關係 (STC 7070 0190), a Chinese term which basically means "relationship" or "connection". Another popular system of transliterating Chinese, the Wade-Giles system, spells it as "kuan-hsi". For American speakers of English, the proper Mandarin pronunciation of that Chinese term can be more easily understood by this spelling: "gwahn-shee". With other Asian languages, of course, the transliteration will be different.

Whatever the spelling, the concept itself is found throughout East Asia (ancient China was the root of all East Asian cultures) and it is an exceedingly important part of the Asian mindset. There probably is nothing as important as this concept in describing Asian social ways — and nothing so different from what we of the West hold as an ideal. Clearly, the concept of guanxi is as important to Asians as the concept of individualism is to Westerners.

Obviously, then, the social application of guanxi by Asians involves more than just the meaning of one or a few connections or relationships. For one thing, it is the key term used to examine the total load of family/ancestral ties, old school ties, influences, obligations, favors due, favors owed, business referrals and continuing business deals, back-door power, political offices, etc. that every Asian is bundled with — unavoidably, as well as by design — throughout life.

Is Guanxi Practiced by Westerners?

By this point, Western readers will surely (but mistakenly) be thinking that maybe guanxi is not such a foreign idea. Before moving on to the specifics of how Asians practice guanxi (and therein lies the real difference between East and West in this matter) let's consider our own ways. Do we of Western cultures also have such bundles of ties, favors, and obligations as noted above? You bet we do! Beyond blood relations, we have old Army buddies, classmates, sports teammates, etc. and we participate in unions, fraternities, alumni associations, police fraternal orders, civic associations, political parties, etc. We understand what it means to marry the boss's daughter, to have

[e] See "On the Chinese Practice of 'Guanxi'" (U.S. Department of the Treasury, FinCEN), a paper prepared for the annual meeting of the International Society for the Comparative Study of Civilizations, Dublin, Ireland, July 1994.

a friend at City Hall, to know someone who can get it for you wholesale, and that a friend in need is a friend indeed. It is not so much that Asians and Westerners have any exclusive activities, it is more that the two groups apply varying amounts of resources and degrees of emphasis and skill in doing similar things.[f]

Business and Crime

Almost every day, some mention is made of guanxi in the business section of most newspapers.[g] Usually, it is in context of a Western entrepreneur going to China, Hong Kong, Taiwan, or Singapore, following the good advice that guanxi is critical to business success in those places and thus finding and paying someone who claims to have the right contacts, then losing his shirt and coming home to complain about the lack of predictability and trust in the Chinese business world. Their common error seems to proceed from (1) an emphasis on getting results in the short term, (2) mistaking guanxi for bribery (although that works, too), and (3) not knowing just who has the right connections at the right place and at the right time.

In the field of law enforcement, similar mistakes are made, but anyone can be excused their mistakes in (3) above, and preparation and training can prevent the problems of (1) and (2). Developing informants is an activity in which guanxi is immediately important, and the truly capable Western officials are already applying guanxi. Less capable officials wait until a critical need is at their feet before they set out to develop informant networks — and then they often just "throw money" at an informant, expecting that money will be a sufficient motivation.[h] With Asians, it often is not.[i]

[f] Consider what East and West have in common as regards a certain class of criminals. Robin Hood, Butch Cassidy, the "Sundance Kid," Ned Kelly, and the various outlaws chronicled in the Chinese classic, *Water Margin,* including the "Flower Monk," Lu Zhishen (魯 智 深, STC 7627 2535 3234) are all admired in folklore for their independence and resistance to authority. To complete the thought of those rogues, however, remember that Robin Hood had his merry band, Cassidy and Sundance worked with the Hole in the Wall Gang, bushranger Ned Kelly had his Kelly Gang, and the several famous rogues of *Water Margin* had their men of the marsh.

[g] An exceedingly perceptive and prolific writer on Asian business matters is Dr. Frankie F. Leung, Adjunct Professor, University of Loyola Law School, Los Angeles, California.

[h] Experienced officers and neophytes alike who attempt to apply guanxi in the execution of their official duties should take care. Most law enforcement managers, especially in the U.S., are aware of the need to pay informants, but they are not aware of guanxi and how it relates to the Asian mindset. This lack of understanding may result in misinterpretations of the actions taken by the officer applying guanxi. Accordingly, it is best to explain the concept of guanxi to one's managers prior to taking any official action with informants.

[i] Special Agent Neil Pitagno, U.S. Customs Service, Newark, NJ, is an especially good authority in this area.

Also, it seems that Asian criminal enterprise (not street-level crime) is best understood as a business venture, which can be of a global scale or dimension, an activity that is run along the same lines as most overseas Chinese businesses, vice the focus on Tongs and Triads. In such businesses, guanxi and profits, not a predetermined structure, direct operations.[j]

The Asian Way

Simply put, Asians focus on the group, and Westerners focus on the individual. Asians accept as normal a need to develop and maintain many circles of useful contacts.[k] They know that each person must deal with a great number of other people in order to make ends meet and get things done. Westerners generally only supplement their more important trust in institutions and law by developing certain personal contacts and favors.

It may not be that Asians cultivate and maintain more relationships with other people than do Westerners, but they surely are more acutely aware of and act on benefits and obligations that attend each relationship. Most importantly, they play personal relationships in a complex and extended way seldom understood, much less practiced by Westerners. The important usefulness of extension in guanxi means that it is possible to receive benefits from other members of a guanxi net who may not be immediately known to the person needing the favor, information, etc.[l] A complimentary consideration is that the individual players may not be aware of the total scheme. One authority puts it this way: "Basically, the art of social action in China is a kind of choreography in which 'guanxi' debts are tapped for particular contributions, and the parts woven into an effective whole of which individual contributors may be quite unaware. A related concept here is 'tuo' (託, STC = 6067), entrusting someone to something for one. It can be used for very serious matters, and not just 'errands'."[m]

[j] Dr. Frankie Leung's paper, *The Myths or Realities of Overseas Chinese Management,* notes "...The overseas Chinese business entities are famous for their lack of a hierarchical corporate structure. If an overseas Chinese structure has ever taken shape, it is more like a family business, with a patriarch at the top, rather than like a Japanese or Western corporation where corporate functions are distributed both horizontally and vertically."

[k] Guanxi provides for the distribution of goods and services, not friendship.

[l] See Special Agent Neil Pitagno's example cited in the paper "On the Chinese Application of 'Guanxi'".

[m] Professor Mark Elvin, Australian National University.

Some Examples

My Chinese teacher from many years ago once called to ask if I could provide him with a few copies of a particular Chinese dictionary. I happened to have several copies of that dictionary on hand, but knowing that my old teacher himself did not need them, I asked who the requester was. I also suggested that if that person would contact me I would ship the dictionaries directly to him. That was a bad mistake. I was thinking in Western ways of efficiency in moving the dictionaries, not in Asian ways of guanxi. My teacher responded in a lowered voice saying that if it was "inconvenient" I should just forget the request.[n] Fortunately, my brain engaged in time for me to salvage the very valuable relationship with my teacher. I said I would get the dictionaries to him the next morning, period. Note that if I had persisted or had shipped the dictionaries directly, it would have cut out my teacher from that guanxi extension — and he, appropriately, would have cut me out of his network. I would have lost him as a valuable source of information and continuing instruction in the Chinese language.

Another simple guanxi example follows. An American detective sought my assistance in tracking down a Chinese murder suspect. He thought the suspect had fled to Taiwan. He needed the suspect's blood type and fingerprints to compare with those found at the crime scene. The problem was, and is, that the U.S. does not have formal diplomatic relations with Taiwan, and the officially prescribed way of obtaining the information would have taken ages, if it was even possible. He would have had to submit his request to the state police, then to Interpol, where it would have been turned around and routed back through the state police to the Federal Bureau of Investigation, where the request would be forwarded to their Legal Attache in the American embassy in Tokyo, Japan, who would have taken the request with him to Taiwan the next time he made a trip there. And would Taiwan authorities act on his request? The Asian way of handling this need was much more direct. I knew a Chinese person living in the U.S. whose father is a retired general officer of Taiwan's army. I asked him (not the father) if he could help, and shortly thereafter I received in the mail copies of the suspect's fingerprints and military and family records, including blood type. The data matched that found at the crime scene. The Taiwan authorities arrested the suspect, the American detective flew to Taiwan and testified at the trial, and the suspect was convicted.[o] Justice was done.

[n] The Chinese term for inconvenient is "bu fangbien" (不方便, STC 0008 2455 0189). It is often used by Chinese as a polite alternative to a frank expression of reluctance, unwillingness, even dislike, as to a particular request or proposal.

[o] The crime was actually the rape and murder of a female business manager. The sentence imposed by the Taiwan court was life imprisonment, not execution, because, curiously, the rape was determined to have taken place after the victim was killed.

Completing the Circle

If you think those stores are finished, you need to be very careful in your study of guanxi. If you already know, however, that the circles were yet to be completed, you are well on your way to practicing guanxi in an effective way. As to the case of the dictionaries, it was only one of a series of favors to and from my teacher. (Between student and teacher, importantly a lifelong relationship, the student shows respect and gratitude and receives instruction and advice.) As to the case of the fingerprints and blood type data, I forwarded the fingerprints and other data to the American detective, sent my Taiwanese friend a very nice bottle of cognac, and bowed out of the scene. What happened subsequently between the Taiwan authorities and the American detective — the more important part of the arrangement, I don't know, although I did give the detective some suggestions on how he could respond.

The important point here is that one good turn deserves another, and no Asian is going to do you a favor without expecting something in return — even though such an expectation may not be explicitly conveyed to you. (Yes, Asians and Westerners alike hate to see someone get away with murder, but business, is business, and if you think friendship is its own reward or otherwise are not prepared to reciprocate favors in some way, you should look for satisfaction outside of police work in the field of Asian crime.) Consider this, too: "Guanxi is a long-term investment. The too-rapid return of a favor is often taken as indicating that one wishes the relationship to cease. Here we are into the analysis of a related concept: 'renqing' (人 情, STC 0086 1906), which may be very roughly translated as 'human feelings [of gratitude for favors received or anticipated]'. In a famous article long ago (perhaps in the *Harvard Journal of Asiatic Studies*) Professor Yang Lien-sheng argued that the basic Chinese virtue was 'bao-en' (報 恩, STC 1032 1869), the return of favours received."[p]

Guanxi Extends Influence

To fully appreciate the important dynamics of guanxi in crime as well as ordinary society, however, you must realize that this Asian phenomenon involves not just a careful measure of favors exchanged, it allows for the great extension of influence through numerous contacts who very likely don't know, or will ever know, all the members of the network. The two examples cited above are extremely simple and illustrate more the exchange of favors than the dynamics of extension. In the case of the dictionaries, the ultimate user/requester could well have been numerous persons removed from my

[p] Professor Mark Elvin, Australian National University.

teacher. In the case of the needed fingerprints and blood type, my Taiwanese contact probably did *not* go through his father to get the records. (His having an influential father was already known, so he already had "clout" and would not have had to actually involve his father.) It is possible that he went through Taiwan official channels, and that officialdom decided it was in Taiwan's interests, in the way of international affairs, to assist U.S. law enforcement. The point here is that it didn't matter what or how many persons were actually involved in moving the request down to the custodian of the needed files — and moving the requested information back to the American detective. The goods were delivered. That is the way guanxi works. The end justifies the means.

Avoid Cynicism

It is possible, I suppose, for Westerners to become rather cynical or skeptical about guanxi. After all, it is in the context of crime that the matter is addressed here, and it is accurate to say that guanxi provides for goods and services, *not* friendship for its own sake. Do not forget, however, that among Asians guanxi is a socio-psychological process for heartwarming good, as well as for cold economic benefit. My teacher was happy to perform his part of the guanxi net in moving the request and the dictionaries. The dictionaries helped someone. My Taiwanese friend was not just coldly providing a favor to get a favor. He is a good person in all the ways we of the West know good people to be, and he knew the world would be better off with the murderer being brought to justice. Goodness, as well as evil, is found everywhere.

Sometimes, however, those of us in law enforcement feel we are running further and further behind the crooks. Indeed, it may always be that way. An observation from the Chinese classic, *Travels to the West,* (西 遊 記[q]), 道 高 一 尺 魔 高 一 丈[r] is translated to this: "As goodness advances by one foot, evil moves on by ten."

[q] STC 6007 6662 6068.

[r] STC 6670 7559 0001 1439 7621 7559 0001 0004.

Appendix D: Overcoming Language and Cultural Barriers in Dealing With Asian Organized Crime

M. CORDELL HART, FINANCIAL CRIMES ENFORCEMENT NETWORK (FINCEN)

Summary

- Western law enforcement agencies, financial institutions, and commercial organizations alike have been alerted to the threat of Asian Organized Crime.
- Most such western institutions are inadequately prepared to deal with the unique language and cultural forms of Asian criminals.
- All need to take advantage of increasingly available training courses designed to provide the necessary language and cross-cultural skills.
- Advances in optical character recognition (OCR) offer hope for computer solutions to problems in dealing with the written form of Asian languages, but Standard Telegraphic Codes (STC) remain the only device suitable for unambiguously listing and tracing Chinese, Japanese, and Korean names in electronic databases.
- There is a desperate need for agreement among Western institutions on the system of Romanization to be used in transliterating Asian names and on the adjustment of databases to accommodate STC.

Background

The greatly increased threat from crime by ethnic Asians, particularly Asian Organized Crime (AOC) in North America, is generally thought to have begun sometime in the early 1980s. The criminals themselves probably know that it started much earlier, but U.S. federal law enforcement agencies only began in the mid- to late 1980s to consider the measures needed to deal with AOC. More recently, financial institutions have taken a direct interest in Asians. "Know your customer" is a key stricture in bank security and a defense against money launderers, many of whom recently have been ethnic Asians. Also, credit card companies have begun to consider defensive measures against Asian crime.

Until the last decade, crime by Asians was largely written off as but another part of life in Chinatown, that exotic area of our cities where inscrutable Asians of all sorts lived. The Hollywood movie, "Chinatown", presented the now-classic line uttered by a police official, "You may think you know what goes on there [referring to San Francisco's Chinatown], but you really don't." Similar police frustrations in dealing with crime in Chinatown, New York, along with some highly accurate observations on the whole range of factors in AOC, were featured in another movie entitled "Year of the Dragon". For this, Hollywood is due our thanks. They picked up on the phenomenon of AOC better and more quickly than did most senior managers in the law enforcement community.

Though some senior managers have grasped the international scope of the AOC threat and are active in adjusting to it, many managers have opted instead to downplay the threat. Usually this is due to concern about their own ignorance of how to go about countering the threat of AOC, their recognition of the required costs in training and equipment, or simply some hope against hope that AOC will be a passing phenomenon. One senior U.S. law enforcement manager, to give an extreme but not uncommon example, once told this writer that he did not believe specialized training for AOC was needed because he had been successful in his career without ever knowing anything about Asian language and cultural matters, Standard Telegraphic Codes, etc. He maintained that a good investigator could deal equally well with any ethnic group. The cost of providing language and cross-cultural training *is* appreciable, in terms of a trainee's time away from the job, as well as the specific costs of instructional fees and study materials, but consider the current alternative. Most importantly, AOC is not going away anytime soon. The Asian criminal's sense of power, derived from the enormous profits of narcotics and alien smuggling and other criminal activities, as well as his sense of immunity from effective police action, will not fade merely with the passing of a generation or two.

The Traditional Response

The problem, simply put, is that few police or bank officials can speak an Asian language and few understand the way Asians think and act. Western police forces have usually responded to needs for certain cultural and language skills by hiring more policemen from the ethnic groups involved. Cultural and language skills are thus acquired along with the person who will actually "walk the beat". But qualified Asians are not being recruited for police work fast enough to deal with the pace of crime by Asians in the West. At present, for example, Fukienese Chinese make up a very high percentage of the narcotics smugglers and violent criminals in North America, yet easily fewer than ten U.S. Federal agents have a capability in that dialect — and even fewer speak the Foochow subdialect. (Note that the term "Asian" is used for convenience in considering the overall phenomenon of crime by ethnic Asians. However, just as Europeans consider themselves French, Italian, German, etc., individual Asians rather thank of themselves as Chinese, Vietnamese, Thai, etc., and it is with such distinctions in mind that specific law enforcement and security measures should be taken.)

Language training for Western law enforcement officers in various Asian languages, particularly Chinese Mandarin, and Cantonese, is increasing, and there have been improved training opportunities in Asian cultural matters. Curiously, however, there remains a distressing misapplication of available skills found among Western police officers. Ethnic Asian police officers, as well as Westerners with Asian language and cultural skills, are not given sufficient outlet and career opportunities for their unique and needed capabilities. Part of the reason seems to be the emphasis law enforcement agencies place on generalized abilities, rather than on specialized skills, for career progression.

Service Needs and Training Levels

Language and cross-cultural (LCC) skills should be dealt with together. In the process of learning a foreign language, much of the relevant culture is learned. similarly, it is most difficult to avoid learning something of the language while making inquiries into a culture. While specific classroom sessions may focus on one or the other, language and cultural skills should be considered as one in planning agency training programs.

Most U.S. agencies consider skill level three, on a language fluency scale of five, to be that required for minimum professional capability. Level one skills are considered survival skills, and level five describes the perfect fluency of native-born and educated persons. (Although not included here, the five skill levels are defined by highly detailed arrays of specific capabilities in speaking, comprehending, and reading.)

Traditional teaching programs generally provide level three skills:

- In 6 months of study in the following languages: Afrikaans, Danish, French, German, Haitian Creole, Italian, Norwegian, Portuguese, Romanian, Spanish, Swedish, and Swahili
- In 10 months of study in the following languages: Amharic Bulgarian, Czech, Finnish, Greek, Hebrew, Bengali, *Burmese,* Dari, Farsi, Hindi, *Khmer, Lao,* Nepali, *Pilipino,* Sinhala, *Thai,* Tamil, Urdu, *Vietnamese,* Hungarian, Polish, Russian, Serbo-Croatian, and Turkish.
- In 21 months of study in Arabic, *Chinese, Japanese,* and *Korean.*

For agencies dealing with AOC, three categories of LCC skills are suggested.

Full and Fluent

Though most agency needs in this category can be met by hiring native speakers of an Asian language — or even by contracting for LCC skills on a case-by-case basis — agencies will want to consider maintaining a limited number of non-Asian officers with full LCC skills (at least level four on the above-noted scale of five) on their staff. Chinese dialects such as Cantonese and Fukienese should be considered, as well as Mandarin. Most often, full LCC skill by an ethnic Asian officer is what is needed, but there are occasions when an Asian target needs to be more assured that he is dealing with a Western official and not some provocateur or security official of an Asian country.

The route to full and fluent Asian LCC skills for Westerners is an expensive one, and agencies should consider carefully those who are nominated for the program. It is exceedingly important that the person selected be one who is thoroughly interested in, and appreciative of, Asians and their culture. Even high skills and accomplishments in police work should not be placed ahead of such interest and appreciation in selecting those to receive training.

Persons selected for this program will also want to consider their own ambitions. Often, it is not a technical skill that will provide them with promotions. They should be reasonably satisfied with "success" as a specialist — and, in the case of certain languages (notably Chinese), they should anticipate the frustration of never fully knowing their specialty. The late and truly great Sinologist, John King Fairbank, told of an encounter with a rival Sinologist — another American — in Shanghai many years ago. Fairbank had already established a great academic reputation for himself, both at Harvard and at Cambridge, and had gone to China, for the first time, to pursue certain studies. He recalled that his rival had been quite interested in just what Fairbank intended to study while in China. When Fairbank told him that he planned to study the language, to paraphrase Fairbank, "He noticeably breathed a sigh of relief, because he knew then — as I was to learn many years later — that many a fine mind had thrown itself into the study of the Chinese language never to be heard from again."

General Competency

Agencies should plan on having many investigators, certainly more than the number that likely will be considered initially, especially supervisory ones, with working level LCC skills at both level three and two. Ten-month programs of study, assuming small classes and intelligent and motivated students, will generally produce level two, and occasionally level three, skills in spoken Chinese. Such skill levels in Southeast Asian languages can be obtained in even less time. For training in Chinese, only Mandarin or Cantonese dialects should be considered. (Mandarin is the easiest to learn of the several Chinese dialects, and it is increasingly the language spoken by ethnic Chinese around the world. Cantonese, however, is the dialect most commonly spoken by Chinese criminal elements related to Triads. It is also the dialect spoken by many Vietnamese criminal elements whether they are ethnic Chinese from Vietnam or Vietnamese who spent time as refugees in Hong Kong.) Tutorial programs will move students along even faster. As with planning for the stable of officers having full and fluent LCC skills, those considered for training to this category should be carefully screened. Even a few months of study are expensive in terms of salary and time away from the job.

Basic Skills

All law enforcement personnel working AOC should have a minimum of LCC skills that will enable them generally to understand Asians and at least one Asian language. They should be able to recognize the written form of the several Asian languages. Occasional classes in cross-cultural matters, even attendance at a conference related to AOC, will be of appreciable value. Survival skills in an Asian language and culture can be obtained through part-time or full-time study in a matter of weeks, or even days, and skills in Standard Telegraphic Codes can be learned in one or two weeks, depending on the particular course and the motivation of the student. In almost every case, candidates for the Full and Fluent and General Competency levels of training/function should undergo Basic Skills training first.

Use of Interactive Video in Language Training

Phenomenal progress in technical devices for language instruction has been made over the last 6 years. Well beyond the effectiveness of instructional audio tapes and programmed texts is computer-assisted interactive video. The first such device was produced by the U.S. Central Intelligence Agency for training in Spanish language. Named "Exito" (Spanish for "success"), it is an award-winning program of instruction proven capable of moving 65%

of students from level zero to level one-plus in only 10 days. Other courses now available are Khorosho (Russian), C'est Tres Facile (French), and Al-Mumtaaz (Arabic). Similar programs for Japanese and Chinese languages are under development. Interested agencies may wish to write to the U.S. Central Intelligence Agency, Office of Training and Education, Washington, D.C. 20505.

Listing and Tracing Asian Names in Electronic Databases

The equipment and procedural capabilities of Western nations' law enforcement databases is formidable. With fair ease and great speed, name traces can be made from practically any office or patrol vehicle. With but a telephone or radio link, names, license numbers, and other identifying data can be checked through a host of federal and state databases. Unfortunately, Western law enforcement officials are all too prone to accept an Asian's adopted Western name without also seeking the individual's original Asian name.

In one incident, an ethnic Chinese heroin smuggler was detained at roadside for a minor traffic violation by the state police in northeastern U.S. As was routine for that state, the officer used his car radio to call for traces on the violator's names as shown on his state-issued drivers license: "John Chang" (example only, not the person's real name). The response was negative, so the officer merely issued a ticket for the traffic violation and released the violator. Much earlier, police in California had received allegations about that person from an informant that he was a major heroin smuggler, and they entered the information in the National Crime Information Center, the primary law enforcement database in the U.S. But the name entered was (again for example, not the real name) "Desheng Zhang", a Romanized version of the person's Chinese name: 張德生 (STC 1728 1795 3932). No match was thus possible, and the smuggler is still at large.

In another embarrassing incident, two U.S. federal law enforcement agencies and one at the state level, cooperated to monitor the activities of a group of Asians known to be arranging to import a large load of heroin. The Asians were considered to be Vietnamese nationals because their identity papers as Permanent Resident Aliens showed them to have come from Vietnam, even though an informant in their midst clearly knew the suspects to be ethnic Chinese from Vietnam. No one bothered to ask the informant about the ethnic origins or language of the suspects. Consequently, when the arrests were made, no Chinese interpreter was on hand to facilitate the attempt at a controlled delivery of the heroin, and no traces on their Chinese names had been requested of authorities in Hong Kong or China to determine other criminal associates of the suspects in the U.S.

Computers and Optical Character Recognition

Many Western law enforcement officials are aware and capable in ways that would have precluded the mistakes noted above, but many more are needed. Advances in optical character recognition (OCR) offer some hope in the field. The former problems of computer storage capacity and speed have been largely overcome. Now, only software challenges remain before completing the development of a total machine interface between character forms of a Chinese, Japanese, or Korean name and their easy registration in a Western-language database. Indeed, one such program, called the "Chinese Recognition Engine", is expected to be on hand at the U.S. Department of the Treasury's Financial Crimes Enforcement Network by the end of 1994.

Already on hand is a similar OCR program for work with Cyrillic, English, German, and French. The "CuneiForm 1.2" OCR system is a multilingual optical character recognition software system that can recognize not only Cyrillic text, but also English, French, and German with an extremely high degree of accuracy. It can recognize printed text from the broadest range of sources, including books, journals, magazines, newspapers, and typewritten materials or computer printouts from dot matrix, ink jet, or laser printers. Its accuracy rate on poor quality second or third generation photocopied materials is unsurpassed.

CuneiForm runs under MS Windows 3.1 or higher on an IBM-compatible 386 PC with a minimum of 4 MB of RAM and 4 MB of free hard-disk space or larger system. It supports 47 families of scanners from 25 manufacturers, including the HP AccuPage® technology.

The system scans and recognizes text, doing an excellent job of automatic page decomposition that can be manually edited before recognition. The recognized text is presented to the user together with the original scanned image for easy editing, with dubiously recognized characters highlighted. It also has a spelling checker that will highlight not-found words and an easy-to-use facility that allows the creation of specialized user dictionaries.

Following editing and correction of any errors, the edited text can be saved as one of two types of ASCII files or in RTF format. These text files must then be exported to a compatible word processing package for processing and printing.

Standard Telegraphic Codes

Even when such software becomes more widely available, however, it may be too expensive for most state and local law enforcement agencies. Accordingly, for the next few decades, Standard Telegraphic Codes (STC) appear the best solution to Western needs for listing and tracing Asian names. Known throughout Asia, STC offer a simple and proven way of recording the words/characters of Chinese, Japanese, and Korean languages. As more and more persons in the West are trained in STC, more STC will be entered in databases, and then more useful traces can be made. Interpol and the Royal Hong Kong Police were the first to advocate the use of STC in law enforcement files. All U.S. federal law enforcement agencies now endorse the use of STC.

An annual training course in STC for U.S. federal law enforcement personnel, and other persons endorsed by them, has been provided for several years now by the U.S. Central Intelligence Agency. The course, 2 weeks in duration, has proven to be an extremely effective piece of training in LCC, as well as the mechanics of the STC system. A more abbreviated course in STC, only one week long, is offered by Diplomatic Language Services, Inc., a commercial firm in the Washington, D.C., area.

Romanized Forms of Asian Names

Still remaining is the acceptance of a standard of Romanization. For Chinese names, the standard in the West was long the Wade-Giles system, but China's Pinyin (which, itself, is the Romanized form for the Mandarin term "spell sound") has been more and more adopted. In addition to being the system formally endorsed, indeed devised, by the Peoples Republic of China, Pinyin has certain advantages over Wade-Giles. Pinyin requires about 20% fewer letters to represent the same sounds than does Wade-Giles, and, unlike Wade Giles which uses apostrophes to denote aspirated syllables, Pinyin has fewer apparent similarities of spelling. Both the Wade-Giles and Pinyin — as well as a host of less popular systems — have arbitrary conventions that must be learned, and none adequately or accurately register the character forms. The Chinese language, for example, is replete with homophones, made only partially more distinguishable by tones. The surnames 張 and 章 (STC 1728 and 4545, respectively) have identical sounds, even with the same tone, and thus the same Romanized form, "Zhang", yet they are importantly different. The bearers of those surnames are careful to offer a distinction based on the radical component — Zhang — of the "li" radical, as opposed to Zhang of the "gung" radical, but all that is lost on non-Chinese speakers or those without training in STC.

As to effective reporting of Asian suspects names in Romanized form, it cannot be stressed too much that the form preferred by the individual, and seen in his travel documents, is of critical importance. Even Asian police sources are not consistent and entirely helpful in this matter. Police in China sometimes provide Western law enforcement agencies with names in Pinyin, even though the suspect is known to use a name spelled differently by the Cantonese pronunciation of his name. Sometimes the Hong Kong police will provide the Romanized form according to the Cantonese pronunciation of the person's name, even though the individual has previously used the Pinyin (Mandarin) form of his name. There is simply no consistency.

Computer Software for STC and Romanized Forms

Computer software is being developed to ease and speed the deviation of STC, various of the more popular Romanized forms, and the several computer codes. One prototype piece of software, entitled the Multi-Lingual Asian Name Identification System, is under development by Pacific Rim Connections, Inc., in San Francisco. It is admirably suited to law enforcement needs, but its development has been slowed by the lack of a commitment from a major law enforcement agency. Somewhat similar software is being developed by the U.S. Department of State. Designed to replace the older Automated Visa Lookout System, it is named the "Consular Lookout and Support System". In both cases, the software consists essentially of a huge inter-relational database, made up of bit maps for characters, STC, the several systems of Romanization, and some miscellaneous data that will enable the user to move to various forms of an Asian name or word into another electronic form.

Benefits for East and West

Solutions for various problems of Western law enforcement agencies will also benefit Asian law enforcement agencies. Developments in OCR, the adoption of similar computer codes (such as Unicode), training in and application of STC and an agreement on a system of Romanization will allow much more effective cooperation between police of Asia and the West. Let us hope that accords can be reached soon.

Appendix E: Chinese Culture and the Practice of "Actuarial" Intelligence

PREPARED BY PAUL DOUGLAS MOORE,
FEDERAL BUREAU OF INVESTIGATION

As my colleagues (Cordell Hart, Douglas Daye) on this discussion panel agree, the Chinese cultural phenomenon of guanxi, that is, the building and maintaining of interpersonal relationships as a means of meeting one's needs, is a key concept in explaining Chinese social behavior. As you may know from what we say here or from things you already have read, individuals seeking to improve their guanxi (i.e., effective social relationships) with others inevitably from small networks; and these networks overlap other small networks. The key to the social interactions in these guanxi networks is the exchange of services, which are viewed as social favors. Those patrons dispensing favors accumulate social capital, while those clients receiving favors incur social obligations. An important consideration is that it is not only possible but quite common for an individual to go to great effort and expense on behalf of a person he has never met nor ever will meet, if the favor thus provided is requested by someone to whom there is a current guanxi obligation. Guanxi interactions are so much an integral and dependable part of Chinese societies everywhere that individuals frequently will try to "go through the back door" through guanxi connections rather than deal with a faceless bureaucracy, even when that bureaucracy ostensibly is the most direct and the nearest route to what is sought.

What I would like to explore briefly in this paper is what some of the evidence has to say as to whether guanxi is an efficient and effective form of behavior. The particular body of data I have drawn upon is observation of Chinese intelligence collection activity in the U.S. over the past 20 years. Because my conclusions are based on both overt and covert activity and this is an academic forum, the reader will have to appreciate that it is not possible to provide specific examples or to explore fully the implications of the simple model I wish to put forward. My hope is that the theorizing I do here may help others interpret their behavioral data in this particular cultural domain.

What we in the Federal Bureau of Investigation (FBI) have determined through our investigations over the years is that, whatever guanxi networks may be to Chinese social interaction, they also are the bedrock of Chinese intelligence collection — both open-source and clandestine — in the U.S. Chinese intelligence collection in the U.S. appears to be a group activity, and it is distinguishable from nonintelligence activity mainly in terms of its objectives, not its methodology.

Western students of Chinese intelligence behavior for a long time have utilized the following example to compare and contrast the Chinese approach to intelligence gathering to that of other nations: If the composition of the sand on a certain beach were identified as an intelligence target by the nations of the world, some countries would solve the challenge by dispatching a submarine to sit offshore from the beach. In the dark of night, a commando team would emerge from the submarine, paddle in a rubber raft to the beach, scoop up a bucket or two of sand, and beat a retreat back to the submarine. Analysis of the buckets of sand would produce a great deal of data. Other countries would task their satellites flying overhead to turn their sophisticated infrared and spectrographic scanners on the beach, and this also would produce a wealth of data. China, however, would approach the problem by allowing 10,000 of its citizens to spend the day at the beach. At sunset they all would go home and simply shake out their towels, and the Chinese would end up with more sand — and more data — than the other nations.

To the FBI and other Western counterintelligence agencies, the Chinese intelligence behavior in this hypothetical example would be considered very unusual, unprofessional, and suspect. For one thing, there would now be 10,000 people who know the "secret" of what happened on the beach; for another, it is both expensive and cumbersome to have thousands of individuals collect a very small piece of intelligence each. While overall we would deem the Chinese effort in this case to be inefficient, there is no way that their results ever could be judged to be ineffective.

My argument is that intelligence collection based on social interaction can be treated as a genuine form of social behavior. If only small numbers of people participate, the activity can be conceptualized and studied with rules and theories designed to predict the behavior of individuals. The success or failure of a given collection enterprise will depend upon the skill and initiative of the individuals involved in it. When very large numbers of people become involved in such collection, however, different rules must be applied, and focusing on the behavior of individuals no longer is useful or enlightening.

This is the point at which I would like to introduce the concept of "actuarial" intelligence. As we all know, actuaries are insurance company analysts who determine the odds of life expectancy and good-health expectancy for enormously large pools of people. They then calculate how much risk-vs.-profit the insurance company will be exposed to if it sets its rates at certain levels for certain groups of people. Based on their observations of large numbers of people, the actuaries know with near mathematical certitude that a certain percentage of people will die each year at a certain average age. Nonetheless, they have absolutely no idea if a particular individual will die well early of that age, at precisely the average age, or well past the average age. They also can calculate the change of risk for subgroups with behaviors such as smoking or skydiving and adjust the rates their company must charge such customers to realize a profit. The essence of their work, however, is that they can "predict" what will happen only to very large groups or to behavioral subgroups of people, not to very small groups, and absolutely not to individuals.

If very large numbers of people join in intelligence activity, some are bound to be skillful, energetic, or just plain lucky collectors. It also is possible to accomplish a large aggregate of collection by taking it in extremely small pieces. When an extremely large number of people become involved, however, it becomes correspondingly difficult to predict the behavior of any single individual. It appears at some point that the weight of numbers just takes over and the problem becomes mainly one of statistics. Hence the notion of actuarial intelligence.

A return to the beach example may better illustrate what I am getting at. If you are in charge of China's intelligence operations against the sand on our hypothetical beach, how do you determine who among your 10,000 countrymen allowed to visit the beach will conscientiously collect for the good of the country as opposed to those among them who will go through the motions while actually only seeking to lounge about and improve his suntan? The answer is this: you don't have to determine anything. If you have 10,000 people visit the beach and shake out their towels afterwards, you will get your desired intelligence no matter what else you do, and you also will get the intelligence no matter what you don't do. Rubber rafts may overturn in the surf, and satellites may malfunction; but 10,000 potential collectors *will* provide a good net intelligence return, even if it may be of uneven quality and quantity when considered at the individual level. If you work with large enough numbers, you don't have to supervise the activities of individuals, for "actuarial" principles will take over.

In almost all countries that seek to locate and take away by fair means or foul U.S. open-source, proprietary, or even classified information, the task of physically laying hands upon the desired data and making off with it usually is directed and controlled by intelligence officers. The "consumers" of intelligence back in the home country tell their government ministries what they need, the ministries establish collection requirements for their intelligence officers in the U.S., and those officers in turn attempt either to collect the desired items themselves or use agents they have developed for just such a purpose. If all goes well, the collected information works its way back to the consumers in the home country.

The strengths of this system are that it is relatively secure, it is centrally directed, it uses intelligence professionals who can do their business with minimal time and effort, and it can collect a large amount of information using a small number of people. In other words, it is designed to be efficient. The weaknesses of this approach are that, often enough, there are not enough intelligence officers or intelligence agents to collect all the items that are requested, what is collected is not exactly what was asked for, it can take too long to accomplish the collection, and interference by the FBI or a similar counterintelligence agency can wipe out large portions of the overall effort in a single stroke. In other words, this professional effort at times is not as effective as the consumers of its intelligence product would like it to be. For such an effort to become more effective, it probably would have to utilize more people and have them work faster and less carefully, meaning that they would be less secure from discovery and ultimately would be working less efficiently. There thus may be a diametric trade-off between efficiency and effectiveness in intelligence operations, with improvements on one side coming only at the expense of the other.

What we in the FBI noticed some time ago was that the Chinese collection efforts we discovered and dismantled had some interesting features in common: the individuals attempting to collect restricted technology or information usually intended to use it themselves, they almost always had sought out the assistance of local Chinese-Americans, they most often tried to collect only small amounts of intelligence, and they did not appear to be under the direction or control of intelligence officers either in the U.S. or China. It was a genuine "cottage industry", and it appeared to have bypassed completely the normal channels in which consumers of intelligence would register their needs with the central authorities and then wait for the desired information to come rolling in. The intelligence officers were in the overall picture, but only in a supporting role, not in the command position the FBI is accustomed to finding them. The intelligence officers often enough were involved in establishing social relationships with the Chinese-Americans involved in the cases, and in some instances the intelligence officers had introduced the Chinese-Americans to the intelligence consumers, but only at the request of the consumers.

Another genuine phenomenon we discovered was that the intelligence officers always ended up establishing social relationships with far more individuals than they ever could hope would become involved in collection activities. This confirmed our belief that the Chinese often enough have a very inefficient approach to intelligence.

I'm sure you see where I am heading with this argument. The picture looks somewhat different when looked at through the prism of guanxi as the organizing structure for both the social behavior and the intelligence behavior observed. By forming social relationships with the Chinese-Americans, the intelligence officers essentially put them "on the map" in terms of guanxi networks. The consumers of intelligence used their connections with the intelligence officers to obtain access to the services of the Chinese-Americans, whom they had not met before. It is necessary to forge guanxi links with as large a number of individuals as possible, since it is not possible to predict the who, what, or when of the favors that may be requested. Not to be forgotten is that the impetus for exchange of favors comes most often as a direct result of actions undertaken by intelligence consumers out to do their own collecting, so no central direction of the overall effort is required.

In counterintelligence eyes, the Chinese collection effort often enough appears to be extremely inefficient in terms of the numbers of people involved, the relative lack of the security brought about by lack of central direction or control, the redundant activities of many of the participants, and the inherent awkwardness of having a large group of people collect small bits of information. In my opinion, the effort appears to be inefficient because it indeed *is* inefficient, and that inefficiency is brought on by the reliance on guanxi as the vehicle through which to accomplish collection.

Guanxi networks, however, are vehicles designed to help individuals overcome unknown future problems reliably, not quickly. As a social mechanism, the Chinese system clearly was built for distance, not speed. It appears to be inherently inefficient but also inherently effective in solving problems. It seems reasonable to conclude that the Chinese use the guanxi model rather than a "normal" approach to intelligence gathering because it simply outperforms the "normal" methodology that other countries utilize.

In my opinion, the evidence is compelling that guanxi networks are a deeply flawed intelligence mechanism. This is owing to the fact that they are really not an intelligence mechanism at all. They are a social mechanism which can be "borrowed" to do intelligence work. As a social mechanism guanxi evidently produces a product that is virtually guaranteed when enough people participate to bring "actuarial" principles to bear. It is a powerful force in Chinese social behavior.

Glossary: English, Chinese, Vietnamese, Sanskrit

The Pinyin transliteration system of Chinese used in the PRC is in **bold** type; Wade-Giles transliterations are in *italics*. Some Chinese characters are taken from Soothill's *A Dictionary of Chinese Buddhist Terms* (Kegan Paul, London 1937).

Amidaism: a form of Japanese Buddhism which focuses on Amida, a Bodhisattva. (see Bodhisattva.)

Ancestor worship: Ji Zu (4385 4371) 祭 祖 This well known, but often misunderstood phrase refers to the historical emphasis placed on Chinese, Japanese, Korean, and Vietnamese family ceremonies to convey respect, duty, and obligations one owes to one's parents and family elders, dead or alive. The family ceremony honoring these values is celebrated during the Spring Festival and usually combines sweeping and cleaning of the family gravesites and/or the family ceremonies before the family lineage tablet. Thus, while the ancestors are honored but not literally worshipped, such ceremonies also propitiate them to avoid their ill-will and to ensure their wellbeing in their fading existence after death.

Bodhisattva: Pu Sa (5476 5646) 菩 薩 A Mahāyāna Buddhist deity who has progressed up the optional ladder of possible rebirths (see) and has attained the position from which he/she/it can attain Nirvāṇa and cease being connected with the world (saṃsāra). However, out of quality of compassion for all other living, sentient beings, the Bodhisattva has vowed to refrain from Nirvāṇa and remains interactive with all suffering beings to help them through his/her/its various methods (Upāyas) to attain Nirvāṇa after which time the Bodhisattva will then, and only then, go to

Nirvāṇa as well. Three popular Bodhisattvas are Amitābha (*O-mi-tuo Fo* in China, Amida Butsu in Japan) and *Guanyin* (*Kwanyin* in China, Avalokitesvara in India, Kwannon in Japan), and *Mi-Le Fo*, the fat-belly "Buddha" whose laughing round face and body is often found in popular statues. This genial popular religious figure appeared only in the Song dynasty (960–1280 A.D.) and usually has a sack and is surrounded by children who are good-naturedly trying to catch and trick him.

Buddhism: Fojiao (0154 2403) 佛 教 One of the major religious, philosophical, and cultural forces to spread through all of Asia. Its founder, Gotoma Siddhārtha , became know as the Buddha, the "Enlightened One", after his enlightenment experience (buddhi) in the fifth century B.C. Subsequently, the Buddha's teachings (Dharma, Pali: Dhamma) slowly spread throughout Asia. Today, the percentages of Buddhists in the following countries are approximately: China: 7%, Japan: 78%, Korea: 45%, India: .07%, Malaysia: 12%, Thailand: 94%, Myanmar (Burma): 88%, Śrī Lanka: 67%, Laos 60%. For example, there are at least three sizable Buddhist centers in the greater Washington, D.C., area.

Boryokudan: Known popularly as "Yakuza", Boryokudan is the preferred name for Japanese organized crime groups (literally, "the violent ones") and is the popular Japanese name for organized crime syndicates. Yakuza, "The Losers", consists of the numerical combination of a losing hand at a Japanese card game.

Ch'an Buddhism: (See **Zen Buddhism**)

***Chi*: Qi** (3051) 氣 Refers to one's vital energies, life force, breath, and a material force, too, when used as a term in medicine or martial arts.

Clock: The character for clock, **Zhong** (6945) 鍾 pronounced in Mandarin Chinese sounds the same (homophonous) as "end", that is, death, and is to be avoided.

Collectivism vs. Individualism: a contrasting feature of Chinese and much of Asian cultures in which greater emphasis is placed upon interests of the collective group than on the interests of the individual. "Individualism pertains to societies in which the ties between individuals are loose: everyone is expected to look after himself or herself and his or her immediate family. Collectivism … pertains to societies in which people from birth onwards are integrated into strong cohesive ingroups, which throughout people's lifetimes continue to protect them in exchange for unquestioning loyalty." (Geert Hofstede, *Cultures and Organizations*, Chapter 3, p. 51ff.)

Americans are generally considered the most individualistic culture in the world; Chinese are among the most collectivist.

Confucius: Kong FuZi "Master Koong" (1313 1133 1311) 孔夫子 Confucius, a highly educated, traveling teacher of social and ethical philosophy, lived from about 551 B.C. To 479 B.C. and founded one of the three major intellectual, ethical, social, and political traditions that influenced all of East Asia and Southeast Asia. For much of Chinese history, Chinese Daoists and the Buddhists (after 200 A.D.) acted in accordance with or in opposition to the developing Confucian traditions. The improtance and influence of the Confucian and Neo-Confucian traditions in all of Asia cannot be overstated.

Contextual pragmatism: (See **Fang Bian**.)

Culture (See **Mindsets**.)

Daoism, *Taoism*, Daojiao (6670 2403) 道 教 Traditionally, Daoism is one of the three major strands of religious and philosophical development during 2500 years of Chinese history. Some of its main emphasis are a gentle sense of naturalness, aesthetic simplicity, a rejection of Confucian authoritarianism, and complex social arrangements.

Fa: Law and Criminal Law (3127) 法 Both Chinese and Americans have thought of law in a pragmatic, utilitarian sense where great emphasis is placed upon the rule-driven ideas of law as a way to maintain public order. However, we also tend to think of law as derived from a transcendental (Judaic-Christian) source, Natural Law, linked together in a logical, rational way; we also think of law as highlighting a higher human morality reflecting human aspirations in humankind for survival and protection. In particular, we tend to think of civil law as protecting the individual against the State and the powerful (due process), where law is (in theory) applied in a fair and equitable manner and conviction must be proven in systematic ways which are socially, ethnically, and gender neutral. Particularly among the Chinese Legalists, there was an element of rule-driven law most Anglo-Europeans would recognize instantly, but on closer inspection would find that such Chinese law usually represented what the rulers arbitrarily wanted and dictated. Thus "law" was usually associated with punishment, applied with regard to one's social rank, and was to be avoided at all costs. However, the exceedingly powerful traditions of Confucian morality played a much more influential role in Chinese history than did any explicit law and/or any nationally sanctioned legal system. In fact, the latter two could hardly be said to exist when compared with the long historical traditions of Anglo-Saxon common law, Napoleonic law, the general Anglo-European evolution of penal law, and the recent invention of professional law enforcement officers. For the most part, Chinese put more faith in the hope of ethically motivated, flexible, and fair administrators than in the nonhuman, mechanically applied rule of law. Thus, within the admirable scope of Chinese civilization and its primary emphasis upon moral awareness and ethical self-cultivation, there is no significant intellectual equivilant of the systemic, rule-governed, checks-and-balance, precedent-driven tradition of either the consistent content, culture-driven acceptance, and quasi-Euclidean style of our fairly coherent legal system.

Face: Mianzi (7240 1311) 面 子 Most Asians, particularly the Chinese, Japanese, Korean, and Vietnamese put great emphasis upon maintaining recognizable personal characteristics which constitute one's dignity, integrity, status, and self-respect. In any social situation, one has a built-in self-interest in maintaining one's own "face", and, with "face", one has a built-in interest in preserving everyone else's "face", This mutual maintenance of "face" preserves the fabric of social coherence and stability. Thus, tact, understatement, polite courtesy, and an occasional "white lie" to save "face" all contribute to interpersonal social stability. Losing "face" is a very severe experience to be avoided at all costs. Thus, avoiding confrontation and allowing everyone to save "face" is strongly supported.

Fangbian: *fang pien* (2455 0189) 方 便 Pragmatic contextualism is the author's interpretation of one of the cultural influences of the fundamental philosophical and religious Mahāyāna Buddhist technical term: Sanskrit: upāya , Chinese: *fang bian*, Japanese: hōben , Tibetan: thabs. The term " upāya " can be paraphrased as "skilled in alternative contextually appropriate means to help others towards Nirvāṇa ." A Bodhisattva — for example, the male Indian Avalokiteśvara or female Chinese Kuanyin and Japanese Kwannon — has many skillful means of adjusting his/her messages to fit the circumstances of the human situation. This idea of "skillful means" is taken to mean that god(s), Bodhisattva, or divine agencies use benevolent strategies, ploys, devices, and/or religious deceptions that change throughout many different lifetimes. This habit of mind has become an integral part of Asian "deep cultural grammars", ways of processing and judging the relationships of information. The fang bian-driven process is experienced as the obvious, common-sense awareness of one's need to judge things in relation to time, place, history, dominant personalities, and long-term social effects of one's decisions on those to whom one has strong obligations and with whom one is socially intimate. In practice, the acculturated Buddhist conceptual habit of upāya /fang bian silently supports the occasional circumvention of the letter of the law, telling the truth and whole truth regardless of the consequences, by using one's talents, luck, and loyalty to one's social guanxi mentors.

Fatalism: a general idea and/or attitude that certain peoples feel that life is largely preordained, that one is generally helpless to alter the future in any significant way, and that one should resign oneself to accepting what happens with an attitude of tolerance and little hope for actions which might prevent certain future events. This is not a true attribute of Asians. Nor is it true of future-oriented Americans for whom optimism about the possibility of altering the future is a cultural article of faith. (Also, see **Fate.**)

Fate, Buddhist: ming (0730) 命 Fate means "destiny", a partial sense of predestination and "that's the way things are". Fate was what can and might happen if one did not take steps such as prayer or formal sacrifice to thwart the approaching situation. It was not the "fate" decreed by God or by Buddhist karma. Thus, good intentions and acting at the right time could allow one to escape a careful prediction of future disaster. Good timing and clever precautions might well master the possibility of an unwanted event. (Also see **Karma(n)** and **Rebirth.**)

Feng shui: (See **Geomancy.**)

Filial piety: Xiao, *hsiao* (1321) 孝 Vietnamese: hieu: Filial piety is a major Chinese and Vietnamese ethical virtue in which formal respect, total loyalty, complete support, and lifelong obedience during the whole of one's parents lives are praised and practiced. Taken on occasion to great lengths, the combination of worship of the ancestors (see) coupled with the great respect shown for age, arranged marriages, the subordination of the individual to the group goals, and the absolute rule (in theory) of the senior male made this value paramount in traditional Chinese societies throughout the world. These ranked relationships can be seen in the famous five relationships of Confucius, namely: (1) kind benevolence in the ruler and loyalty among those ruled, (2) respect and honor for the elders and respectful deference in the younger toward the elders, (3) the father's kindly but stern wisdom coupled with filial piety and obedience in the children, (4) gentility in the eldest brother and respectful humility in the younger brothers and sisters (Vietnamese: de), and (5) righteous behavior in the husband and obedience and proper deference in his wife. Note that these relationships are not relations between equals, but between persons neither of equal worth nor with equal opportunities.

Gangbangers: Common name for members of any street gang or pickup home-invasion gang.

Geomancy: Fengshui, *Fung shui* (7364 3055; 0594 0592) 風 水 Geomancy, a complex set of ancient Chinese ideas and practices reputed to be as old as the 10th century B.C., consists of a body of knowledge and calculated recommendations to ensure that gravesites, construction sites, buildings, architecture, furniture, and other positioned things are placed in harmony with the natural forces and environmental contours of the earth. These natural forces are symbolized by dragons and other semi-mythological beasts of the countryside.

Guanxi: *Kuan-hsi* (See **Networking-Connections.**)

Hungry Ghosts, Holiday or Feast of the: Gui Jie (7607 4634) 鬼 节 (See Holiday, Chapter 17.)

High-context vs. low-context cultures: A high-context culture is one in which — for cultural comfort — most of the needed information is already known to the senders and receivers. Relatively little explicit additional information is required or expected in most everyday situations. A low context culture is just the opposite; substantial amounts of the needed information between persons and institutions is not felt to be already known to the senders and receivers. Thus, in a low-context culture, a relatively greater amount of information is required and *expected* to be made explicit. Rural Asians and most urban Asians live in a relatively conformist, homogenous local culture — in a village or small town setting where "everybody knows everybody and everybody's business" and "everybody knows the rules of the game". Most North American police live and work in a low-context culture, where we rely on formal agreements, an explicit chain of evidence, and contracts more often than in many Asian traditions, especially Chinese and Vietnamese.

Hinduism: a general name for a widely differing range of religious beliefs and practices in India or by people of Indian descent who follow the traditional Dharma, the Sanskrit-based beliefs of the Vedas, the later sacred writings (smrti), and caste-based practices of Indian society for over 2700 years. Some major religious deities are Śiva, Vishnu, Krishna, Gaṇesha, and Braḥman; some examples of the most widely known literature are the *Vedas, Upaṇishads,* the *Bhagavad Gīta*, and the two huge epics, the *Rāmāyaṇa* and *Mahābhārata*.

Human heartedness-humanity: Ren, *Jen* (0088) 仁 Popularly, ren usually is taken to mean the basically good qualities of humane people, the inherent benevolence in all persons. However, the larger question about ren focuses on whether the essence of being human (ren) is basically good or evil. It is a central Chinese Confucian, Neo-Confucian, and Legalist inquiry echoing throughout Chinese history. As a generalization, most (but certainly not all) Chinese thinkers have agreed with Mencius that humans are born basically good but diverge in their behavior because of differences in education, experience, opportunities, and luck. One mainstream response was Confucian moral education through propriety (li), ethical self-reflection, and either universal love (mo-tzu) or graded love based on family relationships and responsibilities (Confucians). Thus, all people were equal only in so far as they were the wards of the benevolent ruler. A contrary response was the dual recommendations to strictly enforce punitive laws to thwart the basic but conflicting desires with which every human is born and the authoritarian belief that humans are basically selfish and only harsh laws and punishments representing the will of the ruler can overcome the chaos that will result if people do not act in accordance with both their social station and their obligations to authorities, whose will is absolute.

Kitchen god: Zao Wang, *Tsao Wang* (3501 3769) 灶 王

Law and criminal law (See **Fa**.)

Li (See **Propriety**.)

Losing Face: diu lian (0016 5245) 丟 臉 (See **Face**.)

Mindsets: As functional adults in a variety of global cultures, everyone generally operates within fairly coherent, consistent sets of ideas about the world. Whether we call these sets of ideas mindsets, cultures, or world views, we unconsciously use them — we swim in them — to make coherent, consistence sense of the world. We anticipate what will happen, who and what we are, and what we value by instantaneous reference to deeply buried but largely unconscious frameworks. Mindsets are those aspects of a cultural tradition we refer to when we examine the largely implicit frameworks of shared ideas, beliefs, social expectations, habits of mind. An important part of a cultural mindset is one's assumptions about the physical and mental furniture of one's self, the relationships between body and mind, and the relations and expectations between self and the world.

A mindset is a "conceptual grammar". That is, cultural frameworks function as grammars function. Grammars describe, shape, and mold a language and also act as reference points to which we refer to get bearings on what can be said, what ought to be said, how to say it, and how to come to know what it means. Thus, culture refers to an integrated, fairly coherent, consistent grammar, a series of overlapping mindsets through which we see ourselves and the world. It is a web of practices (symbols, heroes, rituals), ideas of one's "self" and its characteristics (national, ethnic, generational, class, employment, gender), personality, relationships (between self and society, masculinity and femininity, youth and age, control of aggression, the expression of anger and feelings), and core values/norms.

Mooncake Festival: Zhong Qiu Jie (0022 4428 4634) 中秋 节 (See Holidays, Chapter 17.)

Networking-Connections: Guanxi: *Kuanhsi* (7070 0910) 關係 Both Chinese and North Americans have guanxi networks. North Americans use and support family relations, ancestral ties, old school ties, fraternity and GDI connections, teammates, social and business obligations, duties and debts owed, continuing business deals, co-workers, "back-door" power, etc. Chinese guanxi has additional components that offer greater breadth, depth, and options regarding potential sources of criminal guanxi such as ties of birthplace, village, same-surname associations, and especially dialect, in addition to economic brotherhoods (hui), refugee-camp connections, and other regional ties.

New Year, Chinese Lunar: Chun Jie 春 节 (Vietnamese Tet) (2504 4636); or **Chinese Lunar New Year's Day: Yuan Dan,** *Yuan Tan* (0337 2481) (See Holidays, Chapter 17; Chapter 18 for Vietnamese Holidays.)

Nirvāṇa: *nie pan* (0154 2857) 佛 和 Originally, this was a Sanskrit term for ultimate salvation in Buddhism and is usually taken to mean: (1) the stopping of all karmic forces, good or bad, from the past or present, where none are generated in the future and the cycles of rebirth cease; (2) rebirth in the benevolent, blissful heavens of a Mahāyāna Buddhist Bodhisattva where human problems do not exist, e.g., Amitābha's Western paradise.

Order, patterns in nature: (Vietnamese: ly) 理 The Vietnamese concept of ly, order, pattern, the fitness of things, and regularity in the physical universe is based on the eleventh century Neo-Confucian concept of li which has roughly the same meanings (see Chapter 18). The Chinese used li 3810 to translate the Buddhist Sanskrit "Yukti", reasoning and rationality. Thus, both the Vietnamese and the Chinese had a somewhat similar sense of the regularities and patterns of the world. However, the Vietnamese ly and Chinese li 3810 should not be confused with Chinese li 4409, propiety or ceremony.

PAEF (publicly available explanatory frameworks): PAEFs are collective visions of one's self and one's view of the world that are publicly available in the culture of one's mother language. The content and style of a culture that is public, available, and known by everyone in that particular culture are not the same across the world. Simply put, as functional adults everyone operates with and within fairly coherent, consistent frameworks of ideas by means of which we mature and learn adult rules of the game. All of us have implicit mindsets by means of which we are conscious of ourselves and with which we: (1) try to understand the past, (2) function in the present, (3) anticipate the future, and (4) try to make sense of the world. The content of what is publicly avaliable to a person in a given culture differs considerably throughout the world.

PRC: People's Republic of China (mainline China).

Propriety: Chinese: Li (4409) 理 Propriety, ceremony, or behavioral harmony (Chinese: li; Vietnamese: ly) refers to the proper ways of behaving and thinkings which lead to proper knowledge which leads to proper collective social action. This relationship of propriety (li) was thought to be the behavioral channel through which the humane but natural biological urges and social needs of humans could be shaped and given harmonious behavioral expression as the best of human-heartedness (Chinese: ren, 0088). Because of this, manners, style, and knowledgeable social skills are viewed as both ethical reflections of the very human person behind the face and are not viewed as artificial, put on, or unnatural. In short, human manners and propriety count. The learned development of one's natural good-heartedness is compatible with the recognition of the dark side of human behavior as well as the deliberate development of the best in human behavior by means of an all-pervasive moral sense of human-to-human social manners and self-cultivated, ethical self-knowledge expressed in proper behavior.

Pinyin: The system of transliteration (not translation) adopted within the PRC in which the sounds of Chinese words and names are approximated by English letters. This contrasts with the older Wade-Giles system preferred by the ROC in Taiwan and in much of contemporary academic circles. Drs. Herbert A. Giles and Lionel Giles were British diplomats and academics at the turn of the century who devised a transliteration system strongly related to English. The Pinyin system of the PRC exhibits relationships more akin to European languages than English and is gradually becoming the dominant transliteration system.

Ren (See **Human-heartedness-humanity.**)

Reincarnation: (6034 0936) 業 因 Usually, an Anglo-European interpretation of the Buddhist or Hindu terms "karman" or "gati", destinies after one's death to which one is "re-born". Karma is the general belief about the rebirth of an individual in a form appropriate to the accumulative combination of karmic causal forces he/she generated in this life and in previous lifetimes. The Buddhist traditions generally hold that only a Buddha or a Bodhisattva is aware of his/her/its previous lives; almost all humans are ignorant of them. The particular form of the reborn individual may be one of many different destinies: human, animal, being in hell, etc. Prior to the introduction of Buddhism about 200 A.D., there were no such ideas in China.

ROC (Republic of China): The ethnically Chinese government of Taiwan which fled mainland China in 1947 and 1948 as Mao Zedong's communist government gained control. The PRC claims that Taiwan is a part of China and has vowed to reclaim it.

Superior Man: Junzi (0689 1311) 君 子 A Confucian term to characterize the ethically perfected man, the ideal, perfected man in whom learning, ranked respect, authority, propriety, compassion, and ethical wisdom are balanced.

STC Standard Telegraphic Code: STC is a 100-year-old public code which matches a Chinese character with a number. A number is easier to convey in most modern communication systems than are Chinese characters. The way a Chinese word or character is pronounced — the way it sounds — has no relation to the way it is written. However, the pronunciation of the Chinese ideograph or character is dependent on the Chinese dialect spoken. In other words, the way a Chinese character is written tells us absolutely nothing about how it is properly pronounced. Furthermore, upon hearing the sound of a Chinese character, different people will use quite different English letters to try to recreate the Chinese pronunciation. For example, take the word or character for the common Chinese name "Wang" (STC 3769), which means "king". This has been transliterated in many different ways such as Wang or Wong. STC provides a code by which to switch from nonalphabetic language to representation of Chinese sounds and identify Chinese characters (ideographs) in our alphabetic language. We use STC numbers to make those switches with accuracy and relative ease. This switch is accomplished by matching a specific Chinese/Japanese character or ideograph with a number within the STC code. The use of STC numbers is justified by the fact that they can be more easily transmitted by most telecommunication systems than the nonalphabetic Chinese/Japanese characters.

Thien: Vietnamese Buddhist form of the religious sect known in China as Ch'an and in Japan as Zen; these terms are translations of the Sanskrit word *dhyana*, a level or stage of consciousness in Indian Buddhist meditation. This sect did not exist in India, the birthplace of Buddhism.

Tong: Teng (1016) 堂 The word Tong means "hall" or "meeting place". Tongs were founded in the mid-1800s by Chinese workers and merchants through Triad, shared surname, and other ethnic connections. They were North American self-help organizations which, as with Triads, grew more secretive and more oriented towards criminal activities as their size and power increased. Family name associations and family groups aligned themselves with a specific Tong for protection and individuals aligned themselves to increase the range of their guan xi relationships. Of the over 30 Tongs in the U.S., some strive to fulfill their original benevolent goals, but some are largely bent toward illegal activities in close affiliations with Triads and loose affiliations with street gangs. Professor Ko-Lin Chin's book is an excellent source for Triads and Tongs.

Triads ("Heaven and Earth [Secret] Societies") Tian di hui: (1131 0966 2585) 天 地 會 During the late seventeenth century, groups of Shaolin Buddhist monks had been of considerable help to the authorities. However, according to Triad folklore, when the monks fell out of favor, their monastery was attacked and 108 Chinese Buddhist monks were murdered during a vain attempt to defend their monastery. The five surviving monks formed the basis of the five earliest Triad secret societies which are symbolized by a triangular flag, signifying earth, man, and heaven. The original Triad goals were to overthrow the Qing (*Ch'ing*) dynasty of the conquering Manchu invaders and restore the Ming dynasty. Over many years, their patriotic agendas dwindled as violent criminal elements infiltrated them. With the overthrow of the Qing dynasty in 1912, their subversive activities gradually grew to benefit the powerful members of the Triad. They participated in gambling, narcotics, prostitution, and other illegal activities.

While some Triad organizations direct criminal activities, their major function is to furnish a range of contacts with whom individuals may establish short- or long-term criminal relations. Thus, if members of two separate Triads are seen talking to each other, it does not always follow that both Triads are engaged in developing new criminal activities. With the establishment of the People's Republic of China by Mao Zedong in 1949, Traid members fled to Taiwan, Hong Kong, and other parts of East and Southeast Asia where their criminal activities have increased and prospered. There are allegations that some rogue elements of the PRC government have entered into mutually beneficial arrangements with Triad members. Consequently, the use of a multiple of 108 in a Asian gang member's request for money to a Chinese merchant suggests a Triad connection on the part of the speaker. As a result of the widespread fear of the Triads among most traditional Chinese, this indirect reference to a Triad increases the level of intimidation. (Consult Morgan and Ko-Lin Chin's works in the suggested readings.)

Wade-Giles: (See **Pinyin**.)

Yakuza (See **Boryokudan**.)

Zen Buddhism: a Japanese sect of Buddhism known in China as *Ch'an* and in Vietnam as Thien. These terms are translations of the Sanskrit word *dhyana*, a level or stage of consciousness in Indian Buddhist meditation. This sect did not exist in India, the birthplace of Buddhism, nor was Zen ever particularly popular (except for intellectuals and visiting Americans) in Japan as was, for example, Jōdo Shin Shū, the Pure Land Sect. Zen is primarily known in the West through the writings of D.T. Suzuki, Allan Watts and other metaphysical shoppers and consumers of the "mysteries of the Orient."

Endnotes

1. Asian Organized Crime, Hearings Before the Permanent Subcommittee on Investigations of the Committee on Governmental Affairs, the U.S. Senate, October 3, November 5-9, 1991, p. 64. Underlining is that of the author.
2. Stewart, Edward C., and Bennett, Milton J., American Cultural Patterns: a Cross-Cultural Perspective, Intercultural Press, Inc., Yarmouth, Maine, U.S.A., 1991, ISBN: 1-877864-01-3.
3. Schoenberger, Karl, "Networking Pays Off for Chinese," Los Angeles Times, April 6, 1994, pp. A1 and A8.
4. Tharoor, Shashi, "Growing Up Extreme," Washington Post, July 25, 1993, p. C5. This perspective regarding Black Americans/Afro-Americans and their attitudes towards Africa was also illustrated in an extremely courageous article by Keith B. Richburg in the Sunday Washington Post Magazine, March 26, 1995, pp.17-21, 30-32.
5. Hearings on Asian Organized Crime, U.S. Senate, Committee on Governmental Affairs, Permanent Subcommittee on Investigations, October 3, 1993.
6. Hammer, Michell R. And Weaver, Gary, "Cross-Cultural Considerations in Hostage Negotiations," a lecture by Professor Hammer entitled "Cultural Considerations in Crisis Situations," at the SIETAR International 20th Anniversary World Lecture Series, sponsored by the Calgary Chapter of SIETAR-International, at the Chief Crowfoot Training Academy, Calgary, Alberta, Canada, October 22, 1993, p.8.
7. "The Numbers Game," Time, Vol. 142, No. 21, Fall, 1993, Special Issue, p.15.
8. Ungar, Sanford J., "Counting Us In", a book review of "Who We Are: a Portrait of America Based on the Latest U.S. Census", by Sam Roberts, Times Books, 306 pp. Washington Post, Vol. 14. No. 15, April 10, 1994, p.2.
9. See note 8 above.
10. Hofstede, *Cultures and Organizations: Software of the Mind,* McGraw-Hill, Maidenhead, England, 1991, ISBN: 0-07-707474-2, p. 13.

11. Sowell, Thomas, *Race and Culture: a World View*, Basic Books, New York, 1994, pp. 224-229 (ISBN: 0-465-06796-4).
12. Sowell, Thomas, Race and Culture: A World View, p. 132.
13. Sowell, Thomas, Race and Culture: A World View, p. 159.
14. Sowell, Thomas, Race and Culture: A World View, p. 170.
15. Sowell, Thomas, Race and Culture: A World View, p. 169.
16. To illustrate and confirm this, I counted at least 63% recognizably West European names and only 7% recognizably Asian names in the *1991-1992 Directory* of the International Association of Asian Crime Investigators.
17. *Washington Post*, July 28, 1992, Health Section, p. 5.
18. Meyers, Willard. H., Trans-national Ethnic Chinese Organized Crime: a Global Challenge to the Security of the U.S., Testimony before the Senate Foreign Relations Committee/Terrorism, Narcotics and International Operations Committee, April 21, 1994, Federal Document Clearing House, Washington, DC, Lexis:Nexis, Services of Mead Data Central, Inc.
19. Flanagan, Edward J., Interviewing and interrogation techniques, in *Criminal and Civil Investigation Handbook*, 2nd ed., Grau, Joseph J., and Jacobson, Ben, Eds., McGraw-Hill, 1993, pp.20-3–20-21 (ISBN: 0-07-024156-2).

20a. Imbau, Fred E., Reid, John E., and Buckley, Joseph P., *Criminal Interrogation and Confession,* 3rd ed., Williams and Wilkins, Baltimore, 1986 (ISBN: 0-683-04305-6). Another useful description is that found in Reference 19.

20b. John E. Reid and Associates, Inc., 250 South Wacker Drive, Suite 1100, Chicago, Illinois 60606 (1-800-255-5747).

21. I take it that the precedent on trickery and deceit on which I base this recommendation about the strength of evidence is *Frazier* vs. *Cupp;* 394, U.S., 731 (1969) and in Canada, Rothman, V., *The Queen,* 59 C.C.C. 2nd ed., 30, 1981. States cases sanctioning trickery and deceit are discussed in *Criminal Interrogation and Confession*, see note 20a.
22. See note 8 above.
23. In Chapter 10, standards, definitions, and possible reasons for gang membership are taken from the lectures of Sergeant Tom Purdue, San Francisco Police Department, and past president of the International Association of Asian Crime Investigators. (However, neither Sergeant Purdue nor the San Francisco Police Department are responsible for the content of these remarks; the author bears sole responsibility.)
24. Hannum, Philip, and Lotz, Al, *Nightmare: Vietnamese Home Invasion Robberies, Selected Interstate Cases: 1987-92* an ocassional paper of the International Association of Asian Crime Investigators. Also see William Cassidy's *Fundamentals of Nomadic Vietnamese Armed Robbery Investigation* and Jack Willoughby's *Vietnamese Traveling Criminals.*
25. McKenna, John, The science of the Orient, in *IAACI News*, 8(1), 5-6, January, 1994 (publication of the International Association of Asian Crime Investigators).

26. McKenna, John, The science of the Orient," p. 6.
27. See note 26 above.
28. I am ready to be refuted on specific points or to stand corrected in general — if and only if the counter arguments and the nonsingular mass of counter-examples replicate the level of cross-cultural sophistication exhibited here.
29. The late Mr. David Collier, retired CIA intelligence officer, stated: "The American person says 'To thine own self be true;' The Chinese person says, To the expectations of thine own neighbor be true.'
30. Fukuyama, Francis, Social capital and global economy, in *Foreign Affairs*, September/October, 1995, p.89.
31. This quote and many points of discussion of Chinese views of individuality vs. self-restraint and attitudes toward authority are taken from an unpublished draft of comments by Mr. David Ellsworth Collier, Retired CIA Officer, some of which have been incorporated (with permission) by M. Cordell Hart in his *Chinese* (formerly *Dealing with Chinese*). M. Cordell Hart is a mid-level manager, Financial Crimes Enforcement Network (FinCEN), Department of the Treasury, a former president of the International Association of Asian Crime Investigators, and a former Federal intelligence officer. In addition to Mr. Collier, other contributors to Hart's *Chinese* (1991, FCEN90STO126, Washington, D.C.) were Christopher Ballou, William Donnett, George Harkin, and James Schnell. This is an excellent 20-page introduction to aspects of Chinese culture and is a valuable tool for law enforcement personnel. The address of M. Cordell Hart is Financial Crimes Enforcement Network (FinCEN), 2070 Chainbridge Road, VA 22182, telephone: (703) 905-3662.
32. Carment, William, cited in Bond, Michael H., *Beyond the Chinese Face: Insights from Psychology*, Oxford University Press, Hong Kong, 1991, p.50-60.
33. Perhaps the best translation is *The Scripture of the Lotus Blossom of the Fine Dharma: (The Lotus Sūtra),* translated from the Chinese of Kumārajīva by Leon Hurvitz, Columbia University Press, New York, 1976 (ISBN: 0-231-03920-4).
34. Lee Kuan Yew, quoted in "An elder statesman surveys Asia's future", *Business Week*, November 29, 1993, p.108.
35. The content enclosed in brackets have been added by the author and are not part of Mr. Hart's text.
36. Hall, Edward T., and Hall, Mildred Reeds, *Understanding Cultural Differences*, Intercultural Press, Yarmouth, ME, 1989, p.62ff. (Words in the brackets are the author's).
37. Blustein, Paul, Forging greater China: emigres help build an economic power, *Washington Post*, November 29, 1993, p. C2.
38. Senate Hearings on Asian Organized Crime, Committee on Governmental Affairs, Permanent Subcommittee on Investigations, October 3, November 5 and 6, 1991, Washington, D.C. I have quoted comments prepared by the Subcommittee staff to which I have made a very few editorial and rhetorical changes.

39. This completes the author's uses of the Senate Hearings on Asian Organized Crime, 1991 (see Reference 38).

40. LaMagna, Richard C., Special Agent, Drug Enforcement Administration, Hong Kong Country Office, in *IAACI News*, 8(8), 1,9, May/June 1995.

41. The following paragraphs are not part of the text of the U.S. Senate Hearings on Asian Organized crime and have been added by the author to supplement what is generally known about illegal Chinese criminal activities but not included in the Senate report.

42. Human cargo is hugely profitable to New York's Chinese underworld, *Washington Post*, June 7, 1993, p. A10.

43. Sun, Lena H., Illegal Chinese immigrants arrive home: punishment unlikely, *Washington Post*, July 20, 1993, p. A14.

44. Meyers, Willard H., "Illuminating the Black Economy", Ethnic Chinese Transnational Enterprise Crime and U.S. National Security Interests: Reconciliation or Redefinition?", [No date given]. p. 8 and pp. 31-35; see also previous note 18.

45. See previous note 18.

46. See previous note 18.

47. *Straits Times*, May 31, 1993, and January 18, 1994.

48. CSAOC Intelligence Briefs: Spring/Summer 1995, *IAACI News*, 8(8), 5-7, May/June 1995.

49. See previous note 44.

50. Cao, Glen, *Beijinger in New York*, (transl. by Ted Wang), China Books, 2929 24th St., San Francisco, CA 94110, 1993 (ISBN: 0-8351-2526-2). The theme of the fanatically hardworking immigrant who succeeds financially but loses the warmth and personal security of family and the home culture is a recurring theme in many immigrant novels. The success of such themes is usually based on a combination of cross-cultural voyeurism about immense financial and material wealth and cultural oddities (e.g. strip dancing is a legitimate profession in the U.S.) within which the defects of the target society are contrasted with the contrasting virtues of the homeland. When coupled with a sentimentalized "sob story" in which the warmth and virtues of home are praised and dire woes befall the native-born, the message of the *Wizard of Oz — the best place is that at home* — seldom fails to win favor and fame in the home country even while thousands are fleeing and scrambling to get into the target country by any means. This theme exemplifies the naiveté of the immigrant who fails to realize that everything will change when all of the cultural rules of the game also change and that you cannot have it both ways.

51. Human cargo is hugely profitable to New York's Chinese underworld, *Washington Post*, July 20, 1993, pp. A10, A14.

52. Personal communication from M. Cordell Hart.

53. Human cargo is hugely profitable to New York's Chinese underworld," *Washington Post*, July 20, 1993, pp. A10, A14.

54. Court ruling could spur new wave of immigration from China, *Washington Post*, January 30, 1994, p. A1.
55. Zielenziger, Michael, The new Asian empire: a Mercury News special report, *San Jose Mercury News*, June 26-29, 1994, p.1.
56. Sinclair, Kevin, and Wong Po-yee, Iris, *Culture Shock: China!*, Graphics Arts Center Publishing, Portland, OR, 1990, p.12ff.
57. Bonavia, David, *The Chinese: a Portrait*, Penguin Books, London, 1982, p.16.
58. Examples abound, but here is a representative sample. "In California, there are also 800,000 Toishan folk, many of them fourth generation Americans... Thailand has at least eight million Chinese. The six million citizens of Hong Kong are 98 percent Chinese. The Philippines has three million. The people of bustling Singapore are 75% Chinese, and in Malaysia, 35% of the fold are of Chinese decent. In Calgary [Canada].. There are 42,000 Chinese. Lima in Peru has three Cantonese-language radio stations and there are Chinese daily newspapers in Sydney and Melbourne [Australia]. In Tahiti, 10% of the people are Chinese. And there are growing Chinatowns throughout the world from Amsterdam to Seattle."
59. "Anthropomorphic" means the projection of human qualities on something which is not necessarily human. For example, saying that the "plant knows that it should turn its branches towards the sun to maximize its chances for survival" is anthropomorphism. Humans know things; plants don't.
60. Pye, Lucian W., The China trade: making the deal, in *Harvard Business Review*, July-August, 1986, p.77ff.
61. See previous note 37.
62. See previous note 37.
63. These figures were supplied by Austin Kelly of Citicorp Services, Inc., Tampa, Florida, for the audience at his presentation on Asian Credit Card Cases at the Asian Crime Conference, jointly sponsored by the International Association of Asian Crime Investigators, the Criminal Justice Center, the University of Houston-Downtown, Texas, and the Bureau of Alcohol, Tobacco and Firearms, November 5, 1993, Houston, TX.
64. Sun, Lena H., China's new ideology: make money, not Marxism, *Washington Post*, July 27, 1993, pp. A1 and A12.
65. See note 64 above.
66. Thomas, Pierre, Illegal firearms imported from China, U.S. reports," *Washington Post*, March 9, 1994, p. A4.
67. Kotkin, Joel, *Tribes: How Race, Religion, and Identity Determine Success in the New Global Economy*, Random House, New York, 1992 (ISBN: 679-41282-4). See Chapter 6, The Spacemen Have Landed, pp. 165-200. He also published a summary article of materials from his book in the Washington Post, October 4, 1992, p. C1-2.

68. Kotkin, Joel, *Tribes: How Race, Religion, and Identity Determine Success in the New Global Economy,* p. 169.

69. Mufson, Steven, and Coll, Steve, China offers its oil riches on the open market, *Washington Post,* March 20, 1994, pp. A1, A34.

70. Suro, Robert, Study of immigrants finds Asians at top in science and medicine, *Washington Post,* April 18, 1994, p. A6.

71. See note 70 above.

72. Meyers, Willard H., Transnational Ethnic Chinese Organized Crime: a Global Challange to the Security of the U.S., Testimony Before the Senate Foreign Relations Committee/Terrorism, Narcotics and International Operations Committee, April 21, 1994, Federal Document Clearing House, Inc., Lexis:Nexis, Services of Mead Data Central, Inc.

73. Kotkin, Joel, *Tribes: How Race, Religion, and Identity Determine Success in the New Global Economy,* p. 170.

74. Funabashi, Y., Oksenberg, M. And Weis, H., *An Emerging China in a World of Interdependence,* Trilateral Commission, New York, May, 1994, p. 1.

75. Reischauer, Edwin O., and Fairbank, John K., *East Asia: The Great Tradition,* Houghton-Mifflin, Boston, MA, 1960, p. 19.

76. Reischauer, Edwin O., and Fairbank, John K., *East Asia: The Great Tradition,* p. 21.

77. Reischauer, Edwin O., and Fairbank, John K., *East Asia: The Great Tradition,* p. 23.

78. de Keijzer, Arne J., *The China Business Handbook,* Asian Business Communications, Ltd., Weston, CN, 1986, pp. 2-3.

79. King, Richard, and Schatzy, Sandra, *Coping with the Chinese,* Basil Blackwell Ltd., Oxford, 1991, p. 84.

80. King, Richard, and Schatzy, Sandra, *Coping with the Chinese,* p. 85.

81. Personal communication from Dr. Paul D. Moore.

82. Sinclair, Kevin, and Wong, Po-Yee, Iris, *Culture Shock: China!* Graphic Arts Center Publishing, Portland, OR, 1990, pp. 206-214, (ISBN: 1-55868-060-8).

83. Ho, David Y.F., Chinese patterns of socialization: a critical review, in *The Psychology of the Chinese People,* Bond, M.H., Ed., Oxford University Press, New York, 1987, pp. 1-37.

84. Bond, M.H., Ed., *The Psychology of the Chinese People,* Oxford University Press, New York, 1987, pp. 35-37.

85. Chin, Ko-Lin, *Chinese Subculture and Criminality: Non-Traditional Crime Groups in America,* Greenwood Press, Westport, CN, 1990, pp. 107-108 (ISBN: 0-313-27262-X). This work is probably the best introduction to Triads, Tongs, and Chinese gangs in New York.

86. See note 85 above.

87. Personal communication with M. Cordell Hart.

88. See note 85 above.
89. Meyers, Willard. H., Transnational Ethnic Chinese Organized Crime: A Global Challange to the Security of the U.S., Testimony before the Senate Foreign Relations Committee/Terrorism, Narcotics and International Operations Committee, April 21, 1994, Federal Document Clearing House, Inc., Lexis:Nexis, Services of Mead Data Central, Inc.
89a. Morgan, W. P., *Triad Societies in Hong Kong*, Govenment Press, Hong Kong, 1989, p. 99ff.
90. Sinclair, Kevin, and Wong Po-yee, Iris, *Culture Shock: China!*, p. 21ff.
91. Bond, M.H., Ed., *Beyond the Chinese Face: Insights from Psychology*, Oxford University Press, New York, 1991, p. 64 (ISBN: 0-19-585116-1).
92. In the tightly regulated and censored city-state of Singapore, the Singapore Repertory Theatre group ".. came up with what it called a revolutionary system of self-censorship to deal with a little bit of nudity in a play. A red light was installed at a corner of the stage to alert the audience to flesh-exposing scenes so people can shut their eyes until a bell indicates they can resume watching." This little gem of a cultural anomaly was noted in "American Teenager Awaits Canning in Orderly, Unbending Singapore," by William Branigin, *Washington Post*, April 13, 1994, p.A20.
93. Dikotter, Frank, *Sex, Culture and Modernity in China: Medical Science and the Construction of Sexual Identities in the Early Republican Period*, University of Haiwaii Press, Honolulu, 1995, (ISBN: 0-8248-1676-5).
94. The gap between the desires of the demanding body-as-physical-person (shen) and the calculating self-as-heart-affections-mind (xin) appears to be similar to traditional dualism of Anglo-European Cartesianism, mind vs. physical dualism, rationality and logic vs. emotion and intuition. This Anglo-European view of human beings is illustrated clearly in the popular *Star Trek* series, in the tensions and interplay between Spock, First Science Officer and Dr. McCoy, the physician. However, the Chinese dualism is not based on (two) similar ideas as found in Anglo-European, Western dualism. Thus, the reader would be wise not to read into the Chinese dualism many of the ideas and expectations associated with our ideas of mind/body, etc.
95. Elvin, Mark, Tales of shen and xin: body-person and heart-mind in China during the last 150 years, in *Fragments for a History of the Human Body*, Part II, Feher, Michel, Naddaff, Ramona, and Tazi, Nadia, Zone, Eds., Urzone, New York, 1989, pp. 266-349 (especially pp. 292 to 293ff).
96. Sinclair, Kevin, and Wong Po-yee, Iris, *Culture Shock: China!*, p. 213.
97. Chinese Swaddled, Not Coddled, *Washington Post*, June 30, 1993, pp. 1, 14.
98. Many details of the sections on children, death, and marriage are taken from JoAnn Craig's *Culture Shock*, Times Books International, Singapore, 1982, and from *Coping With China*, by Richard King and Sandra Schatzky, Basil Blackwell Ltd., Oxford, Massachusetts, U.S.A., 1991.
99. See note 97 above.

100. Ibid.
101. Ibid.
102. Ibid.
103. Ibid.
104. Bond, M.H., Ed., *Beyond the Chinese Face: Insights from Psychology*, Oxford University Press, New York, 1991, p. 16.
105. One funeral director located in a large East coast city told me that he knew that he was initially picked because his name was "Lee", an old Virginia family, he assured me. However, he had tried to be accommodating and sensitive to the cultural wishes and practices of the Chinese communities and he had succeeded in securing almost all of the Chinese funerals for over 10 years.
106. Do not kneel although you may see some Asians doing it. It would be best not to presume an unrealistic familiarity with the deceased by kneeling unless you were actually quite close. In other words, do not translate legitimate respect and courtesy into excessive unrealistic gestures of grief. That would be as bad form as bowing too low and too often in Japan!
107. Craig, J., *Culture Shock*, p. 67.
108. Craig, J., *Culture Shock*, p. 68.
109. Payer, Lynn, *Medicine and Culture: Varieties of Treatment in the U.S., England, West Germany, and France*, Henry Holt and Company, New York, 1988 (ISBN: 0-8050-0443-2).
110. Eberhard, Wolfram, *A Dictionary of Chinese Symbols: Hidden Symbols in Chinese Life and Thought*, Routledge and Kegan Paul, London, 1986, p. 185 (ISBN: 0-415-00228-1).
111. Kinkead, Gwen, *Chinatown: A Portrait of a Closed Society*, Harper-Collins, New York, 1992, p. 146 (ISBN: 0-06-016776-9).
112. As with two forms of the same term "kuan-hsi" and "guanxi", the word "chi" is written in the Wade-Giles system of transliterating Chinese sounds into our letter-sound system; an alternative form of the same Chinese character written in the Pinyin system of transliteration would be "qi".
113. Wu, J.N., *Plants and Traditional Chinese Medicine*, The Taoist Institute, location unknown.
114. Kinkead, Gwen, *Chinatown: A Portrait of a Closed Society*, pp. 148-149.
115. Kinkead, Gwen, *Chinatown: A Portrait of a Closed Society*, p. 152.
116. See note 115 above.
117. Chin, Jean Lau; Liem, Joan Huser; Ham, Domokos-Cheng, MaryAnna; Hong, George K., *Transference and Empathy in Asian American Psychotherapy: Cultural Values and Treatment Needs*, Praeger Publishers, Westport, CT, 1993, p. 127ff. (ISBN: 0-275-94493-X).

118. Chin, Jean Lau; Liem, Joan Huser; Ham, Domokos-Cheng, MaryAnna; Hong, George K., *Transference and Empathy in Asian American Psychotherapy: Cultural Values and Treatment Needs*, p. 126ff.
119. See note 118 above.
120. See note 118 above.
121. Ibid.
122. Ibid.
123. Ibid.
124. Indians — Hindu, Jains, and other splinter sects — and Chinese, Japanese, and Korean Buddhists usually appeal to the idea of karman, moral causation to explain the inequalities they observe in life. It is part of their basic world view, their publicly available explanatory frameworks (PAEF) as noted in Chapter 19. The reader is reminded that although the idea of karman as a retributive, morally driven, cause-and-effect force in the whole of the experienced universe (saṃsāra) and allegedly best explains the inequalities and incompatibilities of the experienced world, it is important to point out that the causal theory of karman remains empirically unverified and unfalsifiable. Of course, Hindus and Buddhists and Jains do not consider it unverifiable for the believer, for it is with karman that they explain the moral inequities in the world, and it works for them. In my view, karman constitutes a mere upāya/fang bian/hōben, a fundamental constitutive philosophical presumption inherent within a coherent, consistent religious world view, their PAEF. However, if the idea of a fundamental constitutive philosophical presumption inherent within a coherent consistent religious world view turns you off or merely puzzles you, then you and the skeptic may find equal delight in analyzing: "Is the law legal?".
125. Welch, Holmes, *The Buddhist Revival in China*, Harvard University Press, Cambridge, MA, 1968, pp. 97, 315, note 19.
126. McKenna, John, The Science of the Orient", *IAACI News*, 8(1), 5-6, ?.
127. Tapp, Nicholas, Geomancy as an Aspect of upland-lowland relationships, in *The Hmong in Transition*, Hendricks, G.L., Dowling, B.T., and Deinard, A.S., Eds., Center for Migration Studies of New York, The Southeast Asian Refugee Studies of the University of Minnesota, New York, 1986, p.90.
128. McKenna, John, The Science of the Orient, *IAACI News*, 8(1), 5-6, ?.
129. Craig, J., *Culture Shock*, p. 240.
130. A readable, lively source is *Mooncakes and Hungry Ghosts: Festivals of China*, by C. Stepanchuk and C. Wong, China Books and Periodicals, San Francisco, 1991 (ISBN:0-8351-7481-9).
131. My personal opinion is that for all our directness and consistent attempts at a formalized informality, we Americans are as predictable and consistent in our styles of social interaction as anyone else in the world — no more, no less. Using first names does not really make you any more friendly or "informal"

than anyone else if everybody else does the same thing. (I would not venture to speak of my good neighbors, the Canadians.)

132. Hart, M. Cordell, *Chinese* (formerly *Dealing with Chinese*), Financial Crimes Enforcement Network (FinCEN), U.S. Department of the Treasury, Washington, D.C., 1991.
133. Bond, M.H., Ed., *Beyond the Chinese Face: Insights from Psychology*, Oxford University Press, New York, 1991, p. 59 (ISBN: 0-19-585116-1).
134. Bond, M.H., Ed., *Beyond the Chinese Face: Insights from Psychology*, p. 221.
135. Bond, M.H., Ed., *Beyond the Chinese Face: Insights from Psychology*, p. 225.
136. See note 135 above.
137. Hofstede, Geert, *Cultures and Organizations: Software of the Mind*, MacGraw-Hill, Maidenhead, England, 1991, pp. 49-78 (ISBN: 0-07-707474-2). See also Table 3.1, p. 53.
138. See note 137 above.
139. Geertz, Clifford, *Local Knowledge*, Basic Books, New York, 1983, pp. 59-68.
140. Welch, Holmes, *The Parting of the Way: Lao Tzu and the Taoist Movement*, Beacon Press, Boston, 1957, p.112. Information within brackets was added by the author.
141. Bonavia, David, *The Chinese: A Portrait*, Penguin Books, London, 1982, p. 67.
142. See note 137 above.
143. Hofstede, Geert, Dimensions of national cultures in fifty and three regions, in *Expectations in Cross Cultural Psychology*, Deregowski, J. B., Dzuirawiec, S., and Annis, R.C., Eds., Lisse, Netherlands: Swets and Zeitlinger (quoted in the *Psychology of the Chinese People*, edited by M. H. Bond, Oxford University Press, New York, 1987, p. 227.)
144. Hofstede, Geert, *Cultures and Organizations: Software of the Mind*, p. 28.
145. Lai, Annie, and Harner, Stephen M., *Living and Working in the People's Republic of China: a Cultural Guide*, prepared for the Overseas Briefing Center, Foreign Service Institute, U.S. Department of State, Washington, D.C., 1980, p.26. The following qualification was added in the paper: "This paper was prepared to support training activities. The views expressed are those of the author and do not represent official views of the U.S. Department of State."
146. Schoenberger, Karl, Networking pays off for Chinese, *Los Angles Times*, April 6, 1994, p. A8.
147. See note 146 above.
148. Bond, M.H., Ed., *The Psychology of the Chinese People*, Oxford University Press, New York, 1987, pp. 223-226.
149. Hwang, K.K., Face and Favor: Chinese Power Games, unpublished manuscript, National Taiwan University, 1983, quoted in Reference 148, p. 318.
150. Bond, M.H., Ed., *The Psychology of the Chinese People*, p. 225.

151. This sentence is a paraphrase from a paper by M. Cordell Hart, "Guanxi: An Important Concept for the Law Enforcement Officer", delivered at the Annual International Asian Organized Crime Conference, Boston, March 5-10, 1995. This paper was one of three presented during a panel on guanxi where Mr. Hart was joined by Willard H. Meyers and the author. It is reproduced in Appendix C. A confirmation of these points from a Chinese sociologist may be found in Hwang, K.K., Face and Favor: Chinese Power Games, unpublished manuscript, National Taiwan University, 1983, quoted in *The Psychology of the Chinese People*, p. 318ff.

152. Machiavelli, Niccilo, *The Prince*, (trans. by Hill Thompson), The Heritage Press, New York, 1954.

153. An excellent and easily accessible discussion of the Arthaśāstra and other realistic Indian views about politics, kingship, and the needs and means of political stability can be found in *Philosophies of India*, by Heinrich Zimmer, edited by Joseph Campbell, Meridian Book, New York, 1957, pp. 87-139.

154. Sun Tzu, *The Art of War*, (trans. by Samuel B. Griffith), Oxford University Press, Oxford, 1963, p. *x*. (Foreword by B.H. Liddel Hart). If one wishes to pursue a deeper look at Sun Tzu, although it is now some 20 years old, his translation is an excellent beginning for it offers introductions to Sun Tzu's influence in China, Japan, and Russia and a good bibliography upon which to expand one's particular specialized interests. The Pinyin transliteration of *The Art of War* , "skills of the soldier", is *bing fa*; the Standard Telegraphic Code (STC) numbers are 0365 and 3127; 兵 法.

155. An excellent new publication is *The Seven Military Classics of Ancient China: Including The Art of War*, translation and commentary by Ralph D. Sawyer, with Mei-chun Sawyer, published by Westview Press, Boulder, CO, 1993 (ISBN: 0-8133-1228-0).

156. Yuan, Gao, *Lure the Tiger Out of the Mountains: The 36 Stratagems of Ancient China*, Simon and Schuster, New York, 1991. Contemporary examples from Asian, American, and West European history are offered to illustrate the many alleged applications and interpretations of these terse aphorisms.

157. Sun Tzu, *The Art of War*, Oxford University Press, Oxford, 1963, p. *x*.

158. Yuan, Gao, *Lure the Tiger Out of the Mountains: The 36 Stratagems of Ancient China*, pp. 27, 29.

159. The quotation by Dr. Bergan Evans expresses a counter-position and was brought to my attention by M. Cordell Hart.

160. Chu, Chin-Ning, *The Chinese Mind Game: The Best Kept Trade Secret of the East*, AMC Publishing, Beaverton, OR, 1988. A subtitle/cover comment is "A Guide to Penetrating the Forbidden City of the Asian Inner Business Culture."

161. See note 160 above.

162. Personal communication with M. Cordell Hart.

163. Reischauer, Edwin O., and Fairbank, John K., *East Asia: The Great Tradition*, Houghton-Mifflin, Boston, MA, 1960, p. 15.

164. Reischauer, Edwin O., and Fairbank, John K., *East Asia: The Great Tradition,* p. 17.
165. I am told that the Chinese railroad crews were very good and very fast and that the record for laying the most track from dawn to dusk was earned by a Chinese crew and remains unbroken even today.
166. *A Guide to Chinese Names and Language,* U.S. Department of Justice, Federal Bureau of Investigation, September, 1991. Also, there was an article entitled "A Guide to Chinese Names", by C.F. Anderson and H. Liu Levy in the *FBI Law Enforcement Bulletin,* March, 1992, pp. 10-15.
167. Eberhard, Wolfram, *A Dictionary of Chinese Symbols: Hidden Symbols in Chinese Life and Thought,* Routledge and Kegan Paul, London, 1986, pp. 203-204 (ISBN: 0-415-00228-1).
168. Wang, James J., *Outrageous Chinese: a Guide to Chinese Street Language,* China Books and Periodicals, San Francisco, CA, 1994, pp. 13-14.
169. A readable, lively source is *Mooncakes and Hungry Ghosts: Festivals of China,* by C. Stepanchuk and C. Wong, See previous note 130. Another brief but readable source is *Traditional Chinese Festivals,* by Marie-Luise Latsch, Graham Brash (Pte) Ltd., 227 Rangoon Road, Singapore 0821, 1991 (ISBN: 9971-947-80-3), from which many of these descriptions were paraphrased.
170. Lip, Evelyn, *Notes on Things Chinese,* Graham Brash (Pte) Ltd., Singapore, 1988, p. 23.
171. Latsch, Marie-Louise, *Traditional Chinese Festivals,* Graham Brash (Pte) Ltd., pp. 79-80, 1992, Singapore (ISBN: 9971-947-80-3).
172. I wish to express my gratitude to James P. Delaney, (USCC) Resettlement Program Manager, who, after a talk I gave at MAGLOCLEN (RISS) in May, 1992, sent me valuable outlines of his own and a brief paper by Kim Hong Nguyen; both papers were about Vietnamese culture(s). I have incorporated parts of both papers and have disagreed with parts of both as well. However, my acknowledgment of their materials remains as their comments echo throughout parts of this chapter. Of course, my gratitude for their insights and Mr. Delaney's kindnesses also remains.
173. U.S. Senate, Permanent Subcommittee on Investigations, Hearings on Asian Organized Crime, November, 1991, Washington, D.C.
174. The following is a paraphrase of information conveyed to the author by Lt. Jack Willoughby, New Orleans Police Department, on April 12, 1993. He is the author of *Vietnamese Criminal Activity with an Emphasis on Traveling Criminals,* occasional paper of the International Association of Asian Crime Investigators, 1991. This would be a very valuable addition for the library of every Asian crime investigator.
175. Lotz, Al, and Hannum, Philip, Eds., *Nightmare: Vietnamese Home Invasion Robberies (and Jewelry Store Robberies): Selected Interstate Cases: 1987-1992,* International Association of Asian Crime Investigators, Falls Church, VA, 1992. An excellent series of case studies with commentaries by experienced working Asian crime investigators.

176. Cassidy, William L., *Nomadic Vietnamese Armed Robbery,* An occasional paper of the International Association of Asian Crime Investigators, July 4, 1991. Another valuable publication for the Asian crime investigator in which the text is clear, accurate, and cleanly written. The footnotes are accurate, helpful, and sometimes hilarious.
177. *Vietnamese Traveling Criminals: An Identification Manual,* Bureau of Alcohol, Tobacco and Firearms, Tactical Intelligence Branch, U.S. Department of the Treasury, Washington, D.C., 1994, p. 1
178. FitzGerald, Frances, *Fire in the Lake: The Vietnamese and the Americans in Vietnam*, Vintage Books, Random House, New York, 1972, pp. 15, 57-59, and 144ff.
179. FitzGerald, Frances, *Fire in the Lake: The Vietnamese and the Americans in Vietnam*, p. 17 ff.
180. Much in this paragraph is taken from *Vietnam: a Cultural Profile, Passenger Processing,* Australian Customs Service, March, 1994.
181. Throughout this chapter, I have incorporated, modified, and expanded aspects of the fine summary of Vietnamese culture and immigration history in the excellent book *The Vietnamese Experience in America,* by Paul James Rutledge, Indiana University Press, Bloomington, IN,, 1992, pp. 1-5 (ISBN: 0-253-20711-8). One cannot overemphasize the usefulness of this book.
182. In October, 1992, some 17 years after the Americans left Vietnam, these peoples have apparently concluded their war with the present Vietnamese government. See: "Montagnards End Fight Against Hanoi," *Washington Post,* October 11, 1992, p. A46.
183. Rutledge, Paul J., *The Vietnamese Experience in America,* Indiana University Press, Bloodmington, IN, 1992, p. 6ff.
184. Chin, Shirley Y., *Southeast Asians: a Cross-Cultural Curriculum for Prosecutors and Staff,* unpublished manuscript, 1991. Ms. Chin may be contacted by calling (619) 531-2772 or by writing to her at the San Diego District Attorney's Victim/Witness Program, P.O. Box X-1011, San Diego, CA, 92112-4192. These are excellent materials for all law enforcement personnel.
185. Branigin, William, Vietnamese try to buy American dream, *Washington Post,* February 19, 1993, pp. A1, A26.
186. Rutledge, Paul J., *The Vietnamese Experience in America,* p. 61.
187. Willoughby, Jack, *Wo Fat's Incomplete Cultural Guide,* New Orleans District Violent Gang Task Force, New Orleans Police Department, New Orleans, 1994, p.7.
188. Image of successful Asian Americans only half the story, study concludes, *Washington Post,* May 19, 1994, p. A25.
189. Rutledge, Paul J., pp. 153-154.
190. Nguyen, Kim Hong, Do's and Don'ts in *Understanding Cultural Differences Between Americans and Vietnamese,* Language and Cultural Consultant, Vietnamese Program, Regional Cross-Cultural Training and Resource Center,

Board of Education of the City of New York, pp.1-2, within a paper by Police Officer Al Lotz, entitled *Overview of Vietnamese Crime,* Houston Police Department, 61 Riesner Street, Houston, TX, 77002, 1994.

191. Most of the following points were taken from Neil L. Jamison's *Understanding Vietnam,* University of California Press, Berkeley, CA, 1993, pp. 1-41 (ISBN: 0-520-20157-4). Chapter 1 should be read by all Vietnamese crime specialists.
192. The Vietnamese "ly" and Chinese "li" (STC 3810) are not to be confused with Chinese "li" (STC 4409), propriety or ceremony. the apparent source of this Vietnamese concept was the eleventh century Neo-Confucian Chu Hsi. See Glossary: Propriety.
193. Jamison, Neil L., *Understanding Vietnam,* University of California Press, Berkeley, CA, 1993, p. 19 (ISBN: 0-520-20157-4).
194. *Vietnam: A Cultural Profile, Passenger Processing,* Australian Customs Service, March, 1994, p.10.
195. See note 194 above.
196. Ibid.
197. Jamison, Neil L., *Understanding Vietnam,* University of California Press, pp. 18-19.
198. *Vietnam: A Cultural Profile, Passenger Processing,* Australian Customs Service, March, 1994, p.12.
199. *Education in Vietnam. Fundamental Principles and Curricula,* Indo-Chinese Refugee Education Guides, General Information Series, published by the Center for Applied Linguistics, 1118 22nd St., Washington, D.C. 20037 (telephone: 800 336-3040).
200. See the various articles which outline developments of these Buddhist religious figures and ideas in *Buddhism: a Modern Perspective,* edited by Charles S. Prebbish, the Pennsylvania State University Press, University Park, 1975 (ISBN: 0-271-01185-8). The author's two articles on Buddhist logic and the philosophical school of Madhyamika are now over 20 years old. The latter, however, to my surprise, has been used by several Buddhist groups to introduce serious students to this complex and enigmatic but mind-bending philosophy of emptiness — and the emptiness of emptiness, etc.
201. See Chapter 19: Asian Buddhism and Chinese Confucianism.
202. See Chapter 19: Asian Buddhism and Chinese Confucianism. The introductory section of Chapter 19 offers a more detailed description of the comparative contrasts between Buddhism and Chinese Confucianism and Judaism and Christianity. The Buddhist Contextual Pragmatism and "Truth" section describes in some detail the Mahāyāna Buddhist Chinese background of what I have termed Chinese "contextualism".
203. English, T.J., *Born to Kill: America's Most Notorious Vietnamese Gang, and the Changing Face of Organized Crime,* Morrow Publishing, New York, 1995, p. 238ff.

204. English, T.J., *Born to Kill: America's Most Notorious Vietnamese Gang, and the Changing Face of Organized Crime,* pp 238-239.

205. These lingering ideas were the products of former ways of living which still linger in the mindsets of grandchildren and great-grandchildren. For example, I have been told by Arabs while I was visiting in different parts of what we call the Middle East that some other Arabs whose ancestors were desert-dwelling nomadic Bedouins and who have been city dwellers for several generations still have periodical retreats or "picnics" into the desert where they "feel comfortable and free and at home".

206. Cassidy, William L., *Nomadic Vietnamese Armed Robbery: The Fundamentals of Nomadic Vietnamese Residential Armed Robbery Investigation,* an occasional paper of the International Association of Asian Crime Investigators, November, 1991, p. 4 ff. While Mr. Cassidy was not the first to note this feature of Vietnamese life, he uses it so cogently and so relevantly that his excellent work is a pleasure to read and, as a investigative resource, it ought be in the libraries of all police departments.

207. FitzGerald, F., *Fire in the Lake,* p. 508ff.

208. Rutledge, Paul J., *The Vietnamese Experience in America,* pp. 80-81.

209. Rutledge, Paul J., *The Vietnamese Experience in America,* pp. 80-81.

210. Vandivier, Peter F., *Vietnamese and Thai Names — Law Enforcement Considerations,* published by the Financial Crimes Enforcement Network (FinCEN), U.S. Department of the Treasury, Washington, D.C.

211. These examples were taken from the materials sent to me by James P. Delaney. There was no attribution or any indication of authorship in the materials. My thanks go to the unknown author and Mr. Delaney.

212. *Vietnam: A Cultural Profile,* Australian Customs Service, March, 1994, Appendix 1: Vietnamese Names and Naming Conventions.

213. See note 212 above.

214. STC is the standard abbreviation for Standard Telegraphic Code, sometimes known as Chinese Commercial Code. A reprint of the STC book is available from FinCEN, Department of the Treasury. Other very useful publications are two FinCEN publications, *Distinguishing Between Vietnamese and Chinese Surnames and Vietnamese and Thai Names — Law Enforcement Considerations.*

215. Marian Days is mentioned in James P. Rutledge's *The Vietnamese Experience in America,* p. 138 (see Reference 208). It is also briefly described from a law enforcement point of view by Lt. Jack Willoughby in the *IAACI News,* the publication of the International Association of Asian Crime Investigators, Volume 6, No. 3, September, 1992, p.1. Marian Days is also described in Chapter 17. It is also noted in "Marian Days Celebrated in Carthage", by Janet Theisen, BATF analyst, *IAACI News,* 8(5), 1, 3, September/October, 1994. Detective Rob Harmon, Chief Ed Ellefsen and the Carthage Police Department have been great hosts and have assisted special Asian crime investigators in the pursuit of

criminals at the Marian Days celebrations. Attendence there is a great opportunity for sworn personnel to learn about admirable Southeast Asian families and not so admirable Asian gang bangers, to exhibit wanted posters, to supplement police photo books, and to network with other experienced Asian crime investigators. Detective Rob Harmon may be reached at the Carthage Police Department: (417) 358-2132.

216. Trying to prove the superiority of one religious truth claim over another religious truth claim between major religions as complex and diverse as the religious and philosophical "grammars" of Anglo-European Christianity and Indian or East Asian Mahāyāna Buddhism is intellectually quite complex and difficult. The difficulty can be illustrated (not proved) as follows. Assume that one wanted to claim that one set of religious claims was better or worse than some other set of religious claims. Examples might be "accurate knowledge about how things really are" Theravāda Buddhist) or that "God created the universe but was himself uncreated" (Christian aseity). In claiming one over the other, you would find yourself and your opponents arguing in closed circles — circles in which ideas incompatible with one or the other religion would not be allowed to count against the competing truth claims at issue. That is, in order to prove one set of beliefs best, you would necessarily need to assume some of the standards of best and worst in, say, tradition A. If those standards of a were incompatible with the standards of best and worst in tradition B, then any conclusion drawn from the standards of either a or B could not be justified as superior according to the conclusions of a or B if those conclusion were drawn from the standards of the other. Assuming that each tradition makes no mistakes in coherence and consistency, then the conclusion that one truth claim was superior to another could not be justified without assuming the different and incompatible standards of the other. So, without a means to open the circle to the "different" religious truth claims of either, you would merely be trying to prove what you have already presumed by embracing the standards of one of the two positions. Trying to pass off a conclusion drawn by unpacking what you have already assumed, without regard to the compatibilities of the assumptions of the other contested position, is fallaciously arguing in a circle or fallaciously begging the question; additionally, most religions fallaciously appeal to a built-in "immunizing strategy" which has the system-preserving effect of keeping one's own truth claims immune from any possible counter evidence which could falsify or negate one's own claims. And none of that constitutes an acceptable proof of anything, in anybody's religious or philosophical traditions — anywhere!

217. To put the obvious point in a very ethno-centric way, to greater or lessor degrees, many of these factors also have had similar roles in shaping the national cultures and subcultures of our cultural cousins, the Australians, the New Zealanders, the Welsh, the Scots, and the Irish. And, oh yes, the English — about whom said my Welsh-American father, "If you want to make them happy in their old age, tell them a bloody joke when they are young!".

218. Eastman, Llyod E., Family, *Field, and Ancestors: Constancy and Change in China's Social and Economic History, 1550-1949,* Oxford University Press, New York, 1988, p. 41 (ISBN: 0-19-505270-6).
219. Eastman, Llyod E., Family, *Field, and Ancestors: Constancy and Change in China's Social and Economic History, 1550-1949,* p. 43.
220. Eastman, Llyod E., Family, *Field, and Ancestors: Constancy and Change in China's Social and Economic History, 1550-1949,* p. 57.
221. The author's italics emphasize that the universal, rule-like, quasi-legal principles in which many Anglo-European ethical foundations are *expressed* and often *argued* are not common to Chinese history; this is not to say that these ethical principles were discovered or first articulated in (this) rule-like, quasi-legal style of expression. As Hans Reichenbach stated years ago about scientific discovery (and I paraphrase extensively): The logic of discovery may and often is semirandom, idiosyncratic, and full of personal analogies and other specific heuristic styles. However, the logic of (scientific) demonstration must be rational, theoretically open to public replication, evidence-driven, rigorous, empirically grounded, falsifiable, free from immunizing strategies, where the causal variables should be isolatable, mutually exclusive, and fully exhaustive and the chains of arguments are deductive or inductive with very high probabilities.
222. "Agnostic" means, not that one claims that there is no God or gods (atheism), but that one does not *know* whether there are gods or a God. It is the suspension of belief and/or statements of religious belief based on one's view that he/she has insufficient or inconclusive knowledge.
223. FitzGerald, F., *Fire In The Lake,* pp.14-15, 22, 24, 26, 62-64,147-152, 290-291.
224. Rozman, Gilbert (general editor and author of "The East Asian Region in Comparative Perspective"), in *The East Asian Region: Confucian Heritage and Its Modern Adaptation,* Princeton University Press, NJ, 1991, p. 29 (ISBN: 0-691-02485-5).
225. It seems quite clear that we Americans are more concerned with the public appearance of social equality and social-leveling than Asians; certainly, Americans are more so than the Germans or the French or the Japanese. However, we are apparently less egalitarian than Australians who, for the most part, are even more emphatic about keeping everyone at about the same social level. Personally, I liked Australia and Australians, and I found them the easy people to get along with. However, some Americans have apparently found it difficult to accept that they tend to refuse the kind of grudging admiration and deference we tend to extend to people whose reputations and actions are the result of their own, self-earned actions — the classic American self-made man. That particular Australian cultural value was expressed to me (after several Fosters during a good-natured, interesting argument in a Sydney pub): "We don't want anyone to get above themselves, enh?!". A good first source to look at this cultural variable is *Australians and North Americans,* by George W. Renwick, Interact 2, Intercultural Press, Yarmouth, ME 04096 (ISBN: 0-933662-16-5) phone: (207) 846-5168.

226. Bonavia, David, *The Chinese: a Portrait*, Penguin Books, New York, 1989, pp. 113-114.

227. Rozman, Gilbert (general editor and author of "Comparisons of Modern Confucian Values in China and Japan"), in *The East Asian Region: Confucian Heritage and Its Modern Adaptation,* Princeton University Press, NJ, 1991, p. 199 (ISBN: 0-691-02485-5).

228. Noss, David S., and Noss, John B., *A History of the World's Religions,* Macmillian Publishing, New York, 1990, pp. 249ff. Quotations represent the spellings and/or transliterations of the authors quoted.

229. Kung, Hans, and Ching, Julia, *Christianity and Chinese Religions*, Doubleday and Collins, New York, 1989, p. 131.

230. Kung, Hans, and Ching, Julia, *Christianity and Chinese Religions*, p. 157.

231. In addition to a standard university-level textbook, *A History of the World's Religions,* by David S. Noss and John B. Noss, Macmillian Publishing, New York, 1990, two favorite books of mine on Daoism are the older study by Holmes Welch, *The Parting of the Way: Lao Tzu and the Taoist Movement,* Beacon Press, Boston, 1960, and Arthur Waley's *Three Ways of Thought in Ancient China,* Doubleday, Garden City, NY, 1956, (see the Daoist section on Chuang Tzu, pp. 3-79).

232. Waley, Arthur, *Three Ways of Thought in Ancient China*, Doubleday, Garden City, NY, 1956, pp. 45-46.

233. Ching, Julia, *Confucianism and Christianity: a Comparative Study*, Kodansha International, Tokyo, 1978, p. 53.

234. Personal communication from M. Cordell Hart.

235. Although doubtful, there is some small chance that you might actually find "a professional Sinologist who specializes in Daoism within a discipline relevant to the law enforcement problem at issue!"

236. Hick, John, *Truth and Dialogue in World Religions: Conflicting Truth-Claims,* The Westminster Press, Philadelphia, 1970, p. 146 (ISBN: 0-664-20713-8).

237. If this boggles the mind, remember that this touch of Asian Buddhist "theology" and philosophy is as complicated to many Asians and Asian Buddhists as are the Christian concepts of aseity, theodicy, the Saints, the cult of Mary, the Trinity, or the Anglo-European emphasis on legalism, axiomatics, correspondence theories of truth, and the conceptual stew that has fermented for over 200 years regarding the concepts of Natural Law and human rights. While I admire and prefer the latter to adṛṣṭakarman ("unseen causality") and the śūnya´sūnyatā ("emptiness of emptiness"), I cannot divorce my preferences from either the obvious historical accidents of my own cultural familiarity, nor the recognition that the latter appears quite odd to others.

238. Posner, Gerald L., *Warlords of Crime: Chinese Secret Societies — the New Mafia,* McGraw-Hill, New York, 1988, p. 258-259 (ISBN: 0-007-050600-0).

239. See note 238 above.

240. *Mathews' Chinese-English Dictionary*, rev. American ed., Harvard University Press, Cambridge, MA, 1960.
241. Personal communication with M. Cordell Hart. See Appendix D for Mr. Hart's article: "Overcoming Langauage and Cultural Barriers in Dealing with Asian Organized Crime".
242. This material of Mr. Hearn has been published in the 1993 issues of the *IAACI News*, the bimonthly publication of the International Association of Asian Crime Investigators.
243. See note 240 above.
244. Personal communication with the author.
245. Carr, Gideon, Alien Marine smuggling database network proposed, *IAACI News*, International Association of Asian Crime Investigators, 7(6), 7, July 1993. Mr. Carr is described as the Director, Asian Research Institute, San Diego, CA. Contact is recommended through the editor of the *IAACI News.*
246. *A Guide to Chinese Names and Language*, U.S. Department of Justice, Federal Bureau of Investigation, Washington, D.C., September, 1991.
247. Bozeman, Ada B., *Strategic Intelligence and Statecraft: Selected Essays*, Brassey's (US) Inc., Brassey's Intelligence and National Security Library Series, Washington, D.C., 1992 (ISBN: 0-02-881009-0). The essay "Knowledge and Method in Comparative Intelligence Studies", pp. 180-212, offers an excellent example of her criticisms. Try page 189ff. Philosophical anthropology is an analytical, cognitive subdiscipline of epistemology within philosophy-darśana-xhexue that focuses on how and why people see themselves and act according to those self-views and how we may gain reliable knowledge about these issues. However unfashionable in the federal subcultures of law enforcement and intelligence circles, "philosophical anthropology" — and this is the "dirty little secret" of this book — is the major disciplinary background of this author and of this book.
248. Ibid.
249. Ibid.
250. *Using Research: a Primer for Law Enforcement*, a publication of the Executive Research Forum, 168 p., 1993.
251. One tool which might be of some use to police personnel in screening and training candidates for Asian crime investigations and police and community work is the *Cross-Cultural Adaptability Inventory*, by Collen Kelly and Judith E. Myers (1992). This self-assessment training instrument can be secured from Intercultural Press, Inc., P.O. Box 700, Yarmouth, ME 04096, phone: (207) 846-5181, fax: (207) 846-5181, or by telephoning the offices of Dr. Myers, (619) 294-6822 or Ms. Kelly, (619) 453-8165.
252. Robinson, Richard H., *Early Madhyamika in India and China*, The University of Wisconsin Press, Madison, WI, 1967, p. vii.

Index

C

G

H

I

O

P

U